Social Life in Pre-Reformation Dublin, 1450–1540

PEADAR SLATTERY

FOUR COURTS PRESS

Typeset in 105 pt on 13.5pt CaslonPro by
Carrigboy Typesetting Services for
FOUR COURTS PRESS LTD
7 Malpas Street, Dublin 8, Ireland
www.fourcourtspress.ie
and in North America for
FOUR COURTS PRESS
c/o IPG, 814 N. Franklin Street, Chicago, IL 60610

A catalogue record for this title is available
from the British Library.

ISBN 978-1-84682-790-7

Printed in England
by CPI Antony Rowe, Chippenham, Wilts.

Contents

Abbreviations

Alen's reg.	*Calendar of Archbishop Alen's register*, ed. Charles McNeill, (Dublin, 1950).
Archiv. Hib.	*Archivium Hibernicum*: Irish Historical Records (Catholic Historical Society of Ireland, Maynooth, 1912–).
CARD	*Calendar of ancient records of Dublin*, ed. John T. Gilbert (19 vols, Dublin, 1889).
CDI	*Calendar of documents relating to Ireland*, ed. H.S. Sweetman and G.F. Handcock (5 vols, London, 1875–86).
CIRCLE	*A calendar of Irish chancery letters, c.1244–1509*, ed. Peter Crooks.
CLAHJ	*Co. Louth Archaeological and Historical Journal* (Dundalk, 1904–).
DIB	*Dictionary of Irish biography.*
IESH	*Irish Economic and Social History, Journal of the Economic and Social History Society of Ireland* (Derry, 1974–).
IHS	*Irish Historical Studies: the joint journal of the Irish Historical Society and the Ulster Society for Irish Historical Studies* (Dublin, 1938–).
IHTA	*Irish Historic Town Atlas.*
JRSAI	*Journal of the Royal Society of Antiquaries of Ireland* (Dublin, 1892–).
NHI	*A new history of Ireland*, ed. T.W. Moody et al. (9 vols, Oxford, 1976–2005).
ODCC	*Oxford dictionary of the Christian Church*, ed. F.L. Cross and E.A. Livingstone (3rd ed., New York, 1997).
ODNB	*Oxford dictionary of national biography.*
PRIA	*Proceedings of the Royal Irish Academy* (Dublin, 1836–).
Stat. Ire., 1–12 Edw. IV	*Statute rolls of the parliament of Ireland, 1st to 12th years of the reign of King Edward IV*, ed. H.F. Berry (Dublin, 1914).
Stat. Ire., 12–22 Edw. IV	*Statute rolls of the parliament of Ireland, 12th to 22nd years of the reign of King Edward IV*, ed. J.F. Morrissey (Dublin, 1939).
Stat. Ire., Hen. VI	*Statute rolls of the parliament of Ireland, reign of King Henry VI*, ed. H.F. Berry (Dublin, 1910).
Stat. Ire., John–Hen. V	*Statutes and ordinances, and acts of the parliament of Ireland, King John to Henry V*, ed. H.F. Berry (Dublin, 1907).
Stat. Ire., Rich. III–Hen. VIII	*Statute rolls of the Irish parliament, Richard III to Henry VIII*, ed. Philomena Connolly (Dublin, 2002).
TCD	Trinity College Dublin.

Illustrations

PLATES

(appear between pages 160 and 161)

Acknowledgments

I WOULD LIKE TO EXPRESS my thanks to a number of historians and an archaeologist who read early drafts of this work and offered constructive advice: Dr Colmán Ó Clabaigh OSB, Professor Howard Clarke, Professor Peter Crooks and Professor Terry Barry. Dr Ó Clabaigh pointed out sources of which I was unaware and revealed new topics in Church history worth exploring. Guidance on medieval chant, early polyphony and the Sarum Use was provided by Dr Ann Buckley of TCD for which I am most grateful. Terry McDonald, law librarian at TCD, Roy Stanley, music librarian at TCD and Tony Carey were very helpful with particular queries, as were Caroline Picco of the Cheshire Record Office, Brian Farley and Marie Shields. I would like to thank Dr Frank Lawrence of University College Dublin for reading drafts on medieval music and commenting in detail on them. Dr Theresa O'Byrne very generously read at short notice a number of drafts about Ismaia Fitzwilliam and her spiritual life for which I am very appreciative. Dr Jane Laughton helped open up a new vista on Dublin-Chester trade in the 1470s, sharing with me her detailed notes on trading between the two cities. Sadly, Jane died in 2017; she thoroughly enjoyed a renewed interest in Chester-Dublin studies. She was scholarly and yet immensely generous with her time and knowledge. I am especially grateful to Jane and her family. I owe a particular debt of gratitude to Andrew Slattery who sourced many books on medieval topics, often at short notice. Family members Dr Peter Slattery, Ruth and Stephen Slattery were supportive in numerous ways over the period of the research. I am indebted to Dr Colin Fitzpatrick for allowing me access to his library and to his doctoral research. Michael Mulcahy has shown an enthusiastic and sustained interest in this work through many drafts, for which I am grateful. I would like to thank my wife Bernie for allowing me the time and space to explore and give an account of what has been up to now a hidden and shadowy late medieval Dublin. Mary Ryan of Waterford Treasures Museum was very helpful in offering guidance in the choice of images of the Waterford vestments. Asa Henningsson of the Uppsala University Library facilitated the acquisition of an image of the Uppsala portalan and Dr Albrecht Sauer of the Deutsches Schiffahrtsmuseum in Bremerhaven was also most generous in providing an image of a model of the *Bremen cog*. Dr Mary Clark of Dublin City Library and Archives provided a number of images of medieval Dublin for which I am very thankful. Dr Ruth Johnson, Dublin City Archaeologist, made me aware of the late medieval slipway at Merchant's

Quay for which I am grateful. In my search for suitable photographs, Dr Niall Colfer, Eddie Farrell and Ken Whelan of Dublin City Council were very helpful in supplying images and in facilitating photography. I wish to thank Tim O'Connor for arranging access to the Isolde's tower site for the purpose of photography. In the heritage section of the Office of Public Works at Dublin Castle I wish to thank Dr James Curry for his helpfulness on a number of occasions, and Dr Myles Campbell for his discussion about the Powder Tower excavations. Timothy O'Neill generously supplied his drawing of the Irish mantle for which I am grateful. Thanks are due to Rita Moore for drawing my attention to the image of the St Thomas Becket reliquary and to the trustees of the Victoria and Albert museum for permission to use the image. I am grateful to Dr Niall Brady for permission to use his map of the small ports associated with Dublin and to Professor Robert Bartlett who kindly allowed me use his map of early Dublin immigrants (*c.*1200) taken from his work *The making of Europe: conquest, colonization and cultural change, 950–1350.* Dr Giles Dawkes of University College London advised about the feasibility of drawing a late medieval granary based on a dig in Church Street in which he had been involved and for which I am grateful. Very special thanks are due to Kevin O'Brien for his drawing of the granary. I would like to thank Dr Michael Potterton for his advice on a number of occasions. I wish to thank Jean Farrelly of the National Monuments Service who very kindly explained the particular working of the hagioscope (squint) at Whitechurch chapel, Rathfarnham, Co. Dublin. I am grateful to both Brian McKay O.Carm, prior of Whitefriar Street church and community, and David Twohig O.Carm for the use of the image of 'Our Lady of Dublin' and for information about the history of the statue. Thanks are due to Dr Fergal Donoghue of St Patrick's College, Maynooth, who very kindly took on the task of drawing a number of original maps of Dublin and Co. Dublin to do with debtors, excommunicates, night-watch routes and Dublin city pagents. From Andrew Davis I learned about engraving and Tadg O'Leary of Lisduff, Co. Cork talked to me about driving animals to market. Professor Alan J. Fletcher has been very helpful with guidance about late medieval drama for which I am most appreciative. I wish to thank Dr Connie Kelleher of the National Monuments Service for providing the image of the Drogheda boat.

I wish to thank the Board of Trustees of the Victoria and Albert Museum, London for permission to use the image of the St Thomas Becket reliquary and I am grateful to Oxford University Press for granting permission to use the image of the medieval tallies. I am indebted to Dr Ian Friel for discussion about shipping and marine matters. My thanks are due to Pól Ó Duibhir for his advice about the use of a number of images and to Nick Maxwell of

Wordwell and *History Ireland* who supplied an image at very short notice. I am grateful to Antoinette Prout of the Royal Irish Academy library for facilitating on behalf of the academy the use of Speed's map of Dublin and to Sharon Sutton of TCD who provided images on behalf of the Board of Trinity College Dublin. Fiona Byrne of National Museums Northern Ireland went to considerable lengths to provide an image containing a range of coins minted in Dublin by Germyn Lynch for which I am most grateful. I wish to thank Marinela Mesinschi for compiling work-in-progress bound versions of this work from time to time and for her attention to detail. Where it has not been possible to establish copyright ownership of an image a satisfactory arrangement will be made with owners who come forward.

To Denis O'Shea and the staff of my local library in Raheny and of Libraries Ireland, its interconnected libraries across the country, I wish to convey my gratitude for providing difficult-to-find books. I wish to thank Professor Colm Lennon for reading the manuscript and offering considered suggestions about additions that should be made to the work. I am also grateful to the anonymous reader who offered fresh ideas which have been incorporated into the work. I am very grateful to have had access to the library in Trinity College, Dublin, and wish to thank Mary Higgins, Seán Hughes and other members of the library staff who have been so helpful. Over a sustained period of time, Professor Howard Clarke was interested in the work and encouraging in so many ways. I owe Professor Clarke an immeasurable debt of gratitude.

I alone am responsible for any errors which may remain in the text.

14 January 2019

Introduction

IN THE LATE 1460s, shipmasters making a return voyage from Chester to Dublin on the east coast of Ireland were greeted with a familiar but impressive vista as they came into Dublin bay – to the south the smooth rolling horizon of the Dublin and Wicklow mountains contrasted with the dramatic conical peak of Sugarloaf, to the north the craggy peaks of Howth head and Ireland's Eye. Local experienced masters navigating through the treacherous sandy shallows of the Liffey estuary – John Brette on the *Peter of Dublin*, John Milet on board the *Katharine of Dublin*, and Blak Patrik, master of the *Jenicot Pykard* – would have kept watch for Dublin on the south bank, dominated by Dublin Castle and Christ Church cathedral at about sixteen metres above the river, on the eastern end of a ridge running parallel to the Liffey. John Brette would have had his apprentice Henry Purcell on board who would finish his training at the end of 1469 and become a citizen of Dublin in January 1470. Brette may have allowed Purcell to take command and bring in the *Peter of Dublin* to the quayside, but everyone on board would have known that the more eyes watching the tricky shallows of Dublin bay and the Liffey estuary the better. On the north-facing slopes of the ridge, facing the river, were the homes and shops of tradesmen and merchants. Shipmasters who were familiar with the port knew that, as they eased towards the quayside, after they had passed the prominent landmark of Isolde's tower, moorings were available at timber wharfage on Merchant's Quay and the Wood Quay. At dusk, and in foggy or misty conditions, Dublin was unlikely to be by-passed because all on board would have heard carts rumbling on cobble-stones, church bells ringing, and with a prevailing south-westerly wind blowing would have smelled the city – smoke from hundreds of hearths, dung on every street, and rotting fish guts in the water at the Fishamble Street slipway.

Dublin was a thriving city, the centre of English administration in Ireland with a busy port. Its citizens are recorded as having almost fifty different trades and skills and the city had almost thirty churches and monasteries. There were bustling food markets and a strong municipal authority run by a merchant oligarchy. It was a settlement of foul smells in which pestilence and disease were often rife, an English city in Ireland whose inhabitants spoke English, with an unwanted Irish ethnic group, a city located in a fertile hinterland with a coastline of small ports – Baldoyle, Howth, Malahide, Rogerstown, Rush and Skerries, over which Dublin had control.

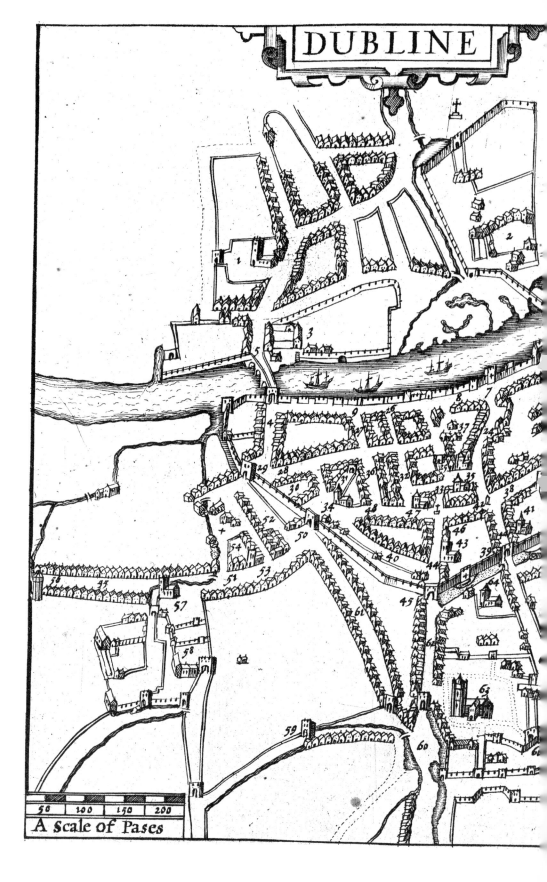

DUBLINE

A Scale of Pases

50   100   150   200

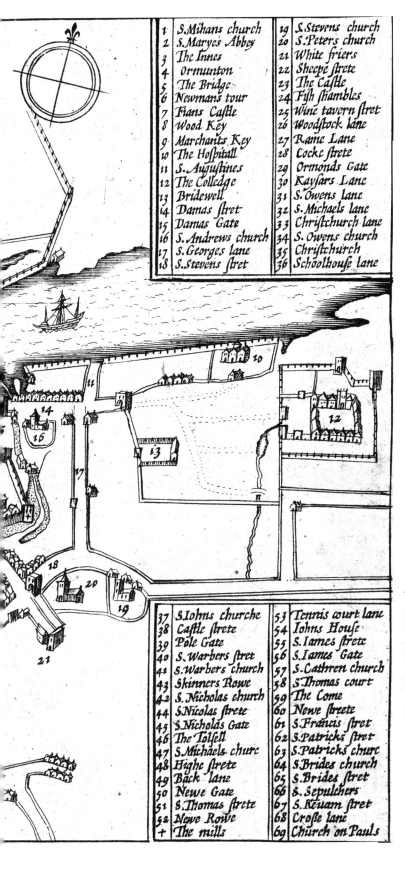

1	S. Mihans church	19	S. Stevens church
2	S. Maryes Abbey	20	S. Peters church
3	The Innes	21	White friers
4	Ormunton	22	Sheepe strete
5	The Bridge	23	The Castle
6	Newmans tour	24	Fish shambles
7	Fians Castle	25	Wine tavern stret
8	Wood Key	26	Woodstock lane
9	Marchants Key	27	Rame Lane
10	The Hospitall	28	Cocke strete
11	S. Augustines	29	Ormonds Gate
12	The Colledge	30	Kaysars Lane
13	Bridewell	31	S. Owens lane
14	Damas stret	32	S. Michaels lane
15	Damas Gate	33	Christchurch lane
16	S. Andrews church	34	S. Owens church
17	S. Georges lane	35	Christchurch
18	S. Stevens stret	36	Schoolhouse lane

37	S. Iohns churche	53	Tennis court lane
38	Castle strete	54	Iohns House
39	Pole Gate	55	S. Iames strete
40	S. Warbers stret	56	S. Iames Gate
41	S. Warbers church	57	S. Cathren church
43	Skinners Rowe	58	S. Thomas court
42	S. Nicholas church	59	The Come
44	S. Nicholas strete	60	Newe streete
45	S. Nicholas Gate	61	S. Francis stret
46	The Tolsell	62	S. Patricks stret
47	S. Michaels churc	63	S. Patricks churc
48	Highe strete	64	S. Brides church
49	Back lane	65	S. Brides stret
50	Newe Gate	66	S. Sepulchers
51	S. Thomas strete	67	S. Keuam stret
52	Newe Rowe	68	Crosse lane
+	The mills	69	Church on Pauls

1 Map of Dublin, 1610, by John Speed. The bird's-eye view of Dublin, appreciated by historians over the years, is technically not a map, one historian describing it as a 'contemporary pictorial representation' of Dublin. Despite the date, the map is regarded as showing the city's medieval street pattern. (By permission of the Royal Irish Academy © RIA.)

This book is concerned with a range of Dubliners, not involved in high politics and not described before in such detail – city governors and administrators; Dublin merchants trading in the city and in England; guildsmen, guildswomen and their apprentices who achieved their citizenship by completing their apprenticeship, and the clergy and their dedicated faithful. In our period, the city had many interesting personalities from every level of society. Jacoba Payn was an innkeeper and brewer who married twice and wanted to be buried close to her first husband; an Italian archbishop, Octavian de Palatio, on his way north to Armagh, offered indulgences at top prices; a bogus king, Lambert Simnel, was crowned in Dublin; a Dublin mayor's widow, Dame Margaret Nugent, ran up debts and owed money to everyone; a government mintmaster, Germyn Lynch, guilty of counterfeiting, was caught and, unbelievably, re-employed again and again and again; an ex-mayor, Janico Marcus, was murdered in a street riot. Successful merchants like Patrick Fitz Leones were managing and controlling the city of Dublin.

Political life

This book is not about high politics, shifts in power, war and military manoeuvres, but it will be helpful to have in mind a chronological framework of events in England and a broad view of the management of the English colony in Ireland in the second half of the fifteenth century. Politically, our chosen period, usually dated in this work as '*c.*1450–*c.*1540', could be said to lie between the appointment of Richard, duke of York, as lieutenant in Dublin (1447) and the dissolution of the monasteries in Dublin in the late 1530s in the Henrician Reformation.[1] The kings who reigned through our period were Henry VI (1422–61), Edward IV (1461–83), Edward V (1483), Richard III (1483–5), Henry VII (1485–1509) and Henry VIII (1509–47).[2] Three of these kings – Edward IV, Richard III and Henry VII – took the kingship by force in what has been called by historians, but not contemporaneously, the 'Wars of the Roses'.[3]

In 1453, the sudden loss of all the English territories in France, other than Calais, brought a sense of unease in England. As a result of the losses in France and the resulting total breakdown of Henry VI, civil war broke out in England in 1455, the first battle of the Wars of the Roses taking place on 22 May 1455 at St Albans.[4] Henry VI was of the House of Lancaster and after 1447 the only surviving descendant of Henry IV in the senior male line. Then, in 1453, his son was born. Ironically, the protector of the realm who acted for Henry VI in his incapacity (1454–5 and 1455–6) was Richard, duke of York, Henry's cousin, and heir of the earl of March who had been passed over for kingship in 1399. Seen as a threat, there was tension at court when Richard was governing on behalf of the king.[5]

In 1459, two battles in England roused York to claim the Crown in 1460; he was attainted and fled to Ireland where he had been a successful lieutenant, the government there dominated by Yorkists protecting him.[6] Returning to England in 1461, and leaving the earl of Kildare as his deputy, York was defeated and killed at Wakefield.[7] However, York's son took the kingship as Edward IV in 1461. Henry VI died in the Tower of London, most probably murdered. Edward was able to enjoy relative political stability in the 1470s. His death in 1483, leaving his son Edward, aged twelve, in line, was too tempting for Richard of Gloucester who seized the throne on 26 June 1483, imprisoning and probably murdering Edward and his brother. In 1485, Richard III lost the Crown in battle to the first of the Tudors, Henry VII, at Bosworth.[8]

In Ireland, in the fifteenth century, the core of English policy was to defend the borders of an emerging Pale territory, partially protected with an earthen bank and a ditch; a chapter in volume two of *A new history of Ireland* – 'The emergence of the Pale' – reflects this development. Absentee landlords, despite requests, refused to come to Ireland to protect their lands. Authority and power were allowed to drift to the great Irish and English lords. In effect, the great magnates – Desmond, Kildare and Ormond – could be chosen to rule the colony with a degree of independence. Anglo-Irish magnates who accepted the office of lieutenant made senior government appointments, controlled the king's council and parliamentary legislation in Ireland, coupled with dispensing patronage. They could not depend on subventions from England but neither were they expected to account for revenue. Once Edward IV was on the throne (1461), the Butlers of Ormond were out of favour because they had backed the Lancastrian cause, and Edward invited the earl of Kildare to take on the deputyship in Dublin and govern the colony, which, with a few breaks, successive earls of Kildare did until 1534 when the FitzGerald power was broken in the reign of Henry VIII. Their period in almost continuous government was also a time of great aggrandisement for the family.[9]

Insecurity and vulnerability are words associated with late medieval Dublin and its hinterland, particularly on the city's southern flank. Dublin, the centre of English power in Ireland, was the front line of defence and attack against the enemy Irish, the immediate adversary being the Irish of north Wicklow and Leinster.[10] Occasionally, municipal meetings were cancelled so that Dublin citizens could join contingents of troops leaving Dublin to deal with the Irish: in the O'Byrne country, led by Sir John Tiptoft, deputy, October 1467; in the O'Connor territory, under the command of Tiptoft, deputy, May

1468; in the O'More country, with Lord de Grey, deputy, October 1478; to devastate the O'Byrne country, led by Gearóid Mór FitzGerald (May 1480); to march under the command of Sir Edward Poynings, deputy, to Waterford and Munster (July 1495).[11] Dublin, perhaps reluctantly, became inextricably bound up with Gearóid Mór's affairs – he held the office of king's deputy, he was commander of an official standing army set up to protect the Pale, and he became a citizen of Dublin.[12] Overall, Gerald FitzGerald (Gearóid Mór), the great earl of Kildare, and later his son Gerald (Gearóid Óg), both of whom served as deputy, and were focussed on personal power and family enrichment, ensured that the borders of the Pale were peaceful and that Dublin was safe. A very recent assessment (2017) credits Gearóid Mór with building up the English Pale as a defensive frontier – 'The English Pale was indeed the Great Earl's principal achievement but largely forgotten legacy as governor and military commander'.[13] Archaeologists have unearthed and reported on Dublin city defences found at a number of sites and a conservation plan for surviving Dublin walls and defences has been published.[14]

Economic life

In late medieval Dublin, all business was done on trust, merchants giving credit to customers living at a distance of 10 or 15 km, as will be seen in new original maps below. John Mold of Malahide, merchant, owed money to merchants in north Wales and Bristol.[15] Intrepid Dublin merchants braved the Irish Sea, which could turn treacherous, to purchase commodities in Chester or Coventry.[16] In the mid-1470s, Dublin merchants used on-board agents to represent them in England, described below in the work of John Wilkynson and Christina Clarke.[17]

   Dublin had many citizen-merchants, 241 in the period 1468–1512, whose goods would have been on show in shops or stored in yards in Dublin.[18] Peter Higeley and Walter Sale had their own businesses and had stocks of brass, lead and pewter vessels, and household utensils and decorations for sale. Richard Boys of Coventry, who had a shop in Dublin, specialized in importing textiles and sold linen and superior cloth. Heavy or bulky goods would have been stored in yards: Peter Higeley had salt, iron, pitch, resin and building materials and John Mold of Malahide had iron, salt, saltpetre and barrels of herring.[19]

   One of the fundamentals of late medieval life in Dublin was the hundreds of indentures signed between master and apprentice (at least 760 in the period 1468–1512) to offer craft training to the apprentice over a term of years.[20] When John White, whose indenture can be read below, agreed to learn the craft of shipbuilding in Dublin from his master, Edmund Lobusby, the agreement involved more than a transfer of craft skills. It was a two-way agreement, the master also offering moral education and leadership, the apprentice responding with a commitment to work, initially unpaid, giving loyalty to his master and being discrete about his business affairs.[21] Success came with qualification in one's chosen craft and the immediate opportunity to become a citizen of Dublin.[22]

Henry VII was fully aware of the long-standing hygiene problem in Dublin, leading to fever, pestilence and death in the city. He knew the streets were filthy with dung heaps everywhere and that 'pestilential exhalations' hung over the city.[23] This was one of the problems faced by Dublin's municipal authority, which was responsible for maintaining hygiene standards in the fish and meat markets of the city. It also fell to the authority to ensure that their city of 6,000 to 8,000 persons, largely non food-producers, would have supplies of grain and flour, especially in winter.[24] The authority was constantly on the watch for those who broke established marketing rules and often appealed to those in the city who had haggards or barns holding grain not to hoard but to put a fair proportion on the market for the common good.[25] Fortunately, the remains of a late medieval barn were unearthed, close to St Michan's, Dublin, and a drawing of the granary completed allowing us to visualize what a late medieval barn would have looked like (see figure 18).[26] Ale was largely brewed by women but men were becoming involved in the industry. Jacoba Payn was from the parish of St Nicholas without, her parish church being in St Patrick's cathedral; she must have lived nearby and was a brewer. She brewed ale, managed a clean inn, fattened pigs in the back yard using kitchen waste, married twice and wanted to be buried close to her first husband in the grounds of the cathedral.[27]

Church life

With the suppression of the monasteries in 1539, Dubliners must have been shocked to see some familiar church buildings occupied by secular authorities and the fabric of other churches stripped away.[28] St John the Baptist's Hospital outside Newgate was thrown down and William Brabazon, vice-treasurer of Ireland, sold roof tiles, timber, glass and iron from the hospital to unidentified persons for sums unknown.[29] Brabazon was also reported as breaking down the church and other buildings of St Mary de Hogges' abbey near Hoggen Green, with its roof tiles and timber carried away to Dublin Castle to be used to repair the castle.[30] In 1539, the Dominican priory north of the Liffey was occupied by judges and government law officers and became known as the King's Inn; the church in St Mary's abbey was used to store artillery and munitions.[31] To the laity in Dublin, when they heard of the selling of church goods, it must have seemed that they might lose the Church they loved.[32]

In the late medieval period, the Church created a magical and other-worldly atmosphere in its liturgies through its use of darkness, candles, coloured vestments, bells, incense and the intoning of plainchant in Latin.[33] Despite reports of expensive indulgences being preached in Dublin, income from indulgences in parish churches seems to have been quite modest.[34] Very occasionally, a priest had the resources to be educated abroad and attend Oxford but most diocesan priests were poor.[35] The laity appear to have been devoted to their faith, but the Church had power and did not shirk from using excommunication where ecclesiastical law was infringed.[36]

Social life

Dublin was culturally English in the late medieval period, but not completely so, recent work drawing attention to the presence of the Irish and their cultural goods in the city and in the Pale region. The records of the proceedings of the Dublin municipal authority reveal the presence of the Irish in the city and their occasional unpopularity.[37] However, that Dublin was English is not in doubt. It has been shown in *Angliores ipsis Anglis* – more English than the English themselves – that Dubliners, from 1172 to the late fifteenth century, were consistently loyal to the Crown (with the exception of the Lambert Simnel episode). In the fifteenth century, Dubliners accepted confirmation of their previous royal charters (1419), attempted to rid Dublin of the Irish and Ulster folk in the city (1450s), required apprentices to be of English birth (1469), and set up defensive measures against the Irish (1461–85). Dublin's loyalty was such that it proved a suitable base for the Tudors when they took a renewed interest in Ireland.[38]

Nevertheless, in Dublin city and county and its immediate neighbourhood, Irish was spoken by persons who were part of colonial society and members of its institutions. Elite families in Meath spoke Irish – the Nugents of Delvin and the Plunketts of Dunsany. On the north Co. Dublin–Meath border the use of Irish nicknames by the Cruise family suggest that they spoke a good standard of Irish.[39] Close to Dublin, the Harolds, who practised a pastoral economy in the march lands of the south county and were Gaelicized, were also qualified butchers in the city.[40] A number of persons of the Irish nation held positions of authority in the Church in Dublin and also served apprenticeships in the city and became citizens.[41]

In the 1530s in Dublin, there was nothing innovative about the desire of government officials who held office in Dublin to seek or accept county seats and lands in Co. Dublin that became available from the monastic suppressions. There was already an established elite in the county, some families with strong city connections. The recipients of county estates in the 1530s included John Alen, master of the rolls, granted the priory of St Wolstan and its lands on the banks of the Liffey, near Celbridge, Co. Kildare, Patrick Barnewall, the solicitor-general, who was granted the convent and lands of Grace Dieu, near Lusk, and Robert Cowley, government official, who was granted the priory of Holmpatrick and its lands, near Skerries, Co. Dublin.[42]

The Sargent family has been traced over a period of 260 years becoming landholders of the first rank in Co. Dublin, with a family member holding the posts of mayor and bailiff a number of times in the 1480s and 1490s. It has been shown that the city and the county were not necessarily separate worlds and that while city families might aspire to being county people, one could occupy and enjoy both worlds; in this regard the families of Burnell, Forester, Tyrell and Ussher have been examined. Although beyond the period of this present work, Colm Lennon's *The lords of Dublin in the age of Reformation* sets a standard for what could be done for the late medieval period in this sphere if more sources could be traced.[43]

In the late medieval period, women had a significant role in the economy, in agricultural work, in domestic service, in brewing and in the crafts, and marginally, though innovatively, in exporting goods. The latter three are discussed below. Other than in brewing, women never dominated in any branch of the economy. Legally, women were constrained by common law but seemed on occasions to circumvent its restrictions. Women were entitled to hold land through inheritance or purchase, although inherited land often reverted to the male line on the death of the recipient. Widows had legal autonomy in the disposal of property whereas a single woman and a wife were legally under the control of their father or husband respectively. In marriage, the husband managed his wife's land, she having no power to sell, transfer or exchange her property without her husband's consent. However, in Dublin, in the available wills, it is very seldom that the 'express consent' of her husband in this matter is recorded.[44] Of the seventy-two wills in the Dublin register of wills, mainly from the 1470s, fourteen were written by married women, with only one stating that she made her will 'by leave of my husband'.[45] Few women adhered to the assumption that they should only bequeath personal jewellery and clothing. Single women could bequeath property but usually had only a few humble possessions. Women were regularly appointed to act as executrix of their husband's will, one study revealing that in 95 per cent of testaments the wife was appointed executrix, the testator showing confidence in the ability of his wife.[46]

Much of the female workforce that had employment was involved in domestic service. We should be aware that the small sample of available wills offers a limited insight into late medieval society in Dublin. Of some 70 late medieval Dublin city and county wills 22 households had one or more servants of either sex, of which 10 households had a female servant.[47] Three merchants in Dublin city had a female servant – Hugh Galyane (Joan Roch, 1474), John Gogh (Benmona, 1472), and Robert Weste (Jonet and Katherine, 1471) – the latter two nursing John Wylde, an English merchant, in his final days.[48] The remaining known rural locations at which there were female servants, who may have been involved in both agricultural and domestic service, are – Balrothery (1476), Clondalkin (1474), Finglas (1475), Hollywood (1471), Rowlestown (1476), and in the parish of St Michan (1477).[49] It is probably safe to assume that Peter Higley and Millane Frayne who had four children, a shop in Dublin and a forty-acre farm near Swords, and had servants, would have included female servants among their employees (1476).[50] The type of work done by women who came to live on farms included making bread, ale and malt, and working as a dairymaid, which would have involved milking cows, making butter, and probably making cheese.[51]

While unpaid, the work of a farmer's wife should not go unrecorded. A study of medieval Suffolk assumes that women undertook household tasks – cleaning, childcare, preparing meals, tending to the fire, drawing water from the well and stitching clothes. It must have been so in Co. Dublin. In Suffolk, there is a shortage of evidence of women working in agriculture but nevertheless it is believed that certain tasks 'were principally the preserve of females, most notably tending to livestock in general and dairy herds in particular'.[52] On sample farms across Co. Dublin in the 1470s, animal totals of cows, sheep, hogs and horses, ranged from 61 to 117. While men concentrated on ploughing, sowing and harvesting, and no doubt repairing fencing and driving animals to the market, it would appear that the overall responsibility for farm animals fell to the farmer's wife. Equally, wives would have assisted with the harvest if required. Some wives had the responsibility of caring for children, balanced occasionally with the availability of a servant. Joan Dansay of Rowlestown, married to Nicholas Duff, would have been responsible for 82 animals; she had two children, Elizabeth and Alexander, but had the assistance of Margaret, her maidservant, who may have milked their 7 cows (1476). Cecily Langan, married to William Walsch, had three children, Katherine, Ellen and Alice; they lived in a parish near Grace Dieu close to Lusk; she had 62 animals under her care, with 12 cows to milk daily (1473).[53] Agnes Lawless of Glasnevin, married to Geoffrey Fox, had 13 cows to milk, and looked after a total of 60 animals; she had two children, Rose and Tom, but could call on the assistance of a servant, John Man (1476). Katherine Wylpite, married to Nicholas Lok of Balrothery, had one child, managed 89 animals, and ensured that 10 cows were milked every day (1474).[54] Richard Porter and Rose Tirrell, whose farm was located possibly between Castleknock and Dublin seem to have had a specialized farm – they kept 17 cows and 100 sheep. There is no clear record of the Porter-Tirrells having children or servants, but they must have had assistance to manage their herds (1472).[55]

It is difficult to estimate family size in late medieval Dublin. In England and Ireland, for our period, the basic information that would facilitate an analysis of family numbers and structure is lacking – no parish registers, no censuses, and no documents that routinely indicate a person's age. Ideally, family size could be explained if contemporary quantifiable information on the following were available – birth control, infanticide, high infant mortality rates, late marriages, infertility because of poor diet, high female mortality, and economic limitations to marriage. Unfortunately, such information is not available.[56] Where data can be collected, it has been shown, for example, in Halesowen (Worcestershire) in the period 1270 to 1349, that marriage was easier and earlier for the sons and daughters of wealthy families.[57]

Bearing in mind the above caveats, wills can nevertheless offer a glimpse into family size. Over seventy wills were examined from Dublin city and county, including a few wills from Co. Kildare, for the period 1457 to 1483. In the wills, 60 couples are recorded as married, with 41 couples having had children.[58] The children mentioned should be regarded as those who have survived into adulthood, no figures being available for the number of pregnancies in families, for babies who died at birth nor the mortality rates of young children. But, again, a word of caution – it is possible that some children, alive at the time a will was written, are not mentioned because they may have received an earlier settlement. The largest number of children recorded in a Dublin family was 4, the children of Millane Frayne and Peter Higeley of Dublin. Peter and Millane had a thriving business in Dublin and a forty-acre farm, pointing to the fact that the children did not want for food. The spacing of their children, 3 young children, not yet of legal age, and an older son, John Higeley, a canon regular in Christ Church, suggests that Millane may have had at least one other child who did not survive, bringing the total number of their children to at least 5.[59] Eight couples had three surviving children and 12 couples had two surviving children. There were 20 couples with one child. Of the 41 families with children, a total of 32 families lived on farms with direct access to food – grain, meat, milk and probably eggs. Of 8 families who had three children, 6 families lived on farms.[60] It is probably safe to assume that family size was reduced by the poor medical care of the day, and by contemporary environmental and hygiene factors. It will be seen below that there were crop failures in Ireland, plagues in rural and urban areas and disease in Dublin, which taken together would have affected child mortality rates in the city and county, probably reducing family size to the levels described here.

New research is being done on those who worked by writing in late medieval Dublin – clerks, scribes and notaries who drafted, witnessed and sealed documents such as charters, wills, contracts and leases. James Yonge was, in his spare time, a historian, but he worked as a notary at the centre of the English administration in Ireland and was possibly assistant to the Dublin city clerk. Yonge has been described as a legal functionary and an attorney, and described himself as 'a notary imperial'; acting as executor in 1434 he earned the significant sum of 20s. Theresa O'Byrne, following her research on James Yonge and the literary world of late medieval Dublin, has published work on Nicholas Bellewe, a legal scribe, and who, like Yonge, was a scribe for hire. Bellewe, as we shall see, worked in the office to do with the Dublin quayside crane, presumably keeping records of merchants names, goods in and out and fees paid. Surviving texts written by Bellewe, often, though not necessarily, of a religious nature, offer clues as to the types of texts that were circulating in Dublin in the fifteenth century.[61] Bellewe found steady work as household secretary to the Fitzwilliam family of Dundrum, Co. Dublin, his hand seen on estate rental rolls but also in religious writings that would appeal to a pious lay audience or specifically to a female audience. It is most likely that pious material in Bellewe's hand was written for Ismaia FitzWilliam of Dundrum, Co. Dublin, probably in the 1430s and 1440s, and will be discussed below.[62] The desire of loyal Dubliners to be English and to be seen as English is reflected in the work of the scribes. In the early fifteenth century, Dublin scribes began to sign the documents they had penned in imitation of their London counterparts. Government officials and scribes in Dublin would have seen many documents from England in the course of their work and often tried to imitate English practices when producing documents.[63]

Crime was alive in Dublin city and neighbourhood. In 1486, in Newgate gaol in Dublin, holding and restraining irons were delivered to the mayor and bailiffs of Dublin. There were iron collars, manacles weighing over a stone, shackles for men's legs and a great chain weighing almost nine stone.[64] In 1525–6, similar manacles and shackles were delivered, including collars for men's necks and a 'bolt for children with two shackles'.[65] There were four prisons in Dublin, at Dublin Castle, the Tholsel, Newgate and near St Mary's abbey. In 1526, Newgate held 7 prisoners, 4 for debt, 2 on suspicion of felony and one for trespass.[66] Typical cases heard at Lucan manorial court in the

1440s concerned charges of trespass, debt, cutting the lord's wood, affray, battery and abduction.[67] Generally, the range of penalties available to the courts included the imposition of a fine, a period in the pillory or that the guilty party should be dragged through the streets on a horse-drawn hurdle. The most serious penalty was imprisonment or execution by hanging.[68] At the beginning of the fourteenth century, crimes of violence were mainly committed by men against men or women, using an axe, a lance, a sword or their fists. Women were attacked, raped, suffered sexual violence and were beaten. Women could be violent and used their fists, took up knives and mixed poisons to hurt, kill and maim.[69] In the early fourteenth century, on the Dublin–Kildare border, a series of crimes were committed through the continuous marauding activity of an outlaw 'rebel English' gang, controlled by Henry Tyrel, a member of a prominent Co. Dublin family. They were mainly involved in cattle-rustling and extortion, and probably seeking protection money.[70]

Entertainment

In the late medieval period, Dublin would have had its share of street entertainers – gamblers and card players, musicians, and juggling acrobats who probably tossed knives in the air. From the thirteenth century there were horn players and harpers in the city.[71] A bull-ring was located in Cornmarket north (1382) where bull-baiting took place under the watchful eye of the 'mayor of the bull-ring'.[72] In the 1490s, apprentices in Dublin had got so out of control that a municipal ordinance was enacted to curb their behaviour – they were consorting in the houses of men and women, drinking, playing cards, throwing dice and involved in 'unthrifty play'.[73] Hoggen Green, east of the city, near All Saints' priory and St Mary de Hogges' abbey, was an open-air space in which a number of entertainments took place, most probably on holy days or on summer evenings – playing at quoits, archery practice, and possibly the staging of morality plays.[74] The declamatory style of the plays, often responded to by the banter of an involved loud audience, may not have pleased the canons in the priory or the nuns in the convent close by whose thoughts were elsewhere.[75] In about 1540, part of Hoggen Green was still considered a pleasure-ground.[76]

Topography

Urban historians find maps useful, indeed essential, in conceptualizing the townscapes of the past. The medieval landscape of Dublin vanished and historians have looked to John Speed's map of Dublin (1610) and John

Rocque's map of Dublin (1756) to visualize the lost urban streetscapes. It has been stated that Speed's depiction of Dublin is not truly a map but rather a 'contemporary pictorial representation'.[77] Despite this and its date Irish historians have traditionally treated it as representing medieval Dublin.[78] Rocque, on the other hand, was a professional cartographer, the value of his map for a medievalist lying in its 'clear and detailed depiction of building plots'.[79] Rocque's map was assessed for its usefulness to medieval research and while some buildings were found not to have been recorded accurately, it was established that Rocque had 'mastered the pattern of the city, to a level of interlocking complexity never before seen for Dublin, or possibly for any other city'. In the history of the mapping of medieval Dublin, three phases have been identified: before 1880, 1880–1970, and after 1970. The best map of medieval Dublin taken from the second phase appeared in *Archaeological Journal* in 1931; compiled by Harold Leask, it seems to have remained unknown and unused. The 1970s saw the beginning of a scientific approach to compiling maps of medieval Dublin, with the publication in *Current Archaeology* (1969–70) of Patrick Healy's map of the gates, towers and town walls of Dublin. The key to the success of Healy's map, which was not perfect, was the use of accurate and comprehensive primary sources along with archaeo-logical evidence.[80] In 1978, Howard Clarke prepared a map of medieval Dublin for the Friends of Medieval Dublin, *Medieval Dublin, c.840–c.1540*, a revised edition appearing as map 4 in *Irish historic town atlas no. 11, Dublin part I, to 1610* (Dublin, 2002).[81] A folded pocket version of map 4 in the above work comes with H.B. Clarke, *Dublin c.840 to c.1540: the medieval town in the modern city* (2nd ed., Dublin, 2002) and would be useful to those who wish to walk the streets of late medieval Dublin with a reliable guide.[82]

A vast amount of archaeological material has been found in Dublin over a fifty-year period and has opened up opportunities to re-consider ideas, to confirm half-established information and to investigate new hidden aspects of Dublin's past.[83] An area in Dublin that has the potential to produce medieval structures and material has been delineated on the *Medieval Dublin c.840–c.1540* map with a broken orange line.[84] The problem for the late medievalists is that the underlying layers in which they are interested are relatively near the surface and may have been destroyed by the intrusion of cellars, piles and trenches for underground services.[85] When finds are made it can be especially rewarding. A site excavated by Giles Dawkes close to the church of St Michan, Dublin, was found to have had a number of late medieval buildings including a late medieval timber-framed granary, mentioned earlier.[86] At Merchant's Quay a late medieval south-north slipway was excavated in 2000, still covered each day by the Liffey at high tide.[87]

2 Isolde's tower base. The tower was built in the thirteenth century and marked the confluence of the Poddle and the Liffey. Incoming mariners knew that when they reached the tower they were moments away from tying up at Wood Quay or Merchant's Quay. (Photo: P. Slattery.)

Geography

The walled town of Dublin was located on the south bank of the river Liffey as its estuary opened out into Dublin bay on the east coast of Ireland. The coast of Wales was 112km eastwards and Chester in England was 225km distant. Much of walled Dublin was situated towards the eastern end of a spur or ridge running west to east parallel to the river and protected on three sides by the confluence of the Liffey and its tributary the Poddle, marked by Isolde's tower (figure 2).[88] The centre of Dublin was about 17 metres (55 feet) above the Liffey with the site sloping downwards and northwards to the river.[89] Dublin had four surrounding extra-mural suburbs which will be discussed below.

To get a sense of the townscape of late medieval Dublin, one should become familiar with two maps in *Irish historic town atlas no. 11*, a text figure, 'Dublin *c*.1300', and map 4, 'Medieval Dublin *c*.840–*c*.1540', in which Dublin can be seen as a somewhat misshapen rectangle fronting onto the south bank of the river Liffey. Dublin's eastern wall, beginning at Isolde's tower on the Liffey, met with the town's southern wall at the Record Tower in the south-east corner of Dublin Castle. The southern wall running westwards from that tower terminated at St Nicholas's Gate from which the town's western wall ran in a north-westerly direction to the banks of the Liffey. The original northern wall left behind due to land reclamation on the south bank of the Liffey, and still a very useful second line of defence, ran from west to east parallel to Pipers' Street and Cook Street to the junction of Fishamble Street and Essex Street West. Today, a fine stretch of this wall can be seen in Cook Street along with St Audoen's Arch (figure 3). Eventually, research would record 20 towers in Dublin's medieval walls and 19 mural and extra-mural gates in Dublin.[90] In the north-west and north-east of the town there were two short town walls facing the river, but otherwise Merchant's Quay and Wood Quay, 400 metres long with intermittent city walls, were open to receive shipping. In the north-west, a bridge across the Liffey to the suburb of Oxmantown was accessed through Bridge Gate.[91]

It will help to be familiar with the location of two major street arteries in medieval Dublin – one artery running from north to south from Pricket's Tower on the quays to St Nicholas's Gate via Winetavern Street, Trinity Lane and Nicholas Street, and the other artery running from west to east from Newgate to Dam Gate via High Street, Skinners' Street and Castle Street. The city aqueduct entered the city at Newgate from a cistern near St James's Gate and ran along this artery.[92] The centre of Dublin was marked at the intersection of these arteries by the high market cross where official civil and church pronouncements were made.[93] In the centre of the walled town were the visual symbols of secular and Church power – the Tholsel, a new centre of city administration, superseding the Guildhall of Winetavern Street, built south of Christ Church on the corner of Nicholas Street and Skinners' Street, and Christ Church cathedral, the most significant church building within the walls. The secular cathedral of the archbishop of Dublin, St Patrick's, and the archbishop's palace, St Sepulchre's, were located outside the walls, 250 to 350 metres south of St Nicholas's Gate. Established intra-mural parish churches c.1300 included St Audoen's located between High Street and St Audoen's Arch, St John's, immediately north of Christ Church, the church of St Mary del Dam at Cork Hill, St Michael's on High Street near the high market cross, and St Werburgh's on Werburgh Street. Immediately east of Christ Church was the fish market on Fishamble Street, the flesh shambles was located along High Street and the corn market was further west near Newgate. The pillory, a wooden frame used to deliver mild belittling punishments, was at a busy place, located at the junction of Skinners' Street and Castle Street at the entrance to Bothe Street, believed to be a centre for shopping. In the

3 (*opposite page*) St Audoen's Arch, Cook Street, Dublin, can be seen today in a stretch of Dublin's medieval wall, 90 metres long. (Photo courtesy of Dublin City Library and Archive.)

DUBLIN CITY WALL AND
GATES 1240 A.D.

THE RESTORATION AND PRESERVATION OF
THIS SECTION OF THE OLD CITY WALL
AND GATES TOGETHER WITH TARGETS MILL
AREA OF SPEED AND LOWER STREET
PART OF DUBLIN CITY CORPORATIONS
CONTRIBUTION TO EUROPES ARCHITECTURAL
HERITAGE YEAR

4 Postern steps leading to a small door in the front curtain wall of Dublin Castle near the Powder Tower. The thirteen steps, about 76 cm wide (30 inches), provided a way in and out of the castle, independent of the main gate. (Photo: P. Slattery, taken with the permission of the OPW.)

fifteenth century, at the bottom of Winetavern Street, a crane operated on Merchant's Quay.[94]

Dublin Castle was located in the south-east corner of the walled town in keeping with practice in some English towns after the Norman conquest by which a castle was built in an angle of an existing town wall. While there was a castle in Dublin before 1176, the castle we know as Dublin Castle had its beginning in 1204 when King John commanded Meiler Fitz Henry to build a strong fortress from which Dublin could be defended and in which the king's treasure could be stored and justice administered. The castle was completed by Henry Blund (Henry of London), justiciar and archbishop of Dublin, in about 1230.[95]

The castle was a large, roughly rectangular courtyard with substantial stone towers in the four corners – starting clockwise from the north-east corner, the Powder Tower, the Record Tower (still standing), the Bermingham Tower and the Corke Tower. The castle's gates were in the centre of the north-facing curtain wall. The first chapel was built in the courtyard in the early 1220s and the King's Hall was built in the 1240s, 120 feet (36.6m) long and 80 feet (24.4m) broad, with glazed windows and a huge rose window, 30 feet (9.14m) in diameter.[96] West of the Powder Tower was a set of thirteen steps, seen today, descending through the north curtain wall leading to a postern or small door that allowed exiting from or entrance to the castle (figure 4).[97] The Poddle flowed along the castle's southern and eastern walls and a moat skirted its western and northern walls, the moat averaging 20 to 22 metres in width and 8 to 9 metres in depth, though the depth was probably lower in the fourteenth century. The moat was crossed by a bridge or causeway.[98]

Dublin Castle was the symbol and centre of English and royal administration in Ireland and the official residence of the king's deputy. The treasury and government armaments were kept in the castle and a number of parliaments were held and courts of law sat in the great hall. Important prisoners were held in the castle. Its defences were never breached.[99] Maintenance done on Dublin Castle in the early fifteenth century was hopelessly inadequate. By 1430, it was reported that the castle, hall, buildings and towers were in a ruinous state and in need of repair to such an extent that the 'books and records of the chancery, both benches and the exchequer' were greatly damaged by rain and storms. It was decided to spend the sum of £13 6s. 8d. on repairs.[100] In 1520, the situation had become worse; the earl of Surrey became chief governor of Ireland, following Gearóid Óg FitzGerald's tenure, and found that Dublin Castle had been allowed to become 'ruinous' and it had to be evacuated in order that it could be rebuilt. The records were in chaos and it was not until the late 1520s that a degree of order was restored.[101]

What did residential Dublin look like in the late medieval period? It would appear that there were two principal house-types – timber-framed houses, made of oak beams, and stone-built houses.[102] The timber-framed houses would have been set on low stone walls and the spaces in the frame or cage-work would have been infilled, plastered and lime-washed.[103] The roofs of stone-built houses would have been supported on timber roof trusses and covered according to choice. In Dublin, both house-types can be traced back to building techniques introduced by the Anglo-Normans in the early thirteenth century.[104]

In 1766, timber-framed houses still survived in Castle Street, High Street, Wood Quay, Bishop Street and Patrick Street.[105] Documentary evidence survives from the thirteenth to the fifteenth century of almost forty houses in Dublin each of which is described as a 'stone house'. It is certain that other stone houses and buildings can be added to this figure.[106] In the 1470s and 1480s in Dublin, agreements continued to be made to lease both types of house and one other basic house-type. In 1476, Thomas Laundey, chaplain, leased a stone house in Ram Lane, and in 1483, John Estrete, leased a property in High Street, and was required to build within eight years 'a new house, with oak beams and a roof of stone tiles'. John Payne leased land at Oxmantown Green in 1485; he was required to 'rebuild with mud walls and straw roof'.[107] In the period 1350 to 1550, one could expect to see a variety of roof coverings in the Dublin area – thatch, stone, stone tiles, stone flags, tiles, boards or wood, and slate.[108]

The streets of late medieval Dublin were paved, requiring, as one would expect, regular maintenance to counter usage by the daily traffic of people, horses and heavily-laden carts. Throughout the fourteenth century, money for paving (and other works) was raised in Dublin by royal permission which allowed the municipal authority to levy customs on goods for a set term of years. In 1336, for example, there was optimistic mention of 'the completion of the paving of the city' and yet, in 1346 and in immediate years following, money was to be used 'for mending the pavement in diverse places where already commenced'. Further royal licences to raise money for paving were granted in 1366, 1374 and 1419. In the fifteenth century, other than in a grant by Richard III in 1485, which mentioned the 'construction and emendation of the walls and pavements' of Dublin, the focus of maintenance in royal grants made to Dublin in 1427, 1454 and 1464, shifted towards the more critical problem of weak and decayed city walls and defences.[109] In Chester, in the fifteenth century, paving was financed in the same way. In 1440–1, in Chester, Miles Paver was paid 6s. 8d. for paving work and in about 1480, John Paver repaired 12 feet of pavement at the rate of a penny a foot.[110]

Streets must have been wide enough for Dubliners involved in the transport of goods to go about their business; the difficulty of negotiating narrow streets is not recorded as a problem in municipal records in the fifteenth century. A street's width was not necessarily consistent, a section of St Nicholas's Street opening out to 33 feet (10m) wide. The opening of the only surviving city gate, St Audoen's Arch, is 10 foot 6 inches (3.2m) in width, and at its apex the headway of the arch today is about 20 feet (6.1m), dimensions well capable of allowing through a well-laden commercial cart. However, stretches of some streets were quite narrow, even down to 8 feet (2.4m) wide, though still sufficient to allow a cart through – at the opening into St Nicholas Street near the junction of High Street and Skinners' Street, at the point where St Nicholas Street became Patrick Street, and at the opening into Bull Alley.[111] Dirt and disease were endemic to the streets of Dublin and will be discussed in detail later. In 1366, in a royal grant to assist paving the streets, the letters patent insisted that the 'lanes are to be cleaned of all dung, dirt and putridity, and kept clean during the prescribed term'. Over 100 years later the problem remained and had become much more serious.[112]

Dublin had four extra-mural suburbs effectively encircling the city, each with its own distinctive character. The suburb of Oxmantown on the north side of the Liffey, located between the lands of the Cistercian St Mary's abbey to the east and the public Oxmantown Green to the west, had three religious institutions – the parish church of St Michan, the Dominican St Saviour's priory fronting onto the Liffey and the enclosed lands of St Mary's abbey. Its streets had a grid-like plan laid out possibly in the late twelfth century. Oxmantown had many of the characteristics of a medieval country town – an urban street pattern, a parish church, a market beside St Mary's abbey, the abbey's harbour on the Liffey, two street gates, and a street called Hangman Lane leading to a place of execution, Gibbet Mede.[113]

Overall, the eastern suburb was semi-rural, characterized by the buildings and lands of four religious institutions – the convent of St Mary de Hogges, Augustinian friars at Holy Trinity friary, the Augustinian priory of All Saints, and St James's Hospital, a hospice for pilgrims going to Compostela in Spain. There were two open spaces, Hoggen Green whose location approximates to College Green, and the Steine, whose location runs along the northern boundary of Trinity College campus. As Dubliners enjoyed the sea air here they were reminded of their pagan predecessors: Hoggen Green contained the Thingmote, once a Viking place of assembly, and nearby there were Scandinavian burial mounds. Further east, the open Steine area was named after a tall megalith that reputedly marked the first Viking landfall in Dublin. A sign that the city was beginning to expand eastwards into this suburb was the Exchequer houses made of stone on the east side of today's South Great George's Street.[114]

There was a strong ecclesiastical feel to medieval Dublin's southern suburb. The dominating focal point of the area was St Patrick's cathedral, the largest medieval church in Ireland. Close by were the chapel and palace of St Sepulchre, the official residence of the archbishop of Dublin, and the mansion of the chancellor of the cathedral, both in Kevin Street. Unbelievably, the lands of the original Dubhlinn church settlement (seventh century) were still largely ecclesiastical in medieval times, their northern boundary demarcated by the curving Stephen Street, the enclosure gradually tapering southwards for 350 metres to the junction of Aungier Street and Bishop Street. There were church buildings – five parish churches, including the southernmost church in Dublin, St Kevin's, a Carmelite priory, a Franciscan friary, and St Stephen's Hospital, a house for lepers. On the Fair Green, just outside Newgate, there was an annual fair of a fortnight's duration. Common pasture was available in St Stephen's Green, unenclosed, and larger than the Green we know today.[115]

There is a distinct east–west component to the fourth suburb of Dublin, the western suburb, which expanded westwards from Newgate along St Thomas's Street and St James's Street in classic ribbon development fashion.

With a higher elevation than the walled city, the suburb with its water cistern at St James's Gate carried a gravity-fed pipe that delivered fresh water daily to Newgate and into the walled city. The most significant religious foundations in the suburb were the Augustinian abbey of St Thomas, and St John the Baptist's Hospital close to Newgate. There were two parish churches, St Catherine's and the church of St James.[116]

* * *

While the foregoing introduction and review shows that Dublin *c.*1450–*c.*1540 can be presented in considerable detail in all its parts, it would be invidious not to give special mention to a series and two works that provide material relevant to the study of late medieval Dublin. The annual volumes of *Medieval Dublin*, edited by Seán Duffy, having first appeared in 2000, contain chapters about late medieval Dublin topics, and other chapters, for example archaeological reports, in which late medieval material can be found. An index in volume ten provides a helpful guide to the first ten volumes. In 1990, twin volumes on medieval Dublin, edited by Howard Clarke, were published – *Medieval Dublin: the living city* and *Medieval Dublin: the making of a metropolis*. There is little of late fifteenth century per se in the volumes, but nevertheless many topics, issues, artefacts and objects are discussed that were part of fifteenth-century Dublin.[117]

CHAPTER 1

Dublin, a Royal English City

O N ASCENSION DAY, 24 May 1487, Dubliners were excited, happy and full of anticipation because they were about to witness a spectacle never seen before in the city – the coronation of the king of England and lord of Ireland in Christ Church cathedral.[1] Dublin had taken to its heart the king-designate, a handsome orphaned boy of ten years, Edward, earl of Warwick, who had been robbed of his right to the throne of England by a usurper, Henry Tudor, now Henry VII.[2] Tudor's tenuous connection with the royal line was put in perspective by F.X. Martin in the 500th anniversary year of these events, when he described the upstart who, in 1485, had won the battle of Bosworth and the kingship of England, as a nephew-in-law of Richard III.[3] Dublin had been a royal city for over 300 years, formed by the granting of royal rights and privileges since 1171–2. Kings had come to Dublin before – Henry II, John[4] and Richard II,[5] but a coronation in a cathedral setting had not been seen in Dublin. Here was history in the making and not to be missed.

The prior of Christ Church, Thomas Harrold, would have ensured that the cathedral was in pristine condition with floors swept and fresh rushes laid.[6] The procession of clergy and lords, wealthy citizens and English dignitaries was magnificent to behold – splendidly robed prelates, richly arrayed lords and knights, the mayor and bailiffs of Dublin, Janico Marcus, Robert Blanchwell and Thomas Benet, the city council, and powerful and wealthy merchants. Stage managing the whole ceremonial was Gearóid Mór FitzGerald, known as the 'great' earl of Kildare, governor of Ireland on behalf of the king of England. With him would have been the chief officers of the lordship of Ireland, including the chancellor, Roland FitzEustace, Lord Portlester, a close friend of FitzGerald.[7] The scions of Anglo-Irish families would have been inspired by the occasion, Edward Óg Plunkett of Meath, son of Lord Killeen, for example, who had Irish kern under his command.[8]

In a smaller Dublin Pale, the number of bishops present was about as expected – Walter FitzSimons, archbishop of Dublin, John Payne, bishop of Meath, Edmund Lane, bishop of Kildare, and William Roche, bishop of Cloyne. Payne, a great friend of the earl of Kildare, gave the sermon and outlined the genealogy of the boy's family to show that he was without doubt,

Edward, earl of Warwick, son of the late duke of Clarence and the next male heir of Edward IV (1461–83) and Richard III (1483–5).[9] Octavian de Palatio, archbishop of Armagh, part of whose diocese was in the Pale, was in Dublin at this time but perhaps was not in the cathedral.[10] If he or anyone had any doubts about the young lad they did not surface publicly on this glorious day.

There was English support for the boy in the cathedral in the person of John de la Pole, earl of Lincoln, a 25-year-old nephew of the Yorkist kings Edward IV and Richard III, through his mother Elizabeth. Francis Lord Lovell, a one-time adviser of Richard III, was also in Christ Church. Another sister of Edward IV, Margaret of Burgundy, schemed and planned on the Continent with her son-in-law, Maximilian, who would later be Holy Roman Emperor, to gather a military force together. Margaret assembled a contingent of 2,000 German mercenaries, devastating with cross-bow bolts and the twelve foot pike, commanded by Martin Schwartz, which arrived in Dublin port on 5 May 1487.[11]

A priest, Richard Symonds, who had tutored the boy and brought him from England to Gerald FitzGerald, was always close to the young lad.[12] The FitzGeralds had given the boy covert support over a number of months when he had been first brought to Dublin in late 1486 or in early 1487, and after communicating with the earl of Lincoln in England and Margaret of Burgundy, FitzGerald and his advisers decided to bring him out into the open.[13] He called a meeting of the nobility of the Pale and its neighbourhood and of the chief citizens of Dublin and told them of the earl's coming and of his claims.[14] At this meeting, the Dublin municipal council, whether they liked it or not, was drawn into the plan.

On 24 May 1487, in Christ Church cathedral, most probably Lincoln and Lovell brought the boy forward to his place before the high altar. He was crowned with a coronet taken from the statue of the Virgin Mary in the nearby St Mary del Dam's church and was to be known as Edward VI. The congregation would have clamoured to see the young king. FitzGerald's best-known lieutenant, Sir William Darcy of Platin in Meath, six and half feet tall, stepped forward, got the boy up on his broad shoulders and walked out into the sunlight to the thunderous roar of the crowd. The young monarch was paraded on the streets around Christ Church, along what is now called Dame Street to an open area, Hoggen Green, capable of holding a huge crowd, and back through the cheering crowds to Dublin Castle and a celebration banquet (plate 2).[15]

Ahead lay, inevitably, an overseas military expedition to fight for the kingship of England, the fleet sailing from Dublin in early June, making landfall in Lancashire on 4 June 1487. The opposing armies began to converge near Newark and met at East Stoke on 16 June 1487. Henry VII had assembled 15,000 men, while the commander-in-chief of the rebels, the earl of Lincoln, had 6,500 men at his disposal. The battle lasted three hours. It was a clear victory for Henry VII and the Lancastrians and was to be the last battle of the Wars of the Roses which had begun in 1455.[16] Local tradition in Stoke has it that a narrow ravine, leading down to the Trent, the Red Gutter, flowed with the blood of the vanquished.[17]

The political and diplomatic aftermath was more drawn out. The boy pretender was captured at Stoke with his tutor-priest and revealed to be Lambert Simnel of Oxford. He was treated reasonably well by Henry and later employed in the king's household.[18] Henry wrote to Pope Innocent VIII on 5 July 1487, naming bishops whom he had been informed had attended the coronation in Dublin – the archbishops of Armagh and Dublin, and the bishops of Kildare and Meath – and in effect seeking their excommunication.[19]

The pope replied by publishing a papal bull on 4 August 1488, *Contra Rebelles Domini Regis*, in which he forbad under pain of excommunication any rebellion against Henry, specifically including the inhabitants of Ireland. But already, in May 1488, Henry had issued pardons to the four prelates whom he had named, adding the bishop of Cloyne to the list of those to be pardoned. He pardoned six abbots and three priors; there was an error made in naming the mayor and two bailiffs who should have been named as Janico Marcus, Robert Blanchwell and Thomas Benet. The citizens of Dublin, so clearly supportive of the coronation, received a general pardon from Henry VII.[20]

In the autumn of 1487, Henry, without actually going to Ireland, had somehow to begin to secure the English colony in Ireland and regain the loyalty of Gerald FitzGerald. He set out to make friendly contacts with Munster, writing on 20 October 1487 to the loyal citizens of Waterford, thanking them for their support.[21] In 1488, he improved relations with Maurice, the new earl of Desmond.[22] In June 1488, Sir Richard Edgecombe, on the south coast of Ireland on the king's business, took the oaths of loyalty of the townsmen of Kinsale, of Lord Barry, of Lord Courcy and of the O'Sullivans.[23]

It was time to deal with FitzGerald and the treasonous citizens of Dublin. Edgecombe arrived at Malahide in north Dublin on 5 July,[24] and was received by a gentlewoman of the Talbot family who 'made him right good cheer'. He learned from Thomas Dartas, almost certainly a gentleman and a citizen of Dublin, that the earl of Kildare was on a four- or five-day pilgrimage and he advised Edgecombe that he should come to Dublin to take his ease.[25] When it became known that Edgecombe was at Malahide, a number of persons visited him – the bishop of Meath, and John Streete, most probably a sergeant-at-law, and others, who brought him to Dublin, where the mayor of the city received him at the Black Friars Gate, and where he lodged with the Dominican friars at St Saviour's on the north side of the city.[26]

The earl of Kildare had already begun to play out a long tortuous diplomatic game with Edgecombe over a seventeen-day period in July. Aware that Edgecombe had arrived in Dublin, Kildare chose not to meet him until about the twelfth day, and insisted that Edgecombe come to him at a monastery in St Thomas Court in Dublin. Edgecombe was livid and 'made not reverence to him nor to the lords' when they first met. He had a royal pardon with him but had no intention of handing it over until three conditions were fulfilled by Kildare and his lords – the posting of bonds, their obligations to Henry VII recorded in writing and their oaths of loyalty sworn in public. For most of the period Edgecombe held his patience but when required he was well capable of losing his temper and raising his voice. To the earl and his council when they made unreasonable delays he spoke 'plainly and sharply'. When the lords sought a pardon for justice Thomas Plunket and James Keating, prior of Kilmainham, Edgecombe spoke 'with right sharp words ... and gave with manful spirit unto the said justice Plunket and prior, fearful and terrible words'. Edgecombe did not trust the Great Earl and when it came to swearing on the Eucharistic host in public at the monastery of St Thomas the Martyr, Edgecombe ensured that his own chaplain should consecrate the same host on which the earl and lords should be sworn. Kildare made his confession during Mass which would have been seen by all present, and was '*assoiled* from the curse of the Pope's bull'. Edgecombe recorded that Kildare held his right hand over the host on the patten and made his solemn oath of allegiance to King Henry VII. The bishops and lords also swore an oath of allegiance.[27]

Edgecombe's reputation went before him to the Dublin municipal authority; the pardoning of the treason of its members must have been dispensed with quickly and without demur from the officials and merchant class, who were well out of their depth. They had wagered all that they had gained in royal privileges over 300 years and were about to lose everything. Early on the morning of 24 July, as they waited nervously for Edgecombe to arrive, they cannot have been other than very humbled and contrite.[28] About nine o'clock, Sir Richard entered the guild hall where the mayor, bailiffs and commons were assembled and there they were 'sworn unto the king's grace upon the holy evangelist ... under their common seal'.[29] Edgecombe insisted that the mayor, bailiffs and commons of Dublin agree to the posting of a bond to pay 1,000 marks to Henry VII. The merchants must have been reeling. Then, Edgecombe added the condition that the preceding obligation would not apply if the mayor, bailiffs and commons maintained their allegiance to

King Henry and his heirs. The privileged governors of Dublin, the municipal authority, and the class from which they were drawn, the guild merchant, realized that despite being guilty of treason they would survive. It seems that Edgecombe brought a prepared royal pardon from England, witnessed at Croydon, dated 25 May 1488, granting a 'pardon to citizens, men, inhabitants and entire commonalty of Dublin for all past offences, forfeitures, outlawries, etc.' In the published record of the quarterly meetings of the Dublin municipal authority, there is no trace of the granting of these pardons nor of any earlier discussions that might have occurred at municipal meetings leading up to the Simnel affair nor at municipal meetings that occurred as news of the battle of Stoke became known in Dublin. The membrane was reported as torn. In short, there are no surviving records of Dublin municipal meetings for the years 1487, 1488 and 1489. Perhaps this is an early example of official redaction.[30]

A privileged royal city

At the beginning of our period, in the 1450s, Dublin city had a population of between 6,000 and 8,000.[31] It was an English city in which English common law applied, and was governed by the Dublin municipal assembly. English was spoken and Irish would have been heard.[32] Dublin was the centre of the English Pale in Ireland, the centre of the four loyal shires of Dublin, Kildare, Louth and Meath.[33] Dublin claimed rights outside the city to take customs at smaller coastal ports from Skerries in north Co. Dublin to Arklow in south Co. Wicklow, a county whose core was controlled by septs of the Irish nation.[34] Dublin was the most important urban nucleus in the country, housed government offices and institutions and was Ireland's most important link with England (figure 5).[35]

On 21 September 1170, Hiberno-Norse Dublin was attacked and conquered by Anglo-Norman-led forces, and the English king, Henry II, who came to Dublin in the winter of 1171–2, consolidated possession of his new territories in Ireland by land grants to loyal knights, and his hold on Dublin by beginning a process that granted a foundation of municipal rights and privileges to its citizens in the period 1171–1229.[36] In the winter of 1171–2, holding court at Dublin, Henry came up with a pragmatic solution that he hoped would produce a loyal thriving city of Dublin. With disaffected Hiberno-Norse leading men expelled to the suburb of Oxmantown on the north bank of the Liffey,[37] Henry granted a charter of rights to people he knew well, the men of Bristol. The Bristollians were granted Dublin 'in toto', to hold it and to settle in it. Here was an invitation to English merchants and

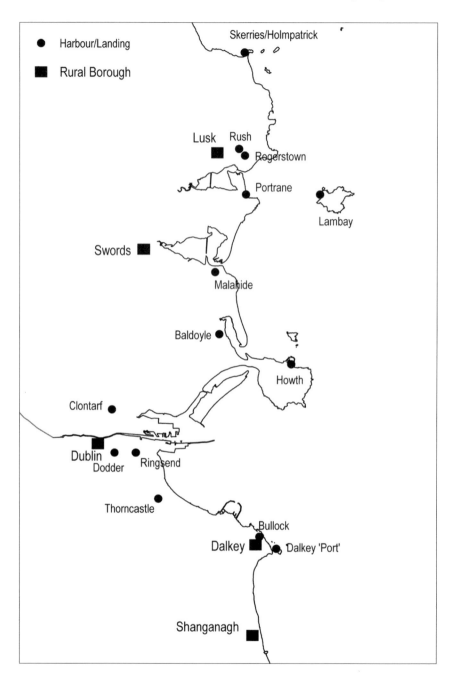

5 Map of the medieval harbours and landing places in the Dublin region showing the medieval boroughs located near the coast. The Dublin municipal authority exercised the right to collect customs at the Co. Dublin ports and at Arklow. (Map courtesy of Dr Niall Brady.)

craftsmen to settle in Dublin and enjoy the same liberties and free customs as were available in Bristol.[38] These privileges were confirmed in a charter of *c.*1174 in which the king spoke of 'his burgesses of Dublin' and 'his free and faithful subjects' in that city.[39] In 1185, when John, son of Henry, was in Ireland, he issued a charter in which the freedoms available to the citizens of Dublin continued to be equated with those available in Bristol. John confirmed that Dubliners were 'to hold the city freely and honourably, with all the liberties and free customs which the men of Bristol have at Bristol ...'.[40] Howard Clarke has referred to Dublin's status in this early period of municipal development, 1171–92, as a 'dependency' and a 'colonial adjunct' of Bristol and a 'political aberration necessitated by the special circumstances of the early years of conquest and consolidation'. That was to change dramatically in 1192.[41]

On 15 May 1192, the citizens of Dublin were generously granted almost thirty 'liberties and free customs' directly, with only a cursory mention of the burgesses of Bristol. Generously, yes, but merchant Dubliners had gone to London and paid for the privileges, meeting John at a time when he needed money and was manoeuvring to take the kingship from King Richard then captured on crusade.[42] At London, Hamo de Valognes witnessed the charter; three years later he would become chief governor of Ireland, 1195–8.[43] Although, no doubt, municipal life had existed for twenty years under the Anglo-Norman dispensation, and earlier in Hiberno-Norse Dublin, John's charter re-energized urban life in Dublin.[44] The privileges granted are listed somewhat irregularly, but fall into three broad categories – judicial, mercantile and tenurial. Citizens would have access to a 'hundred' or town court and could clear themselves by the oath of forty lawful men. Problems to do with land or debts were to be dealt with according to the custom in Dublin. The charter recognizes that Dublin merchants would benefit from being free of payments to do with moving goods – tolls, lastage and passage – and that citizens were entitled to have 'all their reasonable guilds' just like the burgesses of Bristol.[45] It is likely that Dublin's local merchants implied in the charter were already organized in a guild before the charter was written. In the charter, controls on foreign merchants coming to Dublin are unequivocal:

> No foreign merchant shall buy, within the city, corn, hides or wool from a foreigner, but only from citizens.
>
> No foreign merchant shall have a wine-tavern, unless on shipboard, ... No foreigner shall sell cloth in the city by retail.
>
> No foreign merchant shall tarry in the city, with his wares for sale, beyond forty days.[46]

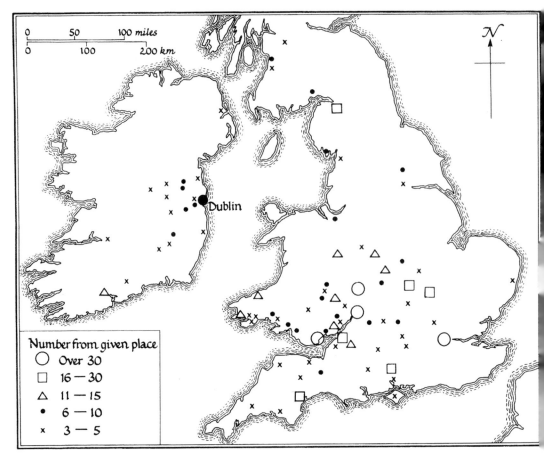

6 Map of the distribution of Dublin citizens, c.1200: origin by toponym; many migrants are seen to come from the Bristol area, South Wales and the Severn valley. (Map courtesy of Prof. Robert Bartlett, taken from Robert Bartlett, *The making of Europe: conquest, colonization and cultural change, 950–1350* (London, 1993), p. 183.)

All citizens were permitted to freely dispose of all tenures within and without the walls of Dublin, and were free to build on the banks of the river provided there was no loss to other citizens or the city itself.[47]

Having access to their own court, the hundred court, to be held once a week, was a great privilege. It meant that citizens were free of the jurisdiction of the court of the feudal lord.[48] The pleas of the Crown were reserved to the king – cases of rape, arson, forestalling and cases to do with treasure trove.[49] With the passage of time, the right of the citizens to their court was challenged by the church in Dublin (1266) and by Edmund le Botiller (1319) in a case concerning a land dispute near Donnybrook. Both attempts were warded off successfully.[50] In fact, the judicial powers of the city's senior office holders were increased – for the mayor and bailiffs in 1419 and for the mayor and recorder of Dublin in 1485 (figure 6).[51]

Early in 1215, King John showed his willingness to grant the fee-farm of Dublin with the city's provostship to its citizens at a modest fixed rent of 200 marks (£133. 6s. 8d.) per annum.[52] Dubliners Sir Gilbert Lyuet, Rauf de la Hore, Thomas de la Cornere, Robert Pollard and others petitioned for the grant of the fee-farm and on 3 July, at Marlborough, John granted it to the citizens of Dublin to be paid in two moieties of 100 marks. Now there would be fewer royal officers in Dublin – the city provostship, the city bailiffs, the custodian of the gaol and the coroner, for example, would be municipal appointments. The city's autonomy had been increased and it would be guarded closely by its citizens.[53] Witnesses to the charter who had strong connections with Ireland included Archbishop Henry of London, Henry, bishop of Emly, William Marshal, earl of Pembroke, Geoffrey de Marisco, Roger Pipard and Walter de Ridelsford.[54]

In the following decade, at Hereford, on 15 June 1229, the citizens of Dublin took a great step forward in municipal power when granted the right to elect a mayor annually. The provost was now subordinate to the mayor and the position of provost was soon duplicated, the officers holding that post eventually being called 'bailiff'.[55] Henry III's charter granted 'permission to the citizens of Dublin, and their heirs, to elect from among themselves annually a loyal and discreet mayor, proper for the government of that city, and who, on his election, shall swear fealty to the king, or to his justiciary in his absence'. The mayor was to hold office for a year at which point the citizens might retain him or elect another.[56] In 1229, we first hear of a common seal of the citizens of Dublin being affixed to a document recording the granting of a plot of land. The bronze matrices of the seal that are pinned together to make a wax seal are extant.[57] From this point onwards, a group of twenty-four burgesses, known as jurats or jurés in municipal government, worked with the mayor and bailiffs in administering the city. The group or council of twenty-four may well have existed since 1215. In March 1220, the citizens of Dublin, writing to the king about a dispute between the city and the archbishop of Dublin, describe their core collective body as the 'twenty-four principal men of the council appointed to preserve the laws and liberty of the city'.[58] It seems reasonable to believe that Dublin, in imitation of London and Ipswich, developed a town council at its change of status in 1215. There were other associated municipal groups – 'the forty-eight' and 'the ninety-six' in Dublin – but it was 'the twenty-four' that was the effective council in the ruling of the city.[59] This reference to other municipal groups is to be found in the 'Laws and

usages of the city of Dublin' dated to the early fourteenth century which stated
that 'the twenty-four are to choose forty-eight younger men. The forty-eight
are to elect ninety-six, and these are to secure the city from ill or damage'.[60]
The two latter groups, known as the forty-eight, the ninety-six or the
numbers, sat in a lower house presided over by the bailiffs. The mayor and
jurats sat in an upper house (plates 3 & 4).[61]

City ordinances required that the mayor and bailiffs be treated with
respect. Fines up to 40s. could be imposed for reviling or insulting the mayor
in any manner or place outside the Guildhall and Tholsel, the centre of
municipal government. Should the mayor have been affronted when on the
bench the fine imposed was set punitively at £10. Equally, bailiffs were not to
be reviled and were protected by a similar ordinance requiring the imposition
of a fine of 10s. Jurats were not to be insulted for which infringement a fine
would be imposed, but most interestingly, should jurats revile or insult each
other, a fine of 5s. was to be imposed – it is not clear if this applied to
altercations in the street or in over-heated debate in the chamber or both.[62]

From 1447 to c.1540, a detailed account of decisions made at Dublin
municipal meetings is extant.[63] By contrast, for city government in Dublin in
the thirteenth and fourteenth centuries we must rely on two municipal books
– the Dublin White Book and the Dublin Chain Book.[64] The White Book
contains material concerned with the properties and rights of the city, the
Chain Book is cited as an authority on the laws and regulations of the city.
The earliest English language entries in the White Book occur in 1471, the
first English matter in the Chain Book appearing in 1486.[65]

Dublin city assembly meetings were held quarterly at Easter, Midsummer,
Michaelmas and Christmas, with the most important meeting taking place at
Michaelmas when the annual surrender of municipal offices occurred and the
appointment of offices for the following year took place.[66] Those appointed
were required to indemnify the mayor and commons against claims by having
pledges acting as guarantors for them and at the end of each year 'to surrender
their wands of office'.[67] The offices that came up for annual appointment
included, for example, buyers for the city, water-bailiff, keeper of the common
prison, keeper of the crane, keeper of the keys of the treasury and master of the
works.[68]

Members of the city assembly were expected to be more than time-servers
and not be diverted to their business interests and away from municipal duties
on the days of important meetings. From the beginning of the fourteenth
century, any citizen who was qualified to serve as mayor and was absent from
the Michaelmas meeting of the city council (at which annual elections took
place) without good cause, would be fined £10. In the same way, bailiffs who

had been elected would be fined for absence without reasonable cause. The problem of absenteeism emerged again and in the 1480s city ordinances directed that members of the assembly be present at meetings and serve in office if nominated for election. In October 1483, for example, a city ordinance required that freemen, nominated to act as bailiffs of the city for the following year, who declined office, absented themselves in the few days following their appointment and did not take their oath, were to be arrested by the mayor, imprisoned until a fine of £10 was paid and deprived of their rights as a freeman of the city. In 1485, the assembly directed, under pain of a 40s. fine for an infringement, that jurés must be present at the mid-September meeting of the assembly to nominate a mayor for the following year. The nominated juré was to present himself for election at the Michaelmas meeting of the assembly a few weeks later or in default pay a fine of 40s. Jurés who did not attend the nominating meeting lost the right to vote for the incoming mayor.[69]

The assembly meetings were continually occupied with regulating the provisioning of an urban people who were not, in the main, food producers – the assembly made and promulgated by-laws to do with the brewing and selling of ale, and the sale of bread, cereals, fish and meat, which will be discussed in a separate chapter. In the second half of the fifteenth century, the assembly regularly discussed a number of topics – the maintenance of the city walls, gates and towers, the efficient provision and maintenance of a fresh water supply, the regulation of the port of Dublin and its facilities, the disposal of human and animal waste, the removal of an unwanted ethnic group, the Irish living in Dublin, and a related problem – assisting the defence of march lands near Dublin against the attacks of the militant Irish, and being involved in expeditions against the Irish on which occasions assembly meetings were prorogued. The recurring topics will be dealt with below.

The twenty-four jurats gradually took more power onto themselves. In 1448, the Dublin assembly decreed that the mayor was to be elected by the current mayor, bailiffs and jurats, the commons being excluded from the election.[70] A city ordinance directed that the annual election of the mayor should take place in the second mansion of the Tholsel, above the house in which the city court is held, with none present at the election except the existing mayor, bailiffs and jurats. It was stipulated that during the election the commons were to be in the house where the city court was held.[71] In 1485, the jurats strengthened their grip on the city further when the assembly decreed that the mayor was to be elected from their ranks.[72] Also, it would seem that the admission of applicants for citizenship and their swearing in was handled solely by the mayor, bailiffs and jurats and took place either at the end of assembly meetings, or at another meeting on the same day.[73]

While citizenship was open to those who had completed their apprenticeship, there were other ways available: birth as a son or daughter of a freeman, marriage to the daughter of a franchise holder, a fine paid by a professional man such as an attorney, and by special grace similar to the modern granting of honorary freedom of a city.[74] Once elected to be a freeman, the trained apprentice was, if called upon, expected to defend his city, the details of which will be discussed in the chapter on guilds.[75]

City defences: walls and gates

In the fifteenth century, the city walls were generally in poor shape. In the reign of Henry VI, on 1 April 1427, for example, in response to the mayor, bailiffs and commons of Dublin petitioning parliament, a royal grant of £20 per annum was to be paid over a twenty-year term from April 1427 for the 'repair, fortification and emendation of the walls and fortalices of the city'. The grant was to come from the Crown rents of Dublin. The Dubliners had argued that the walls and towers were weak and ruined and that they had incurred heavy expenditure on them.[76]

In the second half of the fifteenth century, two charters reflect the urgency of expediting wall and defence repairs. Guarantees were built into the charters and named citizens were given responsibility to ensure that the work was done and that the money was so used. On 13 February 1455, for example, in the reign of Henry VI, it was confirmed that a royal grant of £6 annually over a term of forty years was to be paid to John Bennett, Philip Bellew, William Grampe and James Power, citizens of Dublin; those who were to spend the grant on the repairs and maintenance of the walls and gates, then in a ruined state, were themselves to be supervised by two citizens who had been mayors of Dublin.[77]

A similar royal charter issued by Edward IV at Woodstock on 26 August 1464, reflects the same policy of naming those who will be responsible for wall repairs and the need for urgency. An annual grant of £30 for twelve years, taken from the Crown rent of Dublin, was made to John Bennett, Thomas Newbury, Philip Bedlowe, William Grampe and Arland Ussher, citizens and merchants of Dublin, the money to be spent on the walls, fosses and gates of the city. These men, highly respected citizens, were in turn to be supervised by four citizens elected annually. The charter acknowledged a number of connected problems, which if not attended to, would, it was believed, lead to the loss of Dublin city to the king – the frontiers on the march near the city were devastated and destroyed by English rebels and Irish enemies, the city walls were known to be decayed and weak and the loyal subjects and inhabitants of Dublin were unable to sustain the cost of repairs.[78]

Surviving evidence from the 1460s and the 1490s indicates that the Dublin assembly was aware that a number of city gates and towers were dilapidated both within the walled city and outside it in the western extremities of the city. A range of issues emerge from a reading of the municipal records, both royal charters and minutes of meetings – dilapidation of gates and towers owned by the city, a municipal authority concerned with improving the condition of gates and defences open to possible attack in the western suburbs, a dearth of city funds for necessary repairs and refurbishment and the need for supervision of expenditure, suggesting wastage of money in the past, and perhaps losses through corruption.[79]

The municipal assembly turned to private enterprise to fund their maintenance programmes. In 1455, at Fishamble Street, for example, a tower over the fish slip and the slip itself were in poor condition and needed repair. A thirty-year lease, at 6d. a year, was granted to John Marcus, merchant, to do the necessary work with lime and sand. In 1469, a similar approach was taken by the assembly in the refurbishment of an important gate in the city, the Dam Gate, which gave access across the Poddle estuary into the eastern suburbs. The gate was in a structurally poor state. A property was leased to John Roche, a tailor, for thirty years, at 4d. a year; he was permitted to 'keep the said gate as porter … upon his own proper costs' but was required to bring the structure up to standard, roofing it with oak joists and covering it with slates.[80]

The municipal assembly paid some attention to security in the western suburbs of the city. In 1462, the assembly seized a garden near Crockers' Bars gate at the western end of Crocker Street and gave permission to Roger Penkyston and Thomas Cromall to make a wall of clay on the west side of the garden for the defence of the town. Penkyston and Cromall were to have tenure of the garden until they had recovered the costs for work they had done on the wall. The construction of this clay wall or earthwork may have been an attempt to leave the Crockers' Bars gate less open or less attractive to direct attack from an enemy.[81] Four years later the city assembly noted that the Crockers' Bars gate itself was in a ruinous state and put it top of the list of works to be done in Dublin. In 1466, north of the Liffey in south-west Oxmantown, the assembly decided that the masters of the works of Dublin, their own building department, would make a gate using lime and stone at the western end of Hangman Lane. This was a new gate for Dublin.[82]

The 1460s policy of leasing municipal buildings to citizens who could afford to refurbish them was continued in the 1490s and was probably also used in the intervening decades. John White, merchant, for example, took a lease on Gormond's Gate in 1491 at the west end of Pipers' Street (Cook Street), at a rate of 4d. a year – the complete record of the agreement has not survived but it seems that White was required to build the structure in the first three years of the lease. In July of the same year, Thomas Bellewe and his wife Elizabeth took a lease of fifty-nine years on the tower of the Pool Gate, where Werburgh Street meets Bride Street. The agreement required them to build the tower with lime and stone, their work to be overseen by the mayor and masters of the works of the said city. The tower was to be roofed with oak and slates. In the following year, Reynold Talbot took out a sixty-year lease on what would appear to be Fitzsimon's Tower between Newgate, where Cornmarket meets Thomas Street, and Gormond's Gate at Pipers' Street west. Within two years Talbot was to roof the tower with oak timber and boards.[83]

The night watch

In any thriving city with people coming and going the authorities would be concerned about order and security, and it was no different in 1450s Dublin. Besides having to deal with Co. Dublin being under constant threat from the Irish (see below), especially in the south county, the city authorities were concerned about the number of Irish in the city and within that group the presence of 'all manner of holtaghys' or Ulstermen. Beggars were a problem and scholars walking and begging at night. It seems that the authorities could not differentiate between beggars and friars who were allowed to beg (known as 'questing'), and so passed an ordinance requiring a procedure that must have irritated churchmen greatly – in effect a police line-up of friars in Dublin – Augustinians, Carmelites, Dominicans and Franciscans:

> Also, it was ordained, by authority of the said assembly, that the priors of the four orders of friars bring up their friars with them before [the] mayor and bailiffs of the said city, and there to take their oaths after the tenor of their own charters.[84]

7 (*opposite page*) Map of the night-watch routes in Dublin. Taken together, the routes totalled about 2.6km. Broadly, the three routes covered by the night-watch patrols were: route A, from Gormond's Gate through Bridge Street, along the river frontage, to Cook Street and Pipers' Street; route B, from New Gate through High Street, Nicholas Street, Patrick Street, Rochelle Street, St Audoen's Lane and Gilleholmoc Street; route C from the new Tholsel, through Skinners' Street, Castle Street, Cork Hill as far as the Dam Gate, Bouthe Street as far as the gate in the Taverners' Street, St John's Lane, the Fishambles as far as the tower of St Olave's, and Taverners' Street as far as Winetavern Gate. The second patrol (route B) went outside the city walls, 200 metres south along Patrick Street to St Patrick's Gate. (Map drawn by Dr Fergal Donoghue; the base map is taken from H.B. Clarke, *IHTA no. 11, Dublin part I, to 1610*, map 4.)

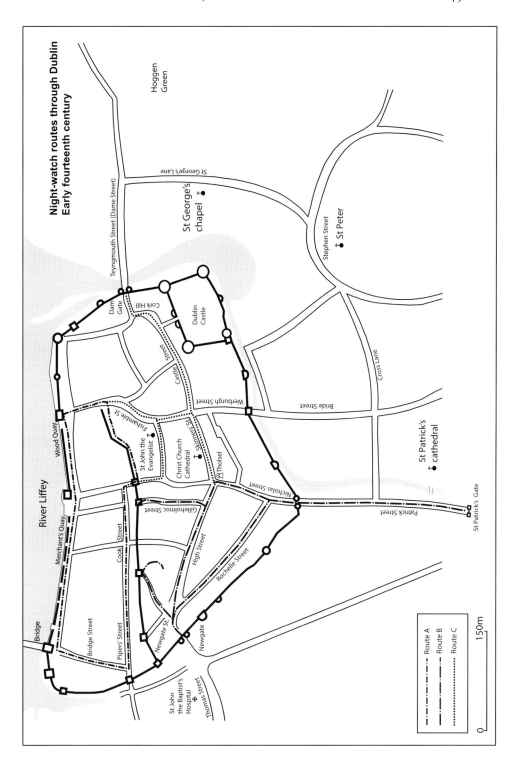

Night-watch routes through Dublin
Early fourteenth century

River Liffey

Hoggen Green

St George's Lane

St George's chapel

Teyngmouth Street (Dame Street)

Dam Gate

Cork Hill

Dublin Castle

Castle Street

Werburgh Street

Stephen Street

St Peter

Cross Lane

Bride Street

St Patrick's cathedral

St Patrick's Gate

Patrick Street

Nicholas Street

Wood Quay

Fishamble St

St John the Evangelist

Skinners' St.

Christ Church Cathedral

Tholsel

Merchant's Quay

Gillehholmoc Street

Cook Street

High Street

Rochelle Street

Bridge

Bridge Street

Pipers' Street

Newgate St.

Newgate

St John the Baptist's Hospital

Thomas Street

Route A
Route B
Route C

150m

0

In the 1450s, prompted by these security issues, the municipal authorities in Dublin re-developed a night watch system and possibly restructured the duties of constables. This was not entirely a new departure. As long ago as 1305, a city ordinance required that three watchmen should patrol the city at night, each having 'three others with him on every night'. It is assumed that this ordinance remained in force throughout the fourteenth century and probably into the mid-fifteenth century, when, for whatever reasons, the night watch patrols as practised were deemed inadequate. Most Dubliners, other than the poorest, seem to have paid for the watch begun in 1305 including widows with property who contributed proportionately with their neighbours. Normally, at this time, mayors and bailiffs were not involved in patrolling and slept safely in their beds. One watchman and his team of three patrolled 'from Gormond's Gate to the Great Bridge and so along the entire of the river bank as far as the small tower opposite St Olave's church and Cook Street, to the gate aforesaid'. The second patrol began 'at the Newgate and so through the High Street as far as the New Tholsel and St Patrick's Gate, together with Rochelle Street (Back Lane), St Audoen's Lane, Gilmeholmoc's Lane [St Michael's Close] and another lane'. The third watchman's patrol covered an area 'from the New Tholsel by the High Street to the Gate del Dam … through the whole fish market so far as the tower of St Olave, with two adjacent lanes, one of which extends from the church of St John to Boue Street (Christchurch Place (west)) as far as the gate in the Tavern Street'. Each watchman was to provide a daily meal to his assistants and if the watchmen found anything amiss on their patrols they were to report to the city bailiffs (figure 7).[85]

The Dublin assembly, in introducing a night watch in 1305, had pre-empted parliamentary legislation ordered to be observed in Ireland from March 1308. Under this legislation, gates in enclosed towns such as Dublin were to be closed from sunset to sunrise. No one was to lodge in the suburbs or in foreign parts of the town, day or night, if the host would not answer for him. Town bailiffs were to carry out weekly or fortnightly inspections for such lodgers and take action if such persons were 'suspected of being against the peace'. In every city, watch was to be kept at every gate by six men from the day of the Ascension to St Michael's day, and they were to keep watch continually all night, from sunset to sunrise. Strangers were to be arrested and held 'until morning' when they would be dealt with. If they should escape, a 'hue-and-cry' was to be made until they were found and brought to the sheriff.[86]

In September 1457, constables were chosen who were to have responsibility for named streets or wards. Many were drawn from well-known merchant families, for example, John Bowland, John Tankard, Walter Dough and Arland

Ussher.[87] Almost a decade later, in 1465, constables continued to be chosen each year for the same purpose and invariably from the same ruling mercantile and skilled stratum of Dublin society. Each group was responsible for a specific named street or an area such as the Key, Oxmantown or St Werburgh's parish.[88]

Table 1.1 Dublin constables and their wards/streets, 1465–6

Patrick Street	Master John Bowland, corviser, Thomas Walsh, James Brown, dyer, William Manning, glover
Nicholas Street	John Higeley, skinner, John Fyan, merchant
High Street	Masters Thomas Walsh, Thomas Wolton, Thomas Barby, Thomas Boys
The Fishambles	John Bennet, James Mulghan
St Werburgh's parish	William Corner, armourer, John More, baker, John Wicom
Cook Street	Harry Eustace, Walter Dough, William Grampey, John Fitz Harry
Sutor Street	Stevyn Harrold, Richard White, glover
Merchant's Quay	Sir Robert Burnell, Arlonton Husher, Nicholas Coke
Wood Quay	John Bryt, John Fowler
Winetavern Street	John Higham, Thomas Palmer
Oxmantown	Nicholas Bowrke, Robert Tywe, Thomas Blake, Robert Fitz Harry, Robert Blanchevyll, Bertylmewe Sylke, yeoman
Thomas Street	John White, Nicholas Bayly, William Walyford
Francis Street	John Barry, butcher
Bride Street	Walter Russell, James Selyman, Thomas Prowt
Ship Street	Richard White, weaver, William Herford, labourer

In October 1457, the constables were involved in night duty and all constables who lived outside the closed gates of the city were to keep in their houses any man or woman they arrested until they were brought to gaol the following morning. In the same month a paid night watch was set up by the assembly; eight men would be chosen to watch nightly between October and Candlemas from curfew time till five o'clock in the morning. In October 1465, John Colleron and Robert Hanwod were appointed as 'waits' or watchmen, taking 4d. from every hall and 3d. from every shop within the city.[89]

Arising from the work of the night watchmen a group of official city musicians was developed in Dublin. There is some evidence that the earliest watchmen in Dublin would have given a signal by using a bell: in around 1316, for example, the public bell was used by day or night to call men to muster. In the fifteenth century, watchmen were known in English as 'waits', derived from the Anglo-Saxon *wacian* meaning 'to watch or guard', and would have signalled the occurrence of a number of events by sounding a horn or trumpet – an imminent attack, an outbreak of fire, marking the time of the day and the arrival of an important person.[90] Gradually, the watchmen became more involved in providing music than in keeping watch. In 1465, mentioned above, John Colleron and Robert Hanwood were appointed as 'waits, within the city'; they were to be well-paid and required to wear official livery; it is possible that they functioned solely as civic musicians.[91] In 1469, Richard Bennet and John Talbot, pipers, were admitted as freemen of Dublin city, and may subsequently have served as city musicians playing a wind instrument. Bennet was granted citizenship by 'special grace' whereas John Talbot had served his apprenticeship with John Clare, a piper perhaps in the Irish tradition, discussed below.[92] In 1498, in Dublin, at the St George's pageant civic celebration, four trumpeters were used, but it was not until 1504 that we hear of 'the office of trumpeter-ship of the city' being awarded to Walter Owrey. He had status: he was to have a chamber, wear 'a gown of the city', had wages of 26s. 8d. annually, and was 'to give attendance daily upon the mayor'.[93] For a number of reasons the trumpeters are not heard of again in city records until the 1560s, possibly because of damaged or abbreviated records, or that the office was allowed to lapse, perhaps due to a shortage of money.[94]

Utilities

From about the middle of the thirteenth century Dublin had a supply of freshwater stored in a municipal cistern or reservoir located south of Thomas Street in the vicinity of St James's Gate. Its precise location is not known. From the cistern an aqueduct was taken eastwards along Thomas Street to High Street to Skinners' Street and to Castle Street, with probable locations for three local cisterns on these streets near St Audoen's on High Street, at the high market cross near Christ Church cathedral and at the junction of Skinners' Street and Castle Street.[95]

In 1450, the Dublin public water system relied on a water course not owned by the municipal authorities, constructed in the first half of the thirteenth century and made up of a section of the river Poddle and two artificial channels. It worked very well. The upper section of the water course taken from a head of water behind a weir on the river Dodder at Balrothery, near Tallaght, was owned by the abbey of St Thomas at Thomas Court. In the

8 Balrothery weir and reservoir near Firhouse, Co. Dublin. Built early in the thirteenth century, the reservoir's diverted waters re-energised the river Poddle which in turn led to the delivery of about 2.73 million litres (600,000 gallons) of water daily to the city. (Photo courtesy of Don McEntee.)

early decades of the thirteenth century, by means of a brilliant piece of engineering, the canons of St Thomas's diverted water from behind the Balrothery weir to flow in a man-made channel and discharge into the river Poddle to provide water for the their community and probably to drive a number of mills (figure 8).[96]

In 1244, when the sheriff of Dublin, advised by the mayor and twelve men of Dublin county, was asked to identify a water course from which water 'can be best and most conveniently taken from its course and conducted to the king's city of Dublin', it seems that everyone in Dublin knew that the only suitable watercourse available was the re-energized Poddle with its enhanced volume.[97] The location on the river where the waters were divided was near Kimmage and was known as the Tongue. It has been calculated that the daily supply of water to the St James's Gate cistern in Dublin was in excess of 2.73 million litres (600,000 gallons).[98]

Connections to the municipal water supply were made by groups and individuals in the city. Possibly one of the earliest public water connections, between 1228 and 1255, was made to the Dominican property at St Saviour's in Oxmantown near the bridge. A water supply was apparently picked up at Newgate using a five-inch diameter pipe that was run northwards and across the bridge. Once the pipe entered the Dominican land its diameter was to be narrowed so that its opening could be stopped by the insertion of a man's little finger. In October 1254, the prior of Christ Church made a formal agreement with the city authorities in relation to their aqueduct; the community was able to receive water from a water cistern near the gate of the priory, the agreement to last for three years. In the middle-to-late thirteenth century costs or annual rents for a water connection were one or two shillings a household – William of Chester paid 2s., William Picot, 12d., and Alexander of Ulster, 12d. with arrears.[99]

In the second half of the fifteenth century, the city authorities employed a man to maintain the water pipes in the city and to make water conduit connections to premises. In 1456, for example, the appropriately named Richard Plummer, was taken on for a year, and was paid 1d. for connecting a shop to the water system and 2d. for installing pipes to the hall of a dwelling, shop connections, close to the pavement, being presumably short and requiring less material and time. In July 1481, beside St Michael's church, near Christ Church, repairs to the main water conduit that went from St Michael's pipe to the pillory along Skinners' Street with its two water cisterns could only be done by demolishing a shop belonging to the St Michael's property. The clergy at St Michael's were reimbursed, the costs of rebuilding the shop totalling 26s. 8d. This may be an early example of building over a water main, unlikely to happen today with the passing of planning bye-laws (figure 9).[100]

It would appear that the Dublin municipal authorities viewed the maintenance of the water course in two reaches – from the head at Balrothery to the Tongue and from there to the city cistern.[101] In late 1455, for example, John Pyll of Templeogue, a husbandman, was sworn 'to keep the water and to bring it as far as the cistern of the city'. In 1491 John Walshe, yeoman, was to have 'the keeping of the conduit of the water from the head of the same at Dodder to the Tongue'. However, if there were floods the mayor and bailiffs of Dublin were to gather a group of men from the city and from the abbeys and monasteries that had mills along the water course to build up the head again at their own expense. There were severe penalties for mill owners who did not repair the head of water – their mill horses would be impounded until they did so and 'paid the keeper for his duties'.[102]

9 Le Decer's fountain in Dublin. In 1308, John le Decer, during his mayoralty, erected this marble water cistern in the Corn Market, Dublin, near the west door of the church of St Audoen.

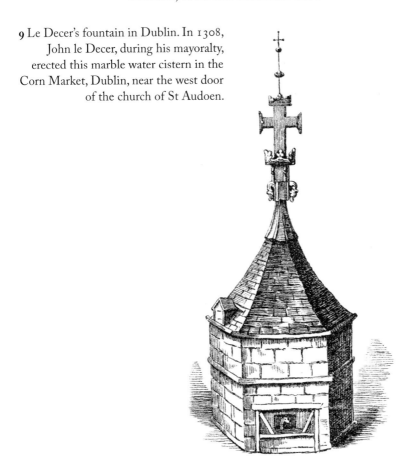

It is clear that at the beginning of the 1470s, there were problems with the security of the water course and with respect for the authority of its keeper. In a strongly worded ordinance the municipal authority marked the gravity of the situation with the level of the fines to be imposed, ordaining that 'whatsoever person or persons enter upon the town ground the which is called the pipe grass, or hinders or disturbs the keeper thereof … that he pay 6s. 8d. as often times as they do so'.[103] The Dublin assembly was constantly vigilant about water quality. In October 1466, the assembly was aware that the piped water supply was being interfered with by pollution from animals, swine being mentioned specifically, and by fishers blocking the river from time to time. Interference was not isolated but occurred in diverse places. The assembly expressed a hope that the water would be made clean and backed this up with ordaining that a fine of one noble (a gold coin worth 6s. 8d.) should be imposed on anyone found guilty of interfering with the watercourse. At the beginning of the 1490s, the city assembly became aware that the banks of the watercourse bringing water to the city cistern had been pastured with horses, cows and swine that were rooting and treading around the banks which had broken and fallen into the river. There were instances where the banks were so broken that the river ran into nearby fields. It was announced that anyone could take such animals and bring them to the city gaol where they would be held until a fine of 6s. 8d. was paid by the owners, with a half going to those who brought in the animals.[104]

The port

In the fifteenth century, the port of Dublin was located on the south bank of the river Liffey overlooked by Christ Church cathedral and Dublin Castle. Importing and exporting took place at Merchant's Quay and the Wood Quay (figure 10). There was a quayside crane with a range of weights up to twenty stone to assist loading and unloading.[105] In autumn 1450, among appointments made by the Dublin assembly to official positions in the city was 'keeper of the house of the crane' which was awarded to John Rodwell (Rothwell), merchant. The tenure ran for a number of years.[106] Later, Nicholas Bellewe was made keeper of the crane in 1457 and he seems to have been re-appointed to the position continuously until at least 1475.[107] Bellewe was a scribe and probably kept records at the crane; he was related to Philip Bellewe who was mayor of Dublin in 1455 and held an official post for the next two years with the Dublin city authorities.[108] Occasionally the office was described as 'keeper of the crane and weights', for example in 1461 and 1475.[109] Nicholas Bellewe's work of transcribing religious tracts will be discussed below.

In 1469, the crane was probably a block-and-tackle affair, worked by porters who were to take in wine, millstones, iron, pitch and resin.[110] In slack times on the quayside, the porters were forbidden to absent themselves or to do other work. They were never to leave the guide rope unwatched; the penalty was a fine of 6s. 8d. and that they would lose their job.[111] In 1489, a new crane was attached to a set of counter-balancing weights ranging from twenty stone to half a stone.[112]

The port was run efficiently and no ship came in or out of Dublin without dealing with port officers. In October 1458, it was made clear that all masters, owners and pursers of all ships whether coming in or going out from Dublin had to produce a ship's manifest of their cargoes. Penalties were severe in the case of non-compliance – a master, owner or purser could forfeit his merchandise and even his ship.[113]

'Foreign' non-Dublin merchants were welcome in the port of Dublin but were required to familiarize themselves with the operating rules of the port. In

10 A late medieval slipway at Merchant's Quay. The visible slipway surface, over 3.5 metres in length, is covered by the tidal Liffey estuary each day at high tide. (Photo: P. Slattery, taken with the permission of Dublin City Council.)

October 1458, for example, any foreign man wishing to purchase hides, deer hides, goatskins, sheepskins, lambskins, yarn, wax and tallow should only buy from a citizen of Dublin. Any foreign merchant bringing iron, salt, wine and coals for sale in Dublin was required to deal with four official buyers who represented the generality of Dublin merchants. If buyers and merchants could not agree about price then there was to be a period of forty days in which they might agree. If nothing was agreed and no sale of the imported goods occurred then the foreign merchants were free to leave with their merchandise.[114] Keeping foreign merchants and their crews in port over a long period was a deliberate tactic to wear down the foreign merchant and force him to sell at a lower price, as was done in England at Ipswich, in the fourteenth century, for example. At Ipswich, and possibly in Dublin, a hosting system operated whereby the incoming merchant could stay with a citizen or man of high renown who would offer advice and through whom the importer could conduct his business.[115]

In relation to the forty-day rule, about Easter 1455, an especially harsh regime was implemented on timber imports into Dublin from Wicklow and other places. The Dublin assembly formally ordained that all timber coming from Wicklow, and from any other place, including slates, boards and gutters, should 'lie upon the key for the space of forty days', and that no man should buy for the purpose of retailing any slates, spars, gutters or timber in that period. A regime of fines was set up for the first, second, and third offence, the fines being set at 6s. 8d., 13s. 4d., and 20s. The fine of 20s. applied in the case of repeating offences.[116]

The essentials of the above regulations were repeated in an ordinance of 1462[117] and then in January 1465 we get a closer look at the working of port procedure. It was enunciated that if any ship of strangers arrived in the port of Dublin, the master, merchants and mariners would be called together by the water-bailiffs and official buyers before they broke bulk. The purpose of the meeting was to address the master of the incoming ship and instruct him to buy only from freemen in Dublin and to familiarize himself with the statutes of Dublin so that he would not feel the need to slander the city and complain of extortion and mistreatment when he left the port.[118]

In July 1466, the assembly enunciated that berthage fees must be paid by everyone tying up a boat in the port. It was a catch-all directive requiring that 'all manner of men, as well freemen as unfreemen, as denizens as foreigns, pay perch money to the water bailiffs of the haven of the said city …'. At the time, mariners would have had to deal with water-bailiffs Walter Rowe and John Goldsburgh. A new directive was more comprehensively worded in October 1483. There were fees to be paid by ships coming to the port of Dublin. The men to deal with in 1483 were the water bailiffs of the day, most likely Richard White and Patrick Penkiston who, allowing for gaps in the record, held these posts continuously from 1480 to 1493. The bailiffs administered two types of mooring. Any man in charge of a ship, piccard, scaff or lighter could berth at a 'perching' or buoy at a cost of 11d. of silver as often as they come in and out. A mariner who occupied the 'plangage' or plankage – whose ship presumably was tied up to timber wharves – also paid fees to the water bailiffs.[119]

From January 1453, customs dues were to be paid on the cargoes of outgoing ships leaving the port of Dublin. No mariner or ship owner was to leave the port without paying customs dues. Infringement would mean forfeiture of the ship and a fine of £10. In January 1456 it was decreed that the mayor and bailiffs of Dublin would collect customs on all incoming and outgoing ships and their merchandise without exception. From October 1454, merchandise arriving in the port of Dublin, such as salt, iron, pitch, resin, coal or any other goods, could be bought only by the official buyers of the city. These were chosen by the city assembly to purchase commodities on behalf of Dublin merchants – the buyers chosen in October 1455 were Thomas

Newbery, John White, John Tankard and Thomas Savage. These office holders seem to have had a tenure of a few years and the office title changed, sometimes perhaps reflecting a current problem. In autumn 1468, the title was 'city buyer of salt and iron', with the following appointees listed as buyers – Simon FitzRery, Arland Ussher, Thomas FitzSimon and John Fouler. In autumn 1470, the official function of the buyers was 'city buyers of salt, iron and wheat, brought for sale to Dublin', reflecting possibly an expected shortage of wheat and flour in the coming winter. The buyers chosen were Thomas Bennet, John Walshe, Richard Stanyhurst and Ricard Chillam. Buyers for the city of Dublin were still being chosen in 1494.[120]

The problem of pigs and refuse

In the late 1450s, swine were on the loose in the streets of Dublin and had become a serious problem. If pigs got free of their owners they could be a formidable animal to control, and of course they fouled the streets and pavements wherever they wandered. In 1458, the Dublin assembly called upon every man that had swine in the city to either drive their pigs outside the city walls or else lock them up so that they could not do harm to their neighbours. The problem had become so bad that pigs were finding their way into halls, porches, cellars or taverns and creating a nuisance. Owners were informed that if pigs were slain or hurt when on the loose they would have no claim against the perpetrators.[121]

Over a decade later, in 1469, pigs continued to destroy gardens and were rooting around in the porches of citizens' houses. It was decreed that it was lawful for any such swine to be killed and that the killers were not to be impeached or be liable for costs. Following a detailed writ sent to the assembly in 1489 by Gearóid Mór FitzGerald, earl of Kildare, about the problem of dung in the city, which will be discussed below in detail, the assembly eventually took a decision to settle the 'kine and swine' problem in Dublin. Probably the combination of two factors – the droppings of cows and pigs abroad causing a health hazard and the problem of bulky difficult-to-control animals loose on the streets – forced the assembly in late October 1491 to insist that cows and pigs be cleared from within the walls of the city by decreeing 'that all that have kine and swine within the walls of the said city, that they and every of them bring not their said kine nor swine within the said walls hereafter upon pain of forfeiture of them and every of them'.[122]

In October 1460, it was understood in Dublin that carters and car men who drew dung out of the city were permitted to carry clay into the city on the return journey. The rates were: two carts of dung for a penny, and four cars of dung for a penny; the rate for a cartload of clay brought into the city was 1½d., and for three cars of clay incoming it cost 1d. If the cart men and car men overcharged they were fined 4d. for each infringement.[123]

From the 1460s, and indeed earlier, the streets and lanes of Dublin would have been covered in a veneer of dung from the droppings of horses, pigs and dogs. Human waste had to be disposed of by each householder and while places were set aside for this outside the city walls many Dubliners dumped waste illegally. The city assembly was concerned about the dirty streets and noxious smells and passed ordinances directing animal owners and city dwellers to dump waste outside the city. In January 1467, cart men and car men were directed not to dump dung in gardens nor within the walls of the city on pain of a 12d. fine. Persons responsible for their family's or animals' dung were directed to take away the waste on the day it was produced. In the following year, Dubliners were reminded of an old city law that commanded them to keep the street clean in front of their household door – that every householder should clean the portion of the street before his own door, 'under a penalty of twelve pence'.[124]

The problem of getting rid of dung from the city was ongoing and some years later, in July 1468, dung was being dumped at unofficial sites such as at city gates by carriers who had cut short their journeys to officially designated sites. There were three such sites – 'without Hankman's lane' in Oxmantown where there were 'holes and pits', a 'hole beyond the Hogges butt' and on 'the other side of St Francis church'. There was a fine of 12d. for each infringement by cart or car men who were paid for their work, and by apprentices and others, such as servants, who were ordered to do this unsavoury work by their masters and mistresses and who, once identified, had to pay the fine of 12d.[125]

The problem continued and in late 1485 it became especially serious at Hangman's Lane where carters and car men cast dung contrary to an old city law. Servants and apprentices, with no choice, still took on the unpleasant task of getting rid of dung in baskets and bags. One man, Thomas Sharpe, was put in charge of keeping the lane clean. Working with deputies he had the authority to bring illegal dumpers to jail. They were released when they paid a 12d. fine, a half of which went to Sharpe with the other half going to the city court. While Sharpe was paid as described, if he failed to keep the lane clean he too would be fined at the higher rate of 6s. 8d.[126]

A decade later, in 1496, the problem of illegal dumping of dung remained. It was known that there was a connection between dung and disease and the problem was taken seriously by the city assembly. Dung was being dumped in the lane behind the fleshambles in High Street and the fine was set at 20s. In late July an ultimatum was given 'that every man put away all their dung that is anent their stables and other places in the said lane by St Bartholomew's day next coming'. A period of about four weeks was given to get the lane clean or the bailiffs would come to apply the law.[127]

It would appear that at the end of the 1480s dirt, dung, disease and smells had become a more serious problem than before. It was no longer a Dublin assembly matter but was being discussed at government level. In a writ sent to the assembly from Gerald, earl of Kildare, received on 14 November 1489, the city authority was commanded by Henry VII to deal with the matter. It was clear that there was a major health problem in Dublin and that immediate action was needed. It was also noted that the smooth running of government was being endangered:

> The king has been informed that dung heaps, swine, hogsties and other nuisances in the streets, lanes and suburbs of Dublin, infect the air and produce mortality, fevers and pestilence throughout that city. Many citizens and sojourners have died in Dublin. The fear of pestilence prevents the coming thither of lords, ecclesiastics and lawyers. Great detriments arise thence to his majesty, as well as dangers to his subjects and impediments to business.

The king commanded that the mayor and bailiffs bring about the removal of all swine from the city and that they have the streets and lanes freed from ordure and prevent loss of life from the 'pestilential exhalations' that hung over the city.[128]

The Irish problem

Attacks by the Irish on Co. Dublin in the late fifteenth century produced a number of reactions from the authorities – the passing of parliamentary legislation, the promulgation of municipal ordinances, the foundation of military guilds and the organizing of military expeditions to go on the attack. In the early 1450s, there were a number of recorded breaches of security in Co. Dublin, involving Irish enemies and English rebels getting closer to the city. Such groups had broken through defences that allowed them to get into Fingal at night, over the ford by the pier of St Mary's abbey and at the bridges at Kilmainham and Lucan. They had killed and robbed persons loyal to the king and it needed a speedy remedy to stop them. Parliament decided to build towers with gates at the Kilmainham and Lucan bridges, and a wall and tower on St Mary's abbey lands.[129]

The Dublin assembly, probably prompted by these and similar incidents, saw a threat from those Irish living in Dublin and decided to clear them from

the city. At the end of July 1454, the Dublin assembly promulgated a comprehensively worded ordinance in which they directed that anyone of Irish blood
and nation, with some exceptions, must leave Dublin within a month – 'that
all manner of men of Irish blood, and women, that is to say Irish nuns, Irish
clerks, and Irish journeymen, Irish apprentices, Irish servants and Irish beggars,
men, women and children, also all manner of Irish householders … that they
and every of them quit by this day four weeks'. An exception was made of
those Irish who had been dwelling in the city for twelve years.[130] Such municipal policies are understandable in an authority whose political and cultural
composition was English. In the fifteenth century, the Irish government and
the Dublin municipal authority were under pressure from the resurgent
Gaelic-Irish who had recovered territory across the island and were knocking
at the gates of the city. Increased military and financial support from England
was needed but not forthcoming with the result that the core of English power
and culture in Ireland was confined to Dublin and the Pale or the four loyal
shires of Dublin, Kildare, Louth and Meath.[131]

   It is useful to define the terms 'Irish' and 'English' in the context of the late
medieval period in Dublin and of the four loyal shires. The term 'Irish' is taken
to mean those of Irish descent or ancestry, though such persons could be
'anglicized' culturally to varying degrees, taking on English language, dress and
customs. Equally, those of English descent in Ireland could become 'Gaelicized'
by having such extensive economic and cultural interaction with the Irish as
to adopt Irish customs. The English of Ireland thought of themselves as
'English' or 'the English of Ireland'.[132] Frame has drawn attention to the
emergence of 'the English of Ireland', a process significantly advanced in the
period 1315–30, in light mainly of the weakening of the old original noble
lordships through a series of dynastic accidents leading to tenurial instability
in Carlow, Kilkenny, Leinster, Meath, Ulster, Wexford and in the south-west.
As a result, the families concentrated their attention on their estates in
England, Wales and France. By 1330, the new earldoms of Desmond, Kildare,
Louth and Ormond had been created and 'a more distinct higher colonial
nobility', who thought of themselves as 'the English of Ireland', began to
emerge as leaders.[133] The core characteristics and beliefs of the English of
Ireland, whether established in Ireland over many generations, with some
Gaelicized, or who were new arrivals from England, were that they were
different from and separate and superior to the Irish, that there was a
distinction in law between the English and the Irish, that they participated in
parliament and that they believed in the connection with the Crown.[134]

   While politically the colonial community in the four shires was English,
economically they relied on the Irish to replenish town populations and to be

agricultural tenants. The Irish on the land ranged from being unfree labourers to having significant land holdings to being higher status Irish with a history of long settlement. Population losses in the English colony from the Bruce war, the Black Death and fourteenth-century famines offered opportunities to the Irish to migrate into the colony and to work on the land, at service, at a trade or in the Church. At the same time, the Irish in the four shires, especially the newcomers, were seen in the shires as a threat to the colonists and their way of life.[135] There were examples of Irish tenants close to Dublin – a small number around Maynooth (1452–3) – Philip McCormyn, Simon Otlgagh and Schan Stanton, for example. In the 1470s, on Ormond lands in Turvey, Rush and Balscadden, likely Irish tenants included – Maryon (*Muireann*), Johannes Kildroght, Thomas Conghur, Evvot Coyng, Thomas Kenan, Agnes Dowlyn and Conghor Coylok[136] The Irish of the four shires continued to improve their social and economic status in the fifteenth century as seen in land transactions. From the beginning of the fifteenth century legislation was passed against trading with the Irish and against Irish persons living in colonial towns. It would appear that exclusionary legislation and bye-laws were applied with some discretion because the Irish were an important element of the economy.[137]

In Dublin in our period the Irish were part, though a minority, of the fabric of society – citizens of Dublin, office-holders, master craftsmen practising their trade in the city, and holding positions of authority in ecclesiastical institutions in the city. A number of anglicized Irish families were fully assimilated into city life such as the families of Shynnagh, Mulghan and Donogh. John Shynnagh was present at the founding of the Dublin merchants guild in 1451 and John Shennagh was bailiff of the city in 1462 and 1463. Thomas Mulghan was a municipal bailiff in 1472 and served as mayor in 1481. Walter Donogh/Donnagh was bailiff in 1449 and 1450 and William Donogh was bailiff in 1473.[138] Intermarriage between Irish and English occurred and citizenship was conferred on an unfree person who married a citizen – in October 1475, in Dublin, John Mulghan, yeoman, marrried to Jenet Sowthren, free woman, became a citizen, and in the same month, Richard Danyell, labourer, married to Cecilia Colman, free woman, was given the franchise of the city. In October 1476, John Ingerame, fisher, married to Anne Kele, free woman, was granted citizenship. It is interesting that Cecilia Colman and Anne Kele, though of Irish descent, were citizens of Dublin, probably through being the daughter or wife of a citizen.[139]

There is some evidence that the Irish poor were also in Dublin. A municipal ordinance was passed (1462) forbidding women to cry or keen out loud in grief for those killed in war or to tear their clothes in sympathy;

keening was an Irish practice.[140] In 1466, an ordinance was passed banning women from wearing saffroned (dyed) smocks and kerchiefs; saffron was a dye that also had anti-lice properties. It seems that clothes dyed in this way were worn openly by Irish women, unacceptable to the authorities, unlike the English practice of wearing a saffroned garment as an under garment.[141] The passing of the ordinances suggest that the numbers of such incidents in the city and the numbers of such women involved were not negligible.

While some musicians in the city would probably have played music in the English tradition, or were civic musicians (trumpeters) – Richard Bennet and John Talbot – others may have played in the Irish tradition – a fiddler, William Kenan, a citizen of Dublin by special grace (1486);[142] a harper, James Hanwodd, a citizen of Dublin by special grace (1487),[143] and piper John Clare to whom John Talbot served his apprenticeship.[144] There is an Irish element in each of the three above – a piper named Clare, possibly from that county, a fiddler with an Irish surname (Kenan), and the harp associated with Ireland. Two were mentored by unknown men of substance, possibly of the merchant class, who knew how to work the municipal levers to raise their man to honorary citizenship, and in turn perhaps give Irish music some status in the city.

In the late medieval period, English was the principal vernacular in Dublin – the dialect of English spoken in Ireland and in Dublin was Hiberno-Middle English. Nevertheless, at various levels of society in Dublin city and county, Irish was spoken. In our period, the large and growing population of Irish peasantry in the four loyal shires spoke Irish and continued to do so in 1515 and in c.1540.[145] Of those Irish who were dissatisfied with their lot in the four shires and had ambition, there was the call of the city and its opportunities for a better life. They came to Dublin bringing their cultural goods with them. In the late medieval period and in the sixteenth century, the elite of Co. Meath spoke Irish – the Nugents of Delvin, Sir William Darcy of Platin and Patrick Bermingham, the chief justice of the king's bench. In the late fifteenth century, the Plunketts of Dunsany would appear to have been bilingual. Being bilingual was not seen as incompatible with loyalty, but not speaking English was seen as suspect. The use of Irish nicknames by a family indicates that Irish was probably known and spoken – Walter Ryagh Cruise and Remon Carragh Cruise of the Cruise (Cruys) family of the north Co. Dublin-Meath region bore the names Ryagh (*riabhach*, swarthy) and Carragh (*carrach*, scabby), strongly suggesting that the family had more than a simple knowledge of Irish. There is evidence that the marcher families of Co. Dublin, the Harolds, Lawlesses and Howels, for example, were Gaelicized.[146] However, it seems that members of the Harold family also participated in city life, eleven being listed as citizens in the Dublin franchise roll, 1468–1512. Three were involved in the meat trade – a probable connection with the marcher Harolds, who practised a pastoral economy in upland or wooded areas – Nicholas (1478) and Richard (1482) were butchers in Dublin, Nicholas taking on Millane Harroll as an apprentice in 1478. Additionally, Richard accepted Richard Coyn alias Tyve as an apprentice, Coyn being Irish (1482). The Harolds had influence with the municipal authorities, two of the family being granted full citizenship – Christina Harolde, 'by special grace' (1482) and Patrick Harolle 'at the instance of the mayor' (1494). In Dublin in the late medieval period, both the English and the Irish were bilingual in order to trade with each other, and yet, the English remained loyal and were seen to be loyal to the Crown.[147]

Although positions of authority in the Church in Dublin were usually occupied by individuals of English stock or background, clergy of the Irish nation occasionally got into senior positions in ecclesiastical institutions in Dublin: Richard Hedyan (Ó hEidigheáin) was prior of St John the Baptist's Hospital without the Newgate in the late 1460s[148] and John Ociretean, who was probably Irish, was prior of the abbey of St Thomas the Martyr in 1475.[149] In the secular domain, despite master craftsmen in Dublin being reminded that they should not take on apprentices of the Irish nation (1468)[150] nor apprentices of Irish blood (1475),[151] persons of the Irish nation were apprenticed in Dublin, completed their seven-year training and were admitted as full members of their guild and to citizenship of the city, the list below showing their chosen profession and date of admission to citizenship.

Table 1.2 Examples of persons of the Irish nation who completed an apprenticeship and were admitted to citizenship of Dublin

John Leyghlyn (Ó Lochlainn)	Merchant	1487
John Kenan (Ó Cianáin)	Tailor	1487
Laghlyn Berne (Lochlainn Ó Broin)	Butcher	1489
Denis Neell (Ó Néill)	Shearman	1492[152]

In a detailed supporting memorandum to do with the exclusionary ordinances of July 1454 above, the assembly advised what the consequences would be for anyone of the Irish nation who lingered on in Dublin or its franchises – they would forfeit their goods and chattels and be imprisoned and not released until they paid a fine and ransom like the king's Irish enemies were required to do. Special commissioners were selected to promote the policy – Sir Robert Burnell and the two city bailiffs, James Blakeney and William Chamberlayn; John Tankard represented the jurats, with the commons represented by Thomas Barby, John Geydon, John Goldesburgh, William Grace, John Power, John Tirrell, Walter Rowe and Harry White.[153]

Attempting to prevent the growth of the Irish problem in the future, the assembly decreed in 1454 that Irish apprentices and Irish servants were not to be taken on in the city on pain of a fine of 40s. in each instance. Attempting to employ Irish persons was deemed a crime – no one from any level of society was to seek or negotiate taking on, favouring or maintaining anyone of the Irish nation on pain of a fine of 40s. The policy did not work and, in October 1455, over a year later, the Dublin assembly promulgated a new anti-Irish ordinance with the severest penalty attached. The general tenor of the ordinance was that certain classes of Irish persons had 'seven days … to avoid the king's city of Dublin' on pain of forfeiting all property found on them and of 'perpetual imprisonment'. The first on the list required to leave Dublin were Ulstermen, followed by Irish beggars, Irish nuns, Irish hermits, Irish clerks, Irish friars, and all manner of beggars that have come 'out of strange parts'. The constables of every ward were to search within their areas and find the Ulstermen and beggars.[154]

In January 1458, the assembly returned to the ongoing problem of the Irish being in their midst, inside the enclosure of Dublin's walls. On this occasion the assembly was concerned with visitors coming to Dublin and lodging at night in the city. The ordinance attempted to tackle innkeepers who were turning a blind eye and allowing Irish men, their horses and horse-boys, to lodge within the walls of the city at night. The fine on innkeepers who took in Irishmen was 6s. 8d.[155]

Despite the efforts of the assembly in the mid-1460s, the problem did not go away, and Irishmen were living in increasing numbers in the loyal counties of Dublin, Kildare, Louth and Meath. In 1465, parliament seems to have accepted the situation and promoted the Anglicization of the Irish in the Pale. The Irish were to wear English apparel and men were to shave above the mouth in the English fashion. After a year they were to swear allegiance to the king. The Irish must set aside their Irish surnames and use instead the names of towns, such as Chester, Kinsale or Trim, for example; or a colour, such as Black, Brown or White; or they could take on a surname based on an art or office – Carpenter, Smith, Butler or Cook, for example.[156] Well into the new century, in the 1530s, the Irish migrating into the Pale was still a problem to the government. The house of Kildare had collapsed in 1534 and a more aggressive attitude to the Irish was seen in government policy-makers. Chief justice Thomas Luttrell, a Thomas Cromwell appointee, wrote to London in about September 1537, advising *inter alia* that 'Irish beggars, rhymers, bards, common women, pardoners, pipers, harpers and the like should not be suffered to come into the Pale'.[157]

There was a threat to Dublin from the midlands and soon after Easter 1468 the Dublin assembly prorogued the conduct of its business because the mayor, bailiffs and commons were in hostile O'Connor country in the midlands with John Tiptoft, earl of Worcester, deputy governor in Ireland.[158] The physical threat to Dublin remained, and in about 1471–2 Co. Dublin's security was breached on its south-western flank. A number of Wicklow septs, the O'Byrnes and O'Tooles, for example, burned the unenclosed village of Saggart. The settlement was regarded as an important protection for Co. Dublin and therefore of Dublin city. The parliament took this incident very seriously and called for over 320 men to be organized into a workforce. A group of 240 men were drawn from the baronies of Balrothery, Castleknock and Coolock, and were to come to Saggart with barrows, spades and pickaxes, and work for three days beginning within an hour and a half after sunrise. Another group, men who might well be termed local, were drawn from the barony of Newcastle and were to work for six days under the same conditions. Their object was to enclose Saggart and its fosses. The work was compulsory, with a system of repeating and increasing fines applied to the labourers to make sure that they would come and complete the work.[159]

Legislation passed in 1465 requiring every Englishman in Ireland, and every Irish person who lived in an English community, to have an English bow with twelve shafts seems to have prompted the Dublin assembly to require the fraternity of St Edmund to manufacture arrows that would be stored in the Tholsel in Dublin. The guild master was Philip Bermingham, with John Weste and Thomas Milton acting as wardens. The guild's chantry was at the chapel of St Edmund in Christ Church cathedral.[160]

Another guild, the Brotherhood of Arms of St George, known as the Guild of St George, was set up in 1474, arising from an inspection of the Pale defences in 1473.[161] It has been described as 'the first real standing army in medieval Ireland', its primary purpose being to protect the Pale which in turn gave a measure of security to Dublin.[162] It was a force of 200 fully equipped men made up of 120 mounted archers, 40 men-at-arms and 40 pages, commanded by its captain Gerald FitzGerald, the eighth earl of Kildare.[163] In 1493, Richard Arland and Richard Stanihurst, masters of the guild, and Thomas Bermingham and Richard Tirrell, wardens, were granted an annuity by Henry VII 'to be expended on the purchase of bows and arrows to be distributed every year among the commons of Dublin who will by force of arms aid in the defence of the loyal subjects against the incursions of Irish and English rebels, in expeditions and hostings'.[164] Often short of funds, the guild was re-established in 1479 and continued in service until abolished in 1494.[165]

In 1471–2, the threat to Dublin came closer. Piers Cruys, civic sword-bearer, and his wife Alison, held two messuages and one hundred acres of land at Crumlin. Cruys was taken by the O'Byrnes and eventually ransomed. In his absence his lands became wasted and there were no tenants to occupy the lands and work them because they were oppressed by the marchers who occupied the boundary lands between the Irish and colonial lands.[166] In 1478, the midlands were also seen as a security threat to Dublin, on this occasion from the O'Mores, an Irish enemy of the king. Again, the mayor, John West, the bailiffs Janico Marcus and Richard Arland, and the commons of the Dublin assembly were absent from municipal business in October 1478 and were in the field with the deputy, Lord Henry Grey.[167] The Dublin assembly did not sit in July 1495 because the mayor, bailiffs and commons were at Waterford on a 'hostile expedition' with Sir Edward Poynings, king's deputy in Ireland. A dutiful scribe in Dublin, marking the absence of the assembly, noted 'Ordinances not enacted'.[168]

* * *

Dublin grew and thrived as a commercial city on the foundation of royal rights and privileges granted to the merchant class, but the flow of royal money to support the city was less than expected. When finance was forthcoming for infrastructural maintenance, spending was often tightly monitored possibly because of previous instances of wastage and corruption. The municipal powers governed Dublin by the passing of laws, insisting on obedience to city ordinances and respect for its governors. Despite its flaws and the perceived threat of the Irish from within the city, and the actual threat on its margins, we can speak of Dublin as a law-abiding and peaceful city. Bearing in mind the constant problem and cost of maintenance – roads, paths, walls and gates, the provision of water and dealing with the near impossible task of waste disposal – the market places of the city functioned well and port infrastructures and procedures worked smoothly. English was the language of the city but Irish was known, spoken by many and heard by everyone. There are moments when the city could be described as decayed, decrepit, smelly and diseased, but with all its imperfections Dublin was open for business.

CHAPTER 2

Merchants and Commerce in Dublin

O N TUESDAY 19 MARCH 1476, in the Cheshire county court, the details of a widespread currency fraud were presented to the justice, Thomas, earl of Derby. The merchants named were from Bradford, Manchester, Stockport and Wigan, and from towns in Ireland – Dublin, Drogheda and Trim. Some twenty merchants from Dublin were involved, many of whom were citizens and some of whom had held office in the city. The indictment recorded that on 2 October 1475 at Burton-on-Wirral the plotters planned the destruction of England's legal coinage, the scheme hinging on getting one English coin to Ireland to be used as a basis for making a die to produce coins. Counterfeit coins were made and were circulating in Chester on 4 December 1475.[1]

The names of indicted Dublin merchants are as follows in the order in which they appear on the indictment roll:[2]

> Thomas Cantwell, John Sweteman, Thomas Berefote, Thomas West, William Bradok, Patrick FitzLeones, Thomas Bedlowe, Robert Forster, Roger Feypow, Richard Parker, Richard Sarswell, John Cru[un?]der, Nicholas White, Thomas Longe, Peter Walsh, Christopher Hegley, Matthew Fouler, John Denys, Nicholas Cordy, Nicholas Mandewe.

To what extent the indictments became widely known in Dublin is not clear; the case of the indicted must have been discussed by their peers, members of the guild merchant and the ruling municipal class, a group perceived as trustworthy and honourable, involved in city administration, law-making and commercial dealing. Did the scandal promote any self-questioning among that group? The counterfeit scheme was the antithesis of what the civic governing class claimed to represent. Of the twenty Dubliners indicted and described as 'merchants', thirteen were listed on the Dublin franchise roll as merchants and citizens.[3] The situation was yet more embarrassing for the merchant class – Richard Parker and Patrick FitzLeones who were indicted had held the post of city bailiff in 1471 and 1473, the second-highest office in Dublin, and Matthew Fouler, also named in court, was a Dublin city bailiff in the year of his indictment (1476).[4] In the following year, with court procedure moving slowly, commercial and municipal life in Dublin seem to have been unruffled. Indicted merchants from Dublin continued to go to England on business – John Sweteman and Christopher Hegeley entering Chester on seven occasions. Matthew Fouler continued to trade in England, sending Thomas Fouler, a merchant and citizen of Dublin, possibly his son, to Chester in early November 1476, and in 1477, John Clerke went to England as Fouler's agent on two occasions in March.[5] Patrick FitzLeones, a member of a respected merchant family, also indicted, was elected mayor of Dublin for 1477.[6]

* * *

In 1450, at the beginning of our period, Dublin, a settlement of about 6,000 to 8,000 people,[7] was a city in which merchants traded successfully, buying and selling, importing and exporting. Since the coming of the Anglo-Normans to Dublin, an economic milieu grounded in royal privilege and law was created in which the work of craftsmen and merchants could thrive. As will be seen, additional parliamentary legislation, refined on a number of occasions, improved safeguards for the use of credit, so vital for the confidence of merchants. True, the local merchants were intent that they themselves should trade profitably but they were also conscious of preserving the name of the port of Dublin as a location which welcomed foreign merchants who would leave Dublin satisfied. Visiting merchants did not meet a free-for-all in Dublin but dealt with officially-appointed buyers in the first instance. Dublin had local resources to feed its people, being situated in a fertile agricultural hinterland well suited to growing and rearing the fruits of tillage and pastoralism – barley, oats, wheat, cattle, horses, pigs and sheep. These in turn were processed into ale, beef, bone, bread, butter, cheese, fat, flour, hides, milk, mutton, pork and tallow. All was not perfect in Dublin – it had a constant waste disposal and hygiene problem, both animal and human; there were skirmishes, raids and attacks from the Irish on Co. Dublin march lands, never involving a breach of the city walls, and, a problem critically to do with shipping – the approaches to Dublin port were difficult and tortuous due to silting and shallows in the Liffey estuary. Earlier we saw that Dublin had a central business district, dominated by the buildings of national and municipal government – Dublin Castle and the Tholsel – with Christ Church cathedral at the city centre. The staple foods of the day could be had in High Street (meat) and at its western end (grain) with fish in Fishamble Street. It is believed that Bothe Street, probably with many retail stalls, was the busiest of streets.[8]

Debts, pie powder courts and tally sticks

By 1450, Dublin merchants had been working for over 200 years in a commercial context in which credit could be obtained and debts registered in a formal way. The time-honoured ways of closing a deal would have been used – the handclasp, the passing over of a small coin and the buying of a drink. Deals were done in the open and in daylight hours with witnesses present.[9] Debts arising from small transactions were not registered formally but simply committed to memory by the participants and a few witnesses.[10] Wealthy merchants could purchase goods abroad wholesale using a well-established banking device, the bill of exchange, which was addressed to a particular party and promised repayment abroad of sums already advanced, that is, money paid into a Florence firm in London could be paid out in Florence.[11]

Earlier, in the event of not being paid on time, merchants on the move from town to town and from fair to fair, requiring prompt payment, could rely on merchant law courts for a speedy decision. They sought and received the services of a court of pie powder at short notice of a few hours – 'pie poudré' signifying the dusty foot of merchants who came in to court with the dust of their journey on their shoes.[12] There are early references to merchant law and pie powder courts in Britain, surviving documentation showing that in the time of Henry I (1100–35) 'a court was an ordinary appurtenance of a fair';[13] in 1226 at Falmouth in England local authorities offered quick justice to a merchant from Bruges 'according to the law of merchants',[14] and in the second quarter of the twelfth century there is a reference to 'piepowdrous' courts in Scotland.[15] The administration of merchant law differed from common law in that it was less formal, used common sense and delivered decisions promptly.[16]

Legislation passed in 1477, applicable in Ireland, recognized that 'diverse fairs' were held in the realm and that attached to every fair was a 'court of pypowders' in which every person coming to a fair 'should have lawful remedy of all manner of contracts, trespasses, covenants, debts, and other deeds made or done within any of the same fairs, during the time of the same fairs, and within the jurisdiction of the same, and to be tried by merchants being [of] the same fair'.[17] For all practical purposes merchant law was almost completely concerned with pleas of debt and contract,[18] and while the legislation repeatedly refers to fairs, it seems that agreements, contracts and debts made and incurred at markets also came within the scope of the legislation.[19]

The pie powder or merchant court was presided over by the mayor (or equivalent officer) in a borough or corporate town or before the steward if the market or fair belonged to a lord. Below the presiding officer a clerk of the market together with a second clerk kept the rolls of the courts. On request from the parties involved in a case, transcripts of the court records could be made, signed with the full name of the clerk along with the recognized device of the clerk which was never to be changed.[20] The court had its own special seal.[21] A notable early feature of the court of pie powder was its summary procedure, requiring that pleas concerning wayfaring merchants 'should be settled before the third tide',[22] as will, for example, be seen below in Dublin. There were local variations in the administration of courts of pie powder. In England, for example, pie powder court proceedings might be recorded on distinct pie powder court rolls or entered on the ordinary plea rolls of the borough court. There are also examples in England of pie powder courts being held in boroughs that did not have a fair or market.[23]

Procedure in the court might follow either of three paths – by 'law' (namely, compurgation) whereby one party made a statement on oath and produced about six persons of reputable standing who swore that they believed his statement to be true; by 'suit', the production of two or more witnesses who would state on oath that they believed, based on their own knowledge, having heard or seen the transaction, that the party's statement was true; by 'inquest', whereby a jury of twelve persons, gave a verdict for one party. In non-jury cases the mayor or steward did not give the judgement, but rather a small group of triers or examiners selected from the merchants present in court.[24]

Sources for the existence of pie powder courts in colonial Ireland and in Dublin are few and fragmented, but enough material has survived to show that this branch of the law was available in the colony before and down to our period of interest in Dublin. In 1323, for example, the clerk of the fair court of the town of Kilkenny, who also did clerical work for the hundred court, was paid for writing the pleas of both courts, and parchment was also bought for a number of courts including the plea rolls of the fair court.[25] Later in the century, in 1385, four men of the town were to be elected barons to hold the pleas of the fair in Kilkenny.[26] In an undated ordinance in *The great parchment book of Waterford*, the court of pie powder was available to merchants at short notice:

> Every estranger or plaintiff or defendant not able to await the common court shall have the court of pie powder from day to day and from hour to hour and he shall give the mayor and bailiffs for their use and to have for their court xx *d*.[27]

In Dublin, from the early fourteenth century, a municipal ordinance required that debts owed to foreign merchants should be settled by citizens within three ebbs and three flows of the tide, a good indication that pie powder courts were available in Dublin in the fourteenth century and most probably in the fifteenth century capable of delivering a reasonably prompt judgement. The good name of the pie powder courts was protected by the Dublin bailiffs who in the event of a debt not being settled would 'pay the amount and arrest the debtor'.[28]

In Dublin around 1450, the administration of pie powder courts continued to be actively promoted in, for example, the south Co. Dublin/north Wicklow area, replicating what was available contemporaneously in Dublin city. Sir Esmond Mulso was given leave to make a town where to him seemed best in the territory of Fercullen, in the frontier of the marches, a key area regarded as a protection for the counties of Dublin and Kildare.[29] In the end, Mulso did not build a town. There has been discussion about the location of the territory of Fir Chualann in the north Wicklow and south Co. Dublin border area, but, according to Price, at the time of the grant to Mulso (1450) the name Fercullen meant the Powerscourt district and Glencree valley of north-east Wicklow.[30] Mulso was given leave to found a town with all the trappings of such a settlement – burgesses, the election of a portreve and bailiffs 'as the citizens of the city of Dublin do at Dublin', the right 'to hold all manner of pleas of trespass, covenants, accounts, debts, and all manner of contracts … arising within the metes and bounds of the said town … in like manner as the mayor, bailiffs and citizens of the said city of Dublin use or have used to do at Dublin'. The community in the new settlement was to have weekly a free market and two four-day fairs each year 'and a court of piepowder to be held there before the barons of the said fair for the time being, of all manner of trespasses, covenants, accounts, debts, and all manner of contracts originating and arising within the said fair …'.[31]

It is safe to say that in the second half of the fifteenth century pie powder courts would have been held in the cities of Dublin, Drogheda, Kilkenny and Waterford. Dublin city and county had a number of markets and fairs at which the services of courts of pie powder would have been available if needed – at Swords, where an eight-day fair began on the vigil of St Columba (8 June); at a fair in Dublin city, beginning on the vigil of St Benedict the abbot (20/21 March); and at a fifteen-day fair at Ballymore Eustace, on the Dublin/Kildare county boundary, beginning on the vigil of St Luke (17 October). There were also markets held at Swords on a Monday and at the manor of Lusk on a Thursday, at which merchants would have been able to seek the services of a court of pie powder.[32]

Currency was used in business transactions, but credit much more so, involving the formal registration of debt, for which there was a final day of reckoning, often at Easter and other days in the year. Under the Statute of

Acton Burnell (1283) and its updating two years later in the Statute of Merchants (1285), recognisances of debts could be enrolled by special government officials in named towns.[33] The enrolments could not be challenged; there were two responses – show proof of payment or discharge the debt.[34] In September 1285, the parliament of Ireland ordained that the Statute of Merchants was to be observed in Ireland and that recognisances of debts could be made in the presence of government or law officers in Ireland: barons of the exchequer, justices of the bench and justices in eyre (or 'justices itinerant') who travelled on a circuit around the colony.[35] Another type of enrolment, quite unofficial, but regarded as binding in London, was the entry of a transaction in a merchant's ledger or daybook.[36]

Two established methods of recording debt were the indenture and the tally. Debts or contracts were recorded in a written bill or bond, with a pair of identical documents written on the same parchment and separated by a zig-zag cut with one being given to each party. Later, in the case of a dispute, the documents could be shown to be genuine or not when matched along the unique indentured cut.[37] For commercial and government transactions the tally had widespread use in colonial Ireland. It was ideally a piece of hazel wood about a foot in length and one and a half inches square in cross profile. On the upper and lower edges notches were cut to record amounts of money, the sides carrying an identical identifying description with possibly the seals of the two parties attached. The tally was divided in two, each stick carrying identical information. The tally began as a tally of credit but it could become a tally of acquitance or a receipt. Governments were inclined to misuse tallies: they would pay a person by tally stating that it could be encashed by a customs office, say, fifty miles distant, which would involve a time-wasting journey.[38] In the period 1440 to 1442 in Dublin, the treasury refused to pay out on fifty-seven known tallies presented for payment, doing so only on foot of a royal writ.[39] Tally amounts were as high as £18, £24 and £30. In the seven tallies referenced below, amounts ranged from £3 6s. 8d. to £18.[40] In England in the fourteenth century there is evidence that the use of tallies declined among merchants but that merchants continued to be reluctant lenders to governments (figure 11).[41]

The method of debt recovery made possible under legislation, described above, was superseded in 1353 by the Statute of the Staple which offered a new system of debt recovery cheaper and speedier than the system it replaced. In Ireland and England, under the new legislation, persons could be pursued successfully for the payment of debts.[42] In Ireland, the cities in which recognisances could be registered and debtors pursued were Dublin, Drogheda, Cork and Waterford.[43] The general intent of the legislators was

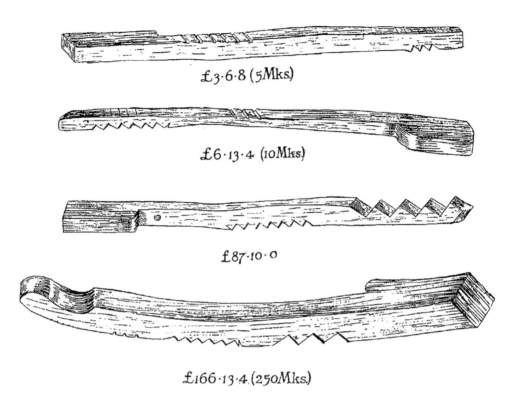

£3·6·8 (5Mks.)

£6·13·4 (10Mks.)

£87·10·0

£166·13·4.(250Mks.)

11 Tallies with notches cut to record the amount of indebtedness between two named persons. Tallies carried an identifying inscription and often the parties' seals were attached. (Image by permission of Oxford University Press, taken from L.F. Salzman, *English trade in the Middle Ages* (Oxford, 1931), p. 27.)

that contracts would be 'better holden' and payments would be 'readily made'. The mayor of the staple in any of the named cities in England or Ireland could take recognisances of debts made before him by a merchant and if the debt was not paid within the term agreed the mayor had the power to 'take and hold in prison the bodies of the debtors' until the debt was paid. He could also arrest the goods of the said debtors found within the staple and deliver the goods to the creditors or sell them at the best price obtainable and deliver the money to the creditors.[44]

Irish persons in England, for example, were pursued for unpaid debts. On 2 March 1469, for example, John Yonge senior of Swords, merchant, John Yonge junior of London, brewer, and John Wymod, gentleman of Middlesex, came before a mayor and constable of the staple and acknowledged that they owed £12 13s. 4d. to John Tatersale, citizen and brewer of London but that they had not paid it. On 15 February 1481, John Broun, mayor of the staple of Westminster, began proceedings that would compel them to make repayment as per the Statute of the Staple. Another case in London involved the indebtedness of Christopher Fleming, the baron of Slane. On 31 December 1493, Fleming recognized his debt of £17 10s. to William White, mercer of London, but the sum was not paid. Within ten months, on 4 November 1484, the mayor of the staple of Westminster instigated proceedings that would compel payment from Fleming. The outcomes of these cases are not known, but it is clear in each case that John Broun, mayor of the staple of Westminster, wrote to the chancellor to compel payment and more than likely the Yonges and Wymond in the first case, and Fleming in the latter case, if found would have been arrested and put in gaol and their goods and property seized and sold to pay the creditors the amounts outstanding.[45]

Some individuals showed in their inventory at the close of their life that they had cut finely, perhaps too finely, the balance between their stated assets and debts. Dame Margaret Nugent, who died in September 1474, the widow of Sir Thomas Newbery, may have been such a person. Her husband had served as mayor of Dublin on five occasions, dying in office on 21 January 1469. Dame Margaret, having probably lived a good social life and in some comfort in those years, seems to have continued in her widowhood to live in this life-style, supported by running up debts with over thirty creditors. Her recorded indebtedness came to £11 16s. 10d. The true figure was higher, unrecorded amounts being due to seven named creditors. If the sum owed to these seven amounted to £2 17s. 10d., then Dame Margaret's debts would have balanced neatly with her stated assets of £14 14s. 8d. Her identifiable creditors came principally from the powerful, the influential and the well-off in Dublin. Dame Margaret was indebted, for example, to Nicholas Sutton (a baron of the exchequer), to Peter Higeley, a well-known general merchant, discussed below, and to Arland Ussher, a merchant who served as mayor in Dublin in the year following her husband's death. The details of her indebtedness to Sutton and Higeley are unknown. Her creditors also included those who held or would hold high municipal office, members of the clergy and gentlewomen. She owed 10s. to John Roche, a vintner, and 5s. to a tailor, John Rendill. It is possible that she had a second tailor, Henry Broun, to whom she owed 12s. The lowliest were to be found among her creditors – Marion Tapister, for example, an ale-seller, of whom we will hear again. Dame Margaret also had debts outside Dublin, in Swords and in Drogheda.[46]

Table 2.1 Select list of named creditors of Lady Margaret Nugent (1474)[47]

Creditor	Amount	Profession, office, status
Sir Nicholas Barry	37s. 6d.	Chaplain in the church of St Michan, Dublin
Sir Walter Ludelow	5s.	Yeoman; citizen by special grace (May 1471)
Dame Matilda Plunket	£3 6s.8d.	Gentlewoman
John Rendill	5s.	Dublin citizen and tailor
John Roche	10s.	Apprentice vintner in 1474; Dublin citizen (Jan. 1477)
John Sawag	4s.	Dublin citizen and merchant; bailiff of Dublin (1476–7)
Elizabeth Sexe	8d.	Gentlewoman, citizen by special grace (Oct. 1474)
Marion Tapister	9d.	Tapster or ale-seller
William Tu (Tyve)	6s. 4d.	Dublin citizen and merchant; mayor of Dublin (1488–9)
Arland Ussher	18s.	Dublin citizen and merchant; mayor of Dublin (1469–70)
Margaret White	3s. 4d.	Dublin citizen and merchant (Jan. 1474)
Robert White	13s. 4d.	Dublin citizen and merchant
John Whiteacres	12s.	Dublin citizen and merchant; bailiff of Dublin (1480–1)

The day books, memorandum books and ledgers or books of account of late medieval Irish merchants have not survived. Few of these types of record survive in England either. In London, a day book from the 1390s belonging to William Maghfield, merchant, is in the National Archives. It contains day-to-day memoranda about his debts and expenses. As his debts were paid they were struck out but the entries are still readable.[48] In Scotland, the ledger of Andrew Halyburton is an invaluable survival; he operated as a merchant in the Netherlands between 1492 and 1503. It seems that once debts were paid there was no good reason to keep daybooks and ledgers and they were eventually destroyed.[49]

There is some evidence that Dublin merchants in the late medieval period recorded business transactions in writing. John Chever, who was a justice of the king's bench, having mentioned that the archdeacon of Meath was bound to him for ten marks, noted that there were other debts 'of which there is mention in my account book'.[50] Two years later, Peter Higeley, a Dublin merchant, pointed out that there was £40 of debt owing to him and recorded 'in the book of shop debts'. Richard Boys, a Coventry merchant visiting Dublin, had two documents showing the indebtedness to him of Nicholas Bourke of Dublin and of Robert Goldsmith, both merchants. One document written by Bourke gave the details of his debt of £17; the second document was an indenture made between them recording Goldsmith's debt of £18 12s. as a result of the purchase of cloth.[51]

Coins and currency

Coin was not used very much in Dublin in the late fifteenth century in everyday transactions and people generally do not seem to have possessed coins. In some sixty examined wills and inventories from Dublin city and county, approved in the 1470s, seven record testators, five men and two women, as having ready money.[52] The most common element found in the group of seven is that found in four who were either merchants, property owners or working at a craft – John Wylde, a merchant from England who died in Dublin, had £20 'money by tale' in his assets; John Mold, a merchant from Malahide, Co. Dublin, left 10 marks (£6 13s. 4d.) ready cash; and Hugh Galliane, a citizen of Dublin city and a property owner, left 40s. in cash. Richard White of Swords, Co. Dublin, was a tailor, with twenty-four debtors in the Swords area when he died. He is recorded in his inventory as having 'in moneys 15s. 6d.'. It is possible that debtors would settle with him from time to time, hence the cash on hand. Joan Drywer of Crumlin was a small farmer, a widow with daughters, who had 13s. 4d. listed in her assets. She was especially generous to the church and friars in her will and was probably so in life, which may go towards explaining her practice of having available cash.[53]

In England, in the fifteenth century – and Dublin's experience reflected this – there was a great shortage of coin and bullion and in particular a great lack of coins of small denominations. The English government, sympathetic to those using coins, introduced the groat (4d.) in the 1340s and then the half-groat, but the mintings of half-pennies and farthings was always insufficient to meet the demand for small change.[54] In 1475–6, the parliament of Ireland accepted that the coin known as the groat minted in the days of previous monarchs – Edward III, Richard II, Henry IV, Henry V and Henry VI – was still circulating in the colony at that time, and it ordained that the groat, the half-groat and the penny from those days be valued at sixpence, three pence and a penny halfpenny respectively, provided the coins were not clipped (plate 5).[55]

The Irish government was actively and continually concerned about the quantity and condition of the coinage circulating and the outflow of silver from the colony. In the 1440s, gold and silver coins were being clipped and the resulting wedges melted down so that bridles and harnesses could be made more ornate.[56] In 1456–7, Frenchmen, Spaniards, Bretons, Portuguese and others, having sold merchandise at colonial ports, were departing from Ireland with silver coins or bullion. The authorities imposed a customs duty of 40*d.* on every pound of silver to stop the flow out of the country with very severe penalties for concealment.[57] The reign of Edward IV saw many enactments made in parliament to do with coinage. From the early 1460s through the 1470s the parliament of Ireland ordained on numerous occasions that new coins in a range of denominations should be struck in Dublin Castle and elsewhere. Minting was to take place in Dublin Castle in 1462, and on a number of occasions throughout the decade (1463–4 and 1467–8) in Dublin, Trim, Waterford and Limerick. Other towns such as Drogheda and Galway were also named as locations at which minting could take place. In 1472–3, coin manufacture was to take place 'in the king's castle of Dublin and no other place' and in 1475–6 it was decreed that coins should be struck in Dublin, Drogheda and Waterford. Parliament, which had been attempting to control Germyn Lynch, the government mintmaster, relented in 1478 from its decision to confine his work to Dublin and allowed him to 'strike, forge and coin' at any location in Ireland.[58]

One name that keeps recurring in our period concerning the minting of coinage is that of Germyn Lynch, goldsmith, moneyer and ship's master[59] who was appointed on 1 February 1461 by Edward IV to be master of the mint in Ireland for life.[60] Throughout more than twenty years as a mintmaster Lynch was repeatedly dishonest and was dismissed a number of times in 1472, 1474, 1478, being finally dismissed in 1484. He had a reputation for producing light-weight coins from bullion supplied to him and would keep the difference for himself.[61] In 1467, he produced an issue of coins on government instructions, one of which coins was a new denomination, a double-groat, followed by the groat, the half-groat, the denier, the half-denier and the farthing, the latter three being silver-copper alloys. Parliament ordained that the coins should be struck in the castles of Dublin and Trim, and in other locations. The double-groat was to have on one side the impression of a face, with a crown, bearing the inscription *Edwardus dei gratia dominus hibernie*, and on the other side, the sun, with a rose in the centre with *Civitas Dublinie* circumscribed. The coin was close to the weight of the English groat and the entire issue was regarded as a devaluation.[62] Lynch continued his work, minting coins of various denominations. In 1470, he was to mint coins in

Dublin, Trim and Drogheda,[63] and in 1473 it was enacted that he should manufacture coins in Dublin Castle solely and was required to turn one fifth of the bullion he received for minting into small coin.[64] He was still working for the government at the end of the 1470s[65] and was dismissed finally in 1484, being described as a counterfeiter.[66]

Dublin merchants

Merchants, despite having a reputation for being hardened businessmen, had another side to their life. In 1471, for example, John Wylde, an English merchant in Ireland, stayed in the house of Thomas West, a Dublin merchant, with whom he possibly had dealings previously. While in Dublin he became ill and was attended to by Jonet and Katherine, the maidservants of a Dublin merchant, Robert West, possibly Thomas's brother. Wylde had appointed his wife Elizabeth and John Swan as his executors but named Robert West as overseer so that he could arrange the funeral and pay 'legacies and debts in Ireland' and execute 'other matters in this testament … until the arrival of my said executors in Ireland'. Far from home and dying, Wylde's trust in the West brothers is reflected in his generous bequests to Robert's maidservants and to his host Thomas West.[67]

Later in the decade, in May 1476, Walter Sale, a Dublin merchant, appointed his wife and son as his executors with the oversight of Thomas Molghane. He and another Dublin merchant, William Grampe, with others, witnessed the drawing up of Sale's inventory of goods. Molghane was a Dublin merchant who in May 1474 had been elected and sworn in as a jurat, one of the twenty-four councillors of the city assembly, and in whom Sale had confidence to carry out the duties of overseer of his will.[68]

In October 1476, Peter Higeley, a citizen of Dublin and a merchant, made Robert Chillame, a fellow merchant,[69] overseer of his will to deal with the legal implications of his underage children *vis-à-vis* his final testament.[70] For whatever reason, Higeley's wife, Millane Frayne, was not given the task of executor. It was not unusual at this time for women in Dublin to take on the duty of executrix – she may not have been interested in being executrix because perhaps she thought she would be too pre-occupied with the care of her children and managing the Higeley's 40-acre leased farm at Killeigh (Killeek), near Swords, Co. Dublin, which she was to inherit from her husband. Peter Higeley's instructions to Robert Chillame were clear: leaving to Patrick and Thomas, his sons, and Agnes his daughter, a third part of his goods, Higeley willed that that third part remain in the hands of Robert Chillame of Dublin, until his children arrive at legal age.[71] Despite the mention of Higeley's farm, his main interests seem to have been as a merchant and a property owner in Dublin, holding a number of houses in Patrick Street and in New Street.[72] However, there is evidence that the ambitions of some successful Dublin merchants did not end at the city walls and that they aspired to being a country gentleman. It has been shown that this could be achieved by a combination of success in business, becoming an office-holder in the city or county and marrying into one of the Co. Dublin or Co. Meath landholding families.[73]

In the 1470s, in Dublin and its commercial neighbourhood, business was transacted between English and Irish merchants involving the use of credit facilities and a degree of trust. In September 1472, for example, Richard Boys, a merchant from Coventry, had 'ten dozen of superior cloth' worth £30 and six dozen of cloth 'in the house of John Broun of Navan' worth £13. Boys also had seven-and-a-half hundredweight of alum, valued at £15, which was 'in the house of Philip Whiteside of Drogheda' and may have been imported for Boys at Drogheda, sight unseen. Boys had a shop in Dublin and goods there were valued at £5. He was also owed 300 goat skins by Robert Goldsmith, merchant. John Wylde, an English merchant, confidently did business in Dublin in November 1471 and had stocks of linen (23s. 4d.), eleven packs of sheep and lamb skins (£6. 13s. 4d.) and seven hundred of yarn, valued at £10. 10s. 0d. He also had with him £20 in cash.[74]

At the close of 1475, an inventory of goods belonging to John Barby was drawn up.[75] It has the appearance of a stock-taking list from a tailor's shop and points to Barby being a tailor. He owed money to two tailors, John Kelly[76] and Henry Russell,[77] from whom he may possibly have bought cloth or trimmings. This inventory, unlike any other surviving will written in Dublin in the 1470s, reads as follows:

> Four gowns worth 20s.
> Three coats worth 5s.
> A long doublet worth 13s. 4d.
> A sword and hanger worth 5s.
> A jerkin worth 2s.
> Two bows worth 5s.
> One pair of sheets worth 2s.[78]

The goods listed below held by Peter Higeley, a Dublin merchant, in October 1476, give an insight into the range of commodities that would be held in stock by a Dublin merchant at this time. Higeley also had a forty-acre farm and it is not surprising to see agricultural produce and equipment listed in the inventory attached to his will. However, the agricultural equipment included in the edited inventory below would seem to be goods for sale and part of the stock of Higeley's business in Dublin. In the 1470s, in Dublin city and county wills and inventories, it was not usual to list agricultural equipment. The inclusion of multiple wagon wheels and ploughs, with additional equipment, suggests that the items are commercial stock available for sale:

> 16 weys of salt valued at £32
> 2 tons of iron worth £9 6s. 8d.
> 4 dakers and 2 hides of leather worth 42s.
> Pitch and resin worth 13s. 4d.
> Merchandise in the shop worth 100s.
> Vessels of brass, lead, pewter and other household utensils worth
>   £10 13s. 4d.
> 4 pairs of wheels with their belongings and wagons worth 30s.
> 3 ploughs with their irons and other belongings worth 5s.
> Boards and laths, with other necessaries for building, worth 20s.[79]

Not all Dublin merchants lived in the city. John Mold resided in Malahide with his wife Matilda Olifer. He died in October 1474. Their household goods were valued at 40s. suggesting that the couple had a very well furnished home and that commerce had been good to them. Mold had a number of commodities in stock:

> Half a tun of iron, valued at 4 marks (£2 13s. 4d.).
> 6 crannocs of salt, worth 13s. 4d.
> 6 crannocs of saltpetre, 16s.
> 10 barrels of herrings, worth 50s.
> 3 nets, worth 10s.
> 5 couples of wheat, barley and oats, worth 40s.

He had £6 13s. 4d. cash on hands, a sizeable sum by contemporary Irish standards. He was a merchant and was possibly involved in fishing also. It is clear that he had done business in north Wales and in Bristol owing money to Robert Oholdernys (12s.) and to Margaret Brydall (2s.), both of Conway in Wales, and to John Baly of Bristol (2s. 9d.). On 16 March 1468, he sailed from Malahide to Chester on the *Trinity of Malahide* without cargo, suggesting that he might buy goods in Chester or go inland to either north Wales or perhaps to the English midlands to purchase commodities.[80]

Trading in County Dublin

By the middle of the fifteenth century, Co. Dublin had a long-established settlement, social, economic and ecclesiastical history that began before the coming of the Anglo-Normans. There was a network of settlements and access roads that was inviting to merchants. Across the county, there were at least eleven market settlements that had become central places with privileges such as the right to hold markets or fairs – Clondalkin, Dalkey, Donore, Lucan, Lusk, Newcastle Lyons, Rathcoole, Saggart, Shankill, Swords and Tallaght. Before 1169, Clondalkin, Dalkey, Swords and Tallaght were almost certainly important central places. Most borough settlements included a pre-1169 church, which would have attracted settlement, while three boroughs were secular in origin – Lucan, at a crossing point on the Liffey, and Newcastle Lyons and Saggart which were royal manors. The fortunes of the boroughs would have waxed and waned over the centuries, but many continued to have the power to attract merchants and trade. While none were towns, all the boroughs were nucleated settlements where roads converged. Dalkey, Swords and Tallaght developed a definite street plan. It is thought that there may have been other settlements with borough status – Finglas, Chapelizod, Crumlin and the liberty of St Sepulchre outside the walls of Dublin. Some recent research, suggesting a higher medieval shoreline than today, would put four of the boroughs mentioned above – Swords and Lusk to the north of Dublin city and Dalkey and Shankill to the south – close to a coastal or maritime location, with all that that would bring in trading potential. Superimposed on this landscape and settlement pattern were the royal manors of Crumlin, Esker, Newcastle Lyons and Saggart, which did not come into being until King John's reign. When his son, Henry III, was farming out demesne lands he kept these four manors under his personal control.[81]

Fortunately, there is quantifiable evidence from the 1470s that illustrates to some degree the geographic 'sphere of influence' of a number of settlements in Co. Dublin – Clondalkin, Howth and Swords. In 1472, the inventory of William Neill, who lived and worked as a tanner in Clondalkin, shows that, of his known debtors, some were located in Dublin, with most found in Ballyfermot, Celbridge, Clondalkin, Kilmainham, Lucan, Newcastle, Rathcoole, Saggart and Tallaght. It is assumed that Neill was supplying finished leather to his customers to be value-added by their manufacture of shoes, straps, harnesses, saddles and so on. The distance of Neill's debtors' home locations from Clondalkin ranged from 5km (Lucan) to 9km (Celbridge), with three locations – Kilmainham, Newcastle and Rathcoole – located 6–7km from Clondalkin (figure 12).[82]

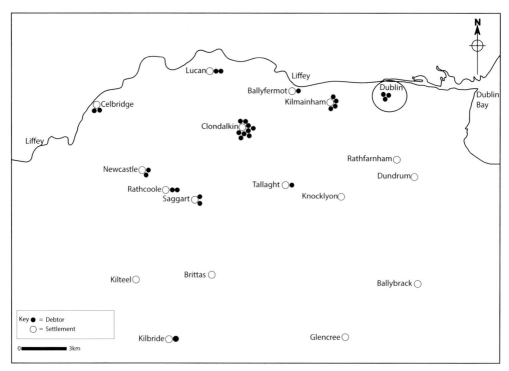

12 Map showing the distribution of the debtors of William Neill of Clondalkin, tanner (1471). Some debtors were 10km distant from Neill's place of business in Clondalkin while one debtor was located 15km from the settlement. There were 9 debtors at Clondalkin, 4 debtors in Kilmainham and 3 debtors in Dublin. (Map drawn by Dr Fergal Donoghue.)

At Howth, in 1472, John Sherreff's inventory listed a total of 41 debtors, 10 of whom were women. Howth had a port used by fishers and Sherreff seems to have acted solely as a local merchant and was not involved in farming. The relatively high percentage of women debtors may be explained through men being away at sea and their wives purchasing family supplies in their own name, two women debtors being referred to in the inventory as 'wife of' a named man. Sherreff's mapped 'sphere of influence' is decidedly asymmetrical as expected from a coastal settlement. He had 23 debtors in the village of Howth and three small clusters of debtors each a short distance west of Howth, at Corrstown (2km), and at Ballybarroke/Kilbarrack and at Baldoyle, both about 6km west of Howth. Testamentary contributions from Sherreff made to local churches confirm and extend this westward component of Sherreff's sphere of activity – he made bequests to churches at Coolock, Little Grange and Raheny, 8 to 10km from Howth (figure 13).[83]

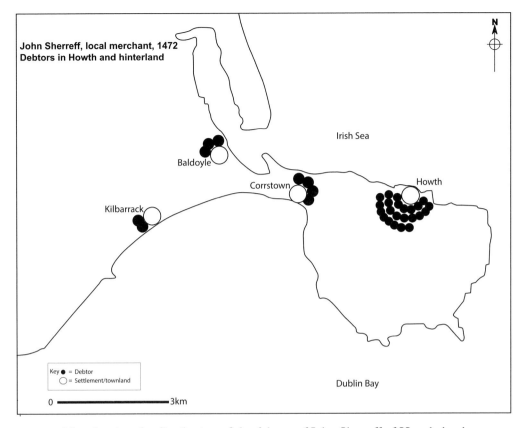

13 Map showing the distribution of the debtors of John Sherreff of Howth, local merchant (1472). Most of the debtors were probably fishermen, or their wives who were named as the debtor possibly when their spouse was away at sea. There were twenty-three debtors clustered at Howth. (Map drawn by Dr Fergal Donoghue.)

Finally, at Swords, in 1476, Richard White had a total of 24 debtors. White did not live ostentatiously, his household goods being valued at 2s., the lowest such valuation in over sixty contemporaneous wills examined.[84] In his inventory, 40 lbs of yarn was valued at 6s. 8d. and his 'tole', tool or trade apparatus was valued at 4s. 4d. White may have worked as a tailor. Sample debts owed to him include substantial amounts of 4s. 11d., 13s. 5d., 9s. 7d., and a very significant debt of 48s. 7d. Of his debtors, 16 were located in Swords, but others were in townlands a short distance from Swords – Rickanhore (3km), Saucerstown and Roganstown (about 5km), Rath and Lispopple (about 7km). He had 1 debtor in Oberstown, 11km distant from Swords (figure 14).[85]

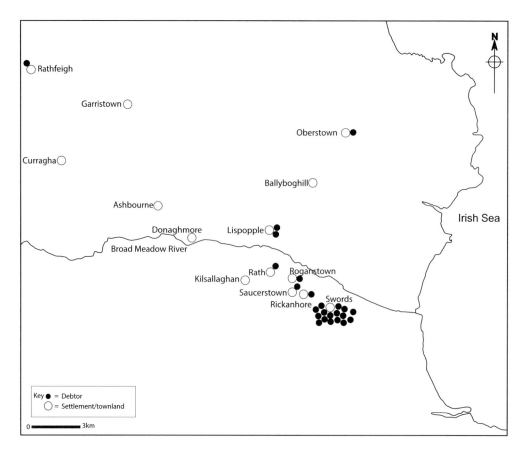

14 Map showing the distribution of the debtors of Richard White of Swords, tailor (1476). Sixteen debtors were clustered in Swords, but others ranged from 3km to 8km from the settlement, with two debtors being 12km and 24km distant from Swords. (Map drawn by Dr Fergal Donoghue.)

In the 1470s, Dublin merchants transacted business in rural Co. Dublin, locations ranging from Balrothery, Tobersool and Balscadden in the north to locations nearer Dublin at Ballymadun, Rowlestown and Finglas. Their clients were farmers with holdings of middle size, on which wheat, barley and oats were grown, and cows, horses, pigs and sheep were reared. Merchants from Dublin were also active at Clondalkin, and at locations near the Dublin–Kildare county boundary at Backweston, Killadoon and Leixlip.[86] In 1476, for example, Nicholas Delaber of Balrothery was indebted to Dublin merchants Patrick Fitzlenys (3*s.*), Bartholemew Rosell (2*s.* 6*d.*) and Richard Arnold (Arland) (8*s.*). In the same year, FitzLenys was also a creditor of Richard Goldynge of Tobersool (6*s.*) and of Joan Usberne of Lusk (26*s.* 8*d.*). Previously, in 1474 and in 1475, William Power of Ballymadun (1s.) and Thomas Fynglas of Finglas (33s. 7d.) were also debtors of FitzLenys. Robert Blanchfield, a Dublin merchant, seems to have traded across the north county, being owed money, for example, in Finglas in 1475 (13s. 4d.) and in Tobersool (6s.) in 1476. Arland Ussher also traded in north Co. Dublin, being owed 2s. 6d. by Alice Cassell of Lusk in 1472 and about 30s. at Finglas in 1475.[87]

Dublin merchants also traded in the south-west of the county. In 1472, William Neill of Clondalkin, a tanner by trade, was owed 26s. 8d. by Robert White, a Dublin merchant. In 1474, Nicholas Ketyng of Clondalkin was indebted to two smiths and two butchers in Dublin – Patrick Lye, Maurice Soggyn, Nicholas Harrold and Richard Harrold. In 1474, Patrick Laweles of Tallaght was a debtor of Dublin merchants John Fyan (5s. 6d.) and Robert Queytrot (22d.), and in 1477, John Borrard of Backweston, 15km from Dublin, was a debtor of two Dubliners – John Rosere (Rossele), merchant, and Patrick Gerrot, smith, both citizens of the city. Dublin merchants also traded beyond the county boundary – in 1467, Margaret Browneusyn of Killadoon, south-west of Celbridge, 18km from Dublin, owed money to two Dublin merchants, John Rossele (8s.) and John Shynnagh (4s.).[88]

Commodities expected to arrive at Dublin port and at the city's markets in the 1330s and 1340s probably give a fair indication of the range of products available in Dublin in our period. The list here is not definitive, and a further list of products on sale in Dublin in the 1470s, with statutory recommended prices, can be found in the chapter below on provisioning.[89] For trade, taxation and customs purposes the quantity, volume or weight of goods was often described using different systems, ranging from simple enumeration – from one 'piece' to a 'hundred', to the use of avoirdupois weight units, and finally to using collective words, sometimes specific to a trade and often archaic today.[90] Corn, wheat and malt for brewing were available in Dublin by the load, and horses, mares, bulls and cows were on the market.[91] Many Co. Dublin farms in the 1470s seem to have had horses surplus to requirements, the animals possibly being bred for selling. Horses may have been offered for sale, for example, by the following, whose total number of horses is shown: Michael Trevers and Joan Goldynge of Balrothery (9 farm horses); Alice Bennet of Santry (8 carthorses); Joan Usberne of Lusk (8 carthorses); Nicholas Duff and Joan Dansay of Rowlestown, Swords (13 carthorses); Joan Steven of Crumlin (7 carthorses).[92] By the 1470s oxen appear to have gone out of use on most Co. Dublin farms and there was probably little demand for them.[93] Wool was available by the stone (14 lbs) and skins came by the hundred – lamb, rabbit, kid, hare, wolf and cat. The skins of stag and deer were offered for sale singly. Goatskins came by the dicker (ten hides), fresh or tanned. Irish or Welsh woollen cloth was taxed by the piece;[94] a piece could have a significant length – fustian could be 30 yards long, buckram 40 yards long, short buckram, 5½ yards.[95] Silk cloth was available in Dublin, with gold, satin or diaper, and baudekin was imported, the richest cloth of the Middle Ages made of gold and silk with embroidery, originally from Baghdad.[96] Various types of cloth arrived in Dublin from Flanders, Normandy and Brabant, and linen cloth came from England and France. Worsted and Irish linen were available by the piece, and sindon or lawn, a very fine linen, could be bought.[97] Salmon were sold singly, while other fish came by the load – fresh, hard or salted. Herring were on the market and measured by the mease, five long hundreds to the barrel, totalling 600 herring. Some commodity quantities used were often terms long associated with a trade – a butt of wine (126 gallons), a load of ashes and a sarpler of wool – a large sack for wool or an equivalent of two sacks of wool.[98] Among the iron goods was Spanish iron, horse-shoes and cart-irons by the hundred, spade-irons, tripods, gridirons, plough-irons, ploughshares and wrought iron. Lead came by the stone, and tin, brass and copper by the hundredweight. Brewing vessels and kitchenware could be bought. Building materials were sold, including large and small boards, most likely from Wicklow, wood, tiles, nails, millstones and hand-grindstones, and barrels of pitch and tar. Local and exotic foods were for sale – honey, butter, cheese, figs, raisins and dates,[99] dried fruits probably coming from Spain or from England via the Low Countries.[100] Salt, woad and coal were imported and for sale in Dublin, firewood was quantified in bundles by the hundred and tan came by the load.[101]

* * *

A relatively attractive commercial milieu was developed in Dublin, which included the use of official port buyers and a number of methods of debt recovery available in both the pie powder courts and under the statute of merchants and statute of the staple parliamentary legislation. Commodities from Britain and the Continent were available in Dublin. Merchants in Dublin began to record transactions in books of account rather than on tallies. Dublin merchants did business across Co. Dublin from Balrothery in the north to Clondalkin in the south-west of the county. At any given time, Dublin merchants would have had a number of creditors and debtors and had creditors in England and Wales. In Dublin city and county, it was usual to have debtors 5–10km distant from the creditor and there are examples of debtors located 10–20km from a merchant's domicile.

CHAPTER 3

Shipping, Navigation and the Irish Sea Trade

WHAT IS IT ABOUT LONG-LOST shipwrecks that they catch the imagination of the public? In Newport, Wales, in 2002, once the importance of a ship find became known – it was a clinker-built ship constructed in the 1460s – public interest grew and a 'save our ship' campaign began.¹ Suddenly, a ship unknown up to then became 'our ship'. An archaeological find can often offer a window into our past activities. Such is the case of the discovery of the 'Drogheda boat' in 2006. Despite what looks like a downturn in fish exports to Chester from the north Co. Dublin coast in the mid-1520s, the herring industry later in the century appears to have been in good shape as revealed by the 'Drogheda boat' and the remains of its cargo excavated in 2007. When raised from river Boyne sediments, 1.5km east of Drogheda, and c.40km north of Dublin, the boat was found to have had 14 casks on board, 13 of which were hogsheads, each with a capacity of 63 gallons. Atlantic herring had been caught, cured and salted in great numbers and stored in barrels for transport to market. The method of preservation, known as the 'Skanian' or 'kaken' method, allowed prolonged storage and preservation up to one year, all pointing to a well-organized fish processing industry at Drogheda. The method of cask storage, directly onto the floor timbers and hull planking, in a ship that had no ceiling planks, suggests that the proposed voyage was to be short, or if a longer journey was proposed that there was a likelihood of cask damage.²

The Drogheda boat was clinker built mainly from oak timber felled on the east coast of Co. Antrim between 1525 and 1535 and was constructed probably close to the timber source in the summer of 1535. The timber was split, worked and finished with axes. The outboard hull of the boat was covered with a sealant, most probably tar, to protect it. Originally it had a stern rudder. A number of plank repairs were done, the final one probably in about 1560. The preserved length of the boat is c.9m, representing almost the entire original length. The Drogheda boat was a locally-built vessel that worked in the Irish Sea and perhaps mainly along the east coast (figure 15).³

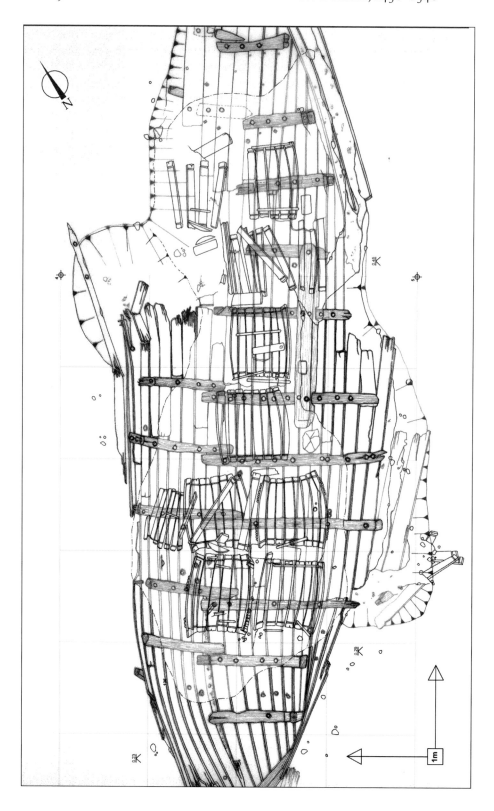

15 (*opposite page*) Drogheda boat wreck overlaid site plans showing plan of the wreck, with structural timbers and lower hold construction; overlaid onto this is the plan of the cargo of wooden barrels and their *in situ* positions within the hold of the wreck when discovered, and prior to excavation. (Drawn by Rex Bangerter, courtesy of the National Monuments Service.)

16 The *Bremen cog*. A model built by Karl-Heinz Haupt, model builder at the Deutsches Schiffahrtsmuseum, Bremerhaven. The original ship, excavated in 1962, had a capacity of 84 tons. (Image courtesy of Egbert Laska © Deutsches Schiffahrtsmuseum, Bremerhaven.)

Ireland's location and situation, an island on the edge of north-western Europe, ensured that it was not quite isolated from Europe and that it was accessible to neighbouring merchants in England and Wales, and to French and Iberian merchants who had Mediterranean products to sell.[4] It required intrepid sailors to reach the island of Ireland and brave shipmasters and crews to cross the Irish Sea to Britain, Gerald of Wales having something to say about that sea – 'The Irish Sea, surging with currents that rush together, is nearly always tempestuous, so that even in the summer it scarcely shows itself calm for a few days to them that sail'.[5] Ships were small in a big sea – 9 metres in length like the Drogheda boat – and were referred to in medieval literature as 'tiny specks' or a 'fragile piece of wood'.[6]

Ships, maps and navigation

It is difficult to be certain about the size of ships operating out of Dublin in the second half of the fifteenth century. The best range of ship types known contemporaneously at one medieval port is that found at Bristol. There were river boats called 'crayers', while the 'picard' class was used for fishing and trading with Ireland. Larger sea-going ships were also known at Bristol, the 'barge', the 'balinger', the 'cog' and the 'caravel'. The cog, a single-masted vessel, with castles fore and aft, was known in the Irish Sea records up to c.1420, having a tonnage capacity of 30 to 240 tons. It was the commonest type of large trading vessel in the thirteenth and fourteenth centuries. A defining characteristic of the cog was that it had a bottom with edge to edge planking that merged into clinker planking towards the stern and the stem; the ship sides were wholly clinker built. The *Bremen cog*, built in 1380, and raised in 1962, had a capacity of 84 tons. The balinger could have one or two masts and was propelled by oarsmen. It had a capacity of 25 to 60 tons; in 1401, a 100-ton royal balinger, *Godegrace*, was built at Ratcliffe on the Thames (figure 16).[7]

The most recent research shows that ships trading between Ireland and England were larger in the earlier years of the fifteenth century than at the end of the century. From 1460, customs records from ports in the west and south-west of England show that ships traversing the Irish Sea ranged from 6 to 30 tons.[8] In the early fifteenth century, sea-going barges were among the most common ships in the Irish Sea. Clinker-built, they used sails and oars, and had a load-bearing capacity of 40 to 240 tons.[9] The *Barge of Caernarvon* is the only identifiable such craft sailing on the Dublin–Chester route in 1467–8. Arriving in Chester on 9 December 1467, while it was probably a lighter and smaller example of its class, the *Barge of Caernarvon* stands out exceptionally in its known carrying capacity, having 102 horseloads and 4 cartloads of cargo and about 20 persons on board; it carried almost 17 tons of cargo. A cartload of goods is taken to be 1 ton (2,240 lbs) and a horseload of cargo is accepted as 2.5 hundredweight (cwt) or one-eighth of a ton.[10] The barge does not seem to have been typical of the ships working out of Dublin in 1467–8 and probably not in the latter half of the fifteenth century. No ship identifiable as

a barge is recorded as sailing between Dublin and Chester in the period
November 1476–September 1477, for which records are available.[11]

Ships similar to the Bristol picards mentioned above, regarded as small in
size (less than 25 tons), worked between Dublin and Chester. Cargoes were
possibly between 6 to 10 tons.[12] Total cargo volumes carried by ships, possibly
of the picard class, entering Chester from Dublin in March–April 1468 were,
for example, 19 horseloads and 6 cartloads on the *Katharine of Dublin*, master
John Milet, with about 20 persons on board; its cargo weighed about 8.5 tons.
There were 15 horseloads and 7 cartloads on the *Katharine of Dublin*, master
Blak Patrick, with about 22 persons on board; it had a cargo of almost 9 tons.
The *Peter of Dublin*, master John Brette, had 62 horseloads and 2 cartloads of
goods and about 21 persons on board; its cargo weighed close to 10 tons.[13]

Until the beginning of the fifteenth century, most ships in England (and
probably in northern Europe) seem to have had only one mast. By about
1410–20, the two-masted ship was being seen in northern Europe, the concept
coming from the Mediterranean, with the first English example built in 1416.
A separate revolutionary development in boat building began in Portugal,
covering a boat frame with planks laid against each other and not overlapping
as in the clinker-built method. These new smooth-hulled boats called 'carvels'
were first seen in Irish waters in 1449. Research may clarify if the *Karvill of
Howth* and the *Carvill of Howth* used on Howth–Chester voyages in 1476–7
were in fact carvel-built ships. A third mast and sail had been developed by the
1430s, and further sail development occurred. In summary, by 1500, the
commonest type of rigging seen in English waters would have been a square-
rigged fore and mainmast and a lateen-rigged (triangular) mizzen. Ideally,
ships crossing the Irish Sea would have been safer and more manoeuvrable
with two or more masts and sails.[14] For such new designs to be used in Ireland
it required that ships be purchased abroad or built in Dublin at the behest of
a wealthy person or partnership. No such entrepreneur in Dublin has emerged
from the records to date. Edmund Lobusby, a shipbuilder, took on an
apprentice in Dublin in 1461, but there is no evidence that a ship was built at
the time, and Lobusby may have made a living by ship repair and
maintenance.[15] Investing in boats was regarded as somewhat unsafe and often
partnerships were formed to spread the risk, even in a boat as small as a fishing
skiff, where, in 1474 for example, Nicholas Wyght of Lusk held a fourth share
of a skiff, value 26s. 8d.[16] Robert Cowley, secretary to Gearóid Mór FitzGerald,
government official, merchant and citizen of Dublin, secured lucrative
government contracts and by 1513 had at least six ships.[17]

There are a number of reasons why the smaller ship was favoured by
owners and mariners. Small ships were unlikely to be commandeered by the

crown in a national emergency, and in adverse weather or in the event of piracy the smaller ship had manoeuvrability. On the east coast of Ireland, in silted Dublin bay, in the long estuary of the river Boyne, and in the narrow creeks of north Co. Dublin – Baldoyle, Malahide, Rogerstown – the smaller ship would have suited better.[18] The picard was one such ship trading between Ireland and England. In 1467–8, the *Jenicot Pykard of Dublin* made five journeys from Dublin to Chester and may have been in the picard class. The weight of its cargoes, ranging from about 5 to 10 tons, suggest that it was a small craft and may have been representative of the typical ship working out of Dublin at this time.[19] The weight of cargoes on the *Jenicot Pykard* that arrived in Chester on 22 October 1467, and on 12 February, 21 May and 2 September 1468 was 7 tons, 4 tons 17.5 cwt, 9 tons 17.5 cwt, and 7 tons respectively. In 1483, the Dublin port authorities named the picard as a type of ship that might moor in Dublin, the other two craft being a lighter (not a deep-sea vessel), and a scaff or skiff.[20] As will be seen below, a number of lighters coming in to Dublin port probably came from Dalkey harbour, on the south side of Dublin bay.

In the late medieval period, Dalkey harbour acted as an outport for large ships destined for Dublin port. Around 1396, the merchants of Dublin, in petitioning the king, noted that 'for want of water there has been no berthage or anchorage for larger ships' whose masters wished to enter Dublin port with 'wines, salt, iron and other wares from foreign parts'.[21] A solution that had developed earlier allowed large ships to discharge their cargoes at the archbishop's harbour of Dalkey, south Co. Dublin, for transfer by smaller ship or lighter to Dublin port, or by road transport. It was believed that the inevitable trading that occurred at Dalkey, for example in 1304, might damage the dominance of Dublin as a trading centre[22] and so, on receiving a petition (*c.*1396, above), the king granted a licence controlling buying and selling at Dalkey in such a way as not to 'prejudice the commonalty of Dublin'.[23] The small ports of Co. Dublin will be discussed below.[24] Dalkey does not seem to have developed much as a port in its own right. Recognized and used as a port in medieval times, it was principally an inward entrepôt port for Dublin. There were little or no port infrastructures, no evidence of customs collected,[25] and no records of ships from Dalkey entering Chester in 1467–8 or in 1476–7 for which detailed customs records are available.[26] In an assessment Dalkey has been described as 'not a port in the full sense'.[27]

It is possible that in the second half of the fifteenth century, ships leaving the port of Dublin, bound for England, may have been of such modest size as to be able to sail down the Liffey estuary on a high tide, navigating around the shallows, and into the Irish Sea without relying on the assistance of any Dublin bay small port facilities. On outgoing voyages from Dublin, mariners knew that if they reached a point beyond Ring's End they had reached Clar Rade (Poolbeg) – 'in English, the clear road for ships' – and the relative safety of deep water and the open sea.[28]

However, if the weather changed for the worse other marine dangers were revealed in the Dublin bay area. At the end of July 1487, for example, Sir Richard Edgecombe, returning to England after diplomatic work on behalf of Henry VII, experienced days of continuous storms at sea before reaching the coast of Cornwall. Edgecombe and his party boarded ship at Dalkey, his small fleet of four ships lying 'at road all night because the wind was contrary to him; and the ships lay in such a road that he could not get them out without peril'.[29] Edgecombe's ship was the *Anne of Fowey*, the remaining three ships being the *Rebel of Dene* belonging to Robert Streete, a barque of Sir John Treffy and a barque of Sir William Brewent. Together, the three ships carried 500 men. Intending to sail southwards, Edgecombe's ships were driven north. The ships got out of Dalkey safely but 'because the wind was contrarious he could make no sail and that night lay beside a place called Howth'. The following day, despite the winds 'being still contrarious', Edgecombe instructed the master to sail, but at four o'clock in the afternoon the wind began to rise and they were glad to reach the relative safety of shelter at Lambay Island, ten miles from Dublin, and there lay all night.[30]

The following day a great tempest arose and there was no sailing done. The storm continued on the next day and in the afternoon it became so stormy that there was a danger of the convoy running aground on sandy beaches or being smashed against rocky coasts. They decided to lie at anchor at Lambay and vowed that they would do a great pilgrimage and prayed that God would cease the tempest and send a fair wind.[31] Once again Edgecombe sailed, but again the wind was 'contrarious' and he had to return to the shelter of Lambay Island because 'so many great dangers were on every side'. The small fleet set out again and anchored at night in the open sea, and there lay all night. This was possibly at a submarine bank off the Wicklow coast. They then sailed to Tuskar Rock off the south-east coast of Wexford where they anchored all night. There 'the wind blew right sore and [there] was right troubleous weather'. They reached St Ives in Cornwall, sailed at night keeping clear of the 'great and perilous' dangers of Land's End and reached Fowey where Edgecombe went on pilgrimage to a chapel of St Saviour. By nightfall all the fleet had landed safely.[32]

In our period, the navigation skills of the shipmasters working in and out of Dublin port would have been rudimentary, as they would have been in any English waters at the time. Most probably, nothing about navigation would have been committed to parchment, everything would have been remembered by rote, by rhyme and possibly by mnemonics – how tides ran at particular points and the sequence of headlands, for example, along the north Anglesey and north Wales coast on the voyage towards the Dee estuary leading to Chester. Apprentice mariners would probably be heard on the quayside rattling off navigational material. A small number of pieces of navigation equipment were available to shipmasters. The magnetic compass was known since the twelfth century and any master crossing the Irish Sea should have had one on board. The sounding lead, a solid lump of lead on a marked line, was useful for establishing the depth under a ship, but a hole on its underside filled with tallow and touching the seabed provided samples that could be interpreted by an experienced mariner. An hour glass was very useful to time a ship's run, or series of short runs, for example on a zig-zag course. These instruments were in use on English ships by the fourteenth century but it is not clear how widely they were used.[33] In the 1470s, mariners measured distance in miles and leagues, but also perceived distance in terms of 'kennings'; the Isle of Man, for example, lay 4 'kennings' from Ireland, 'that is a day and a night's sailing', and Holyhead in Anglesey was said to be 3 'kennings' or '60 miles from the Isle of Howth in Ireland', a reasonably correct estimation.[34]

Maps of Ireland originating in Italy in 1339 (Angelino Dulcert), in 1426 (Jacobus Giroldis), in c.1450 (the Uppsala portalan), in 1500 (Juan de la Cosa) and in 1513 (the Argentine 'Ptolemy'), for example, were used for navigation. They were redrawn by T.J. Westropp in 1912–13. At first sight, the place-name detail is impressive but the shape of the island of Ireland is not correct in any of the original maps and while the maps were used for navigation they were not a basis for safe and accurate coastal work. Dulcert's original map and Baptist Agnesi's map of 1511, for example, have compass bearing lines. On the c.1450 Uppsala portalan, the settlements of Dublin, Malahide, Drogheda, Ardglass and Carrickfergus, for example, are located and named. On the west coast, the place names Sligo, Galway, Limerick and Dingle can be seen. Off the south coast, the Saltee Islands and the Fastnet are marked and named, being useful locators and warnings for mariners but also hazards for shipping (plate 1).[35]

Available also in the fifteenth century were books of sailing directions. While most shipmasters would not have seen these books it is assumed that they picked up knowledge of their contents from other masters in ports like Chester that had ships arriving from the south of England and the Continent. The books were given the term 'rutter' and offered very basic instructions in how to get one from one location to another and make a return voyage. The Landsdowne manuscript is one such rutter,[36] with a few selected sailing instructions and return directions given here, though some in the original are given in reverse order.

> Cape fenister and clere in Irlonde north and south
> The Londis ende and the toure of Watirford north northwest and south south est
> Fro saltais to tuscarde the course is est and west
> From the Skarris unto Arglas the cours is north and south
> The Ilonde of Man and Arglas est north est and west south west
> The Ile of Man and Lambey Ilonde north est and south west
> The Holbe and the Holy hede est and west
> From the tuscarde to the hede of the Skarres for to go clene of all the gronde between tuscarde and Dalcay the cours is north est and south southwest[37]

One can hear young lads on the quayside, aspiring to be mariners, singing out such directions and competing with each other.

Dublin's small neighbouring ports

Dublin's port activities should be seen in the wider maritime context of coastal Co. Dublin not only because the coast had a number of small neighbouring ports but also because the Dublin authority had the right to take customs in these ports. A broad survey of the Chester customs accounts for the period 1427 to 1499 shows that of a total of 332 Irish ships entering Chester, with port names recorded, three-quarters came from Dublin, Howth, Malahide and their vicinity. The number of ships from Howth and Malahide rose during the century, with ship numbers from Dublin and Drogheda dropping because of navigational problems in both ports. While the figures in the table below represent long-distance voyages across the Irish Sea, it must not be forgotten that the same ports, especially the small ports, would have played an important role in developing local economies along the coast of Co. Dublin through unrecorded short coastal voyages.[38]

Table 3.1 Home ports of Irish shipping entering Chester harbour, 1427–99

Dublin	Howth	Drogheda	Malahide	Rush
124	64	42	42	16
Baldoyle	**Rogerstown**	**Portrane**	**Clontarf**	**Lusk**
8	8	7	4	1

There were possibly about fifteen small ports near Dublin, although a contemporary list from 1437–8 mentions seven: Howth, Baldoyle, Malahide, Portrane, Rogerstown, Rush and Skerries.[39] Not surprisingly, the legal basis for Dublin's claim to collect customs and take forfeitures at these ports originated in royal grants made first in 1371–2 by Edward III, that the mayor, citizens and commonalty of Dublin should be allowed take 'the customs and forfeitures of saleable wares coming or passing by land or sea between Skerries and Arklow Head'. A similar grant was made to the 'mayor and commonalty' of Dublin in 1375 to take customs in ports on the same coast.[40]

It was difficult for the Dublin municipal authority to safeguard its interests at the small ports of Co. Dublin. In 1437–8, the authority complained to the Irish government that merchants were not coming 'by sea, as formerly, to the city and its port, but, to the great and manifest injury of Dublin' proceed to the small ports 'where they unload and discharge their merchandise, sell it in the country parts and bring goods thence'. To counter-balance the serious loss of revenue to Dublin that would have funded paving, wall-building and defences, the Dublin authorities were granted royal permission to levy on all merchandise coming to or from the towns involved tolls equivalent to those received by them at Dublin on similar goods.[41]

The problem of revenue loss to Dublin through customs not being collected for the city at the small ports came to a head in a dramatic episode that took place at Howth in autumn 1481. It began with a picard from Milford in Wales discharging coal at Howth without a licence from the mayor and bailiffs of Dublin – Thomas Mulghan, James Barby and John Rosell. Up to that time, the port authorities in Howth, in effect Lord Howth, had paid customs to Dublin, but now there was a change in policy. The mayor and bailiffs decided to stand up to Lord Howth, sending their servants to collect the custom and charge the master and purser of the picard to come to Dublin and pay a fine for breaking bulk without a licence.[42]

When Robert, Lord Howth, refused to pay the custom, the bailiff, James Barby, was ordered by the mayor 'to ride to Howth and take a distress out of the said picard' in lieu of the unpaid custom. An unseemly altercation took place between Barby who had attempted to take a sail from the ship and Lord Howth who tried to stop him. The wrath of the Dublin assembly was roused and the mayor, council, jurés and commons of Dublin decided that they should ride and go together to Howth, which they did, to take some item from the ship equivalent in value to the unpaid custom. How many rode out to Howth that day is not recorded – remember the numbers associated with the Dublin assembly – the twenty-four, the forty-eight and the ninety-six.[43] The honour of Dublin was at stake and it was a short ride of about 11 miles (17.5 km) to

Howth. This was one of the types of situations, as mentioned at the beginning, for which the forty-eight and the ninety-six existed – 'to secure the city from ill or damage'. Probably not everyone was free to go, but a minimum of 100 riders could have set out; with a few hangers-on looking for a day out the numbers could have been as high as 150.[44]

Lord Howth decided to defuse the situation and sent his son Nicholas to the mayor as a guarantee for the unpaid custom and for the offence done to the bailiffs. He also agreed to arbitration by the country's highest law officers, chosen by the mayor, the commons and himself. The arbitrators decided that the mayor and citizens of Dublin should have and enjoy the custom of Howth forever. Lord Howth did not oppose the judgement and his offence done to the bailiffs was forgiven by the arbitrators.[45]

Dublin's trade with France

Ireland had commercial links with the Continent from the earliest times, trading in the medieval period with Normandy, Brittany, La Rochelle, and Bordeaux in Gascony. Merchants brought hides, fish, wool, cloth, frieze and mantles to Normandy and Bordeaux, with Normandy returning pottery, cereals, iron, honey and wine, and Bordeaux exporting wine, honey, cereal products, iron, lead, wool, resin and dyestuffs. Horses and corn were exported to Brittany and Ireland received salt, iron, wine, canvas and linen in return. After the Hundred Years War (1337–1453) between England and France, the trade between Ireland and La Rochelle grew remarkably, especially in the export of wine. In the late fifteenth and early sixteenth centuries, shipping was often in the hands of local merchants, Norman ships being used in Normandy and ships working the ports of Brittany in the hands of Bretons.[46] After 1453, the La Rochelle–Ireland wine trade was run principally by Spanish shippers.[47] All the main ports in Ireland saw some French trade – Sligo, Galway, Limerick, Dingle, Baltimore, Kinsale, Cork, Youghal, Waterford, Dublin, Drogheda and Carrickfergus – but principally the ports of the south-west and south coast. Dublin had a very small share of this trade.[48]

The fourteenth and fifteenth centuries were difficult times for shipping, Richard Britnell referring to a series of wars as the 'so-called' Hundred Years War, and placing that war between 1338 and 1523, 'lasting off and on for well over a hundred years'. As a result, there were recessions, for example, in English and Scottish customs between the 1420s and the 1460s. For safety, ships travelled in convoys and armed men were added to crews to deal with pirates.[49] Irish merchants attempted to trade using safe conducts and in times of truce but this did not always work out satisfactorily.[50] Freight charges rose in the fourteenth century. Quantities of wine imported into England fell between the 1320s and the 1350s and the price of wine doubled. The volume of wine imports into England in the fifteenth century – 10,000 tuns a year – was half what it had been before the Hundred Years War.[51]

In a survey of late medieval trade with Spain, Portugal, France and Flanders, Ireland's share has also been shown to have been either, small, negligible or non-existent in the examined regions. A 'flurry of Irish activity in wine exports' was observed in three available years at Bordeaux in the first decade of the fourteenth century, showing as many as 18 Irish ships (2 from Dublin) at Bordeaux in some years, but even in these years Irish vessels accounted for only two, five and one per cent of shipping at Bordeaux, and two, two and a half, and one per cent of the wine exported.[52]

When Dublin merchants and ships sailed to ports in Normandy, there was no guarantee that the merchants would choose to return directly to Dublin, but might well consider entering ports *en route* to buy or sell commodities. In 1319, twelve Dublin and Drogheda merchants loaded a ship at Dieppe 'with diverse merchandise' to trade in Ireland, their destination possibly being their home ports, with Dublin a port of first call as they sailed up the Irish Sea. In 1335, four Cork merchants – Nicholas Hemmyng, Percival Vincent, Sinolda le Mercer and Adam Recche – shipped wool, woolfells and hides to Normandy on the *Rudecog* of Howth, from which port, near Dublin, they had possibly embarked and to which they possibly returned. Irish oak imported into Rouen in the late 1460s and early 1470s for use in the cathedral and in a local church could have originated from any of the southern ports or from Dublin.[53]

Dublin merchants were granted permission to trade in Brittany: Richard Hegrene, citizen of Dublin, allowed to load and bring 200 crannocks of corn to England and six horses to Brittany in 1358, Thomas Skethe, a Dublin merchant, cleared to go to Brittany and Spain in 1435, and return with salt, iron, wine and other merchandise to any part of Ireland, and John Caunton, Dublin merchant, permitted to export four horses to Brittany or Spain in 1452. Breton ships and merchants were to be seen in Irish ports along the south, south-east and east coast of Ireland, but the journey to Ireland was not without hazard. In 1412, near Dalkey, Co. Dublin, two barges and a balinger sailing from Brittany were captured at sea by a Dublin citizen, John Penkeston and others, 'as a reprisal'; in 1431, a Venetian carrack sailing from Brittany to Dublin, freighted with salt, iron and other goods by Italian and Aragonese merchants resident in London, was captured, and in 1466, Robert, Lord Howth, and others were indicted on a charge of attacking three Breton merchants on a ship carrying wine, salt and iron.[54]

Gascony, acquired by the Crown in 1152, was a major centre of wine production, and Bordeaux was its principal port of export.[55] Individual merchants or small groups of merchants might take the initiative to bring wine directly from Bordeaux to Dublin, while others named a number of destinations such as 'Dublin, Malahide or Drogheda' or 'to Dublin or to Drogheda', to allow for searching out the best markets.[56] From the available evidence there were English or Dublin ships involved in the trade, and merchants from Bordeaux, Chester, Dublin, England, London and Waterford operating in groups or as individuals to arrange shipments. In the fourteenth century, a ship carrying wine called to Dalkey, Co. Dublin (1306), and sailed on to Skinburness in Cumberland, and an English ship, the *Saint Marie*, brought wine to Dublin in 1333–4. In 1405, a Dublin merchant, Geoffrey Gallan, set out for Bordeaux with merchandise valued at 600 marks intent on returning with a cargo of wine. Merchants were sometimes permitted to bring supplies to Bordeaux for the 'maintenance of the king's lieges there': Nicholas Woder of Dublin was so licenced in 1404 and purchased supplies of wine for his return. Gascons came to live in Dublin and Irish merchants lived in Bordeaux: Jenico Markes, a native of Gascony, living in Dublin since he was eight years old, became a citizen and merchant of Dublin, and Bernard d'Irlande, a merchant of Bordeaux, shipped wines on English ships in the 1440s.[57]

As mentioned, groups were involved in the export of Gascon wine to Dublin. Chester merchants, in 1394–5, set out to bring wine to the Irish Sea, naming Waterford, Drogheda, Beaumaris and Chester as possible destination ports, and on 24 September 1449, John Motte, London citizen, Laurence Meryfield, owner of the *Patrick of Waterford*, Germot Ballagh, mariner and master of the same ship, and Robert Broun, ship's steersman, freighted their ship for Bordeaux and intended returning 'to Dublin or Drogheda with the wine of Gascony'. In the same year, a Bordeaux merchant, Bernard Bensyn, arranged with a Bristol merchant, Bernard Brennyng, to ship wine from Bordeaux 'to Dublin, Malahide or Drogheda'. At the beginning of the sixteenth century, in February 1519, two Bordeaux merchants, organized for dispatch to Dublin on the *Pierre de Crozon*, 61 tuns of wine (over 15,000 gallons) and one tun or 252 gallons of a new commodity – brandy.[58] All the major Irish ports were involved in the Bordeaux trade, Waterford and Youghal heading the list, followed by Cork and Kinsale, with, way behind, Dublin, Drogheda and Limerick (plate 6).[59]

In the first half of the sixteenth century, trade with the French ports was disrupted due to occasional fractured and tense Anglo-French relations and a number of wars between the two countries. Henry VIII's first war with France took place between February 1512 and July 1514; it had hardly ended and the new French king, Francis I, sent the duke of Albany, the Scottish claimant, to stir up trouble in Scotland against England.[60] In 1521, England signed a treaty of alliance with Charles V (Holy Roman Emperor) to make war on France, leading to Normandy and Picardy being ravaged in 1522 by the earl of Surrey. England's religious policy and its break with Rome in the 1530s caused relations between England and France to fluctuate. In 1543, Henry went to war again with France, 40,000 men invading from Calais in the following year.[61]

These years were difficult for sea-going merchants and it is no surprise that Irish trade to France was disrupted. In 1512, traffic between England and France ceased and an embargo on ships departing for Ireland or England was imposed at Dieppe and Caudebec.[62] In 1519, the cargo of the *Nicolas* of Rouen was seized at Cork and in September 1522 four English ships patrolled the Irish Sea to hinder communication between Scotland, Ireland and France.[63] The commercial agents of Nicolas Daniel of Rouen were imprisoned at Drogheda in 1528. When war with France was imminent in 1543, Henry VIII advised Lord Deputy St Leger in Dublin that 'all Frenchmen resorting thither must be treated as enemies'.[64]

Dublin–Chester trade, 1467–8

The Dublin–Chester commercial shipping link was strong. The shortest Irish Sea crossing for Dublin-based ships and ships of the smaller Co. Dublin ports was to the coast of Lancashire, Cheshire and north-west and north Wales, whose principal port was Chester. As early as *c*.1125, William of Malmesbury noted that Cestrians exchanged goods for cereals from Ireland, the Irish ports involved being most probably Dublin, Howth, Drogheda and the small ports on the creeks of rural north Dublin.[65] As will be seen, a symbiotic relationship developed between Chester and Dublin, based on the Dublin region's exports of skins and fish that required salt as a preservative, which was available in Cheshire.[66] Despite Dublin's earlier historic connection with Bristol very little sea-going commercial traffic continued with the port. While some business was done between the two cities Dublin ships hardly ever arrived in Bristol. It will be recalled that in October 1474, John Mold of Malahide, a merchant, was a debtor of John Baly of Bristol; equally, in December 1475, Thomas Glayn of Dublin owed 4 marks (£2 13s. 4d.) to Robert Barroun of Bristol. A detailed documentary review of Bristol's overseas trade from the thirteenth to the fifteenth century produced fifty-four references to Cork, Kinsale, Waterford, Wexford and Youghal, and only one reference to Dublin.[67] The whole thrust of Bristol's business with Ireland was to the south-east and south of the country. In a recent major analysis of Bristol's trade in the sixteenth century the pattern remained the same, it being stated that 'Bristol seldom traded with Dublin, which was linked to England via Chester'.[68]

Despite the close commercial ties between Dublin and Chester, there was probably always some friction between their respective merchants. However, the mid-1460s seem to have been a particularly difficult time for Dublin merchants trading into Chester and other locations in England. Dubliners who went to England as merchants were 'arrested, vexed, troubled and imprisoned' on 'feigned and imagined quarrels'. The Dublin assembly was aware that merchants were being imprisoned in Chester and other places. The short-term solution for the merchants was to pay a fine to be set free, but there remained the requirement of their cargoes being restored to them. Despite correspondence with the mayor and commons of Chester the problem continued and the assembly offered to support the merchants either singly or in groups in having their cases heard before the mayor and bailiffs of Chester to recover their goods and have damage made good.[69] The 1470s saw happier times for Dubliners in Chester, and in 1474 six new applicants from Dublin joined the Chester guild merchant, each paying 18*d*.[70]

Table 3.2 Ship arrivals in the port of Chester from Dublin, 1467–8

Date	Ship name	Master
22 October 1467	*Jenicot Pykard*	Blak Patrick
9 December	*Jenicot Pykard*	Blak Patrick
9 December	*Barge of Caernarvon*	–
13 December	*Katharine of Dublin*	John Milet
12 February 1468	*Jenicot Pykard*	–
15 February	*Peter of Dublin*	John Brete
6 March	*Katharine of Dublin*	John Milet
19 March	*Katharine of Dublin*	Blak Patrick
29 April	*Peter of Dublin*	John Brette
30 April	*Katharine of Dublin*	Blak Patrick
21 May	*Jenicote Pykard*	–
17 June	*Katharine of Dublin*	John Milet
4 July	*Peter of Dublin*	John Brette
19 August	*Katharine of Dublin*	Robert Clerke
22 August	*Mary of Dublin*	Patrick Tumlynson
2 September	*Jenicot Pykard*	–
– September	*Katharine of Dublin*	John Brette

In 1467–8, a number of ships, listed below, specialized in the voyage from Dublin to Chester. The regular masters were, Blak Patrick, John Brete (Brette), John Milet, Peter Tumlynson and Robert Clerke. Clerke had served his time as an apprentice mariner with John FitzJohn, a mariner in Dublin, and was granted the Dublin municipal franchise in October 1468. John Brete, based in Dublin, trained his apprentice Henry Purcell as a mariner; Purcell became a franchise holder in 1470. As will be seen the masters did not always command the same ship on the Chester run.[71]

On about 7 December 1467, at the timber wharves in Dublin port, the master of the *Barge of Caernarvon*, mentioned earlier, having had his manifest checked, paid his outgoing customs dues, and his mooring fees to one of the water-bailiffs, John Goldesburgh or Richard White, slipped his moorings and sailed on a high tide into the Irish Sea.[72] He had on board seventeen merchants and their cargoes. The merchants included Martin Eustace, Robert FitzSymond, Mathew Fowler, Richard Stanhirst, Robert West and John Whiteacres, all established merchants and citizens of Dublin.[73] The boat arrived in Chester on 9 December. The details of the cargoes are not available, but the cargo volumes for each merchant were recorded by the Chester customs officers, with examples given here – 28 horseloads for John Whiteacres's goods 'in and out' of Chester; for Martin Eustace the figure was 8 horseloads, for Robert FitzSymond and Richard Stanyhurst the figure was 4 horseloads each. Merchants followed the established customs arrangements at Chester port and city – customs duties were paid on merchandise brought to Chester by land or by sea and by merchants leaving Chester with goods to go inland to other English markets or by merchants sailing from Chester port.[74]

In the second half of the fifteenth century, Irish merchants continued to sail to England to do business. In 1479–80, three Dublin merchants – 'John White, Christopher Hygley and Thomas Lang' – describing how they were 'natives of these parts of Ireland … recent beginners in the occupation of merchandise … freemen of the city of Dublin', claimed that although they were absent from Dublin frequently on business that they should not be charged poundage like strangers but should be treated as Dublin citizens. They added that they regularly sailed as merchants and passengers between England and Ireland and were 'bound for the most part to be in England, buying and selling'. Parliament accepted their claim.[75] Hygley's insistence in 1479–80 that he was a recent beginner in merchandising seems to put in doubt that he was the franchise holder of the same name (Christopher Hege, alias Higley, merchant, married to Katherine Pers) who was enfranchised in Dublin on 21 October 1468. Nor was he a child of Peter Higley, a well-known Dublin merchant, who died in 1476.[76]

Other than the fact that the trio claimed to be 'recent beginners' in 1479–80, their description of their commercial routine tallies with their activities in the late 1460s when they were regularly on the Dublin–Chester sea journey, and especially with those of Hygley who sailed on Dublin–Chester voyages in 1476–7, described below. On 30 April 1468, for example, the cargoes of Thomas Lange, weighing seven horseloads, were carried on the *Katharine of Dublin*.[77] Christopher Hegley arrived in Chester on 3 May 1468 with merchandise, but on 2 and 15 September he arrived as a passenger from Dublin (recorded as Christopher Heyge and Christopher Heggesley), without a cargo, and probably proceeded into the English midlands to buy goods, consistent with his claim later that he was often absent from Dublin on business. Between the two dates, 2 and 15 September, Hegley would probably have purchased goods in Chester or inland, shipped them across the Irish Sea to Dublin and would then have returned to Chester by 15 September and to the English markets.[78] To complete our trio, a merchant named John Whyte entered Chester on 9 December 1467 and on 8 March 1468, carrying cargoes from Ireland to Chester. Whyte does not seem to have had a cargo at Chester on 19 August 1468 and would have been free to go inland to purchase commodities. Of the ships he used, two would have set out from Dublin – the *Jenicot Pykard* and the *Katharine of Dublin* – but on about 6 March 1468, he was on board the *George of Regeston*, with two horseloads of goods, sailing possibly from Rogerstown, a small port in north Co. Dublin. Other Dublin merchants, Robert Rychman and Patrick FitzLenis, were also on board.[79] The person named John Whyte, discussed here, should not be confused with 'John Whyte of Coventry' who seems to have been another merchant who sailed from Dublin and arrived in Chester on 13 December 1468.[80]

One of the most prominent Dublin-based merchants trading out of Dublin in the late 1460s was James Welles. It is assumed he originally came from England; he was enfranchised as a citizen of Dublin in 1469.[81] Earlier, in 1466, he seems to have upset the authorities in Dublin, and was kept in the Tholsel, the principal municipal building in Dublin, in which there was an upper and lower jail.[82] Ten years after being granted citizenship, he was a leading light, as will be discussed later, in organizing the incorporation of the guild of English merchants trading in Ireland, along with Richard Pylkynton and Thomas Whelberde. From December 1467 to September 1468 the record shows his cargoes were carried on the Irish Sea from the ports of Dublin, Chester, Drogheda and Furness. Most of Welles' business at that time, of which we know, was done on ten voyages – eight Dublin–Chester journeys,[83] and two voyages between Furness and Chester (21 July 1468) and between Drogheda and Chester (25 July 1468).[84] Welles' co-founder of the guild of

English merchants trading in Ireland, Richard Pylkynton, was on board a number of ships with Welles and his cargoes on three Dublin–Chester journeys in May, August and September 1468, and in July, on a Furness–Chester voyage.[85] On three of these journeys Pylkynton did not bring cargoes and while he could have been developing his own business as a merchant, it is perhaps more likely that on these occasions the two were working together. In 1477, a decade later, Pilkynton, Welles and Whelberde were still trading on the Chester–Dublin run and probably thinking about how English merchants might organize themselves in Dublin where they must have felt somewhat excluded by the local merchants and municipal authority who made the rules.[86]

Dublin–Chester trade, 1476–7

In the second half of the 1470s, Chester and its outports continued to be busy with sea traffic, the customs officers dealing with ships from Dublin, Howth, Drogheda, Baldoyle and Carrickfergus. Ships originating from ports in Britain included those from Conwy in Wales, Dartmouth and Totnes in Devon, and Holmtown (Peel) in the Isle of Man.[87]

In 1477, Christopher Hegley, Dublin citizen and merchant, was still active in the Chester and English markets, using ships whose home ports were in Chester, Dublin and Howth. On seven voyages across the Irish Sea, Hegley or his factors or on-board agents sailed on the *Karvill of Howth*, the *Katherine of Dublin* (William Cornyssh, master), the *Nicholas of Chester* (John Totty, master), the *Trinity of Chester* (Richard Bolde, master) and the *Trinity of Dublin* (William Andrew, master). On two occasions, Hegley travelled with and was responsible for his own cargo – a cartload of goods each, arriving in Chester on 25 January and on 7 September. On a date in September he arrived on the *Trinity of Dublin* at Chester, without the responsibility of a cargo, prepared possibly to go inland to the English markets. On the four other occasions when Hegley did business in Chester around 24 February, 26 April, 15 July and on a date in August, he appointed 'factors' or on-board agents to deal with his cargoes – Thomas Newnton handling three horseloads of goods in February, Jacob Marley and Robert Not'vile looking after a cartload of goods in April, and Robert Not'vile responsible for a cartload of cargo in July. In August, Hegley asked John White, a close colleague, to manage a cartload of cargo on the *Karvill of Howth* destined for Chester.[88] It seems that the responsibilities and duties given to factors depended on a number of criteria – their age, ability, knowledge, experience and probably the person-to-person relationship they developed with their merchant-employer. This topic will arise again and will be described in more detail.

Other Dublin citizens and merchants were regulars on the Dublin–Chester journey, sometimes using their mature apprentices to manage their goods and look after their affairs. John Savage sent goods to Chester on three occasions in 1477 in January, March and September. Exporting his cargoes of a cartload each to arrive in Chester on 26 January and 26 September, Savage sent his apprentice, Thomas Higeley, in January and almost certainly Thomas was also his on-board agent in September.[89] Since Higeley finished his apprenticeship and became a citizen of Dublin on 3 May 1482, he must have been a mature man when he began his apprenticeship in about 1475, and was therefore sufficiently experienced and able in 1477 to act for Savage.[90] In the same year, John Sweteman, merchant and citizen of Dublin, or his agents, were in Chester or its outports on seven occasions. Sweteman himself made what must have been exploratory journeys to Chester or further inland in England, in February, August and September, seeking to purchase commodities. On about 26 September, with a cargo of three horseloads of goods, he arrived in Chester on the *Karvill of Howth* and possibly moved inland to markets in the English midlands. Sweteman also had an apprentice, Richard Russell, who sailed for Chester and arrived on the *Katherine of Howth* (24 March) and on the *Carvill of Howth* (16 May). Russell did not have goods on board on these occasions and probably sailed for the purpose of travelling to the market at Chester or inland to other English markets; it would seem that on these occasions Russell had the confidence of Sweteman and must have purchased commodities in England on his behalf. On 15 July, Russell, representing Sweteman, arrived in Chester on the *Katherine of Dublin*, managing a cartload of cargo.[91] He later completed his apprenticeship and become a citizen of Dublin on 19 July 1482.[92]

The work of on-board agents

In the Chester customs returns for the period November 1476–September 1477, John Wilkynson stands out as a competent and busy factor or on-board agent. In the period mentioned, Wilkynson worked on ships destined for Chester whose home ports were Drogheda, Dublin and Howth. In less than a year, he made 18 voyages across the Irish Sea and worked for 25 merchants involving 39 transactions, each probably settled on a handshake. Of his voyages, 8 originated in Dublin, 7 in Howth and 3 in Drogheda and while he was probably a Dubliner there is no record of him being a citizen.[93] He was a trusted individual and managed the cargoes of Thomas Tunstall on 5 occasions on ships embarking from Howth (3) and Dublin (2).[94] Taking the Harold merchant family together (Stephen and William),[95] he worked for them on 5 voyages, managing cargoes out of Dublin and Howth. Edward Dughty and Thomas Garnet secured the services of Wilkynson for 2 journeys each to Chester, one journey on behalf of Garnet originating in Drogheda, the remaining voyages beginning in Dublin. John Swan employed Wilkynson for 3 Dublin–Chester voyages in November 1476, and in March and July 1477.[96]

The factors working the Irish Sea route had a responsible role managing the cargoes of their merchant-employers and getting their goods through the customs at Chester. The factors were persons of ability and initiative who under instruction sold goods in Chester or in the English midlands or worked independently selling on behalf of their Dublin employer. We have seen how Richard Russell appears to have worked independently for John Sweteman. In the same manner, John Wilkynson will be seen to work freely in England on behalf of his Dublin employers, meeting up with merchant contacts in Chester or in the midlands, the nominees of his employers, purchasing goods in the English midlands and in Chester for the return voyage to Dublin, and meeting with apparently new merchants and securing new work to manage cargoes on his return journey to Ireland.

Wilkynson's on-board duties often involved managing cargoes from a number of merchants. On three Dublin to Chester journeys, Wilkynson was responsible for four cargoes on each journey. On 2 November 1476, for example, on the *Trinity of Dublin*, he managed the cargoes of four merchants – 3 cartloads, 1 horseload, 1 cartload and 3 horseloads (4.5 tons). In the following year, sailing on the *Katherine of Dublin*, passing through the Chester customs on 15 July 1477, he was responsible for three separate cargoes of 1 cartload each and a cargo of unspecified weight (3 tons). Finally, in August, Wilkynson sailed on the *Mary of Dublin* (John Kenan, master), being responsible for the cargoes of Thomas Tunstall, Edward Dughty, Edward Coly and Brian Wodehouse – 2 cartloads, 1 cartload, 3 horseloads and 1 cartload (almost 4.5 tons). Wilkynson also worked out of the port of Howth, sailing to Chester on at least four occasions. He also worked out of the port of Drogheda in March, May and July 1477. On board the *Peter of Drogheda* (Nicholas White, master) in July, he acted as agent for Richard Waryne, Thomas Coke and Thomas Garnet, being responsible for managing a total of two cartloads of goods through the Chester customs for Coke and Garnet and conducting the affairs of Thomas Garnet at Chester or at locations inland.[97]

The Chester customs records of November 1476–September 1477 occasionally show women working at a responsible level as merchant's agent or factor. Christina Clerke made three journeys from Dublin and one from Howth to Chester in April and in September 1477. In April she was on-board agent for John White, sailing on the *Trinity of Chester* (John Totty, master), managing three horseloads of goods. On 26 April she arrived in Chester on the *Trinity of Dublin* as agent for John White and Robert Lawles, managing 2 tons of goods for the two merchants and dealing with customs officers at Chester. Clerke worked twice again for Robert Lawles on voyages to Chester, on the *Trinity of Dublin* in September, and on the *Karvill of Howth* on about 26 September, managing a ton of cargo on each occasion. Earlier, at Howth, most probably in August, Agnes, wife of William Wilson, was agent for her husband's cargo on the *Karvill of Howth* sailing for Chester, managing a cartload of goods.[98] Both women would have followed the routines of a factor – getting goods through customs and meeting up with a merchant to sell on the merchandise.

It would appear that it was difficult for women to work in shipping, a trade dominated by men, requiring physical strength and absence from home. From the small amount of information we have at present it would seem that the key to entering the trade was a marital or family connection together with knowledge of the functions of a merchant's agent. Agnes Wilson stepped in, possibly in an emergency, to manage her husband's cargo on a Howth–Chester voyage. She probably knew what routine was to be followed at the Chester customs and she or her husband, if he was alive, must have had sufficient confidence that she could sell or move goods on successfully in Chester or in other English markets. Christina Clerke's situation was somewhat similar. She was the wife of John Clerke who had been agent for Mathew Fouler on 21 March and 24 March on ships entering Chester. John Clerke's name does not appear in the Chester customs records from April to September 1477 but the name of Christina Clerke does. It is quite possible that John Clerke was ill, injured or had died, and that Christina stood in for him. Christina Clerke sailed on four ships, working for two merchants who re-employed her to get goods through customs and move or sell them on in Chester or in some other English town, showing that she was an able, competent and responsible merchant's agent.[99]

In the Chester customs accounts recording merchants and their goods destined for Ireland there was often a difference in the quantity or form of the goods carried by a merchant entering the city and leaving the port. Some merchants entered the city by land and exited it by sea with the same quantity of goods – Thomas Tailior of London (5 horseloads) and Richard Waryner (2 horseloads). Robert Tunstall entered Chester by land with 15 horseloads of goods but boarded ship with 2 cartloads, suggesting that he bought a horseload of goods (2.5 cwt) in Chester to bring his cargo up to 2 tons. There were many examples of merchants embarking for Ireland with a greater quantity of merchandise than they had brought into Chester – Thomas

Newman (2 horseloads/1 cartload), Richard Blande (2 horseloads/1 cartload), Thomas Bek (4 horseloads/1 cartload) and Gilbert Walker (3 horseloads/1 cartload). It seems that merchants, returning to Ireland from the English midlands, who entered Chester by land, through the city gates, could either keep their cargoes unchanged, repack their goods in a different form or transact new business in Chester with a corresponding rise in the weight of their cargo. A very small number of merchants embarked for Ireland with less goods than that which they entered Chester by land – William Hey (1 cartload/1 horseload) and John Baker of Coventry (1 cartload/2 horseloads).[100]

In the period November 1476 to September 1477, the majority of merchants in Chester destined for Ireland would have sailed to Dublin, or Howth which would have left them within reach of the city markets. Ships from Drogheda were infrequent callers to Chester, and John Weber and Patrick Symond from Drogheda, each transporting one-ton cargoes, may well have sailed to Dublin first and returned to Drogheda by coaster. Nicholas Clerke of Trim, with a ton of cargo, may have acted similarly on his return journey, having originally embarked for Chester at Baldoyle, a small port in north Co. Dublin. Dublin merchants who sailed home from Chester in 1477 with cargoes, included Thomas Hegley, factor for John Savage (1 ton), James Stokes (1 ton), James Welles (1 ton), John Sweteman (about 7 cwt) and Christopher Hegley (1 ton). Londoners who sailed for Dublin from Chester were John Walssh (1 ton), Thomas Tailior (over half a ton) and Thomas Whilberde (1 ton). There were also a number of Coventry merchants who brought or had goods conveyed to Dublin – John Baker (5 cwt), Robert Baker whose cargo was managed by Richard Lighton (1 ton), John Dwale (about 7 cwt), John Swan whose factor was Robert Lawles (1 ton), and John White 'of Coventry' (1 ton). John Middilton of Doncaster brought 5 cwt of merchandise to Dublin. Thomas Bridde of Manchester brought one ton of goods to Dublin and Richard Bexwik who was most probably from Manchester, and of whom we shall hear again, was at Chester with half a ton of goods ready to embark for Ireland.[101]

Factors or on-board agents also returned to Dublin with cargoes. John Wilkynson returned to Ireland from Chester transporting goods for 10 merchants involving 14 cargoes, less work than he had secured when setting out from Irish ports, but nevertheless a bonus to his income. Most of John Wilkynson's contracts and responsibilities in respect of merchants who employed him in Ireland probably ended when he reached Chester. However, Wilkynson, recognized in Chester as an experienced factor, secured new work to bring commodities to Ireland from seven merchants – Nicholas Herford, John Milnar, John More, Richard Pynchebek, Thomas West, Thomas Weile and Robert Wright, most of whom seem to have been English. Christina Clerke also secured new business from John Weale/Dwale, managing one ton of merchandise to Dublin. Wilkynson continued to get work from three merchants or merchant families who had employed him in Ireland: the Tunstalls, the Beks and Edward Dughty. In Dublin and Howth he had secured work as a factor from William and Thomas Tunstall. In Chester he took instruction from Robert Tunstall to bring 5 cargoes to Ireland. Sailing from Drogheda, Wilkynson had represented Edward Bek on a voyage to Chester but in Chester acted on the instructions of Thomas Bek to bring a ton of goods across the Irish Sea. Wilkynson had been employed by Edward Dughty in Dublin to bring goods to Chester on two occasions. On a return journey he again represented Edward Dughty, entering Chester by land with 5 cwt of cargo, increasing his purchases in the Chester markets to a ton which he then brought to Dublin. It seems that on this occasion John Wilkynson purchased commodities at markets outside Chester, brought the goods into Chester, traded in the city and returned to Dublin, following instructions originally given by Dughty. Similarly, two other factors, Thomas Hegley and John Clerke, worked independently of their merchant-employers having taken instruction from them in Dublin. Hegley, working for John Savage, purchased goods outside Chester and entered Chester by land on two occasions to bring 2 tons of merchandise to Dublin. John Clerke (husband of Christina), factor of Matthew Fouler on two occasions, also transported a total of 2 tons to Dublin, having purchased goods both outside Chester and in the Chester markets.[102]

Little is known of how far into England Dublin citizen merchants travelled in the late fifteenth century. William Worcester (1415–c.1485), topographer and author, and a reliable observer,[103] met 'Bartholomew Rossynell, a youngish merchant of the city of Dublin, on 10 July 1479, while riding from London to Walsingham'.[104] Worcester was on one of his travels and visited London and Walsingham priory in that year. He found Rossynell very informative about the towns and harbours of the Isle of Man.[105] Rossynall was very possibly Bartholomew Rosell (Russell), a Dublin merchant who became a citizen of Dublin on 21 April 1475, gaining citizenship because he was married to a free woman (citizen), Alison Waren.[106] Perhaps it can be assumed that other Dublin merchants also went to London for commercial reasons at this time.

Exports: fish, skins and textiles

The contents of ships' packs in the 1460s and 1470s described above by customs officers as 'horseloads' and 'cartloads' are not known, but Chester customs records from two sample years, 1404–5 and 1525–6, name commodities and these should help to give some insight into what raw materials and finished goods were available in Dublin and exported in the period *c.*1450–*c.*1540. From the 1404–5 customs records a general picture emerges of fish and corn being exported to Chester from the Dublin region and ships returning with quantities of salt available in Cheshire. Also in that year, and probably in other years around that time, merchants from Coventry were regularly involved in Dublin–Chester commerce. The 1525–6 customs returns are especially detailed and will be discussed in the concluding chapter, but it is worth noting here that the returns reveal a substantial trade in skins and textiles from Dublin, including blankets, checkers, fledges, flocks, frieze, linen, mantles, wool and yarn.[107]

In 1404–5, white fish were exported to Chester from Rush and Balrothery and white fish and herring from Malahide. In October 1404, nine merchants imported herring from Ireland to Chester, one of whom brought 3 barrels of herring, each equivalent to 30 gallons in capacity. In January 1405, both Richard de Neuton and Thomas Lede of Malahide imported a last of herring each into Chester – a last being about 12,000 fish or about 12 barrels in capacity. It seems that the coastal waters of north Co. Dublin were very rich in fish stocks at this time. Other products were exported from Dublin but damaged and missing customs records have prevented offering a more complete picture of the range of exports to Chester: John de Hokenhull of Dublin, for example, exported about one ton of iron and Simon de Thornebery (of Chester), sailing most probably from Dublin, exported three pipes of Gascon wine to Chester, each pipe or cask being about 126 gallons.[108] Skins are not listed as a commodity in this sample year and may be concealed in the records behind such terms as 'fardels' (a bundle of unspecified size), 'horseloads' or 'carts [of] merchandise'.[109]

In 1404–5, much of the trade between Dublin and Chester of which we have commodity details was concerned with the export of fish from Ireland and merchants returning with supplies of salt necessary for the preservation of fish.[110] At the close of 1404, two Co. Dublin merchants returned from Chester with cargoes of salt, having probably brought fish to Chester – John Rondull of Lusk (3 tons of salt) and Thomas Blundell of Malahide (4 tons of salt).[111] In the new year, in March, Richard Coyne of Rush and Ralph Wauter of Balrothery exported white fish to Chester and probably returned with cargoes of salt.[112] In the following month, two Malahide merchants exported red herring and white fish to Chester, one returning with over a ton of salt.[113] In July, Richard Coyne again imported fish into Chester and returned with 2 tons of salt and John Wulf also of Rush brought back over half a ton of salt.[114] Inevitably, Chester merchants were involved in this trade. Having come from Ireland to Chester in March 1405 with cargoes of white fish, Richard le Fyssher of Nantwich and Thomas de Wyrvyn of Chester returned to Ireland with 5 horseloads of salt each.[115]

Coventry merchants working from Ireland were involved in trade with Chester in 1404–5 and most probably in other years around the turn of the century. Thomas Dawe, John Leder and John Renell arrived in Chester from Ireland on at least four occasions each and other Coventry merchants sailed from Ireland to Chester on at least two occasions each – John Broun (Bron), John Burbage, John Happesford, John Pycryng, Thomas Russell and John Scarlet. Seventeen other named Coventry merchants voyaged from Ireland to Chester and there were also twenty-three additional visits to Chester by Coventry merchants, which visits would probably have included repeat visits from some of the above-named merchants.[116] Recorded as coming from Ireland, the Coventry merchants most probably came from Dublin or its small ports.

In the fifteenth century, Chester's commerce was built on trade with Ireland. The connection with Ireland and Dublin in particular was Chester's most important and longest-established commercial link. A local Chester poem, said to have been written around 1430, describes the commodities of its trade much of which would have come from Dublin and the small ports of north Co. Dublin.

> Hides and fish, salmon, hake and herringe
> Irish wooll, and linnen cloth, faldinge,
> And marterns good be her marchandie,
> Hertes hides and other of venerie,
> Skinnes of otter, squirrel and Irish hare
> Of sheepe, lambe, and foxe, is her chaffare,
> Felles of kiddes and conies great plenty.[117]

* * *

Navigation methods were simple and primitive, knowledge of the sea was mainly committed to memory, and the experience of shipmasters was important. Dublin port had a shallow estuary and the deep-water Howth harbour was a rival. Ships working out of Dublin seem to have been small.

Dubliners and others imported relatively small cargoes of continental goods into the city. This aspect of Dublin trade was largely unplanned and irregular. Dublin had a close commercial relationship with Chester, many of the cargoes on Irish ships managed by factors or on-board agents. The Irish Sea connection with Chester gave Dublin merchants access to Coventry and the markets of the English midlands.

CHAPTER 4

Guilds and Apprentices

THE INDENTURE BELOW, dated 11 June 1461, belonging to a collection of Dublin deeds, captures the very essence of the medieval guild system, an agreement between a master and an apprentice, over an agreed period of time, in order that the apprentice would acquire the skills of his chosen craft and be invited to join his fellows in the community of the craft guild. Later he could work as a journeyman, learning new skills and in time becoming a master craftsman himself. The master also agreed to offer the apprentice moral training, and physical and material care, in return for obedience, loyalty and work, including keeping the secrets of his master's trade:

> An indenture made between Edmund Lobusby and John White. John placed himself as an apprentice with Edmund for five years after the date of this indenture to serve the said Edmund his master in everything assigned to him in the service of a shipbuilder as becomes such an apprentice for the said term. Edmund shall instruct him in all that shipbuilding to the best of his knowledge and shall treat and teach him honestly and shall also find him in food and drink, in linen clothes and woolen hose and bedclothes suitable to such an apprentice during the said term. John shall conceal the secrete of his master Edmund, shall not damage his goods or chattels, nor shall see it done by others without preventing it so far as he is able, he shall not commit fornication nor marry, shall not gamble, frequent taverns or any disreputable places, shall not absent himself by day or by night without the permission of his master Edmund during the said term under the penalty of doubling the said term. Edmund shall give to John in the fifth year ten shillings for his labour.[1]

In another English city, Bristol, in the first half of the sixteenth century, Irish youths served their time to the trade of ship carpenter. In 1533, Walter Roche from Wexford was apprenticed for seven years to William Evans and his wife Edith. At the end of his term he was given 13s. 4d.[2] In 1547, Thomas son of David Pers of Wexford followed the trade of ship carpenter in Bristol and was apprenticed for seven years to George Naren and Tamson his wife. At the end of his term David became a citizen of Bristol for a fee of 4s. 6d. paid by his master and David was to have the tools of his trade – an axe, a gennet, a borer, a sledge hammer, two caulking irons, a mallet, a hand-saw and other tools.[3]

* * *

In late March 1451, a merchant's guild or fraternity was re-established in Dublin. The merchants had been organized in 1438[4] and earlier, so the setting up of the guild in 1451 by authority of parliament meeting at Drogheda[5] was the beginning of a phase in which a new charter granted 'liberty to establish anew a fraternity or guild of the art of merchants of the city of Dublin, as well men as women, in the chapel of the Holy Trinity in the cathedral church of the Holy Trinity'.[6]

Fifty-one men, led by the earl of Ormond and the archbishop of Dublin, made a formal request to Henry VI to set up the guild. More than forty established Dublin merchant families were represented in the group – Cornwalshe, FitzRery, Chever, Gogh, Grampe, Harrold, Savage, Shynnagh, Ussher and West, for example. The guild was to be governed by two masters elected annually. Liberty was also granted to a chantry of four priests to celebrate Mass every day for the king's health, and for the founders and members of the guild. No foreigner was to buy any merchandise 'in retail or in gross' within the city and suburbs, except from merchants dwelling in Dublin and its franchises. The Dublin guild of merchants was known as the guild of Holy Trinity and their place of worship was Trinity Chapel in the south aisle of Christ Church cathedral.[7] In the 1450s, and almost certainly in earlier decades, as will be explained, the Dublin guild merchant had a tight grip on the proceedings of the Dublin municipal assembly and the formation and promulgation of its ordinances.

What is the origin of the medieval guilds and how and when were they developed in Dublin? When the Normans came to England they found guilds in the Anglo-Saxon towns – associations formed for mutual aid, for attending to religious duties in community and helping a member when ill or a family with funeral expenses. Domesday Book mentions that Dover had a guildhall and that the 'good men of Winchester used to drink their guild' in the guildhall. Drinking was only one facet of guild life; the guilds also concerned themselves with the pursuit of economic self-interest. The early craft guilds practising their trade in given towns in England – weavers, fullers or bakers, for example – were at once friendly societies and also 'coalitions dedicated to the exclusion of outsiders'.[8] In 1171–2, when Henry II granted to the men of Bristol in his city of Dublin all liberties and free customs which they had at Bristol[9] he was in effect allowing the Bristollians to have in Dublin 'all their reasonable guilds' which they had in Bristol.[10] On 15 May 1192, the lord John confirmed this privilege in his grant to the citizens of Dublin – 'The citizens of Dublin shall have all their reasonable guilds as the burgesses of Bristol have or had, and in the most advantageous manner'.[11] But a word of caution, as Robert Bartlett has succinctly put it – 'If town law was marked by freedom, urban organizations insisted that this freedom was for members only'.[12]

Dublin's first guild merchant

The guild that played the formative role in promoting and participating in the self-governance of towns in England in the twelfth and thirteenth centuries was the guild merchant.[13] Like specialized craft guilds the guild merchant had social and religious aspects to its activities: they feasted and drank in the guildhall, looked after the sick and the poor of their families and cared for the widows and orphans of their members. The principal purpose of the guild merchant was to control local trade and to restrict free and full trading to their own members. They also collected tolls and imposed fines for breaches of their regulations. At Ipswich in the early 1200s there were burgesses or free citizens who were not always members of the guild merchant and there were many guildsmen who were not burgesses, for example, at Totnes in 1236.[14] In Dublin, the figures for guildsmen and citizens did not tally either. Taking Philomena Connolly's analysis of admissions to the Dublin guild merchant roll, 1222–65, and of admissions to the Dublin roll of free citizens, 1234–49, the figures for guild admissions, in the available fifteen-year period, are dramatically higher in each year than the numbers acquiring citizenship. A select list is shown in the table.[15]

Table 4.1 Admissions to the Dublin guild merchant and to the Dublin roll of free citizens for select years, 1234–49

Year	Guild members	Free citizens
1234–5	100	41
1236–7	103	46
1239–40	84	27
1242–3	91	25
1245–6	172	31
1248–9	106	27

Nevertheless, in England and in Dublin it would appear that, with the passage of time, the borough or town council and the guild merchant approached more and more closely until they amalgamated and became identical, or 'at least indistinguishable'.[16] In 1419 in Dublin, as craft guilds began to be formed, apprentice tailors, and presumably all other apprentices, could not practise their craft without a licence from their guild and the pre-requisite of obtaining citizenship.[17]

The membership of the early guilds merchant was not as narrow as the name suggests. Salzman tells us that originally the guild merchant cast its net wide and drew in some very small fish. Referring to the rolls of the Leicester and Shrewsbury guilds at the beginning of the thirteenth century he showed a membership, including merchants, of bakers, butchers, coopers, dyers, carpenters, miners, masons and other craftsmen.[1] He could equally and confidently have used the Dublin guild merchant roll, c.1190–1265, to illustrate the same point.[19]

When King John granted Dublin citizens a range of liberties and free customs in 1192 he may well have been responding to a formal request from the Dublin guild merchant already in existence. The guild membership list has been dated as beginning at the latest in c.1190, but it possibly began some years, or even a decade or more, earlier. Membership numbers reached 8,400 guildsmen, with, for dated entries, admissions occurring at an average rate of 112 a year.[20] Almost 170 occupations are recorded on the merchant roll.[21] With a standard rate membership fee of 9s., it has been calculated that the guild had an annual income of almost £50. Membership brought access to the market and the fellowship and support of members. Guildsmen did not necessarily remain resident in Dublin.[22] A cursory survey of their places of origin in Ireland, Britain and the Continent is most impressive. Members came locally from Ballyfermot, Finglas, Oxmantown, Raheny and Swords; and from towns on the Irish coast – Arklow, Carlingford, Cork, Drogheda, Howth, Malahide, Waterford, Wexford and Wicklow; and from inland towns and settlements – Athlone, Carlow, Enniscorthy, Garristown, Kildare, Leixlip, Nenagh, Slane and Tuam. The membership also came from the English west country, and the east and north of England – Bristol, Cardiff, Dunwich, Yarmouth, Carlisle and Furness. The range of continental towns represented in the membership is particularly striking – Antwerp, Cologne, Dinan, Groningen, Limoges, Lucca, Nantes, Paris, Poitou, La Rochelle, Rennes, Tarbes, Valkenberg and Ypres.[23]

The craft guilds and the renewed guild merchant

With the passage of time, the craftsmen were squeezed out of the guilds merchant in England and began to set up their own craft guilds in the thirteenth and fourteenth centuries.[24] This seems to have happened later in Ireland. At the beginning of the second half of the fifteenth century, besides the guild merchant, there were craft guilds already established in Dublin. A charter dated 16 July 1419 granted a licence to a group to found a guild of tailors in Dublin to be known as the fraternity of St John the Baptist. The guild was permitted to have a chantry in St Mary's chapel in the church of St John the Evangelist, Dublin.[25] The guild of shoemakers was established in 1426 and had its chantry in the Lady Chapel of the church of St Michael, High Street.[26] The guild of weavers, established in honour of the Blessed Virgin and All Saints, was set up by charter on 28 September 1446, their chantry chapel being that of the Blessed Virgin in the church of the Carmelite friars in present-day Whitefriar Street. The guild of barber-surgeons of Dublin, older than the comparable London guild, was set up by charter on 18 October 1446, its patron being St Mary Magdalene; they worshipped in the chapel of St Mary Magdalene in the Hospital of St John outside Newgate. The guild of blacksmiths was set up by charter in 1474, their patron being St Loy (Eligius) to whom a chapel was dedicated in St John's outside Newgate, Dublin.[27] The bakers' guild was set up in 1478 and had its chantry in the chapel of St Anne in St Mary del Dam's church.[28] In 1481, a charter, discussed in more detail below, was granted by Edward IV to the guild of English merchants trading in Ireland; their patron was to be the Blessed Virgin and their chantry chapel was in the Chapel of Mary Grace at the bridge end, Dublin.[29] The carpenters, millers, masons and heliers (roofers) of Dublin were incorporated as a guild in a charter granted by Henry VII on 10 March 1508; they met and chose their officers in the Lady Chapel of the abbey of St Thomas at Thomas Court.[30]

We have seen earlier how Dublin's guild merchant was formally re-established in late March 1451. While it is most likely that in the decades immediately before that, say in the 1430s, when it is known that there was an active guild merchant in Dublin,[31] that that body had close ties with the municipal authority, there is no doubt that the membership of the new guild (1451) dominated the proceedings of the municipal assembly. Controlling and directing the Dublin assembly probably could have happened by sheer dint of energy from ambitious and capable merchants, but it was copper-fastened by four significant events in a two-year period – the rewriting of the rules by the members of the nascent guild merchant (14 January 1451),[32] the granting of a royal licence to set up a new guild merchant (late March 1451),[33] the new guild acquiring the facility of a meeting room in the Tholsel, the municipal government building, at the meeting of the Dublin assembly on 20 January 1452,[34] and the decision (1452) by the guild merchant, with one exception, to hold its quarterly meetings on Mondays, a few days before the quarterly Thursday meetings of the municipal assembly. In the case of the Michaelmas quarterly municipal meeting that dealt with elections of officers for the year, the guild merchant held their meeting after this meeting because the outcomes of the municipal elections of officers would affect their own election of officers.[35] It is worth recording the names of the men in whom the guild put their faith in making 'laws and ordinances needful and profitable for the guild' – John FitzRobert, John Bennet, James Dowdall, Philip Bedlewe, Nicholas Clerke, Thomas Sawage, William Grampe and Arnenton Uscherr.[36] It would appear that experienced businessmen attended to guild affairs at their quarterly Monday meetings but must also have discussed the forthcoming agenda and the issues of the day that were likely to surface at the municipal meeting later in the week which many merchants would be attending.

It seems that while the 'Guild of English merchants trading in Ireland', or the fraternity and guild of the Blessed Virgin Mary of the bridge end, Dublin, was established by statute in 1481, it already existed from 1479 and 'was founded in a chapel called the chapel of Mary Grace near the bridge end of the city of Dublin as by letters patent thereof made and shown in parliament more fully appears'.[37] While the foundation date of 1479 has been called a 'primary foundation',[38] supported by Richard, duke of York, lieutenant (chief governor) of Ireland, the legislation of 1481 describes the 'guild of merchants of the aforesaid parts of England coming to this land for the purpose of trading' as being 'anew founded, begun, commenced'.[39] The statute's preamble named and recognized the *de facto* master and wardens (still in office) of the guild set up in 1479 – James Welles, Thomas Whelberde and Richard Pylkington.[40]

Guilds celebrating

While the guilds had chaplains and organized chantries, strictly speaking they were lay organizations with men and women members, although women are seldom mentioned. The guild cultivated a sense of brotherhood, helping members who had come on hard times and settling disputes.[41] At regular meetings the expected business of any organization was conducted – electing officers, drawing up rules and admitting new members. Every year on its patron day the guild met in their church or chantry chapel, dressed in their best, and wearing their distinctive hoods or livery would have attended the celebration of a sung High Mass. Afterwards they would have retired to their favourite tavern where they dined well. Grace was said.[42]

> Christ that bread broke bid his command when he sat among his twelve apostles, Bless our bread and our all, and all that we have, and shall have, and feed us with himself. Amen[43]

In the fourteenth century in Drogheda, medieval trade guilds came under the critical eye of Richard FitzRalph, archbishop of Armagh. FitzRalph had had a reputation in Avignon in the 1340s for delivering unusually outspoken sermons, and after he became archbishop through being noticed by Pope Clement VI,[44] he continued in this vein, preaching in Drogheda, for example, against citizens who did not pay tithes and against merchants and others, he insisted, who did not pay tithes on each commercial transaction (such as buying a bale of cloth) at the point of sale or over the counter. Merchants probably maintained that they could not calculate their profit until the end of the year, whereas FitzRalph believed that the merchants were deliberately avoiding the paying of tithes.[45] In June 1355, he vigorously attacked the guilds and confraternities of Drogheda, seeing them as sinful organizations. FitzRalph argued that guild members take an oath to exclude a certain nation from membership contrary to the law of charity and in this way the Irish were excluded from the trade privileges of Drogheda. He complained that the guilds bound their members to much feasting and spent large amounts of money on candles carried in procession with a consequent loss of alms. He also saw the requirement of guild members to make generous donations to guild funds as another loss to the poor.[46]

Guild apprenticeship and citizenship

In England, the normal period of apprenticeship was seven years, in which the apprentice lived in his master's house. His indentures had to be enrolled, he had to pay a fee to the guild and his family or friends had to give a bond for his good behaviour. He was paid very little, probably about 12d. a year, and was often treated harshly, sometimes being beaten with a rod.[47] Some apprentices in England received additional education, often agreed in their indentures, learning grammar, for example, and how to speak English better. As late as the 1340s in London, two guilds – the leather dressers and pewterers – offered in their ordinances an alternative qualification to a period of apprenticeship for reception into the craft – 'the production of good testimony that the applicant is a competent workman'. The term of apprenticeship could vary considerably but the practice in London was a minimum of seven years, which became the norm in most English boroughs and most probably in Dublin.[48] In 1462 in England, a boy was apprenticed to a haberdasher for twelve years but this was to include two years schooling at grammar and learning to write. In 1494 at Coventry, in a list of apprentices who took the oath of fealty to the king and to the city, the apprenticeship term ranged from five to nine years, with the majority being seven years. In Bristol on 7 March 1543, Nicholas, son of

Henry Harris late of Youghal, a fisher, was apprenticed to John Magott, card maker. The term agreed was for 10 years.[49]

A guide as to how applicants for apprenticeship were assessed in Ireland in the fifteenth century and how apprentices were treated has survived in the royal licence granted to a group who wished to set up a fraternity or guild of the art of shoemakers in Dublin. The royal grant was made at Naas on 4 December 1426.[50] The fraternity had a chaplain, Thomas Lawless, and was entitled to establish a chantry of one or more chaplains who would celebrate daily Mass in the chapel of the Blessed Mary in the church of St Michael in the High Street, Dublin. Under the patronage of James Butler, earl of Ormond, some twenty men and one woman sought royal permission to set up the fraternity. It is clear that men and women could join the fraternity but only one woman, Juliana Lowyn, was named in the founding licence. The guild was entitled to elect two masters to run its affairs, which the guild could replace from time to time.[51] Guilds, such as the shoemakers and weavers, for example, were granted the right to use a common seal in the conduct of their legal and commercial business.[52]

In the shoemakers' guild in Dublin, and almost certainly in other guilds based in Dublin, whenever a person presented themselves to become an apprentice, an interview took place with guild officers. The applicant faced the two masters and the clerk of the guild who were to discretely find out if the applicant was free – not the subject of a prison sentence or already apprenticed to another master, for example. In Dublin, the applicant had to be from the English nation and had to be of good conversation. If the applicant was found to be satisfactory he would be received as an apprentice and within a year would be enrolled by the clerk before the masters on payment of half a mark (6s. 8d.) for the use of the guild. The term of the apprenticeship was seven years.

If the apprentice should run away it was lawful for his master to testify that such fugitive was his apprentice; the master could do this in person or through his attorney having letters testimonial under the common seal of the guild. The master could have the runaway arrested if he was found in cities and towns privileged by the king, such as Dublin, Drogheda, Waterford, Cork and Limerick.[53] Masters in the weavers' guild were more restricted in their search and could pursue the apprentice through the city and in Co. Dublin.[54] If apprehended, the apprentice was brought back to the house of the master and compelled to serve him and finish out his term. When the seven-year term was faithfully served and completed the apprentice was brought by his master and the masters of the guild to the guildhall of the city of Dublin, and by their testimony before the mayor and bailiffs of the city, the apprentice was sworn into the liberty of Dublin and became a citizen.[55] When these rites of passage were first combined in Dublin by ordinance – completing apprenticeship and becoming a citizen – has not been established but it was compulsory in 1419 in the case of apprentice tailors and most probably with all other guild apprentices, the tailors' guild charter stating: 'No one is to exercise the tailor's craft without licence of the master and wardens and without having obtained the freedom of the city of Dublin'.[56]

In the first instance, in order to qualify to become a citizen of Dublin it was usually necessary to have been born in the city or its franchises. One of the categories of persons who were admitted to citizenship was members of the Dublin merchants and craft guilds who had completed their apprenticeship. Other ways of being admitted to the Dublin city franchise were birth as a son or daughter of a freeman, marriage to the daughter of a franchise holder, a fine paid by a professional man such as an attorney, and by special grace similar to the modern granting of honorary freedom of a city. Once elected to be a freeman, the trained apprentice was expected, if called upon, to defend his city and it was ordained in autumn 1454 that an apprentice merchant should 'have a jakebow, sheff, sallet and sword of his own'. Applicants from other guilds were to have a bow, arrows and a sword. The city ordinance directed that the merchants were to present themselves twice a year before the wardens of the merchants' Trinity guild in Dublin. The members of other craft guilds were to present themselves before the masters of their craft (figure 17).[57]

17 An armed apprentice, a drawing taken from the Dublin assembly rolls, autumn 1454. Merchant and craft apprentices about to receive the freedom of Dublin were required to carry arms and were inspected twice a year. (Image courtesy of Dublin City Library and Archive, taken from Dublin City Assembly Roll, 1454.)

In the late 1460s, the Dublin assembly reiterated apprenticeship regulations and the procedure for the correct registration of apprentices. Initially, in 1469, the assembly reminded craftsmen that they should 'take not apprentice but that he be of good English birth', a directive aimed possibly at foreigners but also against young Irish who wished to better themselves. The penalties were severe for enfranchised master craftsmen who would lose their status as a freeman of the city if they did not obey the directive. An unfree man who infringed the ordinance would be fined 40s.[58] The municipal authorities seem to have discovered examples of the exploitation of apprentices in the late 1460s, the instances being more than isolated cases. Late in January 1470, the assembly addressed the craft masters of Dublin who took apprentices for a term of years. The masters were reminded to present their apprentice in court 'within the first year of the term'. There the name of the apprentice was to be recorded with the city recorder and his indenture was to be enrolled. A fee of 4d. was to be paid. If an apprentice was not presented and his name not entered in this way he would not be accepted into the franchise of Dublin in the future after 'he had served truly his term'.[59]

In Dublin, in the 1490s, and probably earlier, it would appear that apprentices and servants got involved in all sorts of misbehaviour in certain houses – eating, drinking, playing cards, throwing dice and other 'unthrifty play'.[60] There was a strong moral tone to agreements signed between masters and apprentices, the indenture signed by the shipbuilder apprentice John White, seen above, covering a range of topics – the maintenance of business confidentiality, protection of property, obeying superiors, absenteeism, gambling, drinking and sexual morality.[61] Apprentices involved in mis-behaviour would have been in the later years of their apprenticeship when they would have had a modest income that might support occasional celebrations; in England, apprentices in their last year could earn wages ranging from 6s. 8d. to 25s. per annum.[62] In the indenture signed between Edmund Lobusby, the master shipbuilder, and his apprentice, the master agreed to pay John White 10s. in the fifth year of a five year term.[63] A city ordinance enunciated in July 1496 called upon men and women to neither suffer nor support the misbehaviour of apprentices in their houses on pain of a fine of 40s. on every occasion that apprentices were found on their premises. The guilty apprentices were put in custody until their masters were satisfied as to the state of their own property and that the fine was paid. Fines in Dublin at this time were usually divided between the courts and the revenue, but on this occasion the fine went to the mayor and bailiffs on the one hand and to the finder of the miscreant on the other.[64]

Guild membership

In the period 1468–1512, at least fifty-three trades were practised in Dublin. It is important to remember that any total numbers for tradespersons for this period, as given below, need to be adjusted down to provide a realistic figure for any given generation in the period. Also, it is important to note that the nature and source of the figures used here and below represent the number of tradespersons in Dublin who became franchise holders at that time and do not derive directly from guild records. There were 241 enfranchised merchants in Dublin in the period, far more than any other trade or craft. Yeomen came next, numbering 127. They are an interesting group who were middle-sized landholders or owners but who were also franchise holders in Dublin city. Their critical part in supplying grain to Dublin is discussed below.

Some trades were represented in the franchise list by only one person – apothecary, furrier, glazier, painter, seamstress and surgeon, but other trades ranged in number from 10 to 40, for example:

Table 4.2 Sample numbers of tradespersons in the Dublin franchise roll, 1468–1512[65]

Butcher	40	Cook	22	Weaver	17	Tanner	11
Smith	36	Corviser	20	Shearman	16	Fisher	11
Clerk	35	Glover	18	Goldsmith	13	Labourer	11
Tailor	29						

In Dublin, master craftsmen trained apprentices in their craft or trade. William Grampe (senior), merchant, took on six apprentices; when they finished their apprenticeship in the years mentioned they became franchise holders in Dublin – Thomas More (1473), Laurence Ellice (1474), Thomas Walsh (1477), Edward FitzThomas (1479), James Rice (1483), and James Stanton (1486).[66] William Grampe, junior, became a citizen through being a son of William Grampe, senior.[67]

With few opportunities for work, it is to be expected that masters offered an apprenticeship to members of their own family. Maurice Sogyn, smith, took on three apprentices who finished their training in 1468, 1469 and 1484. One of his apprentices was David Sogyn, most probably his son. Thomas Cruys, weaver, apprenticed Nicholas Cruys; Nicholas, probably his son, completed his apprenticeship and became a franchise holder in Dublin in 1483. Other examples of likely family members apprenticed to their father are – Millane Harroll, apprentice of Nicholas Harrold, butcher, with Millane completing her apprenticeship in 1478 and becoming a franchise holder; Anastasia Flemyng, apprentice of John Flemyng, smith, completing her apprenticeship in 1480.[68]

The founding charters of several Dublin craft guilds state that the membership would be composed of 'men and women', as seen, for example, in the founding charters of the guild of tailors (1419) and the guild of shoemakers (1426).[69] However, in craft guild records, references to named women are remarkably few. In the founding charter of the guild of shoemakers, rather uniquely, Juliana Lowyn was named, and Margaret Herforde, a sister in the guild of carpenters, is noted as paying 12*d.* to the master of the guild in 1536.[70] Fortunately, the Dublin city franchise roll, 1468–1512 names 71 women who completed an apprenticeship leading to the granting of citizenship in the period. If 'unspecified trades' are discounted, the number of women who became citizens on completion of an apprenticeship in a known craft was 46, the total number of admissions to citizenship (both sexes) following completion of apprenticeship being 760.[71] Of those 46 citizens, 27 served their time with a merchant, and may subsequently have worked in the retail trade. The list of crafts in which women completed an apprenticeship, other than that of merchant, included armourer, butcher, clerk, cook, corviser, glover, justice, painter, smith, tanner and vintner. In all cases above, women were apprenticed to men.[72] However, the Dublin franchise roll records that five women apprentices served their time with women – Rose Fouler, Agnes Wodbone, Rose Downe, Anne Barbi and Joan White, whose trades, regretfully, are not recorded. Each year, the guild membership elected a master and wardens 'for the rule, government and superintendence' of the guild. There are no extant records of women holding these offices.[73]

Table 4.3 Select list of women who served an apprenticeship in Dublin, 1468–1512

Isabel Nangle, apprentice of Thomas Palmer, vintner, 1468
Margery Dennyse, apprentice of John Fouler, merchant, 1470
Joan Laules, apprentice of John Hacket, butcher, 1471
Margaret Dennyse, apprentice of Agnes Wodbone, free woman, 1478
Margaret Lawless, apprentice of William Yonge, cook, 1481
Rose Bron, apprentice of Philip Bermyngham, justice, 1484
Joan Brennan, apprentice of William Kynnedy, glover, 1490
Alice Haghane, apprentice of Walter Armister, corviser, 1493
Alice Cromp, apprentice of Thomas Neuman, merchant, 1496
Genet Blakeny, apprentice of Nicholas Dallagh, merchant, 1501[74]

Wages

In the fifteenth century in Ireland, wages for qualified master craftsmen were tightly controlled by two fourteenth-century statutes passed in England and ratified and proclaimed in Ireland – the statutes concerning servants and labourers (23 Edward III (1349))[75] and the statutes of artificers, labourers, servants and victuallers (12 Richard II (1388)).[76] The first statute attempted, in the time of the Black Death, to control the demand for excessive wages in a labour market depleted by the plague. The statute required that the level of wages should be that which had been offered to tradesmen in 'ordinary years' running up to the year 1346–7. Anyone refusing to accept such wages was to be imprisoned until they obeyed the law. The statute required that tradesmen and workmen were not to take wages higher than what was accustomed to be paid prior to 1346–7, the statute applying to saddlers, skinners, curriers, cordwainers, tailors, smiths, carpenters, masons, tilers, boatmen, carters and all other craftsmen.[77]

The second statute, 12 Richard II (1388), fixed wages for artificers, labourers and servants, stating that these had not been settled for certain earlier. The statute set yearly wages for those with skills needed for working with animals and on farms – ploughmakers (12s.), carters and ploughmen (6s.), shepherds, swineherds, dairy-maids and horse-boys (4s.), and female labourers, able to make bread, ale and malt (6s.). Daily rates were also set – a mower of meadows for the day, 2d., and for the reaper of corn in August for the day, 1d.[78] Daily rates of pay for masons, carpenters and roofers were set as follows: master mason of free stone, master carpenter of free work, capable of being masters of their craft, for the whole day, 2d.; master roofers of slate, master plasterers of walls, for the day, 2d.; coverers of stone, builders of walls, and other labourers, capable of serving the artificers aforesaid, for the day, 1d.[79]

What standard of living might a tradesmen have had at the end of the fifteenth century in Dublin? Perhaps a glance inside the home of Richard Wydon, carpenter, married to Jonet Halgane, may suggest what degree of comfort he and his family enjoyed. They had children some of whom may still have been living at home. Wydon was from the parish of St Werburgh in Dublin and had done some carpentry work for the parish in 1496–7. He died in November 1501. He had a horse valued at 20s. which suggests that it was a superior animal and that he must have travelled widely in Dublin city and county to seek work. The tools of his trade were valued at 20s. It is not known how many people were living in his home but the bedding, described below, suggests that there were perhaps three or four persons. He had a table with three board cloths along with 6 dishes, 5 plates, 2 saucers and 7 candlesticks.

His possessions included a banker or long cushion and 6 cushions. Wydon also owned 2 porcelain cups and 3 silver spoons and had a cupboard in the hall. Practical kitchenware was listed among his goods – a basin and ewer (large jug), a posnet (three legged pot), two small pots and a fire dish. Among his household goods there would have been some well-used tableware not rated or listed by a valuer. In bedding there were three beds – 'a hanging bed with curtains, … a featherbed, another of flokkys with two woolen coverlets'. Additionally the inventory of Wydon's goods included 3 blankets and 3 sheets. There was 8*s.* of silver among his goods. Not a luxurious household, but a home in which there was a hard-won income, a fireplace for heating and cooking, with tablecloths for special occasions, and in which Wydon and his family recreated in some comfort and slept well at night.[80]

* * *

All guilds were inward-looking by nature, concerned with their own affairs, their meetings, the minutiae of their rules and regulations, and their religious and quasi-religious rituals. They also attempted to look beyond themselves to members down on their luck and the widows of deceased members. The seven-year apprenticeship was not only about the acquisition of craft skills but involved a moral education that prepared apprentices for citizenship and for adult life. The training and education was open to women and led to women qualifying in their chosen craft and becoming citizens in their own right. The impact of the guild merchant's four critical decisions taken in the period 1450 to 1452 is most noteworthy as it effectively meant that the guild merchant in Dublin and the municipal assembly of the city became virtually one and the same. These early chapters have been concerned with the building blocks of the city – law, administration, the acquisition of wealth and skills, commerce. The following chapters could be said to be linked to the pleasures of the world and to each other – feeding the body, nurturing the spirit and entertaining the mind.

CHAPTER 5

Provisioning Dublin

IN THE 1470s, in Balrothery in north Co. Dublin, Nicholas Delaber and his wife Margaret Dalton had a holding of about 60 acres, 20 acres of which was left fallow each year. Nicholas had servants and would have had help with the ploughing and farm work. Farming had been good to the Delabers, the value of their household goods being well above average (26s. 8d.).[1] Nicholas was not fixated only on the material, being a member of the guild of the Virgin Mary in St Peter's church in Balrothery, along with neighbours Richard Goldynge, Robert Lanysdall, Michael Trevers and Richard Whitakyr.[2] Delaber made bequests to four churches in the area of Bective, Navan and Trim in Meath, he and Margaret possibly hailing from that area. In his final testament, Delaber bequeathed four nobles (26s. 8d.) to a choir boy, Robert Plunket, who presumably sang in St Peter's and probably sang at the guild of the Virgin Mary liturgies. Like their farming neighbours, Nicholas and Margaret tilled the land for cereal growing and kept animals, with one exception – Delaber had eight acres of peas and beans in the ground, which may point to the fact that he was using a new intensive method of fattening pigs.[3] In England, in the first half of the 1300s, the traditional extensive method of rearing pigs by allowing them to forage in forests was in decline and a new intensive way of fattening was developed which involved sty-feeding animals on legumes, poor quality grains, the by-products of dairying and brewing, and household waste.[4]

This change probably would have come later in Ireland. It is clear that Delaber had all the necessary prerequisites on his farm for the new feeding system – dairy waste, brewing waste, legumes and household waste, to be fed to pigs in stalls. Hired female labourers, who were expected to make bread, ale and malt on a farm, would probably be drawn in to feeding the pigs – in this case Delaber's maid servant, Margaret.[5] Delaber, and perhaps neighbouring farmers, had the necessary combination of resources and initiative to try new approaches to animal production.

* * *

Could the farms of Co. Dublin provide enough food to feed medieval Dublin? The answer seems to be a very strong affirmative. Medieval Co. Dublin in *c.*1300 has been shown from documentary sources to be a grain provisioning zone, with cereals dominating the north county and pasture in south county Dublin supporting animals required for meat and milk.[6] However, a survey of about sixty farms taken from inventories made in rural Dublin in the 1470s reflects a landscape of holdings of mixed farming stretching from Balrothery in the north to Clondalkin in the south-west, with the owners of most farms growing barley, oats and wheat, and rearing cows, horses, pigs and sheep.[7] Some work has been done on the resource consumption of medieval Dublin *c.*1100, using the commodity of grain. Grain is often selected for such studies because it contributed to 70 per cent of the calorific intake in diets of the thirteenth and early fourteenth centuries: it is in bread, brewed in ale, and found in potages and soups. Research has been done on the feeding of medieval London *c.*1300, using a grain allowance believed to be equivalent to 1¼ lbs of coarse bread and a pint of weak ale per person per day. It has been calculated that if the population of Dublin was 10,000 persons, with allowances made for the disposal of cereals in rural markets and for fallow acreage, then 60,000 acres would be required to supply Dublin's grain needs. Pro rata, a population of 20,000 would require 120,000 acres. If only half of the grand total of 400,000 acres available in medieval Co. Dublin within a 30km-radius of the city were put under arable cultivation Dublin's grain requirements would have been adequately met.[8]

Much of this chapter is concerned with the regulation of the sale of the principal foods available in Dublin – ale, cereals, fish and meat – and with the use of workplace and sales locations, the restriction of trading hours by bye-law, the regulation of retail and wholesale practices, the strict application of the guild system at the shop counter, and maintaining standards of hygiene. While

Table 5.1 Statutory maximum prices, 1470

Peck of wheat, 16 pence; peck of oats, 4 pence; peck of barley, 8 pence; peck of wheatmalt, 20 pence; peck of oatmalt, 6 pence; peck of malt of bere, 10 pence.
Peck of beans, 7 pence; peck of peas, 7 pence; peck of rye, 8 pence; barrel of herrings, 6*s.* 8*d.*; mease of red herrings, 4*s.*
A beef, 10*s.*; a cow of the best, 6*s.* 8*d.*; a sheep, 8*d.*; a hog of the best, 3*s.* 4*d.*; a goose, 3 pence; a young pig, 3 pence; a couple of capons, 5 pence; peck of salt, 8 pence.
A gallon of the best ale, 1½*d.*; a gallon of wine of Rochelle, 6 pence; a gallon of wine of Gascony, 8 pence; a gallon of wine of Spain, 10 pence.
A yard of coarse cloth, 2 shillings; a yard of frieze of the best, having the breadth of a yard, 6 pence; a fresh hide, 10 pence; a tanned hide, 20 pence
A peck of coals, 6 pence; a stone of wool, 18 pence; a stone of tallow, 6 pence; a pair of shoes of the best, 4 pence; a pair of shoes for women, 2 pence.[9]

prices of commodities are provided occasionally, it is nevertheless useful to have a wider systematic perspective on the prices of the above commodities relative to each other and to other goods. With the depreciation of coinage from time to time, the Irish parliament found it necessary to fix maximum prices for a range of foods, beverages and other goods, and we are fortunate that such lists, dated 1470 and 1471–2, are extant. The prices in the list above are statutory maximum prices set in 1470, with one exception mentioned in the notes. Merchants were free to sell below the maximum price.[10]

The table below shows government-regulated maximum prices and it is possible that a guide to more realistic prices might be arrived at by considering the valuations of some commodities valued in testamentary inventories made up in the 1470s in Dublin county.[11] Valuations drawn from the inventories of the 1470s show that prices in Dublin city and county were considerably lower than the published statutory maximum prices.

Table 5.2 Inventory valuations and regulated prices in the 1470s[12]

Commodity	Inventory valuations in the 1470s	Government regulated maximum prices, 1470
Cow	5s.	6s. 8d.
Hog	1s.	3s. 4d.
Sheep	4d. to 6d.	8d.

Tillage farmers and pastoralists were at the mercy of the unpredictable weather – they sought moderation in temperatures, sunlight, rainfall and wind, and the avoidance of storms, heavy and persistent rain, frost, drought, humidity, and crop and animal diseases. As expected in any given period, nature could be and was unruly. In Ireland, there were crop failures, for example in 1439 and 1491. In these two years wet weather was the cause of crop failure, with a wet autumn occurring in 1491. The Annals of the Four Masters recorded for 1439 'a plague virulently in Dublin' with '3,000 persons, male and female, large and small' dying from it from the beginning of spring to the end of May. Whatever about the accuracy of the figure, it seems reasonable to accept that many people, above the average, died of plague in Dublin in that year. There were also crop failures in 1434, 1461 and 1497, most probably due to wet weather. Two other crops suffered from summer drought in 1445 and 1462, with an outbreak of murrain, almost certainly anthrax, in 1445. In January 1478, a great wind struck the country, with people, cattle and trees laid low. As many as 180 glazed windows were broken in Dublin. There were outbreaks of plague in Ireland in the years 1446, 1447 and 1448, with other occurrences in 1466, 1478 and in 1489.[13]

In medieval times, two principles guided municipal authorities in their attitude to trading – that there should be a reasonable profit and that the system should be fair to all. There was a feeling against the middleman – that buying from the producer and selling on for profit, without alteration to the goods, was somehow unfair. Therefore, towns' authorities passed by-laws, as was done in Dublin, to prevent three related commercial strategies happening – 'forestalling', the tactic of intercepting goods before they reach the town market; 'engrossing', the buying up of large quantities of a commodity to sell on when the price is good, a group of such merchants in London being known as 'Grossers'; 'regrating', buying wholesale to sell retail. Many of the situations and problems occurring in Dublin to do with the grain and meat trade, and described below, are connected with these strategies.[14]

Grain

The Dublin assembly regularly monitored the price of wheat and malt and took steps to ensure that supplies would be continuously available. It tried to ensure that stockpiling did not occur and from 1455 to 1471 the assembly passed ordinances calling on the haggard men in the city and its franchises to release supplies surplus to their requirements. In October 1455, the city assembly ordered that 'no manner of man nor woman that have haggards of their own within the city, and no man of the country, should buy no corn within the market of the said city upon pain of forfeiting of his corn, and his body to prison, till they make a fine.'[15] Officials were chosen to search and examine in the city the haggards of those disobeying city ordinances. Those chosen to do this work included the merchants Arland Ussher, William Grampe and Nicholas Bourke, and a yeoman Harry White.[16] The Dublin assembly was faced with the problem of how to monitor the men from rural areas, coming in from Co. Dublin to buy or sell grain, men who had their haggards in say, Castleknock, Garristown, Glasnevin or Malahide. The city authorities could identify one relevant enfranchised group, the yeomen, who rented or owned land holdings of middle size, and who would have grown wheat, oats and barley, and held stocks of grain on their farms in Co. Dublin and in their city haggards.[17] In the period 1468–1512, there were 127 yeomen admitted to the franchise of Dublin city. Assembly members would hope to influence such men, citizens or not, to be loyal to Dublin and the well-being of its citizens.[18]

Five years later, in January 1461, the Dublin assembly decreed that anyone who had a haggard in the city, containing grain, should 'buy no corn in the market' and if purchased it was to be forfeited. A few months later, in a time

18 (a) A late medieval Dublin city granary located about 250 metres north of the Liffey, off Church Street, between the church of St Michan and May Lane. The drawing of the granary, viewed from the north-east, is an impression based on the archaeological work of Dr Giles Dawkes reported in *Medieval Dublin X* (© Drawing by Kevin O'Brien); (b) A conjectural cutaway view of the Church Street granary showing construction in progress, viewed from the south-east. (© Drawing by Kevin O'Brien.)

of shortage, it was stated by the assembly that if grain was stored in haggards in Dublin beyond the requirements of the owners it would be lawful 'to take wheat and malt so *ladyt* and bring it into the market and to sell the wheat 4*d*. under the common price in every peck, and the malt 3*d*. in every peck, and the owner to have the money'.[19]

In October 1461, as winter was beginning, the assembly enunciated that any man in the franchises of Dublin who had haggards or corn of their own were not to buy corn in the city market or other corn coming to the city market. The fine for lawbreakers was heavy – 40*s*. as often as a person was convicted. The shortage of wheat was so critical that the authorities added another ordinance, not confined to the haggard men of the city, but including everyone living in Dublin, 'that no man nor woman of the said city, free or unfree, buy no wheat within the said city to sell to no Irishmen'.[20] This ordinance was not directed against Irish persons in the city but rather at those who would sell wheat to the Wicklow Irish and other Irish who were enemies of Dublin. There were anti-Irish ordinances passed in the Dublin assembly in the period 1450–1500, discussed earlier, but in relation to wheat supplies being conserved for Dublin's population in the autumn and winter of 1461, the intent of the authorities seems to have been socio-economic rather than political, and directed at keeping all available grain in the city.

In January 1462, in the middle of winter, when grain and bread were obviously in short supply, and prices high, the city assembly ordained that named officers should search within the franchises of the city for hidden surpluses of grain. Twelve men drawn from the municipal assembly, to be overseen by the mayor and bailiffs, were to do this work. All were men of substance, citizens of Dublin, many from old established merchant families: Sir Thomas Newbery, John Bennet, William Purcell, John Higham, John Bowlond, John Higeley, Walter Sale, merchant, Richard Chalam, merchant, Richard FitzJohn, glover, Richard Geysyng, tailor, Thomas Walsh, corviser and Richard Burton, point-maker. Their task was to search within the franchises of the city and when they found surpluses of corn in storage they were to take possession of them, except what was required by the owners and their household. The surpluses were to be brought to the market and there sold below the market price, the owners receiving the income.[21]

Throughout the 1460s, grain and bread supplies, and their prices, do not seem to have been a major problem in Dublin, but at the end of the sixties a crisis greater than those that occurred earlier began to develop. In October 1469, grain and bread must have been in short supply and it was agreed in the city assembly that the mayor and bailiffs should search for supplies of wheat in the city haggards, the officers to be aided by five jurés – William Grampe,

Thomas Barby, Nicholas Bourke, Master John Boulond and John Walshe, assisted by men from the craft guilds. While some householders in the city must have had no grain others with haggards had some supplies. It was agreed that those who had supplies of grain could keep 'reasonable stuff assigned to their sustenation for the year' while the surplus should be divided in two. One half was to go to the city market to be sold at 2*d*. cheaper in every peck than the best on the market, the other half was to be delivered directly to the bakers at the same price, without the bakers coming to market. Whatever grain was confiscated was ordered to be threshed. This was a serious crisis with the shortage of bread reaching emergency levels.[22]

The Dublin assembly dealt decisively with the problem and with those who failed to help find a solution. Any haggard men who were free men of the city and did not cooperate would lose their franchise and pay a fine of £10; if they did not pay they were placed in custody until they did. Persons who were not free men of Dublin and had partially paid the £10 fine were also placed in custody until the remainder was paid. The crisis continued into January 1470 when haggard men were brought to court and examined under oath to establish what surplus corn they had. If found with a surplus, they were to bring it to market, with a fine of 20*s*. imposed on those who were not compliant.[23]

As the winter of 1470–1 began in October, the assembly drew attention to the problem of regrators, or those who bought wholesale in order to sell retail. The problem must have been sufficiently widespread and critical in October 1470, with the onset of winter, to force the Dublin assembly to speak out as it did. Significantly, the new ordinances attempted to reach out beyond the city into the rural areas of Co. Dublin, if not further afield, and forbid all those that had haggards in the city or outside the city to go to markets or to other places to buy wheat wholesale, either themselves or through their servants, upon the pain of a 40*s*. fine.[24] The ordinance called upon those that had haggards in the country, presumably in Co. Dublin in particular, to bring to the market a proportion of the grain that they were bringing to their city haggards. The ordinance made clear that under a recently made city law the fine for those who did not cooperate and were found guilty was £10. The ordinance also called upon those who had well-stocked haggards in city and rural locations to 'buy no wheat within the market of the said city by themselves nor by no others'. It seems that women were used to circumvent the ordinance; breaking the law merited a fine, but in the case of women or women servants buying wheat in the market contrary to the spirit of the ordinance, the penalty was imprisonment.[25]

The city bailiffs, in October 1471, became aware of the selling of grain outside the Dublin market. The assembly enunciated that haggard owners were prohibited from purchasing grain except in the market places in the city. This was an attempt by the authorities to prevent the activities of forestallers – those who would intercept goods on their way to the Dublin market – so that, buying at rural or outside-the-city prices, they would make a profit selling at city prices. The practice was illegal, and the penalties imposed in Dublin at this time were severe and brought ignominy to the guilty: they were to be fined 100s. and were placed in the pillory to become the butt of passers-by, close to the busy area around Bothe Street.[26]

In 1471–2, the Irish parliament became aware of another aspect of grain supply, grain being exported abroad when there was a shortage in the country. It seems that wheat, rye, meslin and other grains were being exported to England, Scotland and Wales, causing 'great scarcity and famine … among the king's liege people'. People were quitting Dublin. It was decided that anyone who loaded grain to be taken out of the country or anyone involved in the shipping of grain would suffer severe penalties – the grain would be forfeited if found on board ship or being carried to the coast for export. The ship itself would be forfeited to the king and the buyer of the grain was fined 40s. The legislation was effective for one year.[27]

Brewsters and tapsters: monitoring the ale trade

Around 1450, and earlier, ale was brewed in Dublin city, with the city assembly enunciating ordinances to maintain standards. In medieval times in England, and most probably in Dublin, the brewing process and its retail trade were initially dominated by women. Brewing was originally a domestic-centred process, local and small scale. Women were certainly brewing in Dublin in c.1300 and probably earlier. Three early brewing regulations in the Dublin Chain Book were aimed at women-brewers, the ordinances insisting on the highest standards in brewing, and in one instance threatening suspension from her occupation for a year and a day. In Dublin, women brewers were required to pay an annual fee of 2s. a year and a fine of 15d. was imposed if ale was found to be inferior.[28] Brewing gave women status. While women did other work of value – selling eggs, spinning wool, weaving cloth – these occupations did not attract the same level of regulation as brewing. Brewing gave women public recognition, dealing with official ale tasters and other supervising officers who would discuss, assess and review their work as brewers.[29]

The Dublin guild merchant roll, c.1190 to 1265, lists only 2 brewers and 13 taverners in the city, all male. Compared with 57 bakers and 36 butchers contemporaneously in Dublin the brewers and taverners figures look low, suggesting perhaps that not all commercial brewers had been recorded.[30] It is true that most households had the skill to brew at home, but nevertheless the figures suggest that some commercial brewing in Dublin may have been carried on silently by women. Often, the woman brewer's husband was named in court cases as the brewer for legal reasons. In England, there were a number of instances of court cases occurring in which a man was named as a proxy for the woman brewer; one Dublin case is cited below.[31]

In a court case in Dublin in 1308, the abbey of St Thomas the Martyr took an action against twenty-five brewers and taverners who did not give a certain proportion of the ale and mead they had manufactured to the abbey. The grant or custom in question was known as tollboll and amounted to a gallon and a half from every brew. Five women were named – Mabilla Arnalde, Juliana Honicode, Blissina Lotrix and Joan Tyrrell, with Elena Donne being represented by William Donne, probably her husband. The court ordered that in addition to a number of men taverners the said custom should also be taken in future in the taverns of Elena Dunne, Juliana Honicode, Blissina Lotrix and Joan Tyrell. Jurors assessed the abbot's damages, in the case of the women taverners, as follows: Mabilla Arnalde, two marks; Elena Donne, 12d.; and Joan Tyrell, 20s.[32]

The term 'brewster' was applied to female brewers in England, and was used and well-known in Dublin in the second half of the fifteenth century. Equally, the term 'tapster' was applied to women ale-sellers and known in Dublin at the same time. In Dublin, in the early decades of the fourteenth century, municipal ordinances referred to females in the brewing trade as 'woman-brewers', but by the fifteenth century, as will be seen, the term 'brewster' was consistently used in Dublin.[33]

Legislation passed in 1450 in the Irish parliament to do with standardizing liquid measures did not reflect the dominance of women in the liquor trade. While the parliamentary legislation directed that 'no man sell wine, beer or any other liquor in any city or town enfranchised, except it be measures of the king sealed',[34] an ordinance passed by the Dublin assembly in September 1455, prompted by the parliamentary legislation, more accurately reflected the real situation – 'that all manner of women that sell ale within the franchises of Dublin sell after the king's ale measure, that is to say, by the chapping measure, the pint, the quart, pottle, and gallon of the same measure'.[35]

In 1470, the Dublin assembly controlled the price of ale, and directed that the brewsters of Dublin sell a dozen of their best ale for 2d.[36] The tapsters' prices were also set at the same price per dozen, and these prices were to apply 'within house or without house', meaning presumably in taverns owned or managed by women, and outdoors at fairs and markets. Tapsters probably had regular patrons, and Marion Tapister, who in October 1474 was owed 9d. by

Dame Margaret Nugent, probably delivered ale to Lady Margaret from time to time.[37]

By 1481, it would appear that the structure of the personnel in the brewing trade in Dublin was changing or being changed by regulation. In that year, brewers (along with brewsters) were addressed in a municipal ordinance, signifying perhaps that men were already in the trade and that possibly women's traditional position was declining. If this was the case then it mirrors what was happening in England. There is another reason why women began to leave the brewing trade in Dublin, particularly the retail or ale-selling aspect of the trade. The Dublin assembly ordinance (1481) was clearly and consistently anti-tapster in its tone and directives. The ordinance points out that tapsters should not be sold ale by brewers, because, it was stated, they were slow to pay the brewers and brewsters. The ordinance advised that ale-sellers should be such persons as were able to pay and the ordinance went further stating that tapsters should not be allowed 'to sell their ale within house', in a tavern. This may have been an attempt to cull small home-based taverns run by tapsters. The phrasing of the statement that ale-sellers should be of good conversation and English born is taken directly from a standard master-apprentice indenture used in Dublin, seen earlier, and its intent is fairly clear – that a significant proportion of the tapsters in Dublin may have been from the lower levels of society and possibly from the Irish nation, and that they should not be working in taverns in Dublin.[38]

Marion Tapister, mentioned above, whose surname described a skill or office, was probably of the Irish nation. Her first name, Marion, may have been used as an equivalent for the Irish name *Muireann*. Parliamentary legislation passed in 1465, discussed above, called upon those of the Irish nation who wished to live in the Pale, to take on surnames that described an art or an office. Tapister/Tapster was such a name.[39] At this time in England, women in the brewing trade, sometimes called alewives, had every epithet thrown at them – that they were deceptive, disorderly, sexually uncontrolled and that they were temptresses.[40] The Dublin tapsters were not accused of being any of these, but it was clearly stated by the city authorities that the tapsters were not prompt payers and that therefore they were unreliable. The implication that the tapsters may have been of the Irish nation, and therefore unacceptable in Dublin society, is in keeping with the stated anti-Irish policy of the Dublin assembly, discussed earlier.

A fraudulent alewife who appears in a Chester mystery play, 'The harrowing of hell', recalls her misdeeds and points out how she now regrets her actions. The mystery plays, discussed later, appeared in England in the late fourteenth century and were first seen in Chester in 1422.

Some time I was a taverner
A gentle gossip and a tapster
Of wine and ale a trusty brewer
Which woe hath me wrought.
Of cans I kept no true measure,
My cups I sold at my pleasure,
Deceiving many a creature,
Though my ale were naught.
And when I was a brewer long,
With hopes I made my ale strong
Ashes and herbs I blend among
And marred so good malt
Therefore I may my hands wring,
Shake my cans, and cups ring.
Sorrowful may I sigh and sing
That ever I so dealed ...[41]

Jacoba Payn, having probably worked in the 1450s and 1460s during her first marriage, and on into the mid-seventies, may have been one of Dublin's most experienced brewsters. Her second marriage was to John King and they were from the parish of St Nicholas without the walls, Dublin. Her first marriage was to Thomas Paryse. With John King, Jacoba was also, it would seem, managing an inn – they had seven quarters of beef in the larder, six candlesticks and a stock of sheets, blankets, towels and napkins, valued at 9s. 8d. They had about twenty hogs, which would have been fattened on domestic waste, possibly in a yard at the back of their city premises. Many of their possessions included basins, bowls, pitchers and pots. Among their goods was an oven, a brew pan, three pint pots (a brewing regulation measure), leather bottles, and wooden brewing vats worth 4s. Most interesting is the mention of two brand irons in their goods, which could be branding irons to mark a trade name on a cask.[42] In London, in 1453, beer brewers were required 'to make their vessels according to the assize and to have them stamped with their own iron marks'.[43] It is not beyond the realms of possibility that Jacoba Payn brewed a fine ale, but that her husband stamped and sold it as 'King's Ale'. A hard-working woman who at the end wanted to be buried close to her first husband in the grounds of St Patrick's cathedral.[44]

At the end of the fourteenth century a yearly rate of pay was set for female labourers on farms who were able to make bread, ale and malt.[45] On farms that did not have female servants, this work would have been done by the farmer's wife. In the 1470s, across Co. Dublin, it would appear that malt, the raw material of brewing – kiln-dried sprouted grain – was produced on many farms and the brewing of ale would also have taken place on farms. Cecily Langan, a married woman, living in the Grace Dieu area of north Co. Dublin, bequeathed measures of malt in 1473. She most probably prepared the malt and brewed ale on the family farm. The Ketyng-Owyn farm at Clondalkin had wheat and malt in the haggard valued at 20s. in 1474; Alson Owyn probably prepared malt and brewed ale there. In the 1470s, on the Fox-Laweles farm at Glasnevin, Agnes Laweles brewed ale. Agnes had two daughters, Rose and Joan, but chose to bequeath Rose her 'mash tub', which contained malt when used in the brewing process. Rose may have learned the brewing process from her mother and shown an interest in it. She became Rose Sawage, was married with children, and brewing would have supplemented her income.[46]

In Co. Dublin at this time, malt and ale could be purchased. In 1472, Philip Sherreff and Thomas Fennore, for example, owed 10s. for malt purchased at the Porter-Tirrell family farm in the Castleknock area. On face value, Richard Porter and Rose Tirrell were managing a very successful farm but perhaps they should be described as farmer-merchants. Much clearer is the situation in Lusk in 1474 in which Thomas Whyte owed 7½d. to Nicholas Wyght for ale. Wyght and his wife Joan Taillor were involved in farming and fishing but were also local general merchants. Again, in Malahide (1474), Thomas Tynbegh was indebted to a local merchant, John Mold, for twenty measures of malt. Mold is described above as a well-to-do merchant who lived in Malahide.[47]

Testators ensured in their final will that, on the day of their funeral, mourners would be catered for, with expenses being deducted from the estate of the deceased. Alice Bennet of Santry (1471) left bread (5s.) and ale (6s. 8d.) for the mourners at her funeral. In the same year, John Kempe of Hollywood, north Co. Dublin, left 9s. worth of bread and ale for mourners. It is likely that Kempe's maidservant, Jonet, brewed the ale. In 1474, Nicholas Barret of the parish of St Michan left spices and wine (40d.) and bread and ale (40d.) for his funeral day, the ale having probably been brewed by his wife, Isabella Proutfote. Similarly, in that year, Patrick Kenane of Kinsaley, Co. Dublin, provided his mourners with bread and ale (20s.) and meat (12s.), his wife, Joan Pasmor, having most likely brewed the ale. Ellen Kymore of the parish of St Michan, married to John Bulbeke, died in 1477. Her will provided for the supply of bread and ale (15s.) and fish (8s. 6d.) on her funeral day. It is probable that women servants in the Bulbeke-Kymore household, of whom there were a number, would have brewed ale under the direction of Ellen Kymore which would have been used on the day of her funeral.[48] Neighbours, of course, could assist with extra supplies of ale on such occasions – in 1476, John Palmer of Kilsallaghan, Co. Dublin, had a brewing pan as had Nicholas Delaber of Balrothery, north Co. Dublin. Delaber's wife, Margaret Dalton, and their maidservant, Margaret, would probably have done the brewing.[49]

Butchers and the meat trade

The Dublin assembly was concerned with standards and passed ordinances to prevent unqualified persons working in the meat trade. While there may have been a number of reasons for this, including the protection of the apprenticeship system, the most likely purpose would have been to secure the central principle of medieval trade – that the owner of the product retails it to the customer. In trades practised in public it would be obvious to bailiffs that persons other than the master and his indentured apprentice were involved in selling, and a wife or child would be easily observed assisting in a butcher's shop. It was natural that a family member would assist a butcher with sales at a public counter, but the practice was against the law. Twice in the decade commencing 1450, the assembly drew attention to the practice of butchers' wives selling meat. In 1451, meat was only to be sold in the flesh market by butchers; and butchers' wives or other women were prohibited from doing so. In mid-decade the same directive was repeated – that 'no butcher's wife sell flesh'. At the close of the decade, in 1460, the assembly pointed out that boys were not to sell meat at any time of the day – 'that no butcher's boy shall not sell no flesh before or after noon'. Legally, only the owner of the flesh should sell meat and a heavy fine of 6s. 8d. was imposed in the event of an infringement.[50]

A decade later, around Easter 1470, the assembly concerned itself with setting the price for kid, lamb and veal – best quality kid was to sell at 1¼d. a quarter, with seconds at 1d. a quarter. Lamb was to be sold at similar prices. Veal was a luxury with best quality selling at 5d. a quarter and seconds at 4d. A transaction was completed by the buyer putting their silver on the counter, 'upon the flesh board'. The buyer expected to get the cut of meat they had chosen but if this did not happen they could complain to the mayor. If found in the wrong, the butcher faced a heavy fine of 6s. 8d.[51]

It seems that in October of the same year, meat was being sold at locations other than at the shambles of the city at prices below the market price. Certainly, the authorities would have had no control of the prices applying at these illicit locations which would have been undercutting official agreed prices at the shambles. A city ordinance stated that 'the butchers of the said city shall sell no flesh but only in the shambles' at the agreed official price and times. An old bye-law called upon butchers to sell meat to 'none of the country before nine o'clock', that is, not to sell outside the city walls before the markets opened. Meat was not to be sold on a Saturday on pain of imprisonment. Penalties were draconian – a 20s. fine for the first offence, and for the second, loss of citizenship and the butcher was not to practise his craft for one year. The mayor and bailiffs met the butchers and used their discretion to calculate what the retail price of meat should be, based on two factors – 'what every beast cost at the first buying' balanced against the butcher's 'reasonable labour and costs'. Officials recorded the purchase price of animals in a book.[52]

In the early 1480s, it would appear that meat was being sold either at or removed from the fleshambles in Dublin outside of normal trading hours. A well-established ordinance required that meat shall be sold only at the stalls, butchers forfeiting their meat and incurring a fine for any infringement. There were strict rules about when meat should be sold and it seems that either the city bailiffs observed or heard reports that the doors and windows of the shambles were open outside the agreed hours of business. The Dublin assembly put responsibility on the butchers and instructed them to have a keeper of the fleshhambles who would 'lock and stake the doors and windows' of the shambles at all times other than when the shambles was open for business at regulation hours. The masters and wardens of the butchers were warned that if the doors were found open other than at trading times they would be subject to a fine of 6s. 8d. for each infringement.[53]

Fishers and fishmongers

In Dublin in the fourteenth century, the selling of fish occurred at three locations – at stalls in the fishambles, on a boat and from a woman retailer in the street. All the available evidence points to a more-or-less similar situation in fifteenth-century Dublin.[54] The retail fish outlets in Dublin were therefore quite similar to those in England where the sale of fish was only allowed 'in towns, on board ship, or in the fish market'. In England, and in Dublin, the one exception allowed was street hawkers who, in England, were permitted to sell fish 'from street to street' principally to workmen who could not leave their workplace. Such hucksters in London were strictly 'not allowed to take up their stand at any point but must keep on the move'.[55] In Dublin, municipal regulations directed that every woman fish retailer should sell fish sitting in the street with a basket for which she paid a farthing each week to the city authorities.[56]

In the fourteenth century, the Dublin fish market had a variety of products for sale and relied on a number of modes of transport to bring them to market; it was probably much the same in the fifteenth century – fish brought in by the horseload, fish and herrings delivered on four-wheeled carts, men coming in with sackloads of fish, foreign merchants buying fish, fish being sold at stalls, boatloads of oysters brought to the market, herring available fresh or salted, and eels brought to market in loads on a man's back or by the horseload.[57] In our period, there were fishers in Dublin, citizens of the city, discussed below, who would have had the resources to go to sea and land catches from ships at the quayside in Dublin.

Fish supplies were very important in Dublin. When fresh meat was not available, and fish was regularly in demand on Church-designated fast days, it was important that fish supplies be available at regulated outlets. In England measures were regularly passed against engrossers and regraters who bought up fish before they reached the shore and resold them at a profit, thus breaking the great medieval principle that one should not make a profit without cause and that goods should not be sold unaltered for a higher price than the cost price.[58] Dublin assembly ordinances enunciated in 1451 and 1456 reflect this principle. The bye-laws prohibited fishermen's wives to sell fish, with one proviso – 'unless they have purchased it at the seaside'. Infringements drew on a scale of fines, with the third and subsequent offences incurring a fine of 20*s*. The repeated ordinance of 1456 was an attempt to protect the principle outlined above, which it seems was continually under threat. It was quite acceptable for a hawker to buy fish direct from a boat and resell it because the quantity of fish was small in scale. In the case of a few men catching salmon from a boat, one man had to be assigned to sell the salmon at the fishambles. Similarly, in 1460, bailiffs must have found enough examples of boys assisting at fish counters in Dublin to merit promulgation of a new ordinance. The fines were heavy for transgressors, the legislation directing that 'no [fisher's] boy shall not sell no fish after noon nor before noon, but they that own the [fish] shall sell it, upon the pain of vi*s* and viii*d* as oftentimes as they been found guilty thereof'.[59] All three ordinances could have been promulgated to protect a fisher's guild in the Dublin area, that is, that only qualified fishers or fishmongers should sell fish. Salzman, writing about England, states that fishers 'do not appear to have formed any trade guilds' and that the source of any regulations governing their trade is not always clear, coming either from municipal authorities or by self-regulation.[60]

In Dublin, there is some evidence, though tentative, that fishers may have been organized as a group like other trades and crafts in the city. Of eleven fishers who held the franchise in Dublin in the period 1468–1512, only one, Richard Forster in 1485, was granted the franchise because he had successfully completed the normal master-apprenticeship training. His apprenticeship, served with William Hunt, franchise holder and fisher, may point to the existence of a fishers' guild.[61] In 1498 in Dublin, the fishers took part as a named group in a pageant and procession along with other trade groups, though not necessarily as an organized trade or craft guild. This pageant or civic drama is described later.[62]

The Dublin assembly attempted to maintain standards in the fish market by keeping records and by premises inspection. Fishers were expected to run a clean shop – to wash their boards or public counter at the close of business and not to throw fish guts under their boards. A well-known bye-law insisted that 'fish are not to be eviscerated in the fish markets but on the bank at the waterside'. Watchful bailiffs had the right to oversee a fishmonger's shop and if found guilty there was a levy of one groat. Fishers were required by city ordinance to pay the municipal assembly for the right to sell fish at a stall in the fishambles, at a rate of a halfpenny every Saturday. In January 1460, the arrears of customs of some stall holders became so great that bakers, butchers and fishers were threatened with losing their citizenship. The problem continued and in January 1462 at a Dublin assembly meeting, a former custom collector, John Harun, named three fishers who were two years in arrears – Richard Blake, Denys Hayn and Cristofre Drewe. Harun argued that they be compelled to pay or else lose the franchise.[63]

* * *

In the minutes of the Dublin municipal assembly meetings that dealt with the supply of food is one unwritten word – fear. Dublin was a city of 6,000 to 8,000 persons most of whom were not food producers and the assembly members were aware that the responsibility fell on them not to let the city starve. It was a heavy responsibility – to ensure that the city would have enough food in winter. If the assembly members were aware, as we now are, that Dublin's hinterland was well capable of feeding Dublin city, they also saw in our period that engrossers, forestallers and regraters were interfering with the supply of food arriving in Dublin in adequate quantities and at fair prices. And there was always the possibility of the interruption of supplies for reasons outside the control of the assembly – attacks by the Irish in Dublin's hinterland and the fickleness of an entity that can be friend or foe to the farmer, the weather. Somehow, the series of bye-laws passed and fines imposed by the Dublin assembly, and threats of worse, worked to keep the city fed.

CHAPTER 6

The Traditional Church

IN THE MANUSCRIPT COLLECTION in the library of Trinity College, Dublin, there is a late fifteenth-century liturgical book described in 1958 as an antiphonary intended for 'the choral recital of the divine office'.[1] It was later described in 2005 as MS 78, a 'divine office antiphonal designed for use at St Canice's cathedral, Kilkenny', with additions indicating use at Clondalkin in the mid-sixteenth century, the original book dating from probably 1488 to 1500.[2] Marvin Colker's diplomatic account of MS 78 in the Trinity College Library catalogue (1991) in which he classifies the manuscript as an antiphonal with music provides a sound basis on which research can continue.[3] In 1471, William Neill, a comfortably well-off tanner from Clondalkin, bequeathed 40*s*. 'to the parish church of Clondalkin for the purchase of an antiphonar or of a book of lessons'.[4] The terms antiphonal, antiphonary and antiphoner are interchangeable, with the latter term being the standard modern usage. Was the book commissioned at Clondalkin made and could MS 78 be one and the same volume?

When the Reformation came to Ireland MS 78 suffered. In the *Kalendarium* section, the word 'Pope' is erased on the feast days of six popes, but the entry for St Thomas of Canterbury, which was due for erasure, did not receive the same indignity and was passed over unscathed.[5] Eventually, the book was not needed in the new liturgies and it came into the possession of William Gibbons of Clondalkin who wrote his name on it many times, but, one surmises, took care of it until it reached the safety of the Ussher collection and of Trinity College.[6] In 1958, the volume was reported by William Hawkes to be in poor shape, with part of a folio torn off, and folios much thumbed, creased and missing.[7]

It is possible that William Neill's son John, a chaplain attached to the parish of Clondalkin, may have been responsible for the production of the book proposed by his father; he had been involved earlier in the purchase of an expensive chalice, a gift from his father, for a side altar in Clondalkin parish church. Hawkes noted that among the saints listed in the volume, 'Canice of Ossory and Finglas' was given 'special distinction by being written in red' and he felt that one 'could suppose that the manuscript was written in or for the church of Finglas, of which Canice was also the titular, rather than for Clondalkin'.[8]

Family connection may have played some part in introducing the name of St Canice into the volume and indeed the names of saints associated with north Dublin, for example, at Howth (St Fintan)[9], Kilbarrack (St Bearach)[10] and Lusk (St Maculind or Mac Cuilinn).[11] The Neills of Clondalkin were most probably related to a married couple in Glasnevin, near Finglas, Geoffrey Foxe and Jonet Cristore, Jonet probably being a sister of Alson Cristore, William Neill's wife. There were parish and family connections between the Neills and the Foxes. The administration of Jonet's will in 1473 was overseen by John Neill, for example, and Jonet bequeathed 2s. to the parish church of Clondalkin.[12] John Neill, a priest with knowledge of the litany of the saints and probably aware of local devotion to saints in north Dublin through his aunt Jonet, may have been influenced by his background, and directed the scribe of the volume accordingly. Neglected by scholars, there is now a renewed interest in MS 78 and its origins.

* * *

In late medieval England, and most probably in Dublin and the Pale, there was a schema of instruction for the laity covering the essentials of the Christian faith to be delivered each year in the vernacular in four sermons by every parish priest. The themes were constructed around fourteen articles of faith to be found in the creed, the ten commandments, the two precepts to love God and one's neighbour, the seven works of mercy, the seven virtues, the seven deadly sins and the seven sacraments.[13] Widely used in the late Middle Ages, these core beliefs and practices were to be found in a work, *Ignorantia sacerdotum*, originally promulgated at the Lambeth council in October 1281.[14] In 1526, in a diocese next to the archdiocese of Dublin, Armagh *inter Anglicos*, it was required reading for priests.[15] The instruction, chapter nine of the Lambeth council documents, adapted and translated into English in 1357 and known as the *Lay folk's catechism*, was 'imitated or directly used in dioceses all over England up to the Reformation'. In 1425, the bishop of Bath and Wells had the chapter translated into English and had it placed in every church in his diocese at a cost of 6d. a copy.[16] From the foregoing we can be confident that the contents of *Ignorantia sacerdotum* were preached to Dubliners in the second half of the fifteenth century and that it outlined the core of their beliefs.

The call to worship and prayer

At this time Dublin had twenty-seven buildings in which Christian worship took place. There were two cathedrals – Christ Church and St Patrick's – and fifteen churches. There were also ten buildings described as abbeys, friaries or priories, and a chapel. In Speed's map of Dublin (1610) churches can be seen

19 Chapel at Grange Abbey (Little Grange), Baldoyle, Co. Dublin. Some architectural features suggest a fourteenth-century date for part of the church; the west gable was capped by a double-arched bellcote. A bell found locally in 1972 was possibly used at the chapel. (Photo: P. Slattery.)

with a belfry or tower that would have housed a bell or bells. Other church buildings would have had a bellcote on a gable carrying from one to three bells.[17] Bells were rung to call the faithful to Mass and to other religious ceremonies. In the case of a triple bellcote, one bell called parishioners to Mass, another was an Angelus bell, while the third announced a death in the parish. There were bellcotes in Co. Dublin in the 1400s: at Grange Abbey, west of Baldoyle; a double bellcote at Kinsaley and triple bellcotes at Howth and Hollywood in north Co. Dublin (figures 19, 20 & 21).[18]

The bell tower in St Audoen's church in Dublin was most likely built in the early fifteenth century, its lower walls probably built earlier. Although four storeys high the purpose of the tower was to house bells that would call parishioners to prayer.[19] Another possible reason for a high tower is that it is visible from a distance and while it may have offered reassurance to the faithful it has been described as a way of dominating a community.[20] Church towers

20 Church of St Nicholas, Kinsaley, Co. Dublin. The church, which has a double bellcote, was dedicated to St Nicholas of Myra and was subservient to the mother church at Swords. (Photo: P. Slattery.)

were built with additional functions – at Newcastle Lyons, Co. Dublin, as a residence (late fourteenth/early fifteenth century), at Baldongan, Co. Dublin, with fortress-like features.[21] There were bell-towers at Balrothery and at Swords, both of which stand today.[22]

Three bells at St Audoen's were cast in 1423 either in Bristol or in York and today are the oldest serving hanging bells in Ireland.[23] The bells were dedicated to St Audoen, to the Blessed Virgin Mary and to the Holy Trinity and All the Saints. Traditionally it was believed that a Dublin bell-founder, John Kyrcham, may have cast the bells but this is unlikely now. Kyrcham did work for Christ Church cathedral. Buried at Christ Church, he was described as 'artifex campanarum nostrarum' – our bell-founder.[24] Three bells at Howth were inscribed as follows: IESUS CRISTE MISSERERE NOIBS;[25] SANCTA MARIA PRO NOBIS AD FILIUM; NICHOLAS MVN CVR OFMEBIGINER[26] (figure 22).

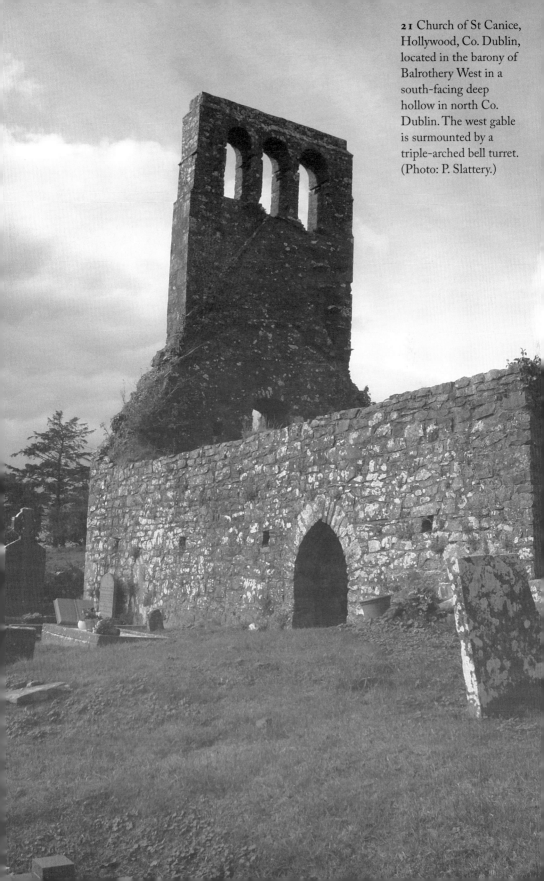

Church of St Canice, Hollywood, Co. Dublin, located in the barony of Balrothery West in a south-facing deep hollow in north Co. Dublin. The west gable is surmounted by a triple-arched bell turret. (Photo: P. Slattery.)

Church bells, used several times throughout the day, needed maintenance to work efficiently. At St Werburgh's church, Dublin, bells were regularly repaired. In the period 1481–4 John Cradoke did repair work on the bell wheels and bell frame that required carpentry and the purchase of nails and boards. Later, in the year October 1484 to September 1485, Cradoke was paid for repairing the bell wheel on two occasions at 3d. each per job. On one of these occasions he supplied boards for the steeple at a cost of 3d. Around the year 1490, the sanctus bell – an external bell that would indicate to those outside the church the approach of the most solemn moment of the Mass – was taken down and repaired on two occasions. In each instance costs were as follows: taking the sanctus bell down (2d.), mending the bell (6d.) and setting up the bell (2d.). In 1495, there were further maintenance costs for the sanctus bell on three occasions costing a total of 10d.[27]

In the Western Church, in medieval times, liturgy and music were shaped by local or regional practices and traditions. The term describing church practice was the word 'use', there being a number of such 'uses' on the Continent and in Britain and Ireland. The Sarum Use gradually became pre-eminent in England, and in 1457 was stated to be accepted in nearly the whole of England, Wales and Ireland. The Sarum Use liturgy and music was essentially Roman, with allowance made for local elements, the name 'Sarum' being derived from the original diocese of Old Sarum in the south of England, which was moved to New Sarum or Salisbury in 1219.[28] At the synod of Cashel in 1172, the Irish bishops agreed to formally accept and use the practices of the English Church, probably as performed in the south of England. The statute reads as follows: 'And so let all divine services (*omnia divina*) be administered in all parts of the Church on the model of Holy Church, as is observed by the English Church'.[29] In the diocese of Ferns, for example, in the episcopacy of John St John (1223–53) and most probably during the episcopacy of Bishop Ailbe Ua Máel Muaid (c.1186–1223), the cathedral chapter's constitution followed the English or Anglo-Norman model of having a dean, precentor, chancellor and treasurer to manage the cathedral's spiritual and temporal affairs.[30] Ailbe was aware of reforms in the universal Church and of the workings of the English Church – he had been suffragan in Winchester in 1201 and 1214 and had attended the fourth Lateran Council in Rome.[31] Writers have suggested that from 1172 the liturgical practices of Salisbury cathedral known as the Sarum Use were to be observed in Ireland but in fact the Sarum Use had not as yet been codified.[32] By way of clarification, there were five usages in Britain – Bangor, Hereford, Lincoln, Salisbury and York – which are described as being dialects within the Roman rite.[33] It is agreed that the Sarum Use most probably was not codified by

22 (a) The belfry at St Mary's, with its external stairway and its three bell openings of one above two, is probably of fourteenth- or fifteenth-century construction. The openings are about .76m wide and about 2.1m high. The external stairway allowed the bellringer to reach the belfry to tap or strike the bells, it being assumed that the bells did not swing. (Photo: P. Slattery.) (b) Three bells from the church of St Mary, Howth, Co. Dublin are now at Howth Castle. The bells were made in the fourteenth or fifteenth century, their diameters being 0.6m, 0.66m, and 0.73m. The bellfounder is unknown but tradition has it that the bells may have been cast in Italy. (Photos: P. Slattery, with the permission of J. Gaisford-St Lawrence.)

bishop Richard Poore in its final form until the period 1219 to 1225.[34] The codification gave Salisbury 'unparalled status and authority'.[35]

Nevertheless, from the end of the twelfth century into the new century Dublin looked to and maintained contact with the diocese of Salisbury. In 1186 at a Dublin provincial council meeting in Christ Church cathedral, Archbishop John Cumin re-committed the diocese to Church practices at Salisbury. In the early 1190s, Cumin raised St Patrick's to the level of a collegiate church of secular canons, and Henry of London, Cumin's successor, took decisions that brought the chapter of St Patrick's more into line with English secular cathedrals and 'in particular with the chapter at Salisbury'. On 30 April 1225, Henry was present at the consecration of the first phase of the building of the new cathedral at Salisbury begun in 1220. So also was Stephen Langton, archbishop of Canterbury. A consignment or consignments of oak were sent to Salisbury from Dublin in 1224 and used in the roofs of two, if not all three chapels consecrated at the time. Travelling under royal protection, the timber may have been either a royal gift or have come from the archbishop. Dendrochronological tests have shown that the oaks were felled in the spring of 1222 near Dublin.[36] With leadership coming from Dublin's two cathedrals, ecclesiastical practice was set firmly on the adoption of Salisbury cathedral traditions, liturgy and music. In March 1216, a letter from Innocent III to the canons at St Patrick's was about the canons emulating those at Salisbury and not the wider issue of liturgical use.[37]

Priests, the Eucharist, vestments and the hours of the church

Two separate liturgies would have been celebrated daily in Dublin cathedrals and churches – a sung Mass, and the daily prayer of the church known as the divine office or 'hours', which will be discussed below. The parts of the Mass known as the 'ordinary', and described as invariable, included the Kyrie, Gloria, Creed, Sanctus, Canon and Lord's Prayer. Other parts of the Mass, called the 'proper', varied with the church calendar, according to the festival or eccle-siastical season, which included Advent, Christmas, Lent, Easter and saint's feast days.[38] Daily Masses celebrated in the smaller churches of Dublin city and county were probably not as grand as a medieval High Mass celebrated on Sundays and major feast days which had the potential to be 'a major musical production that unfolded in every church, cathedral and monastery. It required architectural space, furnishings, books (increasingly), vestments, candles, and above all people to sing …'[39]

The Eucharist remained central to the beliefs of the faithful. Most believers in Dublin would have received communion once a year at Easter, and also at the time of their death. What was important to the believer in the fifteenth century was seeing the elevated host at Mass – that moment when the priest was heard to say '*Hoc est enim Corpus Meum*', 'For this is my body'. Candles were used to light up the church the better to see the host and a sanctus or sacring bell was rung to warn worshippers absorbed in their own prayers to look up.[40] In the 1490s, parishioners in St Werburgh's and in parishes across Dublin city and county would have heard the sanctus or sacring bell signifying the approach of the consecration of the bread and wine.[41] The practice of using a sanctus or sacring bell at Mass, begun in the twelfth century, was to focus the attention of the congregation on the approach of the consecration of the elements.[42]

In many churches architecture made it difficult to witness the host being elevated. The view of the altar from the west end of the church, the congregation end, to the east or liturgical end of the church would have been impeded by one or two screens – the choir screen or pulpitum (which had doors which could be opened) and a second screen to the west of the choir screen called a rood screen over which there was a rood or representation of the crucifixion.[43] The rood was supported on a beam, on which one or more lights burned constantly, so that the rood-beam was often called the 'candle-beam'. These were the principal lights of the church.[44] In the 1480s and 1490s, St Werburgh's parish church in Dublin had a 'rode loft' and its rood lights were regularly maintained.[45] Rood screens do not survive in Ireland, but in England the dado or panelling of the lower half of the rood screen was or could be pierced by a row of elevation squints or viewing holes to suit kneeling worshippers. In Dublin this would have happened where possible and practicable, for example where panelling was painted with flowers rather than images of saints.[46]

To afford a view of church altars, particularly at the consecration during the Mass, squints were also cut into the stone walls of a number of Dublin churches – at St Audoen's, and at Whitechurch chapel, Rathfarnham, Co. Dublin, in which there is a squint in the centre gable of a small bi-cameral chapel.[47] This squint was probably used to assist a chantry priest to synchronize the celebration of his Mass with a parallel Mass in the chapel, particularly at the moment of the consecration.[48] At St Audoen's, three squints can be seen today which were originally located on the first floor of a building that abutted the south side of the church. While that building is not extant today, the role of the squints can be explained. If one stands inside the church and looks at the squints from the east end of the south nave, it seems that their purpose was to provide the occupants of the adjoining building with a view of the south nave and its dedicated altars below.[49] In 1430, royal permission was

23 (a) The church of St Audoen, Dublin. In an adjoining building (not extant), three squints or hagioscopes at first floor level facilitated a view of the south nave and of a number of dedicated altars which in turn allowed observation of the consecration and elevation of the bread and wine during Mass. (Photo: P. Slattery.) (b) (*opposite page*) A squint or hagioscope at St Audoen's today, now outdoors, but originally indoors, permitting members of a lay religious guild a close overview of the celebration of Masses which they had requested. (Photo: P. Slattery.)

granted to fourteen individuals in the guild of St Anne to have Masses said in St Audoen's – in a chapel of St Anne to be built, in the Lady Chapel, and at the altars of St Catherine, St Nicholas, St Thomas and St Clare, and while such individuals could have attended Mass close to the altars, they or members of their entourage could also have viewed the liturgy using the squints[50] (figure 23 a & b, plate 7).

One aspect of the liturgy, noticed even by an unsophisticated congregation, was the changing colour of the priest's vestments used throughout the year. In the Sarum liturgical calendar used in Dublin there would have been '182 feasts on specific dates, with others of varying date from year to year'.[51] The cycle of liturgical colours associated with the changing feasts would have been strictly regulated, with

> the exclusive use of white throughout Eastertide and feasts and octaves of the Blessed Virgin Mary, even when these seasons included feasts of another colour; red for ordinary Sundays, including those after Trinity, rather than ferial colours; green or blue for ferial days of Trinity and Epiphany; yellow for feasts of confessors; brown, grey or violet for Advent, Lent and other vigils and fasts; the Lenten Sunday and Passiontide colour was red ...[52]

Altar frontals, and drapes for lecterns and statues were also used to match the vestment colour of the day.[53] That said, a sequence of colours used at different seasons of the ecclesiastical year is first found in Jerusalem in the twelfth century and Innocent III wrote about liturgical colours, but a standard sequence in general use in the Western Church did not become established until more recent times.[54]

The ritual vestments attributed to the different grades of clergy developed in the early years of the Church. All clerical grades wore the amice, alb and cincture. The amice consisted of a rectangular piece of linen worn around the neck and shoulders while the alb was a full-length garment with narrow sleeves, usually of white linen. The alb was tied at the waist by a cincture. The major clerical orders – sub-deacon, deacon, priest and bishop – were distinguished by their elaborate outer garments. Made from expensive fabrics coloured according to the liturgical season, and often embroidered, these were: the stole, somewhat like a scarf, worn in different ways by deacons, priests and bishops; the maniple, an ornamental band of cloth, worn on the left wrist or forearm by priests and bishops. A subdeacon's outer garment was a tunicle, knee-length with sleeves. The deacon wore a dalmatic, decorated with fuller sleeves. Priests wore a chasuble, a full-length sleeveless garment, for the celebration of Mass.[55]

In the late fifteenth century, two archbishops who died in Dublin, Michael Tregury (1471) and John Walton (1490), owned sets of vestments or liturgical clothes.[56] Michael Tregury had one blue cloth of silk and five towels for the altar. He also had two chasubles and three albs.[57] John Walton had borrowed vestments from his former monastery at Osney in Oxfordshire – one pair of vestments of green damask and six rochets (full-length surplices), which he instructed to be returned. To his prebendal vicar in St Patrick's cathedral, according to tradition, he bequeathed his surplice and amice, and to Christ Church cathedral he bequeathed one pair of vestments of bord Alexander of a yellow colour.[58]

In medieval times, wealthy benefactors presented sets of vestments to religious communities and cathedrals in, for example, Clogher, Galway, Limerick, Waterford and Wexford.[59] In 1510, Cornelius, archdeacon of Kildare, bequeathed fourteen pounds of silver to buy a cape of blood-red velvet for St Patrick's cathedral.[60] Gerald, the great earl, FitzGerald was a generous benefactor of St Patrick's and on one occasion presented one pair of vestments of cloth of gold tissues to the cathedral. In his last will and testament he bequeathed his best cloak of purple and cloth of gold to make vestments.[61] Vestments in well-endowed wealthy cathedrals must have been magnificent to glimpse in candlelight with a whiff of incense in the air against a background of intoned plainchant. None survive from Dublin cathedrals or churches but a collection of late fifteenth-century vestments has survived from Waterford cathedral, consisting of four Benediction copes and a set of High Mass vestments.[62] In the past, the vestments, while reported correctly as having been dulled by time and wear, were also recognized as being of superb quality. The original colours were reported to have been brilliant emerald green or ruby on a yellow/gold background. Some idea of the cloth's magnificence can be gauged from the striking colours together with the designs of pomegranates, flowers and fruit whose giant stalks swing rhythmically across the width of the cloth. The collection has now been fully restored and can be seen in Waterford.[63] While the velvet may well have come from a Florentine loom, the faces of the figures on the vestments and the details of architecture, of dress and armour are late fifteenth-century Flemish.[64] Most experts agree that the cloth in one cope in the collection, the Magi cope, was woven in Florence in c.1480.[65] It is quite probable that the richly endowed cathedrals and churches of Dublin would have had vestments of such beauty and quality (plates 8 & 9).

Not all was magnificence and in parish churches altar cloths and vestments had to be routinely maintained, repaired and replaced. In St Werburgh's church, in the 1480s, five yards of linen was purchased for altar cloths for St Martin's altar. Linen was purchased to make rochets or full-length surplices (5s. 10d.) and six surplices were made at a cost of 2s. Twelve surplices, three albs, four altar clothes and three towels were washed at a cost of 10d. In 1496–8, a cope's linen foundation was repaired and silk was bought to repair the parish's best cope.[66]

Around 1450, the Church in Dublin would have recognized seven clerical orders – priest (including bishop), deacon, sub-deacon, acolyte, exorcist, lector and door-keeper. A boy could move up through these orders and become a priest. Promotion was by age or length of service, but favour and preferment would, of course, speed up promotion. Priests were ordained by a bishop as were deacons, both ranks being invested with a chasuble and stole respectively. Sub-deacons and orders below that level were not ordained but were appointed and admitted at a Mass through the presentation of their instruments of office – a paten for a sub-deacon, a candle-holder or wine-cruet for an acolyte, an exorcist receiving a book of exorcism prayers, a lector receiving a book of scripture lessons, with church keys being presented to a door-keeper. A singing boy might graduate directly to lector or acolyte in his teens. He could expect to be deacon at twenty-five and a priest at thirty.[67]

It is difficult to construct a systematic account of the lives of diocesan priests in Dublin in the second half of the fifteenth century because of a lack of diocesan records. We must therefore look to a neighbouring diocese, in particular the southern region of the diocese of Armagh *inter Anglicos* in the pre-Reformation 1500s to attempt to throw some light on what priestly life may have been like in Dublin in our period. Similar to Dublin city and county, the region had rural parishes and contained a large town, Drogheda, and was English territory.[68]

An aspirant to the priesthood in Dublin had in the first instance to be educated in order to put himself forward to be trained as a priest. The best schools were those within the monasteries, such as at St Mary's abbey in Dublin, an institution that was in exceptionally good order at the end of the fifteenth century,[69] and in the *studia* of the friaries whose schools existed solely to educate clerical candidates accepted for formation.[70] The orders of friars were also interested in fostering vocations in young men and on the Continent the Franciscans and Dominicans set up grammar schools to give a grounding in literacy and the arts. It is believed that a school dedicated to St Thomas Aquinas in 1428, located on Usher's Island on the Liffey, and run by the Dominicans in the fifteenth century, was such a school and would have been open to their own postulants and others. Youths used to flock there for the study of philosophy and theology including young men from Oxmantown on the north side of the Liffey, who may have been influenced by the Dominicans of St Saviour's priory in their neighbourhood. Such a school would have been available to young men who were considering applying to become a trainee diocesan priest.[71] There were also educated citizens in Dublin, clerks, scribes, grammarians and notaries who if under-employed might tutor students. There were thirty-five clerks in Dublin in the period 1468 to 1512.[72] The granting of citizenship to Thomas Brasyl, a master in grammar (1477), and Thomas Bron, a notary public whose apprentice clerk John Stanton became a citizen in 1485, informs us that along with the clerks, there would have been a cohort of educated persons in Dublin, not recorded as citizens, who were capable of tutoring at grammar school level.[73]

Dublin had no university and formal training for the priesthood was not available. As elsewhere in Christendom, young men were trained for the priesthood by a form of apprenticeship, tutored by a parish priest, learning Latin, imitating the liturgical actions and gestures of the priest, while acting as both server and servant to the priest over a period of years. The results of the process varied, depending on the quality of the teacher and the student. Promotion or preferment would not have come easily for priests.[74] If Armagh diocese *inter Anglicos* is a guide, most priests would have spent their lives being an auxiliary chaplain at a chantry chapel, in a lord's household or as an assistant curate. Only a minority reached the position of parish priest. Those with degrees in canon law could secure a position in diocesan administration.[75]

In 1493, John FitzLenes, prebendary of Howth, and Richard Eustace, prebendary of Swords, had the opportunity to pursue education and study at the university of Oxford for a period of five years, which on completion would greatly enhance their opportunity for promotion in the Church.[76]

A basic requirement of a parish priest was to be resident in his parish. In early sixteenth-century Armagh *inter Anglicos* absenteeism was not a serious problem and presumably it was not a problem in Dublin city and county in our period.[77] John FitzLenes and Richard Eustace were absentees from Dublin but they had been cleared by parliament in 1493 'to absent [themselves] out of this land for the space of five years next ensuing'. Both were entitled to enjoy the profits and rents of their assets, including tithes, while absent.[78] The priest was required to say Mass on Sundays and holydays and on some other days in the week and to recite the office publicly on those days. He also had to administer the sacraments and perform other duties – baptism, matrimony, churching women after childbirth, conducting the funeral liturgy, visiting the sick and anointing the dying. A parishioner's confession had to be heard in preparation for receiving the Eucharist at Easter.[79]

A priest's fundamental duty was to instruct his flock in the tenets of their faith and he could do this in short homilies at Sunday or other Masses, but he was also expected in the late Middle Ages to deliver at least four sermons a year based on the contents of *Ignorantia sacerdotum*, referred to earlier. If a parish priest felt he was not up to it, he could invite another priest or a member of any one of the four mendicant orders to deliver a sermon to his parishioners. The four orders of friars, Augustinians, Carmelites, Dominicans and Franciscans, were well established in Dublin and trained to preach and, as we shall see from bequests, were very popular and highly regarded by Dubliners.[80]

While the details of individual bequests to diocesan priests in both Dublin city and county are available for the 1470s, we must again look to the diocese of Armagh *inter Anglicos* in the early 1500s for guidance on the sources of priests' incomes in Dublin. Several factors that shape the incomes of all parishes should be borne in mind – parish size, the physical geography of a parish, its socio-economic environment, whether it is urban or rural, local practices concerning financial support for the clergy, and any endowments the local church may possess. Briefly, the sources of clerical income were great tithes or the tithes collected on corn and hay – one acre from every ten acres each of both wheat and oats. Altarages were another tithe levied on produce other than grain or hay – on fish, on the profits of trade and on wages. Personal tithes on the profits of shopkeepers and merchants were to be collected but were difficult to assess and claim. In Armagh *inter Anglicos*, and probably in the diocese of Dublin, parishioners were expected to give offerings to the local priest three times a year. A priest was entitled to charge fees for the administration of a number of sacraments, conducting the funeral service and the churching of women. The canonical portion was a levy on the moveable goods of a deceased person; it could be 10 per cent or 20 per cent, but in Dublin it was a punitive 33 per cent. If exacted fully it would have been very harsh on the poor. Depending on the size of glebelands, a rural-based rector might be able to grow a significant amount of his own food. The glebelands of the townland of Slane, Co. Meath, ranged from 2 to 20 acres, with a median of 5 acres. The incomes of beneficed clergy have been calculated for clergy in Armagh *inter Anglicos c.* 1540 and in summary it has been found that the vast majority were poor, and five may have been desperately poor indeed.[81]

The divine office of the church or hours was based on the passing hours of the day from the darkness of midnight to the light of day and back to the returning darkness. Its structure of interspersed prayers, reading and singing would have taken place daily in Dublin's monastic communities. On any day, the hour known as vigils was held a little after midnight closely followed by matins. Lauds took place at dawn. Prime, terce, sext and none (the little hours) took place at the first, third, sixth and ninth hours of the day respectively, beginning at 6 a.m. Vespers were held at dusk and compline before retiring to bed. The entire psalter was to be recited in one week. While it was accepted that performing the night hours was gruelling, the celebration of the divine office was an enriching experience for the participants.[82] Three important canticles were assigned to a particular hour of prayer: the *Benedictus*, the song of Zacharias, the father of John the Baptist, was sung daily at lauds; the *Magnificat*, the song of Mary, was sung at vespers; the third gospel canticle, the *Nunc dimittis*, the song of Simeon, was sung at secular (but not monastic) compline.[83] In Ireland, a wise abbot or prior allowed some flexibility in summoning friars or monks to celebrate the divine hours because of the shorter days of winter and the longer days of summer. Allowance was made in Dominican friaries to adapt the hours and this was also most probably done in the houses of other friars and monks.[84]

The clergy of the two cathedrals and the canons, friars and monks of religious communities in Dublin began the chanting of the divine office in the darkest hours of the night when the city was quiet and asleep – the Augustinians on Cecilia Street, the Carmelites on Whitefriar Street, the Dominicans on Church Street and the Franciscans on Francis Street, as well as Arroasian nuns at St Mary de Hogges' abbey, Cistercian monks at Mary's abbey and canons regular of St Augustine at Christ Church Place, Hoggen Green and Thomas Court.[85]

Map of Ireland taken from the Uppsala portalan *c.*1450, showing, for example, Waterford, Dublin, Howth, Malahide, Drogheda, Ardglass, Carrickfergus, Sligo, Inishbofin, Galway, Limerick, Dingle, the Fastnet and the Saltees. In 1913, the map was redrawn by Thomas J. Westropp showing place names more clearly. (Image courtesy of the copyright owners, Uppsala University Library.)

2 Lambert Simnel depicted in a mosaic in City Hall, Dublin. Simnel is held aloft on the shoulders of Sir William Darcy of Platin in Meath after his coronation on 24 May 1487 in Christ Church. (Image courtesy of Dublin City Library and Archive.)

3 & 4 The common seal of the city of Dublin in the thirteenth century, whose bronze matrices are extant. The first recorded use in Dublin of such a seal was in 1229. On the obverse side is a triple-arched castle, with two archers, two trumpeters, and two men blowing horns. In an arched doorway is an armoured figure with shield and sword and over the doorway three human heads. The theme on the reverse of the seal is maritime –

a galley in full sail, fish in the sea, an anchor, and embattled platforms on the ship, fore and aft. There are four figures on board, one with a crown, a woman facing him, a man offering a cup and in the stern a sailor hauls the bunt of a sail. (Images courtesy of Dublin City Library and Archive.)

5 Coins minted in Dublin. *Top left*: Edward IV penny, struck in Dublin 1465–7. *Top right*: Edward IV groat, struck in Dublin 1472–8 and minted by Germyn Lynch or one of his associates. Lynch's work is recognizable by a G on the breast of the monarch. *Bottom left:* Edward IV half-groat, struck in Dublin 1472–8. *Bottom right*: Edward IV double-groat, struck in Dublin *c.*1467–70, the entire issue being regarded as a

devaluation. The verso of the double-groat bore an image of the sun with a rose in the centre, while the other coins carried a cross and pellets design. All the coins showed the mint name, *Civitas Dublinie*. (© Copyright image, courtesy of National Museums NI.)

6 A Spanish ship carrying iron that came into Dublin port before Christmas 1455. Capable of carrying more than 100 tons, it is the sort of vessel that would have been engaged in the Bordeaux wine trade. It is a two-master with a forecastle, aftercastle, and a topcastle on the main mast. The Dublin assembly minutes (1456), in which this piece of documentary graffiti is found, state that the ship had 'come in', surprisingly belying the oft-repeated statement that large ships did not come into Dublin due to shallows and silting in Dublin bay and the Liffey estuary. (Image courtesy of Dublin City Library and Archive, taken from Dublin City Assembly Roll, 1456; advice from Dr Mary Clark, Dr Ian Friel and Dr Pat Wallace.)

7 Chapel at Whitechurch, Rathfarnham, Co. Dublin. A bicameral medieval church whose centre gable has a small chancel arch and a squint. The small lower opening in the wall in the distance was used by a chantry priest to help synchronise his Mass and its consecration with a parallel Mass taking place at the main altar in the chancel or sanctuary. (Photo: P. Slattery.)

8 The Magi cope, front, a benediction cope in the collection of the late medieval church vestments associated with Waterford. There are four copes in the Waterford vestment collection, the embroidery dealing with the Creation, the life of Christ, the Last Day and the Salvation of Souls. (Image courtesy of Waterford Museum of Treasures.)

9 A dalmatic, a T-shaped High Mass garment, with open sleeves and sides, in the Waterford vestments collection. It was worn by bishops and deacons. Made from green silk velvet, with an asymmetrical pattern of plant ornament, it is decorated by embroidered bands called orphreys. (Image courtesy of Waterford Museum of Treasures.)

11 TCD MS 78, a late fifteenth-century antiphoner. The illustration shows plainchant notation for the opening lines in Latin of the canticle, the *Magnificat*, sung at Vespers every day, the song of praise sung by Mary when her cousin Elizabeth greeted her as the mother of God. This *Magnificat* setting uses the *tonus peregrinus* mode.

> My soul proclaims the greatness of the Lord
> And my spirit exults in God my saviour;
> because he has looked upon his lowly handmaid.
> Yes, from this day forward all generations will call me blessed,
> for the Almighty has done great things for me.

(© Copyright image with the permission of The Board of Trinity College Dublin; *Jerusalem Bible*, Luke, 1:46–9.)

10 (*opposite*) The statue of Our Lady of Dublin can be seen today in the church of Our Lady of Mount Carmel, Dublin, commonly called Whitefriar Street church. It is a life-size figure in oak compared stylistically to sculptures in the Henry VII chapel at Westminster. Tradition has it that it originally belonged to St Mary's Cistercian Abbey, Dublin, survived the iconoclasts and was in use in the Church Street area in 1749. With new church building it was disposed of and in 1824 was bought by a Carmelite priest, Fr John Francis Spratt, in a secondhand shop in Capel Street. George Petrie, the antiquarian, saw its crown for sale in a jeweller's shop – a double-arched crown similar to that seen on Henry VII coins. Unfortunately, its outer white coating and hidden multi-coloured paint from the medieval period was removed in 1914. (Image courtesy of the prior of the Carmelite order, Whitefriar Street, Dublin.)

12 A St Thomas Becket reliquary casket, made in Limoges, France, *c.* 1180–90, gilt-copper and champlevé enamel on a wooden core. It measures 29.9 cm high, 30.5 cm wide and 11.4 cm deep. It is believed to have housed relics of Becket taken by his friend Benedict to Peterborough abbey in 1177. (© Victoria and Albert Museum, London.)

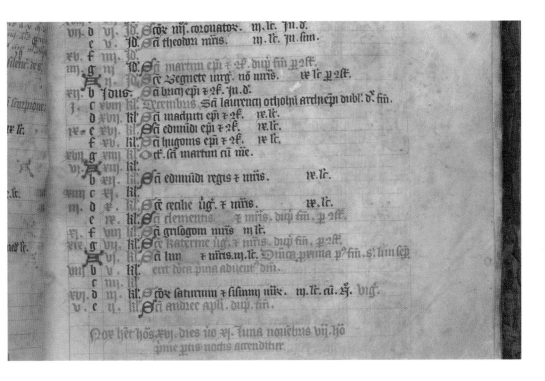

13 A late fifteenth-century liturgical book, TCD MS 78, a manuscript antiphoner, associated with Clondalkin, Finglas, Glasnevin and Kilkenny. With the passing of the Act of Supremacy, such books were censored; in the lower half of the image the title *Pape* (Pope) was erased in respect of Pope St Clement and Pope St Linus. (© Copyright image with the permission of The Board of Trinity College Dublin.)

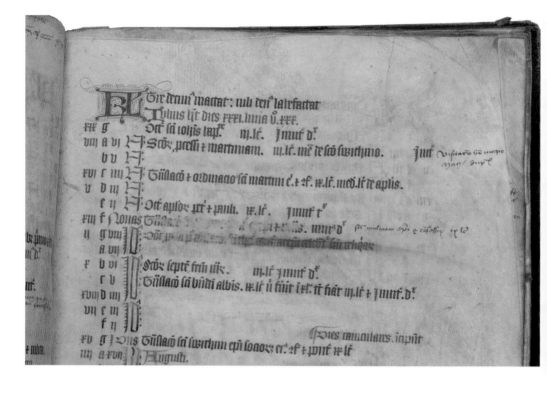

14 A liturgical book censored in the Reformation, TCD MS 79, a manuscript antiphoner originally the property of the church of St John the Evangelist, Dublin. The illustration shows the work of a sixteenth-century censor in the ninth and tenth line, the feast of the translation of St Thomas Becket and the Feast of Relics having been erased. (© Copyright image with the permission of The Board of Trinity College Dublin.)

Devotion to Mary and the saints

Within the Sarum Use it was possible to create liturgy and music in honour
of a saint or an occasion. The most popular of these devotions was Marian and
by about 1250 in England a Marian memorial service, sung after compline in
the evening, had been developed. It was known as the *Salve* service after the
Marian votive antiphon *Salve Regina*. In time, the Little Hours of the Virgin
came to be sung after each of the regular hours of the divine office. Such
liturgies must also have been practised in Dublin. Marian practice in England
is probably a good reflection of the history and development of Marian
liturgies in Dublin down to the late fifteenth century. In England, from the
mid-twelfth century onwards, Mary inspired new services, new chants and
polyphony, but also the building of architectural spaces in which to house
Marian liturgies that were particularly made accessible to lay congregations.
England took the lead in this with the daily morning Lady Mass and evening
Salve service performed outside of choir, usually in a specially-built hall within
the church called the Lady Chapel. These services became the most important
occasions for regular attendance at church by the laity, especially devout
women.[86]

By the mid-fifteenth century, the beginning of our core period of interest,
Dublin's cathedrals and churches had well-established Mary chapels, Marian
liturgies and statues of Mary. Christ Church cathedral had a Lady Chapel
dedicated to the Blessed Virgin Mary. It is not clear when the chapel, 60 feet
long (18.3m), was built – possibly in the late thirteenth/early fourteenth
century – in the north-east corner of the cathedral.[87] In 1414, an altar was
consecrated in honour of the Virgin, probably a new and more elaborate altar
to replace that in the Lady Chapel. Another early chapel in the cathedral
dedicated to St Mary Alba and St Laud was known as the 'White Mary
Chapel', probably because it had an image of Our Lady made of white stone
or made of wood and painted white.[88]

As part of a building programme in St Patrick's cathedral a new Lady
Chapel was built in the 1260s. An earlier Lady Chapel existed in St Patrick's
in 1235 in which a lamp on the Blessed Virgin Mary's altar burned and in
which the Mass of the Blessed Virgin Mary was frequently sung. The new
chapel must have been an enhanced location for a dedicated Marian liturgy.[89]
If St Patrick's followed the pattern of other major ecclesiastical centres, such
as Salisbury, it would probably have hosted a daily Lady Mass in the Lady
Chapel around midday, with a sung evening Marian office.[90]

Clergy in cathedrals and churches within the Sarum Use did not always
slavishly follow Salisbury's lead. St Patrick's cathedral produced a body of
original Marian material for use in the new Lady Chapel from about 1310

onwards which it is believed was used until the fifteenth century. It has been noted that of forty-two proses or poetic texts set to music in honour of the Blessed Virgin Mary found in the Dublin Troper, twenty-four can 'lay greater or lesser claim to being considered either Dublin compositions or Dublin adaptations' – both the texts and melodies are regarded as Dublin compositions. Examples of Dublin Troper proses identified as almost certain to have been composed in Dublin are: *Regina celi flos Carmeli, Gaude Garbrielis ore Virgo* and *Mellis stilla maris stella*.[91] With St Patrick's as centre of the archdiocese of Dublin, these and the other Marian melodies can hardly have been confined to the cathedral liturgies and must have become known in Dublin city and county in the fifteenth century and learned and sung by the faithful (plate 10).

Parish churches also had chapels and altars dedicated to the Blessed Virgin Mary. Buildings and objects and celebrants associated with her and her liturgy were often referred to by parish proctors, and most probably in colloquial language, as 'our Lady's altar', 'our Lady chapel', 'the Mary chapel' or 'the Mary priest'. In St Werburgh's church, in the early 1480s, Edmund Carpenter, who took his name from his trade, was hired for 'the making of the altar of our Lady chapel', raw timber and possibly finished boards being purchased for the work. The same man repaired 'our Lady's tabernacle' and made benches for the Lady Chapel. 'Our Lady coffer', a locked chest, may have been used to accept the offerings of the faithful at anytime and at the celebration of Marian liturgies. In around 1490, work was done on the Lady Chapel roof. Later in the decade it seems that a 'Mary priest', or priest who specialized in celebrating Marian Masses, lived on parish property, in the Mary priest's chamber.[92] At this time and into the early years of the new century, the Mary priest was to be paid quarterly it seems, by a group of parishioners, not formally licensed as a chantry nor organized as a guild.[93]

Within the Sarum Use, local variations known as 'tropes' were made to the texts and music of the standard liturgical books of the day. New saints and new feasts were added to church calendars throughout the later medieval period.[94] A number of surviving liturgical manuscript books used in Dublin had local or local interest saints' names added in the fifteenth and early sixteenth century. An antiphoner owned by the church of St John the Evangelist, Dublin, originally had seven Irish feasts but more than twenty Irish saints were added, along with others of Dublin city interest – St Audoen, St Olave and St Werburgh – after whom Dublin churches were named.[95] The list of Irish saints' names added to the manuscript are associated with ancient church sites in the diocese of Dublin or in the English Pale. A short selection of troped saints of Dublin city and county interest are given below.[96]

Table 6.1 Saints troped in a Sarum Use antiphoner used in Dublin, showing the saint's liturgical name and Irish name and his connection with Dublin[97]

St Berus/Bearach	gave name to Kilbarrack
St Canice	patron of the church of Finglas
St Fintan	devotion to in the parish of Howth, and gave name to 'Fintan's well' in Sutton South
St Magrus/Moshagra	of Saggart
St Maganus/Maighneann	of Kilmainham
St Micheas/Michan	gave name to St Michan's church
St Mobhi	of Glasnevin

The clergy, the laity and church discipline

In the 1460s, the religious institutions of the archdiocese of Dublin seem to have been in good order, with visitations being made to cathedrals, priories and convents, resulting in satisfactory reports. The surviving visitation reports of seven religious institutions are few, brief and damaged, and yet we have a fair overview of the procedure as practised in Dublin. The majority of communities visited in April and May 1468 were in Dublin city, while two were in north Co. Dublin – the convent of Grace Dieu, 4km south-west of Lusk, and the monastery of Holmpatrick near Skerries.[98] Archbishop Michael Tregury made visitations to the two Dublin cathedrals and to the monastery of St Thomas the Martyr,[99] while the remaining four visitations were conducted by Robert Waren, precentor of St Patrick's cathedral. On 27 April, Waren visited the priory of All Hallows and the abbey of St Mary de Hogges, both in the eastern suburb of Dublin.[100] On 4 May he visited the priory of Holmpatrick, possibly accepting the hospitality of the monks on the nights of 4 and 5 May, and then travelling on 6 May to visit the priory of Grace Dieu.[101] Despite the brevity of the visitation material, there is internal evidence to show that the visitations went a good way towards establishing an accurate report on each house. We have therefore some insight into the leadership skills of the priors and the quality of the daily routine of community life in the houses visited.

Dean John Alleyn of St Patrick's cathedral, for example, stated that he had visited cathedral prebends, a statement that could be checked easily; the Holmpatrick community reported frankly that local farmers legally held a chalice belonging to the priory, the silver chalice having been pledged by a former prior; in Grace Dieu the nuns were interviewed separately, a method that would help elicit the truth in a community and in the same convent the entire community complained 'greatly' about their archbishop, Michael

Tregury.[102] The reports of the visitations suggest that there was an openness about the exercise and that responses concerning religious houses and their leaders were made candidly and courageously, indicating a self-critical and healthy Church.

Christ Church cathedral and community were visited in April 1468 by Michael Tregury. All was found to be in good order though Tregury was concerned 'about the great age and infirmity of the prior', William Lynton, and wished that a coadjutor be chosen by the canons to look after the estates and possessions of the house. On the following day, 26 April, St Patrick's cathedral was visited and the dean, John Alleyn, declared that all the prebends of St Patrick's were visited except for Howth and Mulhuddart and those 'in the Irish parts and also in the marches which he had not dared to visit on account of the disturbances of the wars'. Alleyn assured the archbishop that all the canons, petty canons and vicars visited by him were subject to correction and obedient to him and reported that he was occupied in correcting those visited. At the priory of Holmpatrick, on 4 May 1468, the archbishop learned from the prior that all the canons were 'obedient and subject to correction' and that the divine offices were celebrated 'according to the resources of the house'. The community members at Holmpatrick reported that the prior, James Cogan, 'conducts himself with propriety in all matters and governs the house well'.[103]

Convents of nuns were also visited – St Mary de Hogges' abbey, near Dublin (27 April 1468) and St Mary of Grace Dieu in north Co. Dublin, a community of six nuns, led by the prioress, Dame Elena Haket, visited on 6 May 1468. Haket reported that all the nuns were sufficiently subject to correction and obedient, that the house was in a satisfactory state and that the divine offices were celebrated. Dame Alson Taylour, whose name was listed next to that of the prioress, and may have been a sub-prioress in the community, spoke well of the prioress and the house, saying that the prioress conducted herself 'with propriety in all things'. Three nuns – Margaret Ward, Katherine Haket and Anne Gelluys – were 'questioned one by one' as to the prioress and the state of the house and concurred with the sentiments of Alson Taylour.[104]

What were Church expectations of the laity in the mid-fifteenth century? The most detailed description of the laity's duties in Ireland at this time is to be found in a series of decrees approved by a synod of bishops from the Munster ecclesiastical province meeting at Limerick in 1453.[105] A likely leading bishop at the synod, who may have put his stamp on the decrees, was John (of) Mothel, bishop of Limerick, an Augustinian canon regular from Kells Augustinian priory in Ossory, a diocese in the province of Dublin.[106] In a largely universal and uniform Church it perhaps is not unreasonable to assume that the duties and standards required of the faithful, and indeed of the

24 Map of ecclesiastical provinces and dioceses in thirteenth-century Ireland. (Map drawn by Derek Waite, Hull University.)

clergy, in a neighbouring ecclesiastical province may be a fair guide as to what was required of the laity in Dublin. The synod directed that church buildings should be 'well constructed … in nave and chancel, in roof and walls, inside and outside … according to the means of the people'. Cemeteries, often located beside a church, were to be kept clean and walled-in at the expense of the people. It was decreed that parishioners of every parish should have the following in their parochial church at their own expense – a missal, silver or gilt chalice, an amice, alb, cincture, maniple, stole, chasuble, surplice, a baptismal font of stone neatly constructed and well covered, and a suitable vessel for keeping the chrism for the use of the sick. Every church was to have at least a statue of the Blessed Virgin Mary, a cross and statue of the patron saint of the church and a becoming vessel consecrated for the body of Christ.[107] The task for the laity was formidable but could have been tackled successfully in either of two ways – by strong lay voluntary leadership at parish level or by responsibility and power being devolved formally to lay churchwardens or proctors. The role of churchwardens and their responsibilities in a Dublin parish at the end of the fifteenth century will be described in detail below.

The synod required the faithful to cease from all civil works on Sundays and church holidays and to come together in the churches to hear Mass. On Sundays and church holidays the church bell was to be rung three times before commencing Mass and the other divine services. On those days, with presumably a full congregation in the church, there was to be public denunciation of anyone who had been excommunicated and of any of the following – contractors of incestuous and clandestine marriages, defrauders of legitimate heirs, those who had fixed false boundaries, usurers, coiners of false money, strikers of the clergy, and those who had plundered churches and cemeteries.[108]

The ecclesiastical court of the archdiocese of Dublin used excommunication to maintain discipline in the Church and control the clergy and laity. While excommunication was a censure, its purpose was medicinal – it was hoped that the excommunicate would seek absolution, be reconciled to the Church and restored to his place in society.[109] Excommunication was the ultimate weapon of the Church, removing the excommunicate from the communion of the faithful. In a unitary Christian society, excommunication came close to complete ostracism, the excommunicate being cut off from the Church's body as a scandalizing member and treated as a pariah. The excommunicated person was separated from the Christian community – *separatio a communione fidelium*.[110] From the thirteenth century onwards, the canonists made a distinction between minor and major excommunication – minor excommunication separating a person from reception of the Eucharist, from celebration of Mass and possibly attendance at Mass. It could be imposed and removed by any priest who had jurisdiction in matters of conscience.[111]

The censure of major excommunication was of greater significance, separating the excommunicate not only from the Eucharist but from the mystical body of Christ, that is, the Christian community. By the thirteenth century, canonical teaching reserved the power to impose major excommunications to certain prelates – bishops, archdeacons, deans of cathedral chapters, abbots, and laymen empowered to act as ecclesiastical judges. The excommunicate lost all religious rights, he was excluded from entering a church and separated from the company of the faithful and from pleading in secular and ecclesiastical courts. If a cleric, the excommunicate was not to enjoy a benefice nor perform any ecclesiastical acts, but must continue to recite the daily office. The excommunicated person was denied ecclesiastical burial.[112]

In Ireland, in legislation passed in 1404, the sentence of 'greater excommunication' was deemed appropriate for those who violated ecclesiastical liberty and who daily placed 'impositions and illicit burdens' on the lands and possessions of the bishop of Cloyne and his clergy, that is, lay persons who, for example, against the will of the bishop, insisted on undue contributions from the Church and on the 'sustenance of horse and foot within that county'.[113] In 1467–8, when the thirty-year Wars of the Roses was over a decade old, and loyalty to the Crown and to a royal dynasty had become an issue in England, the Irish parliament called upon the archbishops and bishops of Ireland to command their subjects 'to be attentive and obedient to our sovereign lord the present king', Edward IV. Any subject who disobeyed the command after warnings were given over a period of forty days was to suffer the sentence of the greater excommunication, which involved being 'suspended from the sacraments of Holy Church, to wit, from the sacrament of matrimony, purification, communion, the holy extreme unction and burial'. The subjects of excommunication in this instance were never to be restored to the sacraments until they agreed to obey their sovereign lord and to be his subjects and liegemen.[114]

The meaning of 'contumacy' in canon law in our period was set by the canonists in the twelfth and thirteenth centuries; they were virtually unanimous in relating contumacy to procedure in ecclesiastical courts. Put simply, contumacy was regarded as disobedience to a court order and to the law itself. One could be guilty of being contumacious by failing to come to court when cited, by leaving the court before a case was concluded, or by refusing to obey the decisions of a court.[115] One would also be guilty of contumacy by hiding so that the citation or summons to court could not be made or by impeding the citation in some way. It is believed that contumacy for non-appearance was the most common form of contumacy.[116]

The Church was assisted by the royal power in pursuing excommunicates on the run. The action by which the Church requested the royal chancery to arrest a named excommunicate was known as 'signification', but that power to 'signify' was normally restricted to residential bishops.[117] The power to signify could be granted to others by parliament on the direction of the king. In 1481, for example, Roger, abbot of the house of the Blessed Virgin Mary of Mellifont, petitioned and was granted the right to signify to the Irish chancery to cause writs to be made from time to time for the taking of excommunicates 'as is accustomed on the signification of a bishop for the taking of excommunicated persons'.[118]

The act of excommunication was publicly and fearlessly implemented by the Church whatever the status of the accused. In 1478, in a case in which the 'the tithes, fruits and all other profits' of the parochial church of St Bride of Martry in the diocese of Meath were taken by the bishop of Meath and others, the pope appointed delegates to hear the case at Killeigh, Co. Kildare, where the accused were 'to come and show their title and claim that they had to the said church'. When the accused – William, bishop of Meath, John White, archdeacon of Meath, John Darcy of Platin, Richard Botiller and others – did not respond to the citations sent by the delegates and 'appeared not', they were declared to be contumacious. They were formally excommunicated at the busiest crossroads in Dublin at the high market cross, beside Christ Church cathedral and the municipal building, the Tholsel.[119]

The solemnity and gravity of the public declaration of excommunication is probably best seen in the case of Thomas Bathe, knight, who repeatedly broke the law by lying, deception, slander and robbery. When Bathe refused to restore stolen goods, as commanded by the Church, Esmond, formerly bishop of Meath, excommunicated him:

> Whereupon the said bishop in execution of the command of our said most Holy Father and by his authority, at Navan upon a market day there kept, in solemn procession in the said market in the full time thereof, excommunicated the said Thomas for the said contempt, pronouncing openly against him the psalm of David, *Deus laudem*; and moreover declaring, decreeing and adjudging there by the said authority, that in any town into which the said Thomas should thereafter chance to come, in which there was any church, no baptism or burial should be had, or Mass sung or said within three days after his residence there.[120]

The archdiocese of Dublin, acting through its ecclesiastical courts, insisted that individual members of the laity (and clergy) maintain standards and that they be brought to book 'for offending against the moral law, church discipline and for disobedience of their mandates'. With the exception of one ecclesiastical court case in Dublin concerning two curates, the surviving court records from the late 1470s are concerned with lay discipline. On 15 April 1478, the parish curates of Rathmichael and Killiney, in south Co. Dublin, were suspended from the divine offices for contumacy in 'not certifying a mandate citatory against Edmond Walsh directed to them' – in effect neglecting or refusing to serve a court summons on Walsh.[121]

In 1478, between 4 April and 30 May, 27 lay persons were excommunicated in the Dublin diocese.[122] In court the defendants would have been under oath.[123] As in the courts of the diocese of Armagh *inter Anglicos*, court cases occurred in the Dublin diocese at the behest of diocesan court officials or at the instance of others, often a local cleric or a neighbour of the accused.[124] It is useful to list the known parish locations of the accused individuals to illustrate the frequency of excommunications and the geographical stretch of the arm of the Church in an eight week period in April-May 1478. Excommunicates are named in the chronological order of the court sessions at Tymon, Killester, Balrothery, Swords, St Kevin's parish (Dublin), Malahide, Little Grange (Grange Abbey), St John the Evangelist (Dublin), St Nicholas within the walls (Dublin), Swords, Kells, Dublin, Garristown, Rathmore, Swords, Lusk, Leixlip, Swords and Dublin[125] (table 6.2). If the rate of excommunication was maintained, it would have produced an annual total of over 180 excommunications a year.

Table 6.2 Named excommunicates of the archdiocese of Dublin, April–May 1478, with their parish, likely parish or home location[126]

Excommunicate	Parish/home location	Date
John (Shane) Ballowe	Tymon	4 April
Conoghour M'Kegyn	Killester	4 April
John Hamlet	Balrothery	11 April
John Scot	Swords	11 April
Anita Kelly and John Ryagh	St Kevin, Dublin	15 April
Henry Russell	Malahide	15 April
Thomas Ryland	Little Grange	-
Geoffrey Huchoun	St John the Evangelist	18 April
Matilda (wife of Henry Russell)	St Nicholas within the walls	22 April
John Conoghour	Swords	2 May
John Ledwych	Kells	6 May
Robert Flemyng	Dublin	6 May
William Owel	-	20 May
William Loghane	Garristown	20 May
David Walleys and his wife	Rathmore	20 May
Conoghir Ocasy	Rathmore	20 May
Richard Flemyng	Swords	20 May
Patrick Hossey	Lusk	28 May
William Horwych	Lusk	28 May
Thomas Baly	Lusk	28 May
William Gerrote	Leixlip	27 May
John Lutterell	Swords	-
John Mole	Swords	30 May
John White	Swords	-
Nicholas Lok	Dublin	-

Little is known of the personal details of those excommunicated in the Dublin diocese in the late 1470s, and less has survived of the records of the charges against them other than that of being guilty of contumacy. A number of those excommunicated were possibly of the Irish nation – Conoghour M'Kegyn of Killester, John Conoghour of Swords and Conoghir Ocasy of Rathmore. Merchants and gentlemen were excommunicated – John Hamlet, merchant, of Balrothery, and John Lutterell, a gentleman, most probably from Swords. Two curates from Rathmichael and Killiney, discussed above, were suspended from the divine offices. Married persons and married couples were excommunicated – Matilda, wife of Henry Russell of the parish of St Nicholas within the walls, Dublin, was excommunicated, as were David Walleys and his wife of the parish of Rathmore.[127]

In England, surviving records concerned with excommunications show that all levels of society were subject to excommunication – lords of the manor, knights, bailiffs, reeves, gentlemen, citizens of cities, men and women, and those from virtually every trade and craft. In the records of excommunication cases in England, the details of the crime with which persons were charged are known in many instances – the cleric who neglected his celibacy, the woman given in concubinage, a thief, an adulterer, a perjurer, and there were suits concerned with testaments, tithes, benefices and marriages. In a case in Salisbury, seven men assaulted a cleric, and a husbandman, Hugh Knyght from Exeter – most probably mentally unstable – 'blackened the chin and nose of the image of the Virgin with a burning candle' and gibed at the image, 'Mable, ware thy berde'.[128]

The Armagh *inter Anglicos* diocesan court operating *c.*1520 was 'peripatetic within the diocese'[129] and there is evidence that this may have been so in the archdiocese of Dublin in the 1470s. On 11 April 1478, for example, John Hamlet of Balrothery and John Scot of Swords were excommunicated, suggesting that the court operated in north Co. Dublin on that day.[130] The excommunications of William Loghane of Garristown and Richard Flemyng of Swords took place on 20 May indicating that the ecclesiastical court was in session again in north Co. Dublin, possibly in Swords. Interestingly, on the same day at Rathmore, in the barony of Naas, court officials dealt with three excommunications in two separate cases, one case involving Conoghir Ocasy, and another in which David Walleys and his wife were the accused.[131] It would appear therefore that two diocesan courts dealing with excommunications were in session on that day in two widely separated locations in north Co. Dublin and in Co. Kildare. Finally, three cases recorded consecutively in the surviving register, only one of which was dated 30 May, involving three men who were excommunicated – two from Swords, John Mole and John White,

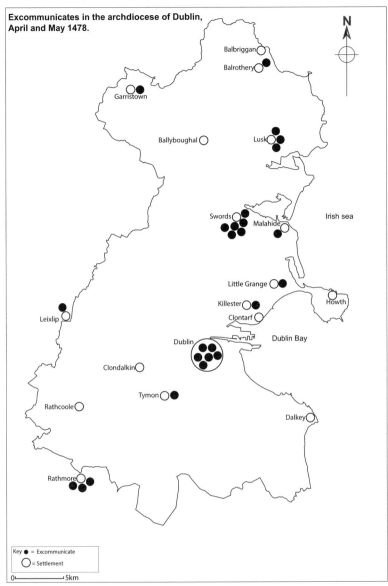

25 Map showing the distribution of excommunicates in the archdiocese of Dublin in a two-month period in 1478. (Map drawn by Dr Fergal Donoghue.)

and another person, John Lutterell, who was named by a parishioner in Swords – would seem to suggest that the Dublin diocesan court was in session in Swords on that day (figure 25).[132]

Excommunication was the last step in attempting to bring church members into line, with the procedure requiring the accused to be summoned to court 'at the instance' of a named person. Often, it seems, that that person was a member of the laity, but there are examples of the accused being summoned to court at the instance of members of the clergy, church officials or diocesan officials in Dublin such as Roger Don.[133]

Table 6.3 Excommunications at the instance of clergy and church officials in the archdiocese of Dublin, April–May 1478

4 April 1478, Sir William Panton, prebendary of Tymon, south County Dublin, naming John/Shane Ballowe.
11 April 1478, Sir John Plant, prebendary of Howth, naming John Scot of Swords.
15 April 1478, the holy water clerk at Malahide, Walter Canton, naming Henry Russell of Malahide.
[15 April 1478], Sir Robert Byrsale chaplain, naming Thomas Ryland of the parish of Little Grange.
2 May 1478, Roger Don, apparitor of the ecclesiastical court of Dublin, naming John Conoghour of Swords.
[30 May 1478], Patrick Cantoun and Richard Meyler, proctors of the work of the church of Lusk, naming John White of the parish of Swords.[134]

In 24 cases brought before the court, no one escaped the wrath of the Church. In the parish of St Kevin in Dublin, Anita Kelly and John Ryagh were excommunicated 'on account of their contumacy before us', which may mean that both of them were disrespectful to the court. In Lusk in another case, three men were excommunicated – Patrick Hossey, William Horwych and Thomas Baly.[135] In a case in Dublin – could it have been a case concerning infidelity? – Matilda, wife of Henry Russell of the parish of St Nicholas within the walls, was excommunicated on 22 April 1478, 'on account of her contumacy incurred before us', at the instance of Isabelle, wife of Richard Nagle of the same parish.[136]

Away from public worship and liturgies in grand cathedrals, remote from busy parish churches and harsh excommunication tribunals, Christians developed an interior life. Despite devotion to Our Lady and the saints, the core beliefs of the faithful were Christo-centric. One type of prayer practised was affective meditation 'in which the emphasis is on making aspirations of love towards God, rather than on formulating precise petitions or engaging in discursive reflection'.[137] In affective devotion, 'characterized by mental and emotional involvement with the various life situations of Christ',[138] believers focussed, for example, on the Passion of Christ and the Five Wounds. In the fourteenth and fifteenth centuries, the Passion became 'the chief concern of the Christian soul'.[139] The Crucifix was liturgically central to English men and women in the late medieval period and the Passion matched this as a subject of affective meditation. In time, the Passion became 'without any rival the central devotional activity of all seriously-minded Christians'.[140] The Jesus of prayer in the affective tradition is loving and tender.[141] Affective devotion also became an important feature of Irish (Gaelic) devotional life in the fourteenth and fifteenth centuries.[142] Devotion to the Five Wounds of Christ was one of the most popular cults of late medieval Europe, including England. It grew in popularity right up to the Reformation.[143] It was known in Dublin. Another affective meditation used the 'Seven Words on the Cross' – the seven sentences uttered by Jesus on the Cross – as a means of affectively approaching the Passion. And one of the most popular of all prayers in late medieval England structured around the Seven Words was the *Fifteen Oes of St Bridget*. English in origin, the *Oes* were composed most probably in the devotional world of Richard Rolle of Yorkshire (*c.*1300–49), a hermit and spiritual writer, and his disciples, and the English Brigittines.[144]

Ismaia Fitzwilliam of Dundrum manor, Co. Dublin, was interested in and practised affective meditation in the 1430s and 1440s. Among her pious reading material was a bound manuscript volume that brought together four booklets of religious material transcribed in the hand of Nicholas Bellewe of Dublin.[145] Bellewe, a scribe whom we met earlier, working at Merchant's Quay, Dublin, was household secretary at the family home of William and Ismaia Fitzwilliam (née Perers), daughter of Edward Perers, marshal of the English army in Ireland. The couple had two sons.[146] In Ismaia Fitzwilliam's manuscript volume, there is a wide variety of reading and meditative material – a meditation on the Lord's Prayer, interspersed with prayers incorporating litanies of Irish saints; a Latin meditation on the Eucharist and an account of a woman mystic's vision of Purgatory. There is also a confession using the seven deadly sins and the Ten Commandments as a guide. The *Fifteen Oes of St Bridget* are included in the volume,[147] all the fifteen 'Oes' conceived as pleas of mercy to a merciful Saviour who through his suffering formed 'an enduring bond of endearment and tenderness between him and suffering humanity'.[148] A number of works by Richard Rolle of Yorkshire, notably an excerpt from his *Meditation on the Passion* (A), *The Commandment, Desire and Delight*, and also his *Form of Living*, are incorporated in Ismaia's collection.[149]

It would appear that Nicholas Bellewe may have been more than a scribe, possibly writing original religious material – a prose meditation on the Five Wounds, a prose work called *The Laddre of Heuyn*, and a meditation on the Lord's Prayer mentioned above.[150] One meditation transcribed and translated by Bellewe may have been used by a community of nuns or may have been created for women's affective devotion.[151] Community members of two convents of nuns in Dublin – Grace Dieu near Lusk Co. Dublin and a community at St Mary de Hogges abbey on the south side of Hoggen Green in the semi-rural eastern suburb of Dublin – may have taken up the practice of affective meditation. The Grace Dieu community was involved in the education of young ladies from the colonial community and the nuns at St Mary de Hogges were mature women who had to be thirty years of age before they would be accepted into the convent.[152] Tantalizingly, we are left with a question – was Ismaia Fitzwilliam alone or were others practising affective piety in Dublin? The answer must be a strong affirmative. Based on the evidence available, it is highly likely that lay and religious practised affective prayer in Dublin from the 1420s onwards.

* * *

The Church in our period was an organization which made clear what was expected of the clergy and laity. Diocesan visitations to monasteries and convents were made and members of the Church both clerical and lay were excommunicated regularly for, it would seem, transgressions to do with ecclesiastical court procedure. Its buildings and bells dominated Dublin and in a drab world it offered colourful mysterious liturgies and the promise of a better life. Against a background of a male-dominated society, and indeed a remote male deity, there was the intercessory power of local saints and Marian liturgies, and the possibility of developing a personal relationship with the Lord.

CHAPTER 7

A Changing Growing Church

W E HAVE SEEN THE PRESCRIBING, disciplining and excommunicating Church in action, but this description, if left unqualified, would give an unbalanced view of the late medieval Church in Dublin. In 2009, the proctors' accounts of the parish church of St Werburgh in Dublin, dating from 1481 to 1627, and containing a series of twelve proctors' accounts, eight of which belong to the pre-Reformation period, were published. Familiar to scholars in their archival repository, their uniqueness was known, and it was accepted that the accounts should be published, providing, as they do, an insight into the workings of a Dublin parish. The accounts clearly show at St Werburgh's 'a remarkably well-ordered parochial community in which the laity played an essential role'.[1] Not only do the accounts reveal the day-to-day detail of parish activities, but, for our period, point out the presence of lay proctors (churchwardens), elected by parishioners, working and participating in virtually all aspects of church and parish life.[2]

The office of churchwarden or proctor was not new and was known in England in the second half of the thirteenth century. At Bath, for example, in 1349, the churchwardens received rents and bequests, paid wages and were involved in buying, selling and arranging for the maintenance of church goods.[3] In 1454, at St Werburgh's, two proctors leased to chaplains land owned corporatively by parishioners, and in 1471, in the nearby parish of the church of St John, Dublin, two churchwardens leased land 'with the consent of the parishioners'.[4] The proctors of St Werburgh's, John Grene and Thomas Day, show in their accounts (1496–7) the extent of their involvement in church administration: they received income from rents due on leased church properties, from pardon money and from the regular sale of tapers (lights); they made payments for work and materials to do with repairs to gutters, chimneys and roofs. The proctors recorded costs involved in making, repairing and washing vestments, and the repair of the Mary priest's chamber.[5] The class of people who sought election to the office of proctor in St Werburgh's may have been similar to the parishioners of the parish of St John who were citizens of Dublin and qualified in their respective crafts of baker, butcher, glover, goldsmith, merchant and pewterer – successful men, careful in keeping business records, possibly office holders in their craft guild, and prepared to give service to the Church.[6] In 1496–7, Grene and Day, proctors at St Werburgh's, purchased extra paper 'to make the book of account'.[7]

* * *

It would appear that virtually all parish churches were rebuilt in the fourteenth and fifteenth centuries, suggesting that the replaced structures were probably wooden, modest and inadequate.[8] Many reasons have been offered for this phase of re-building or extending parish church buildings, closely connected with the desire by the community for Masses – the enormous loss of life and horror of the Black Death (1348–50), the psychological legacy of pessimism about the brevity and fragility of life that followed from that, the Church's teaching on the final judgement and the sufferings of hell and Purgatory, and the keeping of the feast day of Corpus Christi becoming universal in the West in the fourteenth century.[9] The increased desire for Masses fell on the parish churches in particular, it being believed that monasteries, with their established daily routine, could not accommodate the flow of Masses required.[10] At the church of St Audoen, for example, the building was extended a number of times and, as will be seen below, many altars were built.[11] The increasing desire for Masses came from the laity – from individuals and from groups of parishioners, from chantries and religious guilds, both rural and urban. It is possible, in this period, to get insights into the piety of individual members of the laity, there being some evidence to show that many testators did not seek the celebration of Masses for themselves, leaving this decision to the discretion of their executor, believing this to be more effective in saving their soul, that testators were very conscious of their obligations to the poor, and that some found that images of saints (as opposed to relics) assisted their prayer life.

Plainchant and polyphony

At the beginning of our period, c.1450, plainchant was sung in the cathedrals, convents, friaries and monasteries of Dublin, though polyphony, which was performed in earlier times in Ireland, began to develop anew. There is evidence of polyphony in Ireland from the twelfth century and in Dublin in the early fourteenth century, which will be discussed below.[12] Plainchant could trace its history back to Roman and Frankish chant, related to each other.[13] By the late seventh century, several major centres of chant and liturgy had evolved in western Europe in, for example, Rome, Milan, Toledo, Braga (Portugal), and in Gaul, in Anglo-Saxon England and in Ireland. Under Charlemagne the Frankish liturgy and music began to dominate.[14] It is believed that the earliest chant in Dublin was brought to Christ Church cathedral by two Dublin bishops – Gilla Pátraic OSB, known as Patricius, bishop of Dublin (1074–84), who had come from the cathedral-priory of Worcester, and Bishop Donngus OSB (Donatus) who ruled the Dublin diocese from 1085 to 1095. Both men would have been trained in plainchant – and Donatus was consecrated by Lanfranc of Canterbury who brought in reforms leading to an Anglo-Norman liturgical and chant tradition.[15] Equally, as described earlier, the archbishop of Dublin, John Cumin, in the 1190s at his seat in St Patrick's cemented Dublin's connection with Salisbury cathedral and no doubt with plainchant.

A number of liturgical volumes of the Sarum Use, used in Dublin in the fifteenth century, carrying plainchant notation, are extant. One volume known as the Dublin Troper is associated with St Patrick's cathedral (the core of it was written in *c.*1300),[16] another, an antiphoner, whose possible connection with the Clondalkin–Finglas area of Co. Dublin was suggested at the beginning of the previous chapter,[17] while three volumes (two processionals and an antiphoner) were the property of the parish church of St John the Evangelist which stood close to Christ Church cathedral (plate 11).[18]

The greater portion of each of the three volumes from the parish of St John the Evangelist has plainchant notation. The fourteenth-century processional carries musical notation and there are rubrical directions for texts and prayers to be said or sung at each procession on Sundays and festivals throughout the year. A second fourteenth-century processional has been described as for the greater part notated. The volume includes texts to be sung according to the season, the feast day and the occasion. There are also melodies and antiphons in honour of Mary, including the *Regina Coeli* and the *Ave Regina Caelorum*. An antiphoner belonging to St John's was intended for choir use in the chanting of the divine office. The greater part of the volume is notated, there being sixteen four-barred staves in red to the page, accompanying sixteen lines of text. The psalter bound within the volume is notated only for the antiphons before and after each group of psalms and for the first words of each psalm.[19]

In Dublin, in the second quarter of the fifteenth century, or perhaps in the mid-century, while not a wholly new sound, polyphony was beginning to be heard more frequently. The newly organized development of polyphony in Dublin, singing simultaneously in two or more voices, can be dated possibly to the 1430s, or perhaps to the 1440s, in St Patrick's cathedral, but there is evidence to suggest that polyphony was known earlier in Dublin and elsewhere in Ireland. While plainchant dominated church liturgy, polyphony was in the wings for a long time waiting to come on stage. It is possible, for example, that Bishop Pátraic of Dublin, mentioned earlier, who brought plainchant to Dublin may also have brought polyphony.[20] In pre-Norman times, Winchester had a reputation for polyphony, the Winchester Troper containing 173 two-part polyphonic organa.[21] Two aspects of pre-Conquest church music emerge from the early eleventh-century troper – that music was important in Anglo-Saxon liturgies and that polyphony was established and advanced.[22] In twelfth-century Ireland there is evidence of the existence of polyphony in a manuscript known as 'Cormac's Psalter', the scribe inserting an enchanting collophon, a short piece of three-part polyphony, in which he identifies himself and asks to be remembered:

> Cormac wrote this psalter, pray for him
> You who read these things, pray for yourself in every hour.[23]

In the same century or in the early thirteenth century, a Gradual, believed to have come from a Benedictine house at Downpatrick, contains an Easter processional antiphon, *Dicant nunc Iudei*, in a setting for two voices.[24] The Dublin Troper, associated with St Patrick's cathedral from around 1310, but with later additions made to it, contains a polyphonic setting for three voices of *Angelus ad Virginem* (a thirteenth-century English or French song) notated in Dublin,[25] and closer to our own period in an early fourteenth-century missal, originally belonging to the Augustinian canons regular at the church of St Thomas the Martyr, Dublin, three pages of composed two-part polyphony show that church music was presented in a polyphonic setting in Dublin in the fourteenth century.[26] The above body of evidence, small and fragmented, points to a possible wider picture of multi-part singing in the Irish Church from the twelfth to the fourteenth century, which research may more fully reveal.

In the fifteenth century, polyphony was known in remote rural areas, as at Smarmore, Co. Louth, and it is tempting to speculate in what other small parish churches was such knowledge available and put into practice. Around 1430, it seems that possibly a schoolmaster-priest at Smarmore wrote polyphonic musical notation for a dance-tune on slate. The notation was not liturgical and it was scribbled but nevertheless the writer seems to have been a trained musician and at ease with writing measured music in bars of equal notation.[27]

Not everyone was pleased about innovation in music. The tradition of plainchant in western Europe was very strong and with that the concept of keeping that sound pure and unadulterated. In 1228–9, a Cistercian monk, Abbot Stephen of Lexington, came to Ireland on official visitation to Cistercian monasteries. There is a possibility that some of his complaints could be formulaic and standard and not to do with a specific religious house. Among monastic practices of which he was critical was any tendency in a community to introduce changes to the traditional form of plainchant:

It is decreed that the rules of the order in chanting and psalmody shall be followed according to the writing of blessed Bernard. No one shall attempt to sing with duplicated notes against the simplicity of the order. Otherwise anyone who transgresses in this, and the keepers of the chant unless they immediately restrain the aforesaid disobedient persons, shall be on bread and water on the day following and shall be flogged in chapter without dispensation for as often as he does so.[28]

Despite the fears of Abbot Stephen, and of others no doubt, innovation occurred in church music. While the documentary evidence for polyphony in St Patrick's cathedral in the fifteenth century is negligible, Dubliners would have heard this style of choral singing. Given that St Patrick's looked to Salisbury for guidance in liturgy and music, we can be confident that as Salisbury began to train boy singers and practise polyphony, St Patrick's would have followed. The three-part polyphonic composition *Angelus ad Virginem* is regarded as unique and has been rated as an 'outstanding' composition and is the only known such work from Dublin. The Dublin Troper – a working reference book or day book containing musical material such as Kyries, hymns, songs, sanctus settings, Glorias, guidelines for confession and formal oaths to be taken by canons – began life in the early fourteenth century in St Patrick's and was used throughout the fifteenth century and into the early sixteenth century.[29] A choir that performed such a work as *Angelus ad Virginem* must surely have had other polyphonic compositions in their repertoire. Musicologists would classify the melody as improvised polyphony, although in this case someone happened to write it down. By the end of the fifteenth century *Angelus ad Virginem* would have been dated.

It is likely that boy singers were heard in St Patrick's at the end of the fourteenth century, as they were certainly in Salisbury in the later fourteenth century. For St Patrick's the evidence is circumstantial.[30] In England, towards the end of the fourteenth century, there was a fashion for increasing the number of singing boys in the choirs of newly founded collegiate churches and in using boys' voices in the music of the daily Lady Mass, which by this time was usually observed in most great churches.[31] The use of boys' voices and polyphony was first noted in St Patrick's cathedral in 1431.[32] Arrangements for the training and development of six boy choristers came the following year with archbishop Richard Talbot's charter in favour of St Patrick's. The boys were to be trained 'according to the use and constitution of the said churches of Sarum and of ours'.[33] The boys at St Patrick's would have sung the plainsong of the daily Lady Mass and votive antiphons in the Lady Chapel, and possibly also at other Masses celebrated within the cathedral. They would have improvised a descant to the plainsong according to contemporary practice. Composed polyphony involving boys would not have arisen in the English context, and in Dublin, until close to the middle of the fifteenth century.[34]

It is useful to get an overview of the development of polyphony and the emergence and function of boy singers in church music in the period *c.*1390 to *c.*1450. We must largely rely on sources to do with mainland England to suggest what might have been developing in Dublin. In about 1390 in England, while the music of the church was still principally delivered by plainsong, the number of English institutions performing written composed polyphony numbered about 35 to 40, in secular cathedrals, collegiate churches and in household chapels of the king. By *c.*1450 there were 65 such establishments.[35] The membership of these choirs in terms of numbers was quite wide, ranging from 50 to 60 down to about 12 members, with some ensembles in monasteries having 3 or 4 members. Monastic establishments excepted, the choirs would have included boys' voices which would not have been used in the performance of polyphony. What is likely to have happened is that in the most enterprising choirs in England provision was made 'to ensure that the boys were taught the skills of descant – that is, the improvisation at sight of a line of melody above a given plainsong'. Research very strongly suggests that in the period *c.*1390 to *c.*1450 in England boys were not involved in the performance of polyphony and it is most likely that the situation was similar in Dublin. By the end of the fifteenth century the performance of composed polyphony had emerged in England as one of the splendours of the Church.[36]

It would be fifty years before Christ Church cathedral would set up similar training for choristers as was available in St Patrick's in 1432. From 1480, singing boys could be heard in Christ Church. In that year the cathedral authorities set up a group of boys to sing in the choir and in the Lady Chapel. Funded by Thomas Bennet, a former mayor of Dublin, it was agreed to provide for the sustenance and musical training of four boys, described as *paraphonistae*. They were to be trained in plainsong and polyphony – 'set song or priksong and other more learned musical chants'.[37] Some years later, in 1485, John Estrete funded a Mass to be sung every Thursday in perpetuity in the chapel of St Laurence O'Toole in Christ Church. The Mass was to be sung 'with plain song and set song', although Estrete was unsure of the polyphonic skills of the boys and would settle for plainsong.[38] In view of his doubts it perhaps comes as no surprise that a renewed effort was made in 1493 to put the training of boy choristers on a firmer footing. In August 1493, the prior of Christ Church, David Wynchester, and his community, agreed to establish a music master to teach four boys 'plainchant, polyphony, descant and counter, with the intention that the aforesaid master and boys shall have the care each day of a Mass for the Blessed Mary …'. The boys were to be fed and clothed and rooms for sleeping and teaching were to be provided. This initiative was funded by a combination of incoming rents on three properties and the offerings of the faithful at the relic of the holy staff of Jesus (*Baculus Ihesu*) in the cathedral.[39] The vocal abilities and standards of the choir at this time, in the 1490s and at the turn of century, are not known. It is believed that while a beginning had been made the choral standard would not have come close to the best choirs in England. Regretfully, neither music nor details of its repertoire have survived for this period.[40]

Purgatory, pardoners and indulgences

Dubliners in the late fifteenth century would have believed in Purgatory without question and would have made spiritual and testamentary decisions based on that belief. Purgatory as a doctrine of the Church flowered in the second half of the twelfth century, the Church having inherited the concept in its earliest days from other religions and civilizations. The early Church got interested in what might happen to the soul between the death of an individual and the last judgement and by the fourth century the great fathers of the Church, Ambrose, Jerome and Augustine, developed the idea that certain sinners after their death might be saved by some sort of trial. Their ideas developed into the late twelfth-century belief in Purgatory. In relation to time, Purgatory lies between death and the last judgement, while spatially it is found between hell and paradise. Trial by fire was seen as its worst torment, but fire was equally recognized as a purifier. A modern scholar writing about Purgatory, and knowing that there was work in progress on Purgatory going on in the church in the 1100s, could still write: 'I am convinced by my research and textual analyses that Purgatory did not exist before 1170 at the earliest'. All changed when Innocent III became pope in 1198 and he proclaimed and recognized that part of the Church was 'the army that is in Purgatory'.[41]

In the twelfth century in Europe, running parallel with the development of ideas about Purgatory, there was discussion about sin and confession. The debate among theologians considered the difference between voluntary sin and sins committed due to ignorance. Venial or small sins were discussed and the distinction between vice and sin, the latter being seen as consensual, and the distinction between guilt and punishment were debated. The idea that penance should be done regularly in one's life and not simply after committing a great sin or as one approached death was discussed. Finally, another idea emerged – that secret sins required secret penance and that public sins required public penance. This was to lead to the decline and eventual disappearance of public penance. In 1215, at the Fourth Lateran Council, all this work led to the declaration that all adult Christians, men and women, must make an auricular confession once a year.[42] It is against this background of sin, confession and Purgatory, well established in the fifteenth century, that believers in Dublin in c.1450 to c.1540 developed their spiritual lives and their relationship with God.

It was possible to shorten one's time in Purgatory by gaining an indulgence or pardon of, say, forty days. This remission was not gained easily – penitents had to have truly repented, sincerely confessed their sins and been absolved of all serious sin. Despite being forgiven, the penitent always received a penance from the priest. The harsh penances of the early medieval period – long pilgrimages and many days fasting – were replaced by compassionate and practically minded pastors who imposed milder penances involving prayer, fasting or alms giving, which remitted the time that would have been involved in the old style harsher penances. It was argued that the unfulfilled balance of a penitent's debt of penance could draw on 'the treasure of merits acquired by Christ and by his saints'. Somehow, by late medieval times, the remission-of-time procedure applied also to the souls in Purgatory, and the living could gain indulgences for the souls in Purgatory and so 'shorten their torments'.[43]

But inherent in this new procedure – the combination of sin, confession, penance, indulgences and Purgatory, and the all-important element of money – was a time-bomb. In the ecclesiastical sense the Church gained great power from the newly developed system of the hereafter, based on supervised prayers, alms, Masses and offerings made by the living on behalf of the dead. The concept of Purgatory allowed the Church to develop the device of indulgences into a source of great power and profit, which in turn became a dangerous weapon that was ultimately thrown back against the Church.[44] While an individual could generate indulgences through his spiritual life, special indulgences were promoted by the Church, sometimes using an agent for this work; such a person, who was called a 'pardoner', was usually a priest but could be a lay person.[45] There were pardoners in Ireland working in the Munster and Dublin ecclesiastical provinces, men of initiative and independence, to whom bishops did not take easily. In Dublin in 1320, Archbishop Alexander de Bicknor put limits on the rights of pardoners to absolve penitents, specifically precluding them from absolving anyone guilty of murder. The intention of one canon was that wandering pardoners were to be strictly controlled.[46] Again, in Dublin in 1367, Archbishop Thomas Minot published a lengthy canon attacking the abuses of pardoners and directing that they should not enter any diocese without the express permission of the bishop.[47] In 1453, at the synod of Cashel, close episcopal control of pardoners is evident again when they 'were banned from the province, apart from those who belonged to the order of St Patrick, unless they received special permission from a bishop, which had to be renewed annually'.[48] The absence of comment about pardoners at the synod of Cashel in 1511 may suggest that pardoners had been integrated into the life of the dioceses and no longer posed a threat to the established order.[49]

In our period, in the cathedrals and churches of Dublin, the faithful would have sought the granting of indulgences for their own souls and the souls of their departed loved ones. Hard evidence is not in abundance but there is enough in the surviving fifteenth-century financial records of St Werburgh's to suggest how parishioners, and most probably those in other parishes in Dublin city and county, would have gained an indulgence. The St Werburgh's records show that sums of money recorded as 'pardon money' or a 'pardon offering' were in fact indulgence offerings – in England, and in Dublin it would appear, an indulgence was more commonly called a 'pardon'.[50] Parishioners, following the usual Church-prescribed directions for gaining an indulgence, probably involving a combination of praying, fasting and making a confession, made a monetary contribution or 'offering'. In one entry in the accounts wax or candles were related to 'the pardon' and it is possible that in St Werburgh's there was a shrine lit with candles at which the penitent prayed and at which there was a collection box to receive offerings. In two instances the accounts relate pardon money to All Hallows Day on 1 November (All Saints Day), the day before All Souls Day, at which time of the year the faithful would have especially remembered their loved ones and prayed for indulgences or pardons for their souls. In such incomplete accounts annual totals of pardon money are difficult to assess – 5s. 3d. (1495) and 4s. 2½d. (1496–7). Considering the value of money at the time, it does seem likely that pardon offerings would have been made in small denomination coins, probably as low as a farthing. By any reckoning, the pardon money totals in St Werburgh's look modest.[51]

Not so in the case of Octavian de Palatio of Florence, papal nuncio in Ireland, who targeted the wealthy in his promotion of an indulgence announced by Pope Sixtus IV. De Palatio came to Ireland to become archbishop of Armagh and in October 1477 began promoting a plenary indulgence to be gained in Dublin and Drogheda.[52] He was in effect seeking support for a crusade against the Turks who a generation earlier had taken Constantinople in 1453.[53] He explained that the pope had announced that the faithful would gain an indulgence if they visited churches in Ireland appointed by the papal nuncio and recited certain prescribed prayers. The nuncio named the churches in which prayers should be said – the cathedrals of Christ Church and St Patrick and the church of St Thomas in Dublin, and the

26 Seal of Octavian de Palatio, archbishop of Armagh, who offered an indulgence in Dublin at top prices; a nineteenth-century engraving of an original medieval bronze seal reported as in perfect condition in 1874–5. (W. Reeves, 'Octavianus Del Palacio, archbishop of Armagh', *JRSAI*, 4th series, 3:21 (Jan. 1875), pp 350–2.)

church of the Blessed Virgin Mary in Drogheda. Penitents seeking the indulgence were required to say three times the seven psalms with the lections or alternatively the Lord's Prayer and angelic salutation, namely, the *Ave Maria* sixty times. A monetary contribution was to be made 'for the aid of the cross and holy faith'. De Palatio set contribution levels commensurate with a penitent's role in society – archbishops, bishops, earls or countesses, 2 marks (26*s.* 8*d.*); barons or baronesses, 1½ marks (20*s.*); nobles or doctors, 1 mark (13*s.* 4*d.*), and all others half a mark (6*s.* 8*d.*), 'provided they be penitent and have confessed'. The plenary indulgence was available for a period of two months beginning from about 1 October 1477 (figure 26).[54]

Chantries and religious guilds

Two Church-related developments – chantries and religious guilds – that flourished in the fifteenth century brought a number of advantages to the laity. Any person or group organizing a chantry or religious guild was able to create regular opportunities to be physically close to the action of the Mass either in a chapel or at a side altar and they could also decide the timing, frequency, location and content of the Mass to be spoken or sung for the repose of the souls of their benefactors and loved ones.[55] A 'chantry' had three meanings – a fund, a chapel or a group of clergy – a fund that supported the building of a chapel, that chapel being known as a chantry chapel; clergy chosen to conduct Masses in such a chapel were themselves known as a chantry; a fund that supported specific clergy to say or sing Masses at established side altars in monastic or parish churches was also known as a chantry.[56] The very earliest chantries in England and Ireland seem to have been attached to monasteries, but in England there was a shift away from setting up monastic chantries in the late thirteenth century.[57] The decline in the practice of having monastic chantries seems to have been slower in Ireland, two chantries connected with friars surviving into the late thirteenth and early fourteenth century: a perpetual chantry in Dublin, supported by the exchequer and maintained by the Carmelites of Dublin who said Mass within the precincts of Dublin Castle, ran from 1335 to at least 1428;[58] in June 1394, another order of friars, the Augustinians, said a chantry Mass in the chapel of St Thomas the Martyr in Dublin Castle.[59] As late as 1385, at the Benedictine monastery of Fore in Westmeath, a chantry was set up consisting of the prior with three chaplains.[60]

In the second half of the fifteenth century chantries were set up in Dublin city and county: in Christ Church cathedral, in parish churches in Dublin city and in north Co. Dublin at the chapel of St Doulagh. In 1458, for example, John Chevir, clerk and keeper of the rolls in chancery, was granted a licence to found a chantry of one or two chaplains in honour of St Sythe the Virgin at the altar of St Sythe in the church of St Michan in the town of Oxmantown in the suburbs of Dublin.[61] On the same day, Edward Somerton, a justice, was granted permission to found a perpetual chantry of one or two chaplains in honour of the Blessed Virgin Mary at the altar of the Blessed Virgin Mary in the church of St Nicholas near the high cross in the city of Dublin.[62] In the parish of St Werburgh, in 1482, Lady Maude Plunket established a chantry, funded by a property that she had made over to the parish. Her intention was that the parish authorities should find a priest to sing at Our Lady's altar in St Werburgh's for the souls of William and Margaret Boxseworth, for her own soul and all their generation. One priest was to be chosen by Lady Maude or her daughter Elizabeth Plunket in the event of Lady Maude's death, 'and the other priest at the choice of the proctors of St Werburgh's and so from priest to priest when needful'.[63] In c.1506, John Burnell of Balgriffin, Co. Dublin, set up a chantry in the chapel of St Doulagh, the celebrant to be John Young, chaplain, and his successors. Burnell made over properties to the chantry that would generate an income of £4 a year (figure 27).[64]

A covenant made in October 1485 between John Estrete, sergeant-at-law, and the prior of Christ Church cathedral, that a canon would say a Mass of the Holy Ghost and other divine services in the chapel of the Holy Ghost, then called St Laurence O'Toole's chapel, illustrates well the idea that in chantry and similar agreements the laity were closely involved with the celebrant in shaping and controlling the liturgical content of the Mass. Estrete's endowment of the cathedral drew on a pension and rents that the cathedral could enjoy forever. Masses were to be said for Estrete's named benefactors and family members, the benefactors being the king, Gerald, earl of Kildare, Sir Roland FitzEustace, treasurer of Ireland, Thomas Dowdall, squire, Richard Stanyhurst and Master John Fleming.[65]

The officiating canon was to recommend the king, the earl of Kildare, Sir Roland FitzEustace and many members of the Estrete family to the prayers of the congregation and it was agreed that he would recite

> the psalm *De Profundis* and orison *Inclina domine aurem tuam ad preces nostras* before the *Lavabo*; that the great bell be rung before Thursday Masses; that a 'still' evensong, compline and *De Profundis* be said every Sunday and holiday for the benefit of the said persons and souls; that, when dead, the souls of the various persons shall be prayed for, the obit of John, the founder, being kept yearly on the Thursday and Friday of 'Witson' week, and *Dirige* being said ...[66]

Here indeed was a member of the laity, admittedly powerful and wealthy, seeking and obtaining liturgies and readings tailor-made to his requirements. There would have been some discussion between Estrete and the prior to agree the contents of the covenant but it is clear that Estrete got what he wanted.

The laity could also organize additional Masses by founding religious guilds with strong financial assets that could support priests in celebrating Masses at locations, times and frequencies chosen by the guild. This led to the development of side altars or the building of new chapels dedicated to a named saint from which the guild took its name.[67] At such altars, managed by lay people, it was possible for the laity to get closer to the priest more easily than at a high altar. For the laity, access to the Mass was more frequent in the later Middle Ages; it was a service which the better-off could pay for and also time to suit their requirements.[68]

Little is known about the activities of the Dublin religious guilds but they should have performed three basic functions. First they would have shown a presence in the church to which they were attached, maintaining a great torch or candle lit on Sundays and holy days at the elevation in the Mass. Second, the guild would have sought prayers and alms from their members for the repose of the souls of their deceased brothers. In time, guilds were wealthy enough to fund a chaplain who would celebrate Masses regularly for guild

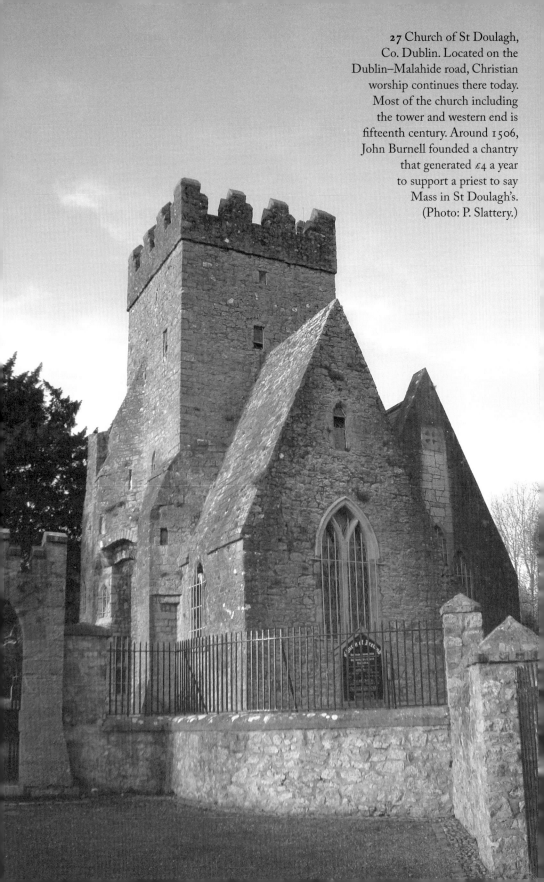

27 Church of St Doulagh, Co. Dublin. Located on the Dublin–Malahide road, Christian worship continues there today. Most of the church including the tower and western end is fifteenth century. Around 1506, John Burnell founded a chantry that generated £4 a year to support a priest to say Mass in St Doulagh's. (Photo: P. Slattery.)

members and deceased brethren. Finally, guilds promoted charity and a sense of community. The guild members met once a year on its feast day when they attended Mass, held a general meeting and concluded with a guild dinner.[69] The guild probably had a distinctive livery, at the very minimum a hood.[70] In north Co. Dublin in the guild of St Mary it may be that the guild had a red hood and a blue gown: Richard Whitakyr of Bremore, near Balrothery, Co. Dublin, was a member of the local guild of St Mary, along with Nicholas Delaber, Robert Lanysdall and Michael Trevers. Whitakyr bequeathed 'my blue gown and my red hood' to Christopher Eliot, and one or both of these items may possibly have been a part of the guild's livery.[71] There would have been an entrance fee and annual subscription, a modest enough amount, but set at a level that would have excluded the very poor.[72]

In 1450 in Dublin city, a number of religious guilds flourished. Such guilds were essentially religious in character, their purpose being to regulate the devotional lives of their members.[73] At the church of St John the Evangelist, Fishamble Street, the guild of St John the Baptist was established in 1418.[74] The guild of St George Martyr was established in 1426, and royal permission was granted in the same year to rebuild a chapel on All Saints' priory land in honour of the Virgin Mary and St George Martyr. The guild, to be based in the chapel, was to support one or more priests celebrating Mass every day forever. It is believed that the chapel was rebuilt by 1433 and that the annual pageant held on St George's day, 23 April, which will be mentioned below, may have been instituted in that year. It became the religious guild of the Dublin municipal assembly. A parallel but separate organization, the military guild or brotherhood of St George was discussed in chapter one.[75] In 1430 the guild of St Anne was established, the guild chantry being at St Anne's chapel in St Audoen's, Cornmarket; the guild supported six priests saying daily Mass at six altars dedicated to St Anne, the Blessed Virgin Mary, St Catherine, St Nicholas, St Thomas and St Clare. The guild of Corpus Christi was established in 1444, the guild chantry being at St Katherine's chapel in the church of St Michael and All Angels, High Street. The guild of the Blessed Virgin Mary and St Sythe, described in more detail below, was founded in 1476, supporting the celebration of daily Mass in St Michan's church.[76]

In Co. Dublin in the 1470s, a number of religious guilds existed – the guild of St Mary at St Peter's church, Balrothery, a guild at the church of St Mary, Balscadden, and a guild at St Mary's church Mulhuddart, established in 1445.[77] In late medieval times in rural England, religious guilds were ubiquitous and it is not surprising to see similar guilds, though few in number, developing in Co. Dublin at this time. By the end of the Middle Ages in England religious guilds were as much a rural as an urban phenomenon. Most villages had at least one guild, and that sense of religious belonging that the guilds offered was available to most adults.[78] In Co. Dublin, the founders of rural-based guilds may have been encouraged to set up a guild by the presence of a number of guilds adjacent to their area – the guild of St Anne established in 1437–8 in a chapel of St Anne newly built and annexed to the chancel of St Peter's church, Drogheda, towards the north,[79] and two guilds established in Co. Meath, at Dunsany in 1465 and at Skreen in 1474–5.[80] Those who founded religious guilds in rural areas may also have been aware that at Stamullin, in 1458, Robert Preston, Lord Gormanston, had founded a chantry of two chaplains, one clerk and four boys in honour of St Christopher Martyr. A new chapel was to be built there outside the walls of the chancel of the parish church of St Patrick.[81] It is interesting to consider what the singing function of the boys may have been in 1458 – were they singing plainsong or performing in a polyphonic setting? It is believed that composed polyphony was beginning in Dublin city at about mid-century and we have seen that polyphonic compositional skills were available in one rural area, Smarmore, Co. Louth.

Of the Dublin religious guilds, most is known about the affairs of the guild of St Anne at St Audoen's. Established in 1430 by royal licence, named laypersons were given permission to found a chantry to support six priests who would celebrate Mass at St Audoen's, one to celebrate in a chapel which was to be built and dedicated to St Anne, one in the Lady Chapel, and one at each of the four altars for the souls of the king and the founders, brethren and sisters of the guild.[82] The four altars in the church erected prior to the establishment of the guild were dedicated to St Catherine, St Nicholas, St Thomas and St Clare.[83] The royal licence allowed men and women to be members although no women are named in the licence nor are the names of any women listed among the known masters and wardens of the guild in the period from 1435 to 1539.[84]

The new chapel of St Anne was erected on the south side of the nave, running parallel to it. Later, in 1455, Roland FitzEustace (Lord Portlester) had a chapel erected in St Audoen's in honour of St Mary, known as the Portlester chapel, by extending St Anne's chapel eastwards. Each chantry priest was assigned an altar when appointed and was allotted an apartment. The priests appear to have been given a salary of eight marks a year (£5 6s. 8d.). While they were expected to sing at all divine services the guild for its part was to provide everything necessary for singing a Mass – 'bread, wine, wax, chalice, Mass-book, vestments, etc.'[85]

In the middle of our period, 1476, a new religious guild and chantry was founded in Dublin – the guild of the Blessed Virgin Mary and St Sythe the Virgin, the intention of whose members was to have Mass celebrated 'daily in the parish church of St Michan forever'. The guild members were permitted to choose a master and two wardens and establish a chantry of two or more chaplains 'to sing and celebrate and do other praiseworthy things', the latter possibly referring to looking after the welfare of each other, of parishioners and of the poor. The founding members, aside from the bishop of Meath, Lord Portlester, and Robert Dowdall, knight, were drawn from the merchant and municipal ruling class of the city – James Aylmer, Simon FitzRery, Arland Ussher, Thomas FitzSimon, Robert West, William Tyve, Robert FitzSimon, William Donagh, Thomas Mulghin, Robert Blanchville, Bartholomew Silke, Thomas Blake and Peter Bartholomew, many holding the posts of bailiff, juré or mayor in and around the 1470s. The guild was free to acquire lands and assets to the value of £40 per annum to sustain the guild and chantry.[86] There was more to the religious guilds than the spiritual, and an assessment of the St Sythe guild points out that 'besides conferring spiritual benefits, participation in the fraternity of St Sythe reinforced political, social and commercial links between the founders, strengthened local suburban identity and cemented relations with the colonial administration'.[87] Other guilds and chantries founded in Dublin, involving members of the laity, would have brought similar benefits (figure 28).

Relics and images

While St Patrick's cathedral was primarily associated with the archbishop of Dublin and in that sense was the centre of the ecclesiastical province of Dublin, Christ Church cathedral was affectionately regarded as the spiritual centre of Dublin and the wider Pale region.[88] It attracted pilgrims to its Masses for local saints – St Fintan of Howth and St Begnet of Dalkey for example – and to its collection of relics, the most famous of which were the *Baculus Ihesu*, reputedly given by Christ to St Patrick, and a miraculous crucifix. In the second half of the fifteenth century the faithful believed in the efficacy of praying in the presence of relics of the saints. Relics of Irish saints were in the collection – the bones of St Patrick, St Brigid and St Columba. For the believing faithful, the efficacy of some relics must have been perceived as especially powerful – a thorn from the crown of thorns worn by Jesus and a piece from the cloth in which he was wrapped when an infant.[89]

---

28 (*opposite page*) Church of St Michan, Dublin. Said to have been founded in 1095 by a colony of Norse settlers, it was for six centuries the only Dublin city parish church on the north side of the Liffey. The Masses of a religious guild founded in 1476, whose members were of the merchant and municipal ruling class, were sung here. (Photo: P. Slattery.)

Research has been done on what relics and how many were in the Holy Trinity collection in the late medieval period. Sixteen relics were brought to Dublin in about 1030 by Dúnán (Donatus), the first bishop of Dublin who had come from one of two Irish Benedictine houses in Cologne. These are regarded as the founding relics of the diocese.[90] With losses and additions the number of relics listed in the cathedral's book of obits totalled forty-two.[91] It has been calculated that the earliest year in which the collection would have been assembled is in about 1250.[92] Little is known about many of the relics – whether they were corporeal or an object associated with a saint, or when and from whom they were acquired. In the period with which we are concerned the most important relic in Holy Trinity was a pre-Anglo-Norman crucifix, the Speaking Crucifix, large, heavy, very difficult to move and very impressive to look at. The most significant Irish relics were the *Baculus Ihesu* and the marble altar of St Patrick, both of which, according to one account, were sent to Dublin from Armagh in about 1180. It is likely that the *Baculus* was not left plain but was adorned with metalwork in copper, silver, gold and precious stones. Irish saints' relics in Christ Church were those of Patrick, Brendan, Brigid and Columba. With the early Dublin diocese connections with Worcester and Canterbury it should not be surprising to find that Christ Church had relics of two Benedictine bishops of Worcester, Oswald and Wulfstan, and had relics of St Thomas Becket of Canterbury. From the Continent relics of St Nicholas, bishop of Myra (in Turkey), were probably acquired from Bari in Italy after 1087 when his remains were transferred there. The relics of St Catherine of Alexandria it seems could have been acquired from Rouen where devotion to her was promoted.[93] There was a great devotion to Catherine in the Middle Ages, notably in France, and she is the patron saint of young women, wheelwrights, attorneys and scholars. Nicholas is regarded as the patron saint of sailors, churches and children.[94]

Little is known about how the Christ Church relics were presented to the cathedral congregation and its pilgrims. It is probable that they were stored in chests and taken out on special feast days and occasions. The likelihood is that they were housed in a feretory (feretrum), a reliquary that in the fourteenth century would have resembled a miniature church, 'rectangular or cruciform in plan, complete with buttressed walls, traceried windows, steeply pitched roofs surmounted by spires, ridges and pinnacles'. In late medieval times several feretories including the *Baculus Ihesu* were kept in a great chest stored between the high altar and the east window of the quire. The chest was damaged in 1461 in a masonry fall but the *Baculus* survived undamaged. The feretory would have been carried in procession on special feast days and would have attracted the prayers and monetary offerings of the laity.[95]

In late April 1497, two issues to do with pilgrimages and sanctuary offered by the Church seem to have flared up in Dublin. The Dublin municipal assembly was moved into action at the instance of David Wynchester, prior of Christ Church.[96] It would appear that pilgrims were being attacked – it is not clear by whom, but most probably by those who had powers of arrest – and when seeking sanctuary were pursued. James Prendergast and Robert Lynne, clergy from Armagh, were injured when they tried to visit the cathedral.[97] The Dublin assembly accepted that 'no pilgrims that come on pilgrimage to the Blessed Trinity [Christ Church] to the Holy Rode or *Baculus Ihesu* or any other image or relic within the said place, shall not be vexed, troubled nor arrested, coming nor going, during his pilgrimage'.[98] The assembly agreed that anyone seeking refuge and succour in Christ Church would not be hindered from going there and would not be arrested within the precinct of the cathedral and that the long-established privileges of sanctuary would 'stand in their full effect without any interruption or contradiction of any citizen or inhabitant' of Dublin.[99]

In the fifteenth century, in the English Church of which Dublin was part, the faithful were no longer solely reliant on relics as a means of prayerfully communicating with a saint or interceding with the Lord. They began to assist their prayer life by praying before images of a saint rather than by the use of relics. In late medieval wills, references to saints were usually concerned with bequests of lights, money, or ornaments to existing images of saints that had attracted the notice and devotion of the testator. Whereas early medieval devotion to the saints was often centred on their relics, the use of images of saints became more popular in late medieval times.[100] In the 1470s in Co. Dublin, testators left bequests to shrines or images of saints in their local churches reflecting most probably a devotion that they had cultivated in their lifetime. In 1472, for example, Alice Cassell of Lusk left one robe to the image of St Mary in the chapel of St Maurus in Rush, near Lusk, the gift of a robe suggesting that the image was a statue, either of stone, plaster or wood. Other bequests made in and around the 1470s show devotion to Our Lady and the saints cultivated through the use of images – in 1475, Philip Taillor of Lusk left 12*d.* to the image of St Katherine of Lusk and John Browne (1481) left 2*s.* to the image of St Mary of Swordlestown. Presumably, these images were statues, but could have been paintings or carved wall panels; what is important, however, is that the image was the conduit through which the testator sought the attention and intercession of the saint. In Swords, in 1474, Robert Walsh bequeathed modest sums to maintain the lights (candles) of St Katherine and of St Brigid, in St Columba's parish church. It seems reasonable to assume that these lights illuminated images of the saints in the church, and that there was special devotion to the two saints in Swords through the use of the images.[101]

In 1471, William Neill of Clondalkin, left 6s. 8d. each to the altars of St Brigid and of St Thomas, towards the maintenance of the lights of the altars in the parish church. Not only does Neill's bequest show a devotion to the two saints but it identifies two side altars, named after saints, at which very probably liturgies to do with the saints, often controlled by the laity, took place.[102]

The faith of the people

We have seen how the faithful developed their spiritual lives around attendance at Mass, confessing their sins, acquiring indulgences that would shorten their stay in Purgatory and going on pilgrimage to holy places. The laity believed that their petitions and prayers to the Lord could be affected through intercessory prayers to Our Lady, to local saints and in the presence of the relics of the saints. The better-off in society organized the setting-up of scheduled chantry Masses and religious guilds which assisted not only their prayer life but also developed community cohesion and solidified the connection between the civic and religious elements of society.[103] Some of the religious and community concerns, interests and preferences of late medieval Dublin believers, identified in their final testaments, are described below.

There was a long tradition among Christians in England and Ireland that as one became aware of the onset of death, one's last confession should be heard and a will should be written. A common characteristic of medieval wills was that the testators made bequests for the 'health of their souls'.[104] One study of medieval wills, which included surviving late fifteenth-century Dublin wills, has described the range of social classes of the testators as being wide, from wealthy merchants, comfortable traders and craftsmen to small farmers and fishermen. Another analysis of Dublin wills, mainly from the 1470s, based on the portion of the testator's estate to be given to the Church, described the generality of testators as 'middling folk'. The detail of these wills allows the piety of the testators to be revealed and assessed.[105] When a parishioner was seriously ill, a diocesan priest was usually called, a will was made, the testator's confession was heard and it would be agreed that the burial would take place at the local parish church. There was always a transfer of money, freely given, to cover the expenses of the funeral service and refreshments for the mourners, some of whom may have travelled a long distance.[106] In fourteenth-century Dublin, penitents were given directions on how to approach confession, the advice standing the test of time and applying in our period: to come frequently to confession and to be compliant, submissive and culpable in their attitude. Penitents were to come prepared, to be honest, impartial and truthful and to give a complete account of their sins.[107]

Both the Church and the laity had a strong sense of parish. Normally, those who died were buried in their parish church grounds, but some testators chose otherwise, having probably already discussed the matter with their parish clergy and with the clergy managing the chosen burial ground. In Dublin wills available for the 1470s it is recorded that nine testators wished to be buried in the parish churches of St Michan's, north of the Liffey and of St Kevin's on the south side of the city. The parish church of Margaret Yong, in which she wished to be buried, was not named in her will, and it has not been identified. Both Margaret Obern and Dermot Carryk bequeathed money to the vicar of St Kevin's, Richard Trevers, and Margaret Obern left a bequest towards the repair of the church of St Kevin. The location of their farms are not known, but Margaret's surname of 'Obern' with its 'O' prefix, indicative of an Irish surname, and Irish 'O' and 'Mac' surnames among her and Dermot Carryk's debtors and creditors, suggest that their farms were possibly located between St Kevin's church and Tallaght, where it seems there were many individuals of the Irish nation.[108]

Of the six testators wishing to be buried at St Michan's, one was not involved in agriculture – Dame Margaret Nugent, a widow, relict of Sir Thomas Newbery, former mayor of Dublin, who died on 21 January 1469. Five testators had holdings that they farmed with their spouse: John Cor, Nicholas Barret, Alice Sex, Nicholas Haylot and Ellen Kymore.[109] Margaret Nugent left all her affairs in the hands of three clergymen at St Michan's – and, once debts were discharged, the residue was to be given to the chapel of St Mary the Virgin in St Michan's. She wished that ornaments and other necessaries be purchased for the chapel. John Cor and Nicholas Barret left similar donations to the high altar of St Michan's (20d.), Cor and Nicholas Haylot bequeathing other donations to the works of St Michan's. Nicholas Barret made a bequest of 6s. 8d. to the altar of St Sythe in the south aisle of St Michan's and to the works of St Mary's chapel in St Michan's. Barret did not forget about other Dublin churches in his bequests and left donations to Christ Church and the house of the Blessed Virgin Mary near Dublin. Nicholas Haylot left 2½ lbs of wax to the chapel of St Mary at Dublin bridge.[110]

The locations of the farms of those who wished to be buried at St Michan's are not known, but their religious bequests may suggest their whereabouts. Nicholas Haylot made three bequests to the churches of Donaghmore, Chapelmidway and Killeigh, in the Dunsoghly-Swords area. Haylot's farm may have been located in this area or adjacent to it, or he or his wife may have come originally from that part of north Co. Dublin. Ellen Kymore left donations to the churches of Cloghran and of Santry (2s. each), suggesting that her and her spouse's farm was possibly located around that area of north Co. Dublin, or that she or her husband, John Bulbeke, may have hailed from that area originally. The most interesting item from this group of bequests is to do with Nicholas Barret who bequeathed 12d. to the works of the chancel in the church of Glasnevin. Earlier, in 1453–4, a Nicholas Barret leased a tenement in Glasnevin from the prior of Christ Church – a meadow beside the river Tolka near Glasnevin bridge. It may be that Barret, despite having farmed at Glasnevin, wished to be buried at St Michan's with which he had become familiar as he regularly made his way from Glasnevin to the city markets.[111]

Four testators in the cohort available from the 1470s chose to be buried at Christ Church in Dublin – James Selyman, John Gogh, Thomas Glayn and Peter Higeley. Two were merchants, Higeley and Glayn; Gogh and Selyman appear to have generated their wealth from land. Gogh, Higeley and Selyman were citizens of Dublin. John Gogh left a monetary bequest and a missal to the canons at the cathedral. Thomas Glayn left 10s. to the works of Christ Church and Peter Higeley bequeathed 20s. to the cathedral. Higeley's son was a canon regular of the cathedral and Peter left him 13s. 4d. yearly during his life. Glayn and Higeley also made bequests to each of the four orders of mendicant friars in Dublin.[112]

A number of testators chose to be buried in the grounds of churches belonging to friars in Dublin – Richard Boys and John Wylde, two merchants from England, electing to be buried in the grounds of the friars preachers or Dominicans. Wylde left £4 to be equally divided between the four orders of friars in Dublin. John Roche, possibly a vintner, chose to be buried in the church of the Augustinian friars, leaving a bequest of 3s. 4d. to the community. Walter Sale wished to be buried in the grounds of the Franciscan friars to whom he bequeathed 20s., and an additional 6s. 8d. to be equally divided between the four orders of friars in Dublin.[113]

Individuals had their own reasons for choosing a place of burial other than in the grounds of their parish church. Michael Tregury, archbishop of Dublin, described how he wished 'to be buried in my beloved metropolitan church of St Patrick, Dublin', at the corner of the altar of St Stephen, the first martyr. Jacoba Payn was married twice but wished to be buried in the cemetery of St Patrick's cathedral, 'near the burial place of Thomas Paryse, my former husband, deceased'. Hugh Galliane wished to be buried at the church of St Mary del Dam and bequeathed 13s. 4d. for repairs to the belfry and maintenance of the north wall of the church. John Chever, chief justice of the king's bench, who wished to be buried in the monastery of St Mary the Virgin, left £16 13s. 4d. for a thousand Masses to be said for his own soul – his offering worked out at a rate of 4d. a Mass.[114]

Testators were mindful of family and community and made provision for those who would gather together on the funeral day. In November 1471, John Wylde made provision for those who would be present at his funeral, asking his executors to arrange for wax, wine, ale, spices and other necessaries connected with his funeral. Two years later, John Cor, who was buried at St Michan's, put his wishes more bluntly: 'I leave on the day of my funeral for all expenses about my corpse, 2 marks' (26s. 8d.). Nicholas Barret, who was also buried at St Michan's, itemized the likely expenses for his funeral: 'to the priests and clerks on the day of my burial, 4s., for spices and wine, 40d., for bread and ale, 40d., for wax, 6s. 8d.'. Dame Margaret Nugent, who had given instructions for all her property to be sold off, simply stated: 'I will that my funeral expenses be creditable'. Ellen Kymore knew that she must make provision for relatives and friends who might come from as far away as Cloghran and Santry on her funeral day. She provided 'for a burial place, 3s. 4d.; for wax, 4s. 8d.; for priests and clerks, 8s.; for bread and ale, 15s.; for fish, 8s. 6d.'[115]

Those near death were aware that they would be judged by their actions towards the poor and the weak. The seven corporal works of mercy – to feed the hungry, to clothe the naked, to visit the sick, for example – became more important in late medieval times.[116] In Dublin, bequests were made to St John the Baptist's Hospital or to what testators named as the house of the poor of St John, without the Newgate, at the eastern end of Thomas Street. In the 1470s donations came from all parts of Co. Dublin – 5s. 1½d. from Nicholas Ketyng of Clondalkin, 5s. from Patrick Kenane of Kinsaley and 2s. from Agnes Laweles of Glasnevin. William Neill of Clondalkin responded to the call to feed the hungry and left sufficient funds to St John's to allow the inmates enjoy a 'threefold repast' as had been done by others.[117]

One's final testament offered a last chance to respond to the poor. Richard Boys, a merchant from Coventry who died in September 1471 in Dublin, left a considerable sum, 10 marks or £6 13s. 4d., to provide clothes for the poor – 'I leave 10 marks to buy woollen and linen cloth for clothing poor people in gowns and shirts'.[118] Another English merchant, John Wylde, who died in Dublin in November 1471, cancelled some of his debts, forgiving 'John Walthow all the debts which he owes me. … I will that what is due to me in Ireland by debtors able to pay shall be recovered, and that other debts due by poor people unable to pay may be remitted, at the discretion of my overseers'.[119] Joan Stevyn of Crumlin, who died in 1481, had a similar attitude, advising her son in her will 'that he take and receive certain of the said debts from those able to pay, but remit those due by the poor and by people unable to pay, as I for the health of my soul and that of the said John my late husband, forgive and remit them'.[120]

Towards the end of the fifteenth century, testators came to believe that 'any activities organized by one's executor for the 'wealth of my soul' was more effective if undertaken in a spirit of charity than if done merely mechanically as a matter of duty'.[121] It is interesting to note that of 67 wills proved in Dublin in the 1470s, 51 testators did not seek to have any Masses said for the good of their soul but relied solely on a more or less formulaic sentence in their final testament which called upon their executors, as did Nicholas Wyght of Lusk (1474), for example, 'to dispose of all my [available] goods for the health of my soul according to the disposition of the Church, as they shall answer to God'. For whatever reason, 5 testators did not use the above formula nor express any interest in having Masses said for the good of their souls.[122]

The remaining 11 testaments, while carrying general directions to look after the health of the testator's souls, also provided more specific instructions. Five testators bequeathed money to have thirty Masses, known as the Trental of St Gregory, said for the repose of their soul.

> The Trental of St Gregory was [a] … complex devotion, much and increasingly favoured by fifteenth-century English testators. It involved the saying of thirty Masses spread out over a year, three each in the octaves and using the Masses of the Nativity, Epiphany, Purification, Annunciation, Easter, Ascension, Pentecost, Trinity, the Assumption of the Virgin and her Nativity, together with daily recitation of *Placebo* and *Dirige*.[123]

Alice Bennet of Santry (1471), William Neill of Clondalkin (1471), Alice Cassell of Lusk (1472), and Nicholas Barrett of the parish of St Michan's (1474), stated respectively: 'I leave … for thirty Masses, 30*d*.'; 'I leave for a Trental, 10*s*.'; 'I leave to the priests celebrating there [Lusk] to celebrate the Trental of St Gregory, for my soul, 10*s*.'; 'I leave … for a Trental, 10*s*. 5*d*.'. An English merchant, John Wylde, chose to be buried in the grounds of the friars preachers or Dominicans in Dublin (1471) and left 30*s*. 'for three Trentals to be celebrated for my soul'. While clearly there was an element of self interest in the above bequests, the testators were also aware that their monetary contribution was supporting the daily work of the clergy.[124]

For medieval people, as for all generations, the great fear was to be forgotten in the silence of death. But for those who were well-off, ways and means were found by which one's name would be remembered, repeated and not forgotten by the community.[125] Obsequies of remembrance celebrated for departed souls on the seventh and thirtieth day after burial and on the first anniversary were known as the week's, month's and year's 'mind' of remembrance, and on All Soul's Day in November every soul was remembered by the Church.[126] Earlier in this work, we witnessed the establishment of more complex remembrance strategies – perpetual chantries of one or more priests being set up, and testators making arrangements to have a trental of Masses said for their soul, at each Mass of which the benefactor would be named. Yet another way to be remembered was to link one's name to a bequest given to the Church – a liturgical book, vestment, chalice, altar cloth or towel.[127] A number of Dubliners bequeathed such gifts to the Church in their final testament.

Desiring to be buried in the chapel of the Holy Trinity in St Patrick's cathedral, Dublin, John Gogh, merchant, who died in 1472, bequeathed a missal to the altar of the same chapel, the book probably bearing his name, a reminder of his generous gift: 'I leave to the altar of the [chapel of Holy Trinity] one missal to remain there forever … I appoint the masters and guardians of the said chapel overseers of the said missal'.[128] In 1473, Alice Whyte of Garristown bequeathed 10*s.* 'to make a chalice for the church of Garristown'; the lip or foot of such chalices was often inscribed with the name of the benefactor and would be seen by the celebrant at the sacring, but even if not seen, the donor's name was symbolically raised to God at the elevation.[129] Michael Tregury, archbishop of Dublin, made provision in 1471, that his two salt cellars of silver and overgilt be used to make chalices for St Patrick's cathedral, Dublin, and in 1475, Joan Drywer of Crumlin arranged in her will for the gilding of a chalice in her parish church; she also bequeathed 'an overcloth for the altar' of the church of Aderrig. In Glasnevin, in 1473, Jonet Cristore, who it will be remembered was related to the Neill family of Clondalkin who had given a chalice and antiphoner to their local church, left a bequest to buy a cope for the parish church of Glasnevin.[130]

* * *

An outstanding hallmark of the period is the flowering of lay participation in parish governance through the work of elected proctors or churchwardens. Wealthy members of the laity, working with chantry priests, were able to choose Mass readings to suit their needs and intentions. The setting up of lay-organized religious guilds also allowed the laity to be physically close to the liturgical action of the Mass. Traditionally, the laity believed in the efficaciousness of praying in the presence of relics of the saints to assist securing their needs, but now they also prayed before images of the Blessed

Virgin and the saints for the same reason. Members of the Church believed in Purgatory and in seeking indulgences that would shorten their stay there. In testamentary bequests, conscious of their duty to the less well-off, the laity made contributions to the poor and cancelled debts owed by them. Church members were generous to the clergy and the mendicant orders by way of monetary contributions and liturgical gifts and the laity in Dublin city and county had a steadfast belief in the traditional Church.

CHAPTER 8

Dramatic Presentations

FOR A NUMBER OF REASONS, the early Church was deeply hostile to the dramatic presentations available in imperial Rome – ranging from gladiatorial combats to obscene comedies. Such activities were associated with paganism, and the general pursuit of pleasure was seen to conflict with the ascetism of Christianity.[1] From the earliest times, Christians were forbidden to attend theatrical performances or to appear in them.[2] With the coming of the Dark Ages the pagan shows disappeared but the desire to entertain and be entertained never died. All was not dark, however, and in the tenth century there were two significant developments. Hrosvit, a Saxon nun, wrote a number of edifying comedies, imitating Terence, and Ethelwold, an English monk, described the 'praiseworthy custom' of celebrating the death and resurrection of Christ by a dramatic work that used mime and dialogue. This was performed during or after church liturgies.[3] Across medieval Europe, entertainers singly and in groups, carrying with them the germ of the theatre and its skills and tricks, wandered and put on shows – acrobats, animal trainers with bears and monkeys, ballad singers, jugglers, mimics, story tellers and wrestlers – until a time when the theatre would 'offer a spectacle much superior to that of the little troupe of musicians and wandering singers'.[4]

Drama and the Church

In the Church, within the Sarum Use, religious ceremonies other than Mass and the divine office were developed, becoming settings for ritual elaboration and the development of new chants – processions, short services (memorials) in honour of a saint or other occasion sung after lauds or vespers, including Marian memorials, and the Little Hours of the Virgin sung after each of the church hours of the day. Processions were one such type of ceremony, winding their way through the church, into the grounds and sometimes into the local streets. Salisbury missals reveal the details of ceremonies at Holy Week and Easter using a dramatic approach and separation of character roles for the reading of the passion texts. Fully sung Latin liturgical dramas were developed – the *Visitatio sepulchri*, for example, at the end of matins early on Easter Sunday morning. The *Visitatio sepulchri* as performed in Dublin will be described below.[5]

The Sarum Use practised in Salisbury was renowned in Europe for the splendour of its liturgies, particularly its processions in which large numbers of clergy, choir and acolytes were assembled wearing colourful vestments. Processions included banners, bells ringing, lanterns, singing and the carrying aloft of the Eucharistic host and relics. The most splendid of the church processions was that which took place on Palm Sunday.[6] At Salisbury, the procession included four stations – at locations north, south and west of the cathedral, and at an inside station before the rood.[7] Towards the end of the thirteenth century, Salisbury had adopted the custom of having two processions to re-enact Christ's entrance into Jerusalem – the main procession, the crowd, meeting a smaller procession representing Jesus and his disciples at the first station.[8] The outdoor procession at Salisbury would have moved in a clockwise direction from the northern first station to the south station and on to the west station at the west door before entering the cathedral to come to the fourth and intramural station at the rood.[9]

It can be reasonably expected that the Palm Sunday procession as presented at St Patrick's in Dublin would have been quite similar to that of Salisbury. At Salisbury, the liturgy began with the distribution of palms, accompanied by the singing of two antiphons. The first station took place outdoors beside a cross near the cemetery of the laity north of the choir. Two clerks carried the Blessed Sacrament and relics on a catafalque.[10] The Sunday gospel was read and the antiphon *En rex venit* was sung for the adoration of the Eucharist. The relics were venerated by song and genuflection.[11] The procession moved via the east end of the cathedral towards the second station, on the south side of the cathedral. Seven boys 'in a high place' sang the refrain *Gloria laus et honor*. This was repeated by the choir. A lighted lantern and banners accompanied the reliquary.[12] The procession moved again, this time to the west door of the cathedral; there, three senior clerics turned to the people and sang a verse which included: 'It is expedient for you that one man die for the people than that the whole race perish'. Everyone filed singing into the cathedral through the west door to come to the fourth station.[13] The cross, covered for Lent, was uncovered and the master of ceremonies, genuflecting to the rood, sang *Ave* to the choir's *rex noster*; this was sung twice more at a higher pitch each time. The crucifix on the high altar was uncovered, the procession had come to an end and the Palm Sunday Mass began.[14]

Easter Sunday morning provided the most dramatic action in the liturgical year. On Good Friday, in Dublin's two cathedrals and most probably in other Dublin churches across the city and county, the cross and host would have been deposited in the Easter sepulchre at a side altar with lighted candles. Then, on Easter Sunday morning, before dawn, in a church lit only by the sepulchre candles and the pascal candle, with all present carrying unlit candles, a liturgical action began in which priests approached the sepulchre to raise the cross and return it and the host to the high altar. The priests approaching the sepulchre intoned an antiphon in a low voice with the choir responding; this happened three times with the voices becoming somewhat louder and louder each time. Thurifers censed the sepulchre and the priests lit their candles from the sepulchre candles and from these all the candles in the church were lit. The priests returned to the high altar with the host and the cross and intoned 'Christus resurgens' and the choir responded. All the bells in the church were rung and all images and crosses in the church were uncovered. The liturgical performance was a most impressive combination of the use of darkness and light, music and incense.[15]

On Easter Sunday morning, immediately following the above liturgy, some Dubliners would have been present at a liturgical drama, Visitatio sepulchri, about the visit of the three Marys to the tomb of Christ. The sung play was staged in the church of St John the Evangelist just north-east of Christ Church. The work is Ireland's earliest fully extant play. There are other versions of the Visitatio, but modern commentators describe the Dublin drama as exhibiting 'the most dramatic skill and literary finish' and having 'a clear sense of dramatic feeling'. It seems inconceivable that Christ Church did not also stage a production as good as that available in St John's, whose Augustinian canons would have performed in this liturgy from around 1400. Internally, the dimensions of St John's were about 70 feet (21.3m) long by 35 feet (10.7m) wide. With the sepulchre located at a side altar on the left of the choir area, at the east end of the church, each Mary separately approached the choir entrance where they sang a lament. Moving forward centrally in the choir and still separated they each sang a second lament. They then moved forward to the high altar singing in unison. Approaching the sepulchre on the left of the choir, the first and second Mary sang in turn of their intention to anoint the body of Christ. The third Mary questions who will roll back the stone at the tomb entrance. An angel appears and with the entrance opened the three Marys enter and seek Christ's body. Not finding the body they emerge to announce that Christ has risen. Making their way to a mid-point in the choir the three Marys intone their share of the Victime paschali sequence. They meet the apostles in the middle of the choir; the apostles run to the sepulchre and emerge to sing of the truth of the resurrection. The presiding celebrant begins the Te Deum and the characters of the play leave the choir and retreat westwards to the congregation end of the church.[16]

Morality and mystery plays

Two types of drama written in Middle English emerged in the late medieval period, the mystery play and the morality play. Neither term was used by the audiences or authors of the day. Both genres were concerned with death and salvation, the mystery plays set in historical time from the beginning of the world to the last day, the morality plays in everyday time, in the lifetime of an individual. Mystery plays (known also as miracle plays, cycle plays or civic drama) are known to have been presented in Chester, York and Wakefield.[17] Similar plays were also presented in Dublin in the second half of the fifteenth century.[18] In mystery plays the story of man's salvation was explored using biblical settings ranging from the Creation to the Last Judgement, the *dramatis personae* being easily recognized personalities – Adam and Eve, Abraham, Annas and Caiaphas, Christ, Our Lady and Pilate.[19] The characters of morality plays are personifications of concepts or abstractions – Life, Death, Health, Wisdom and Mercy, for example.[20]

A dramatic morality play, 'The pride of life', was seen on stage in Dublin in the early fifteenth century. Written in Middle English in Dublin in around 1400 or shortly after, 'The pride of life' is the earliest known text of an English morality play.[21] Found in the archives of Christ Church, and incomplete as the surviving text is, it has been described as 'unique in these islands' and hard to exaggerate its 'cultural significance to medieval Dublin'. In a society in which disease, poor diet and death were never far away, the play seeks to offer comfort to a people fearful of death and to show that divine providence will ultimately prevail.[22]

The action of the play is structured around a combat between a protagonist and an antagonist, the protagonist's overthrow, and eventually his regeneration through his soul being saved by the Virgin Mary. There are thirteen roles in the play that with doubling could be played by six actors – the king of life and the king of death, two knights (health and strength), a bishop, a queen, the messenger Solace, the Virgin Mary, two devils, the body and the soul of the king of life and Christ.[23] It seems that the playing area for 'The pride of life' was set out on a number of separated stages on scaffolds; it is believed that the presentation could have been done using as few as two stages with a higher figure of five stages being possible. If the playing area was set out with three small separated stages on scaffolds, two stages would include a tent into which an actor could be concealed whenever stage directions required. Two stages would also have been arranged with a throne each for the king and bishop. The multi-stage set up, known as place-and-scaffold, allowed the action to be switched to a new locale while interval music was played on another stage (figure 29).[24]

29 The staging of 'The pride of life'. From two to five stages could be used for the presentation, depending on the resources available, with one stage in use for the dramatic action at any given time. Stages not in use could be prepared for subsequent scenes with the spaces behind their screens serving as changing rooms. (Drawing by Marion Gunn, University College Dublin.)

On balance, it is likely that 'The pride of life' was not kept hidden within Christ Church, but was performed at an open public location – inside the city walls at the high market cross at the junction of High Street and Skinners' Street, or outside the walls at Hoggen Green, for example. At such locations, the audience would have initially stood about talking and it would have required a loud declamatory style of delivery from the actors to catch and engage their attention. It is believed that, when appropriate, the audience would have been treated as participants in the cast. While the intent of the dramatist was serious, at times the action of the play with audience participation could have become quite boisterous.[25]

Civic celebrations

It is clear that the Church played a major role in developing dramatic presentations seen in cathedrals and in church settings. The earliest dramas were church liturgies, particularly associated with Palm Sunday and Easter Sunday. Even when not liturgical, early plays like 'The pride of life' do not stray too far from moral and religious topics and personalities – 'The pride of life' dealing with the saving of a man's soul. Another authority, the civil authority in Dublin, also promoted dramatic presentations, in particular street pageants on festive occasions. While not a scripted dramatic work, the riding of the franchises of Dublin by the members of the municipal assembly of Dublin, was a grand public spectacle, led by the mayor, bailiffs and assembly of Dublin, 170 in number, in which citizens could participate either as riders or as street spectators. The driving force behind this event and the street pageants presented by the Dublin trade guilds (whose presentations were typically biblical) was both civic and secular – celebrating and confirming the independence and sovereignty of Dublin, and city life.

Early on 4 September 1488, when the tide was low, the mayor of Dublin, Thomas Meyler, and his two bailiffs, William Englyshe and Robert Boys, with the aldermen (jurats) and commons of Dublin, set out to ride the franchises of Dublin, or demarcate the territory of the city. There would have been as many as 170 on horseback, which must have attracted a good-sized crowd, including other riders, despite the early hour. It was the occasion of both a legal exercise and a commemoration of a time-honoured event – 'lyke as ther fore fadres enformed and taght them how they shold ride their fraunches'[26] – recalling the time when Henry II oversaw the first perambulation of the Dublin franchise in 1171–2 and John commemorated it twenty years later. In 1327, the citizens of Dublin used the perambulation to help secure royal affirmation of their rights.[27] The municipal assembly rode the franchises in 1455 and also in 1486.[28] In 1488, the exercise was taken very seriously by the civic group, but on that day there were certainly moments of what can only be described as the farcical and the comical.

Initially, a fitting formal gathering could have taken place outside the Tholsel at the high market cross. Then the group could have headed slowly eastwards through the streets, coming together again in Hoggen Green before moving along the south bank of the Liffey and coming to Ringsend, Poolbeg and the *Bar Fote*, east of which there was a strand. Here, a man cast a spear into the sea to mark the eastern boundary of Dublin; not satisfied with this, a yeoman, William Walshe, rode out into the sea 'at low water as far as he might' and cast a spear into the sea to extend the boundary further. Riding inland the civic group came to Merrion, Simmonscourt and Donnybrook, and worked their way back to the built-up city entering by St Kevin's Gate to reach St Sepulchre's and St Patrick's Close. In the urban area, the group must have attracted the notice of the public, especially when there was controversy involved. The group went through private property, described below in more detail, came to the Coombe and went out through Coombe Gate to Cow

Lane and on to Dolphin's Barn. They crossed the rivers Camac and Liffey in their peregrinations and had difficulties on Christ Church lands described below. Taking the road to Glasnevin they came to Ballyboght and crossed the Tolka bridge and returned to Dublin.[29]

When the group was in the area of St Patrick's Close, a small selection on foot from the group – the select group surely must have been small – went 'through an orchard' and through gardens to a house, through which they went into the street. Heading south, they went through the house of William Englyshe[30] and 'over the roof of another house' in Patrick Street[31] and through the gardens till they came to the Coombe and into Cow Lane. At one stage the group came up 'against the prior of Christ Church's barn', the prior making 'a way for them into the barn' by providing 'a ladder to a window at the west end of the barn' at Grangegorman manor. It seems that there was a boundary stone in the barn floor and the mayor chose a citizen, John Savage, and his mace bearer, Richard Whyte, 'to trye how the francheis went' in the barn. One man was put through the window on a ladder to get onto the barn floor where he found a stone marking the boundary between the franchise of Dublin and the prior's franchise. After a long day, when the perambulation was complete, 'they departed and every man went home to their lodgings', the mayor and his companions having done their duty in demarcating the city boundaries.[32]

In 1422 in Chester, a city with which Dublin had had social, religious and commercial connections over many years, mystery plays began to be staged in association with Corpus Christi processions. The plays were actively supported by the civic authorities, the trade guilds being responsible for their production. There were fines for non-appearance or if actors forgot their lines. Two-tier mobile wagons were used as stages and dressing rooms. The great Biblical themes were explored, such as *The Fall of Lucifer, The Creation, The Flood, The Nativity, The Slaying of the Innocents* and *The Last Supper*. The plays contained a mixture of serious matter and humour, but the comedy was crude and slapstick.[33]

By the second half of the fifteenth century it would seem that street pageants were established in Dublin and threaded their way through the streets on the feasts of Corpus Christi, St George and St Patrick, Shrove Tuesday being included in a decree of 1466. Such processions were regulated and controlled by the Dublin assembly, often down to the finest details. Some visitors to the city seem to have taken at least a three-day holiday on these occasions, 'coming, going and abiding a day before and after' to celebrate the feast day and view the pageants.[34] The entertainment content of the shows as put on in 1498 in Dublin must have included dramatic action and speech, as was happening in neighbouring Chester for over sixty years. Scripts of lines to be delivered in Dublin are not extant, but there is some tentative evidence that 'acting' occurred. In Dublin, the Tailors' guild staged the same show, about Pilate and his wife, in 1498 and in the 1550s, their records in the mid-century mentioning an actor playing Pilate and an actor playing on Corpus Christi day.[35] It is not inconceivable that in 1498, on the streets of Dublin, in the English tradition, spectators waited where they were and actors arrived in a succession of pageant-wagons at each stopping-place and repeated their play, the actors impersonating characters through word and gesture and dramatic animation.[36]

The Dublin municipal assembly regulated the contents of the street pageants and most probably the order of precedence of the guilds responsible for each show appearing in the procession. In 1498, sixteen presentations, mainly drawn from biblical scenes, appeared in the Corpus Christi pageant. The order in which they appeared may not always have been true to biblical sequence or chronology. The participating craftsmen or groups of craftsmen making presentations were as follows: glovers; corvisers; mariners, vintners, ship carpenters and salmon-takers; weavers; smiths, shearmen, bakers, slaters, cooks and masons; skinners, house carpenters, tanners, embroiderers and porters; stainers and painters; goldsmiths; hoopers; tailors; barbers; fishers; merchants. The mayor of the bullring and his bachelors made a presentation on horseback and the haggardmen and husbandmen bore an image of a dragon. Any guild which did not comply with municipal requirements and standards was liable for a fine of 40s.[37]

Contemporary descriptions of the pageant presentations reveal the regulatory hand of the municipal authorities – Adam and Eve with an angel carrying a sword following; Cain and Abel with an altar and offerings; the shepherds with an angel singing *Gloria in excelsis Deo*. In one presentation in which the skinners and others were responsible for building the body of a camel, the porters were 'to bear the camel'. In the same presentation by the skinners, Our Lady and her child were to be 'well apparelled, with Joseph to lead the camel'. The goldsmiths were to present 'the three kings of Cologne, riding worshipfully, with the offerance, with a star before them'. The haggardmen and husbandmen had the great responsibility of carrying an effigy of a dragon, the recognizable symbol of the Dublin municipal authorities, reminding everyone, even on a carnival day, who was in charge in Dublin.[38]

30 (*opposite page*) Map of the most likely route of the Dublin pageant plays in the late fifteenth century, with the assembly of wagons taking place west of Newgate and the route terminating in George's Lane (South Great George's Street). (Map drawn by Dr Fergal Donoghue; the base map is taken from H.B. Clarke, *IHTA no. 11, Dublin part I, to 1610*, map 4; the routeway is taken from the work of Dr Alan J. Fletcher, with permission.)

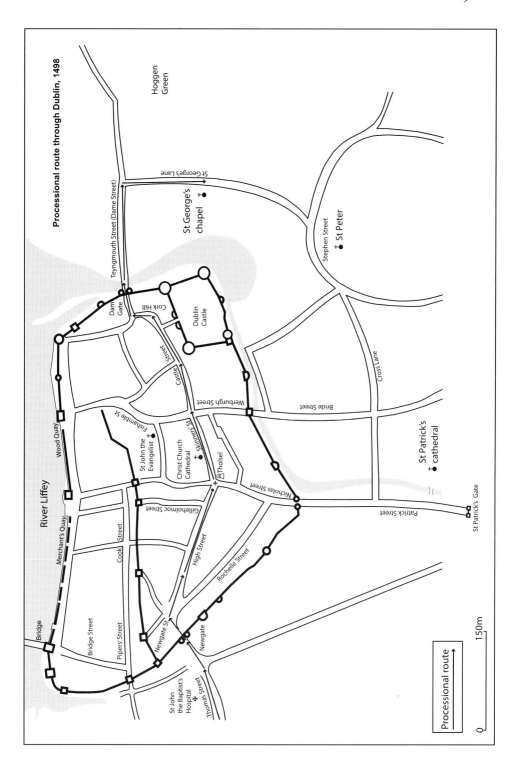

It seems that while the Dublin street pageant presentations would probably have been fairly similar on the feast days of Corpus Christi, St George and St Patrick, each procession may have had its own character. The Dublin authorities were very specific about their pageant requirements on St George's day. The mayor, for example, was to find an emperor and an empress with their followers 'well apparelled … and two maidens to bear the trains of their gowns'. He was also to find 'St George a horse-back' and the bailiffs of the day were to find 'four horses with men upon them, well apparelled' to bear the pole-axe, the standard, the emperor and St George's sword. St George's chapel, the destination of the procession, was to be 'well hanged and apparelled', and was to be fitted with cushions and have its floor covered with rushes on the day.[39]

In the late fifteenth century, the most likely route taken by the Dublin pageant procession would have been as follows. The wheeled horse-drawn wagons would probably have assembled near the Hospital of St John the Baptist west of Newgate and outside the walls of the city. Entering the city at Newgate, the entourage would have proceeded eastwards along New Gate Street (Cornmarket) and into High Street to its junction with Skinners' Street at the high market cross. The market cross area was overlooked by the Tholsel, the municipal headquarters of the city, from which the procession could be viewed proudly by the city fathers. The route continued eastwards along Skinners' Street to its junction with Castle Street where the pillory was located. Continuing eastwards along Castle Street with Dublin castle on the right, the route turned left into Lorimers' Street (Cork Hill) followed by a right turn through Dam Gate, crossing the dam on the Poddle estuary and on into Teyngmouth Street (Dame Street). Finally, the procession took a right turn off Dame Street into George's Lane (South Great George's Street) and would have arrived at St George's chapel on the right (figure 30).[40]

CHAPTER 9

Continuity and Religious Revolution

I N DUBLIN, EARLY IN THE SIXTEENTH CENTURY, the routines of many institutions and organizations remained unchanged. The agendas of the monthly meetings of the Dublin municipal assembly were much the same as in previous years and administration of the merchant and craft guilds followed the established pattern. Dublin merchants controlled the Dublin assembly as before and did business principally with Chester and in the English midlands as they had done in the fifteenth century. The work of the Church continued at parish level and in the daily and seasonal round of liturgy, prayer and worship in the cathedrals, monasteries and convents. However, it would be simplistic and disingenuous to ignore or deny that there were signs of change coming in Dublin and from abroad. We, of course, have the advantage of hindsight and the opportunity of having an overview of the changes or events that promoted change in the fifteenth and early sixteenth century in Ireland, England and on the Continent.

A number of such inter-related changes and events that took place at this time are to do with Ireland emerging from the medieval world into the early modern. From 1494, the Irish parliament was tightly controlled by the king and his council through the enactment of Poynings' Law, one historian stating that the law made 'a clear watershed between medieval Ireland and the Tudor period'.[1] Another farewell to the medieval period was the fall of the house of Kildare through the revolt of Silken Thomas FitzGerald in 1534, bringing to an end the long period in which the lord deputyship was controlled by Anglo-Irish feudal magnates.[2] In the 1530s, Thomas Cromwell attempted to create a modern role for those magnates, transforming them into true agents of the Crown within a 'framework of a properly controlled government'.[3]

Change in Europe and the New World

On the continent of Europe especially, there were new ideas and achievements in many branches of knowledge including in painting, architecture, religion and geographical discovery. Leonardo da Vinci was producing some of his most renowned work – 'The Last Supper' painted between 1495 and 1498, full of realism, movement and drama, and the 'Mona Lisa', painted about 1502, using da Vinci's technique of *sfumato*, which produced blurred outlines and mellow colours, conveying an indistinctness, vagueness and mystery leaving something to the viewer's imagination.[4] Architects in Italy were designing new buildings and seeking wealthy patrons to fund their proposed buildings, designed for their beauty, proportions and spaciousness. Brunelleschi's dome of Florence cathedral was built between 1420 and 1436, but almost a century would pass before his building methods, based on the work of ancient Greek and Roman architects, would be followed by architects outside Italy. The last phase of the Gothic style was worked out, for example, in England in the wonderful chapel at King's College, Cambridge, begun in 1446.[5] There were new ideas in religion also. The first we hear of Martin Luther is in 1517, when his 95 theses about indulgences came to be regarded as a call to reform the Church. In the next few years, Luther challenged the primacy of the pope and the infallibility of general councils of the Church. By 1520, he was encouraging the German princes to abolish tributes to Rome, the celibacy of the clergy, Masses for the dead, and many other Catholic practices.[6] It is possible that English ships were fishing off the Grand Banks of Newfoundland in the 1480s. In 1497, John Cabot, who was living in Bristol, set out for America on 2 May on the *Matthew* with a crew of eighteen, under royal letters patent granted by Henry VII. He sailed from Dursey Head, Co. Cork on *c.*22 May making landfall on 24 June in Newfoundland and returned home on 6 August. It was England's closest connection with North America thus far. In 1502, a ship sent from Bristol returned with 216 barrels of salted cod, perhaps the first such cargo to arrive in England from Newfoundland.[7]

The Tudors look to Ireland

Around the turn of the century there was the beginning of a new approach in London to the government of Ireland. The Tudors did not know Ireland and realized that they must 'discover' it and establish facts about it so that they could develop appropriate policies. In September 1537, Sir Anthony St Leger, a future lord deputy, arrived in Ireland with four royal commissioners to enquire into the state of government and society in Ireland, and to investigate how Ireland might be made orderly and civilized. It is known that the group came well briefed, armed with 'writings and muniments'. They must have been familiar with a bound volume, a compendium of manuscripts known today as the Hatfield Compendium, a copy of which they may have had with them, which contained historical and geographical information about Ireland and descriptions of contemporary political, socio-economic and military matters, the documents originating from persons in Ireland loyal to the Crown.[8]

The contents of the volume were both informative and prescriptive. While the 14,000 words of the compendium of eight documents were copied by a clerk in 1537 for Thomas Cromwell, the documents were already known to government, some as early as in the 1490s and in 1515.[9] The first document in the compendium, Patrick Finglas' Breviate, about the original acquisition of Ireland by the king in the twelfth century and the subsequent decay of the English colony, was written in 1515 by Patrick Finglas of the village of that name in Co. Dublin. Finglas, who would become king's sergeant, justice of the common bench, chief baron of the exchequer and a member of the Irish privy council, updated his Breviate on a number of occasions up to 1537. In that year, the policy of Lord Grey, the lord deputy, and the Irish privy council, of which Finglas was a member, was the 'winning of Leinster', for which approval a memorial was sent to Henry VIII. The sentiments of the memorial dovetailed neatly with Finglas' Breviate which recommended the redistribution of abbeys and castles on the borders of the Pale. Also, sentiments in the memorial and in the Breviate about the quality of men needed to colonize were similar – the memorial spoke of the original colonists who 'sought neither for delicate fare, neither desired they to lye in walled townes upon soft beddes', the Breviate stating that the lands should not now be given to men 'who coveyte easye beds ne good fare'.[10] The hand of Finglas was on both documents.

A document, dated to the 1490s, described the military power of leading Irishmen, stating how many fighting men each had, the total coming to over 22,500. Another document, dated about 1515, named all the havens (ports) around the coast of Ireland, in effect listing locations where customs could be collected and where ships could land.[11] A collection of documents, probably written by William Darcy of Platin, administrator and undertreasurer of Ireland, and dated around 1519, or possibly from the early 1520s, attempted to show the revenue-raising capacity of Ireland. The entire compendium provided royal servants with a 'crash course' in information on Ireland. The early Tudors wished to 'reform' government in Ireland, but to do this they had first to 'discover' Ireland using well-developed, informative, and often advisory documents emanating from Dublin and the Pale.[12] In September 1537, officials in the Irish government in Dublin and Thomas Cromwell who had briefed St Leger's royal commissioners were intent that the Crown should be more involved in Irish affairs. With the collapse of the house of Kildare in 1534, they believed that the time had now come to march against the Irish and extend the borders of the Pale.[13]

The established routines of life in Dublin in the early sixteenth century

The records of meetings of the Dublin municipal assembly in the early years of the new century show patterns of agendas, appointment to offices, and decisions and agreements made, similar to those recorded at municipal assembly meetings fifty years earlier.[14] Annual elections for the posts of mayor and bailiffs continued to take place and a formal 'surrender of offices and appointment of officials' was included in the October meeting of the assembly each year. Still short of money, the Dublin assembly continued to lease towers over city gates: in 1502, the tower over the Whitefriars Gate at the western end of Stephen Street Lower was leased to Nicholas Kenan, chaplain at St Patrick's, and the tower over the gate at Crokers' Bars was leased to Thomas Moyr in 1503 (elected bailiff in 1502), both for 31 years at 12*d.* a year, lessees normally being expected to bring the property up to standard.[15] Routine maintenance continued in public utilities, water pipes being maintained by David Wallace appointed in 1504. His job was to scour the openings of the pipes for which he was paid 6*s.* 8*d.* a year. Corruption had not gone away and it seems that some of those seeking office in the city offered money to lords, ladies and others who might be able to influence decisions. An old problem remained, the illegal dumping of dung, with fines being imposed to control it. All was not routine and in late July 1503 a meeting of the assembly received an inquest report on the body of John Plate, merchant who was identified by a jury and who on 5 June 1503, it had been agreed, 'went into the water of the Liffey' at, it seems, the Slype near the bridge in Dublin and was drowned.[16]

At the beginning of the sixteenth century, in the period 1510–15, the proctors' accounts of the parish of St Werburgh in Dublin show the parish following a similar pattern of activities as it had done in the late fifteenth century. The parish had a number of properties, in Swords and in Dolphin's Barn for example, and incoming rents from these were diligently recorded by the proctors. The authorities in St Werburgh's ensured that buildings were well-maintained and a variety of tradesmen – carpenters, plumbers and roofers – were employed. The accounts show regular payments for building materials – laths, lath nails, lime, pitch, slates and timber. Purchases of items needed for liturgical use were as would be expected – bread and wine, wax for Pascal candles, the renewal of a rope for the sacring bell. On special festivals rushes were purchased and strewn on the floor. The proctors made an inventory of the church's precious liturgical objects:

Cross of silver gilt with a stone 60 ounces
Thurible or censer of silver gilt 30 ounces
Paxboard of silver gilt *c.*6 ounces
Buffe of silver gilt 4 ounces
Chalice of silver gilt 15 ounces
Chalice of silver gilt 16 ounces
Chalice of silver gilt 14 ounces
Chalice of silver gilt 12 ounces

A covering was bought for the stairs leading to the rood beam or loft which topped a timber screen that stretched across the width of the church in front of the altar; the beam, a hallmark of the medieval church, carried a crucifix and many candles or lights.[17]

In the new century, community life at Christ Church Augustinian priory and cathedral continued busily. The dual functions of Christ Church were presided over by one person, William Hassard, for example, prior of the community and dean of the cathedral from 1520 to 1537. The community numbered about ten or eleven canons, about equal to similarly-wealthy Augustinian houses in England in the 1530s. In Dublin, the daily routine of the canons would have included prayer, study, reciting the Mass and the daily office, and holding a chapter meeting that included a rules review and the business of the day.[18] Some members of the community were involved in parish work outside the priory – Thomas Water, for example, was a Mary priest in St Werburgh's in 1513, receiving 10*s.* for the Christmas quarter.[19] The priory had benefited over the years from endowments of buildings and lands from which it derived income. Necessarily, its eighty-five urban dwellings and over 10,000 acres in Co. Dublin were managed efficiently by the community to support themselves and their work. The manors of Grangegorman, Clonkeen and Balscadden owned by the priory were operated by appointed managers. Lessees of small urban properties were usually offered a thirty-one-year lease on, say, a house and garden. In the 1530s and 1540s, Christ Church's income was estimated to be £100 to £160, the average of Augustinian houses in England being about £200.[20] Boundary disputes occurred and most could be resolved easily. In September 1500, in the Liffey tidal estuary, demarcating fishing rights with stakes and stones at five locations was not easy for John Warde and Thomas Bermyngham, as they worked in the shifting mud and sand along the north bank and estuary of the Liffey from Dublin to Clontarf where Christ Church, St Mary's abbey and a number of merchants had fishing rights. The work of Warde and Bermyngham was closely overseen by an abbot and a prior, canons, monks, notaries, clerks and others, totalling at least fifteen persons.[21]

In St Patrick's cathedral in the early decades of the new century, traditional life went on – choir books were bought, candles were lit, chalices and patens were re-gilded and hoods were repaired for the clergy. A new crucifix was set up in the rood loft and routine maintenance was done to the fabric of the building. Vicars choral and six boy choristers sang the services. The cathedral was well endowed with its income derived from sixty benefices throughout the diocese. While Christ Church cathedral was located on the high ground in Dublin and had strong links to the city, St Patrick's, located outside the city walls, was firmly connected to the archbishop and the diocesan administrative structures housed in the cathedral. The government in Dublin would have been aware of the legal knowledge of the cathedral's educated canon lawyers and would have consulted them, some of whom were Oxford graduates. Many of the cathedral's men were drawn from the great Anglo-Irish families of the Pale. None of the canons were of the Irish nation.[22] St Patrick's practice and promotion of the Sarum Use in matters liturgical would have been as strong as ever.[23] As John Alen, the archbishop, was compiling his register of documents in what would be called the Calendar of Archbishop Alen's Register, the authorities in St Patrick's in the 1520s began to do likewise – put order on its collection of documents, which included charters, papal bulls and acts of parliament pertinent to their property and rights. The compilation would be known as *Dignitas decani*.[24]

The merchant and craft guilds continued to function in the new century, offering training to apprentices, maintaining discipline among its apprentices and members, and dealing with rule infractions. In the 1540s, for example, a practice had developed among merchants of intercepting ships about to enter Dublin port laden with wine and drawing off the 'flower and best' of it for personal use. It was enacted by the guild that this must cease until wines were fully discharged at the city crane and cellared, tasted, allotted and divided among the purchasing merchants according to practice.[25] A new guild of carpenters, heliers (roofers) and masons was founded in 1508. Although craftsmen with those skills were to be found in Dublin from the thirteenth century, this was the first time they were organized as a separate guild. The carpenters and roofers dominated guild proceedings in a guild that also had masons, millers and painters as members. From its foundation to the 1550s, the master and one of the wardens of the guild was a carpenter, with the second warden always a roofer. Possibly, the number of masons who were members was low because masons traditionally worked in roving bands and companies under a master, and were seldom settled long enough in one place to be enrolled as freemen. The guild register included a variety of members: Margaret Herforde who joined the guild in 1536, 9 mason members in 1555 and 6 joiners recorded as members in 1560. It is seldom that journeymen are mentioned in surviving Irish sources and interesting to surmise to what locations they might have travelled to find work and practise and improve their skills, either in the Pale towns, in Cork, Limerick or Waterford, or in England.[26]

9.1 Select membership of the carpenters' guild, 1547 and 1560: carpenters, roofers and journeymen[27]

Year	Carpenters	Journeymen carpenters	Roofers	Journeymen Roofers
1547	23	24	10	5
1560	16	11	5	3

In the new century, Hoggen Green, east of the city walls, continued as 'a civic rallying place', having seen a judicial burning for blasphemy in 1328, archery practice, military drills and dramatic presentations.[28] Earlier, above, it was suggested that theatrical plays were staged on the Green. That tradition continued and in 1506 the Passion of Christ 'was played on the Hoggen Green' and in July 1523 a miracle play about the life of St Laurence (third-century deacon and martyr in Rome) was performed on Hoggen Green, his martyrdom by slow burning over a gridiron providing stuff for dramatic treatment.[29] At Christmas 1528, eight plays to which Silken Thomas FitzGerald was invited were presented in Dublin with the 'stage put up on Hoggen Green'. The guilds in the city staged six plays, three sacred and three secular, while the priors of St John of Jerusalem, Blessed Trinity and All Hallows in Dublin presented two plays, one of which was about the Passion of Jesus and the other about the several deaths suffered by the Apostles. Three guilds presented neo-classical subjects, about Bacchus, Vulcan, and 'the comedy of Ceres, the goddess of corn'.[30] If the plays were presented daily, starting on Christmas Day, the last play would have been staged on New Year's Day. Most probably, all the plays would have been place-and-scaffold performances, as described earlier in the staging of *The pride of life*, and would have been in the medieval tradition of production and choice of subject matter.[31]

Business with Chester and the rise of Liverpool

The Chester customs accounts for the year 1525–6 are replete with information on ships, merchandise and merchants involved in the trade with Chester, suggesting Dublin to have been a textile manufacturing and exporting centre at the time and also, probably, in the last quarter of the fifteenth century. In 1525–6, over fifty ships passed through the customs at Chester, with ships arriving from ports in Ireland, England, France and the Iberian peninsula – Bilbao, Caminha, Concarneau, Dublin, Howth, London, Milford, Penmarche, Southampton and Workington, for example. The principal ships that carried Dublin merchants and their cargoes to Chester were the *Francis of Dublin* (master William Edward), the *Michael of Dublin* (master William Brisell), the *Michael of Furness* (master Thomas Wele), the *Michael of Wallasey* (master Henry Aynesdale), the *Patrick of Chester* (master Edward ap Herri) and the *Trinity of Dublin* (master John Massy). The *Mary of Regeston* (master Edmund Luces) possibly came from Rogerstown or one of the small north Co. Dublin ports.[32]

A cursory review of the merchants aboard these seven ships shows that, as we have seen in the 1460s and 1470s, many were citizens of Dublin and held or would hold municipal office – Thomas Barbe (mayor, 1530), Walter Eustace (auditor of account, 1532), Walter FitzSymon (mayor, 1533), Nicholas Gaidon (mayor, 1532), Nicholas Hanckoke (auditor, 1533), Simon Lutterell (bailiff, 1532), William Newman (treasurer, 1531), Nicholas Queytrot (auditor of account, 1532), Robert Shillyngford (auditor of account, 1531), Walter Tirrell (bailiff, 1531),[33] William Coytrod/Queytrot (citizen, 1510), Walter Fyan (citizen, 1508), Henry Gaydon (citizen, 1506) and Oliver Wrentche (citizen, 1500).[34]

The broader strokes of the 1525–6 records show that Dublin merchants mainly exported hides, skins and textiles, with some significant quantities of herring arriving in Chester in the early part of 1526. Ireland had a long-established tradition for selling hides or skins, though many Irish ports other than Dublin were involved in the trade with Bristol and European ports – Carrickfergus, Cork, Drogheda, Galway, Limerick, Waterford, Wexford and Youghal. Known cargoes of Irish hides in the fourteenth century ranged from 3,700 to 13,000. Extraordinarily, peaks of 34,000 and 24,000 Irish hides were imported into Pisa in 1466–7 and 1482–3 respectively.[35] Skins exported in 1525–6 included those from the following animals – badger, calf, deer, fox, goat, lamb, marten, otter and sheep. In the Chester customs records for the year 1525–6 the numbers of hides and skins arriving in Chester from Dublin compare favourably with the fourteenth-century trade mentioned above, with over 4,500 skins and about 300 hides arriving on 25 April on the *Michael of Dublin* and over 10,000 skins passing through customs on 16 June on the same ship.[36] In its only recorded voyage into Chester in 1525–6 the *Michael of Wallasey* carried over 2,200 skins and about 200 hides. The *Patrick of Chester* carried about 860 skins and 400 hides on 16 April and 1,680 skins and 20 hides on 31 May. On 15 August, over 5,850 skins were landed from the

Francis of Dublin.[37] If the visit of the *Mary of Regeston* to Chester on 8 September was from Rogerstown or any other small port in Co. Dublin – Nicholas Gaidon, a citizen of Dublin and a future mayor of the city was on board – then its cargo of more than 5,640 skins and 30 hides would bring the grand total of hide and skin imports from Dublin to Chester in this year to about 34,000 skins and 1,800 hides.[38]

Three merchants contributed markedly to the final skin total that year – Henry Gaidon of Dublin who imported 2,400 skins on 15 August, Nicholas Hankok who brought around 2,570 skins to Chester on 16 June, and Alexander Bexwik who landed almost 4,360 skins on the same day.[39] Bexwik was an energetic merchant, importing goods from Dublin into Chester on eight occasions in 1525–6.[40] Alexander Beswyke was a bailiff in Dublin in 1526, having the confidence of his fellow merchants in being elected to office, and presumably the same man we have been discussing.[41] He was possibly related to Richard Beswik of Manchester, a merchant who in 1495 paid a fine of 20 marks (£13 6s. 8d.) to the Dublin municipal authority to acquire citizenship. Between 1470 and 1500, Richard Bexwick, Thomas Bridde and Richard Tetlow, all Englishmen and described as 'clothiers', were involved in business in Chester. Richard Beswyk also acquired an interest in properties in Dublin before his death in 1511. If known to each other it is likely that Alexander Bexwik would have learned the nuances and needs of the English markets from Richard. While Richard seems to have remained in Manchester in the early years of his citizenship, he took on an apprentice in Dublin, Michael FitzSymon, who became a citizen in 1504. Alexander Bexwik and FitzSymon must have in time become acquainted in Dublin. On 28 August 1526, the two arrived in Chester on the *Trinity of Dublin* and probably worked together in getting Bexwik's goods through customs, FitzSymon importing a token 3 mantles but Bexwik having to deal with 22 items – 11 packs, 9 fardels and two 'cribbes' of glass.[42]

The cargoes of ships sailing from Dublin in the mid-1520s suggest Dublin city and its immediate neighbourhood to have been at that time a market and most probably a manufacturing centre for a range of textiles – blankets, checkers cloth, frieze, fledges, linen, mantles, rugs, yarn and the Irish mantle or heavy woolen garment. Wool was also available and exported. Textile production in Dublin seems to have been at a level that created marketable quantities of flocks (wool refuse or cloth shavings) that were sold abroad – an early example of exported re-usable waste from Dublin. There is every reason to believe that the products listed above must also have been manufactured in Dublin in, for example, the second half of the fifteenth century – the Dublin city franchise roll (1468–1512) lists 8 dyers, 16 shearmen and 17 weavers – and

it should be recalled that Dublin in the time of its first guild merchant, *c.*1190–1265, had a range of skills, and craftsmen remaining in or passing through Dublin, associated with the textile industry – blanket makers (6), dyers (38), fullers (13), mercers (72), weavers (22) and wool beaters (6). A list of textile products and quantities exported to Chester in 1525–6 is in the table below; unfortunately, rug exports cannot be quantified because they were included in a 'checkers and rugs' category (total imports about 800 yards), but fortunately other cargoes of checkers cloth were dealt with separately in the customs records. Noteworthy importation figures at Chester in 1525–6 for Dublin textile products include over 3,200 yards of checkers cloth, over 9,160 lbs of yarn (over 4 tons) and 134 stone or more than three-quarters of a ton of flocks (figure 31).[43]

31 The Irish mantle: a heavy woolen garment popular in Ireland and exported abroad. (Drawing courtesy of Timothy O'Neill, after Dürer.)

Table 9.2 Chester port, 1525–6: imports of textiles, yarn and wool from Dublin[44]

Blankets	46 yards	Flocks	134 stone	Mantles	227
Checkers	3,241 yards	Frieze	121 yards	Wool	213 stone
Fledges	40 yards	Linen	965 yards	Yarn	9,164 lbs

Chester had seen good times but by about 1540 the boom was on the downturn. In the period 1463–1563, Chester's population grew from about 3,000 to about 5,000. It had an undeveloped hinterland that was poorly drained. One of Chester's major roles was to act as an *entrepôt* for inland towns.[45] A number of factors began to interplay and bring about the city's trade decline. Traditionally, it was believed that the silting of the Dee estuary leading to the port of Chester had caused the city's trade slump – the use of anchorages at the outports of West Kirby, Redbank, Heswall, Gayton, Neston, Newquay, Denhall, Burton, Shotwick and Portpool drawing attention to the difficulty of access to the city. While silting was a serious problem, and was to become more serious, Chester had administrative and customs control of the small ports, their imports being brought to Chester in small vessels without customs loss to the city.[46] The bulk of the incoming trade was from Ireland, Brittany, Spain and Portugal. When the continental element of the trade came under threat in a time of worsening political relations with France and Spain in the later years of Henry VIII's reign, the greater proportion of imports came from the Irish and coastal trade. Most of Chester's trade was in the hands of outsiders over which Chester merchants had no control. By about 1550, Irish and coastal trade accounted for 95 per cent of all inward sailings to Chester.[47]

Chester merchants were not inclined to invest in local or Irish trade, preferring to focus on continental ventures. In the fifteenth century they were not shipowners (though they became so in the sixteenth century) and tended to use ships from other ports. When Chester trade began to pick up in the 1490s the local merchants were slow to respond so that in the sixteenth century they were only responsible for little over 10% of the import trade through Chester. Dubliners dominated this trade, particularly in the period between 1520 and 1540; and many of the Dublin merchants sailing to Chester were municipal office-holders in Dublin, as we have seen. By the end of this period, Liverpool port was posing a significant threat to Chester; the council responded in 1541 by commencing a new quay at Neston, ten miles downriver from Chester, but the effort came too late.[48]

After 1450, the trade in exporting salt from Chester to Ireland ceased and Ireland appears to have sourced its salt supplies from France. The tradition of Coventry merchants coming to Dublin or to Chester to acquire Irish wool for the manufacture of Coventry cloth came to an end. It seems that changes in fashion, and competition from the coarse cloths of Worcester, Shrewsbury, Lancashire and Yorkshire, brought about a decline in this aspect of Coventry's trade.[49] From the 1490s, the textile industry had begun to develop in south-east Lancashire, and Liverpool, a rival port on the Mersey estuary, was best located to serve it. From 1500 Drogheda merchants had largely 'abandoned Chester in favour of Liverpool' and by the reign of Edward VI (1537–53) Chester merchants were apprehensive of port activity at Liverpool. By the mid-1530s, Liverpool was described as being the natural entrepôt of Irish yarn, required for the expanding Lancashire cloth industry.[50]

The Henrician Reformation in England

It is worthwhile looking closely at how the Henrician Reformation worked in England – the speed and comprehensiveness with which it took place, the fact that it was based on law and legislation and had the semblance of legality, the doctrinal changes made, and the ruthlessness by which it was accomplished – because it reveals what was likely to be proposed for Ireland.

The unleashing of Protestant ideas and reforms in the 1530s in England, arising from the close cooperation of Henry VIII, Thomas Cromwell, the MP for Taunton who had strong reforming zeal, and Thomas Cranmer, a Cambridge don, the new archbishop of Canterbury who had reforming tendencies, led to revolutionary constitutional and religious changes in England and eventually, and to a lesser degree, in Dublin, the Pale and the English territories in Ireland. Henry had a personal problem – he wished to divorce his wife, Catherine of Aragon, and marry Anne Boleyn. As the 1530s advanced it will be seen that through parliamentary legislation it became legally possible for Henry, married to Catherine of Aragon, to get an annulment and marry again. By 1527, Henry had tired of Catherine and was in love with Anne Boleyn. He began a long six-year search for an annulment that came in 1533 from Thomas Cranmer who also declared as valid Henry's marriage to Anne, which had taken place secretly in January 1533. Thomas Cromwell entered the king's service in 1529 and became a strong advocate of Protestantism and the concept of the royal supremacy in Church and state. In 1535 he became vicar general and vice gerent in spirituals, the chief adviser and instrument of the king in all ecclesiastical matters. He was also the chief intermediary between Henry and the Reformation parliament. Thomas Cranmer, convinced that specifically English matters were not the concern of the pope, gathered university opinion together in favour of the king when his divorce proceedings were not going well. Henry quickly arranged for Cranmer to be consecrated archbishop of Canterbury when the see became vacant. It was Cranmer who was significantly instrumental in overthrowing papal supremacy in England, a Supremacy Act in 1534 declaring Henry 'supreme head' of the English Church, and a Treason Act forbidding denial of the supremacy.[51]

Henry, and indeed Cromwell, were aware of a number of concerns to do with the Church in England and its relationship with Rome – that the clergy took an oath to the pope (and not to the king), that the laws of the Church in England did not depend on royal sanction and that monastic institutions functioned independently of the bishops and were answerable only to official visitors sent by the pope or by the superiors of the orders. The king was also concerned that the annates or first fruits (a portion of the first year's income of a new bishop) were paid to the papacy, that appeals in testamentary and matrimonial cases were sent to Rome, and that approval for a bishop-elect came from the pope. As early as 15 May 1532, the clergy in England surrendered to the demands of Henry and agreed to make no new canon without royal licence and to submit all its existing canons for examination. Effectively, the king was now supreme in all ecclesiastical matters. It is surprising to note that in one decade, the 1530s, a range of bills was drafted by Cromwell and passed in parliament to settle the above issues to the satisfaction of the government. During these years England disentangled itself and the English Church from the clutches of Rome, and by the end of the decade the English Church now found itself subservient to the English state.[52]

By 1536 the Church in England was in an uncertain state, with the king attached to the old faith, Cranmer and Cromwell moderate in reform and extremists using 'wild teaching and revolutionary preaching'. A clear definition of the faith was needed, which came in the form of the Ten Articles of the Church of England issued by the government in July 1536. The sacraments of baptism, penance and the Eucharist were upheld, the Eucharistic presence being described as corporal and substantial, no mention being made of transubstantiation. Justification was said to be attained by contrition and faith joined with charity. Images were allowed as representations of virtue but were not to be worshipped. Using the intercession of the saints, reciting prayers and celebrating Masses for the dead were retained as practices, with a suggestion that prayers to saints and prayers for the dead were of no value. The articles were binding on the clergy.[53]

In the following year, the four lost sacraments were brought back and there was to be a Bible in English placed in every church. In 1538, a royal injunction on ecclesiastical affairs drew attention to superstitious practices, and the use of prayer addressed to the saints in procession was strongly discouraged. Throughout 1538 centres of pilgrimage were attacked, wonder-working images were shown to be bogus by reformers and even Becket's shrine at Canterbury was demolished. He was no longer to be regarded as a saint and his name was to be erased from all liturgical books. His images were to be taken down in all churches and chapels.[54] In Dublin, there would have been a strong tradition of devotion to St Thomas Becket, the church of St Thomas the Martyr having been founded in 1177 by Henry II whose knights murdered Becket in his cathedral in Canterbury in 1170. St Thomas's was soon transformed into an abbey and later generously endowed by King John (plate 12).[55]

A backlash came in 1539. England was divided between the old religion and the emerging reformed Church. The outcome of discussion in parliament and among the bishops showed a majority for orthodoxy supported by a parliamentary statute, the act of six articles, which were doctrinally strongly Catholic in tone. There were penalties for those who opposed the articles, which asserted 'transubstantiation, the need for auricular confession, the sanctity of monastic vows, communion under one kind only, the justness of private Masses, and the illegality of clerical marriage'. Cromwell, despite this loss, did not lose his position, and he and the reformers awaited better times. Still in power, Cromwell ensured that the statute was never fully used against the reformers.[56]

One aspect of the Reformation – the dissolution of the monasteries, which began in 1536 – is especially associated with the Henrician reforms. Attacks on clerical property and the dissolution of monasteries had occurred in the past, Thomas Cromwell having assisted Cardinal Wolsey in suppressing a number of small monasteries to provide college endowments. Monasteries attracted notice in late-medieval times for their wealth, the possible moral laxity of their monks and an undue emphasis on the contemplative. Henry has been accused of using dissolution to augment his treasury; the dissolutions increased the revenue of the Crown by over £100,000 a year (a figure roughly equal to the total royal income in c.1530). Begun in 1536 with the smaller houses the entire process of dissolution was completed by the spring of 1540. From January 1535, evidence against the monasteries was gathered by a group of visitors sent by Cromwell to a fraction of the monasteries involved, one historian putting it that the visitations were 'never intended to mend but always to end' the monastic institutions. True, land and buildings became available for use by others, but buildings, works of art and libraries were also destroyed.[57]

In 1536, the *modus operandi* of the officers of the court of augmentations of the king's revenue became apparent. They visited monasteries, accepted the surrender of the buildings and lands, surveyed the monastic lands, made inventories of lead, gold, silver and precious stones, moved monks to bigger houses, granted pensions to those who wished to leave the religious life or found benefices for those who wished to remain. Monastic debts were paid off by the government. There was opposition, the most notable being a northern rising against the reforms and the dissolutions known as the Pilgrimage of Grace (October 1536 to February 1537). It was put down by the government by using the tactics of stalling and breaking promises. Terror hangings followed in the northern provinces including the executions of the abbots of the bigger monasteries of Kirkstead, Whalley and Jervaux. Throughout, the south had remained tranquil and loyal. Nevertheless, in the autumn of 1539, the abbots of three great abbeys in the south – Glastonbury, Colchester and Reading – were hanged for treasons 'they probably contemplated but barely had yet committed'.[58]

The Reformation comes to Dublin

Henry VIII and Cromwell made plans to extend the Reformation to Ireland. This would need legislation passed in the Irish parliament and the right man on the ground to give leadership. The man they chose to be archbishop of Dublin, where there was a vacancy, was George Browne, an Augustinian friar and committed reformist from London, known personally to Cromwell. He was a professional preacher and was experienced in preaching to socially influential congregations.[59] On Easter Sunday 1533, it was he who announced Henry VIII's marriage to Anne Boleyn, six weeks before Henry's marriage to Catherine of Aragon was annulled.[60] He arrived in Dublin in July 1536 and made a reticent start in his first year.[61]

Dublin was different from London; the Pale was small and Browne would have had no influence on the Irish nation. In Dublin he was resisted by his clergy and opposed by leaders in the Irish administration. Of twenty-eight of his most senior clergy he reported that he could scarcely find one favourable to reform. Lord Deputy Leonard Grey seems to have made no secret of the fact that he was for the old religion, released Catholic dissidents from jail, and believed that, politically, a softer approach was needed in matters of reform to keep the colony together. In difficult circumstances, Browne did not flinch from his pastoral work.[62] In April 1538, he issued a series of injunctions to do with, for example, the royal supremacy and clerical discipline, that the Our Father and the Creed should be taught in English, and that the meaning of the Eucharist should be explained. Later in 1538, 'the second Royal Injunctions of Henry VIII, 1538', published in England in October, were published in Dublin, Carlow, Kilkenny, New Ross, Wexford, Waterford and Clonmel in several of which towns Browne preached. He met with two archbishops and eight bishops in Clonmel and offered them the oath of supremacy which they took.[63]

One of Browne's tasks was to have parish liturgical books censored. However, on 8 January 1538, Browne reported to Cromwell that when he required the 'name of the bishop of Rome', namely, '*Pape*', to be cancelled out of liturgical books, he found that, even though he had sent his own servants to the churches on that specific task, 'my authority is little regarded'. Browne described how he could get no one to preach or support the supremacy of Henry VIII in the Church – 'neither by gentle exhortation, evangelical instruction, neither by oaths of them solemnly taken, nor yet by threats of sharp correction, can I persuade or induce any, either religious or secular, since my coming over, once to preach the word of God or the just title of our most illustrious prince'. He pleaded that he needed the support of the secular powers in the form of shire sheriffs to assist him in implementing the censorship of liturgical books. It is clear from Browne's letter to Cromwell in January that he had been struggling unsuccessfully in this work in 1537.[64]

At the end of 1538, Browne would be required to have feast days excised from liturgical books. Already, in 1536, the feast of St Thomas Becket's translation (7 July), recalling the solemn re-internment of his remains, had been abolished.[65] Now, in 1538, over a number of days in September, Becket's shrine at Canterbury was dismantled.[66] A royal proclamation, dated 16 November 1538, stated that Becket was no longer to be named nor called a saint and that his name be 'erased and put out of all the books …'[67] The Feast of the Relics was to be excised from the Church calendar and books, most probably on foot of a directive in the second Royal Injunctions (1538) which required that 'pilgrimages, fiegned relics, or images, or any such superstitions' were to be recanted and reproved by the clergy.[68] The censorship of liturgical books in Dublin is discussed below.

The first session of the Reformation parliament of 1536–7 worked well, quickly passing legislation dealing with supremacy in the Church and disentangling the Church in the colony from established procedures to do with the papacy and transferring them to the Crown. The bills were prepared in London in the summer of 1535 and brought to Dublin in October by John Alen, master of the rolls. There were six measures in all, designed to correspond with the English legislation in which the royal supremacy was given statutory expression. Each bill was separately concerned with the supremacy, succession, slander (against the monarch), first fruits, appeals, and a faculties or ecclesiastical dispensations bill. Within a month of the first session of parliament opening on 1 May 1536, the first five bills were passed in both houses. The faculties bill was passed in the final session of parliament at the close of 1537.[69] It is worth repeating – the supremacy legislation went through parliament speedily and smoothly.

The passage of the bill 'for the suppression of certain monasteries' in Ireland was not so straightforward. Introduced in the second session of the Reformation parliament in September 1536, it was passed at the close of 1537. Two other bills also under consideration – that a customs levy traditionally spent locally would now go to royal coffers, and that there should be an annual tax of one-twentieth imposed on incomes – were seen by the professional classes, along with the monasteries suppression bill, which would jeopardize their stewardship of monastic leases, as an attack on their vested interests. They decided to resist the monasteries bill. Patrick Barnewall MP from Swords, the king's sergeant-at-law and solicitor-general, was outspoken is his opposition and bravely led a deputation to the king to defend the monasteries.

The government eventually compromised and the commons, seeing that the customs levy bill would now be set aside, and that the one-twentieth tax would apply to the clergy alone, no longer opposed the bill. Late in the day, the bishops mustered some courage along with the clerical proctors but buckled in the presence of royal commissioners sent over by Henry VIII to supervise the autumn session of parliament and conceded the monasteries bill.[70] With negotiation in 1539 it was agreed that six monasteries could remain in certain circumstances in view of the lack of inns and educational centres in Ireland and in Dublin. The three Dublin institutions agreed were St Mary's abbey, the resort of persons of reputation who came to Dublin from England, Christ Church, where the king's deputy often lodged and where parliaments where held, and the convent of Grace Dieu, a centre of education for the young ladies of the Pale. In the case of Christ Church, the Irish council responded to protests in Dublin and it was agreed to constitute it as a secular cathedral according to its original foundation, the clergy accepting membership of the reformed Church.[71]

In 1539, George Browne became a member of two high-powered commissions for the suppression of images (3 February) and for the dissolution of the monasteries (7 April). The work of the commissioners and the measures that they implemented in 1539–40, in particular the destruction of the religious houses of the Pale, resulted in the Henrician Reformation finally getting under way after a wobbly start. It was Browne's best period as a reformer.[72] Lord chancellor John Alen, vice-treasurer William Brabazon, Archbishop George Browne, Robert Cowley, master of the rolls, and Thomas Cusack, an experienced government official, had been empowered as commissioners to take the surrender of all monasteries and to suppress them.[73]

Destruction and urban change in Dublin

The method of taking possession of a monastery or convent, its lands and assets was the same in Ireland as described above for England. Arriving at the house in question, the commissioners would demand the seals of the institution and either break them or keep them for the authorities. All household goods, church goods, including vestments, and harvests were taken to be sold. Lead, bells, plate, jewels, principal ornaments, gold and silver were to be kept for the Crown. Outstanding debts and wages were to be paid. Many monks received pensions. The community were told to depart, the buildings were then locked and held for the king along with its leases and lands.[74]

The city of Dublin benefited directly from the monastery dissolutions act. The buildings, assets, lands and leases of the priory of All Saints (All Hallows) were surrendered by its prior, Walter Hancocke, on 16 November 1538 and granted forever to the mayor, bailiffs, commons and citizens of Dublin by Henry VIII on 4 February 1539.[75] Other former religious-owned buildings and lands were becoming available and those in powerful positions expected that they would receive a grant or that the opportunity might arise by which they could plead their case. Not everyone would be pleased. John Alen, master of the rolls, lawyer and administrator, who hailed from Norfolk, was granted the priory of St Wolstan on the banks of the Liffey, near Celbridge, in 1536, with all its lucrative spiritual and temporal possessions. Later, Alen sought possession of St Thomas's abbey, Dublin, from Cromwell but was disappointed.[76] Making an early plea in 1537, George Browne, archbishop of Dublin, noting that the convent of Grace Dieu, near Lusk, Co. Dublin, was near his manors of Swords and Finglas, wrote to London seeking the convent and its lands should they be suppressed. Suppression came in October 1540 with the formal surrender of the convent by the prioress, Alison White. Browne must have been more than irritated when he heard that the house and lands were to be granted to his old enemy, Patrick Barnewall, the solicitor-general, who earlier had opposed the suppression. In October 1540, the house, church and other buildings of Grace Dieu were reported to be in good condition. After dissolution, Barnewall and his family supported the community of nuns who were relocated to nearby Portrane until they were discovered in 1571.[77] Robert Cowley, government official, sought possession of the priory of Holmpatrick and its lands which he was granted in August 1537; it was to become his residence. In the 1530s, he had been adviser to Cromwell on Irish affairs; later, in 1539, he was made master of the rolls.[78] To William Brabazon came the site and lands of St Thomas's abbey on 31 March 1539 with its lucrative leases. It is no surprise to discover that Brabazon took possession of the abbey a year-and-a-half before it was suppressed. Although he had more than a whiff of corruption about him, he was granted the abbey and its lands for distinguished service: he was vice-treasurer of Ireland, a commissioner to take possession of monasteries, and brave in the field of battle. He also had a powerful patron in Thomas Cromwell.[79]

We have seen how some monastery and convent buildings became homes and residences for the rich and powerful. Not all buildings fared similarly or as well. The priory of friars preachers (Blackfriars or Dominicans) was surrendered on 8 July 1539 and almost immediately the buildings became lodgings for judges and law officers of the Crown, who thought it better to be housed together in one building to do their work more efficiently. The building became known as the King's Inns.[80] In November 1540, the buildings of St Mary's abbey came into the possession of Sir John Travers, master of ordinance in Ireland. The abbey had not been suppressed in the 1537 act but suppression went ahead anyway. The church of the abbey was converted into a storehouse for artillery and military supplies.[81] The properties of the former Franciscan friary in Dublin were leased to a number of individuals in 1541–2, including to Thomas Stephens, a Dublin merchant, who was reported to have pulled down the church and convent and sold the corbels, mullions and marble altars in England. On 15 June 1542, Thomas Luttrell, chief justice of the king's bench, a position to which he was appointed in 1534 in an Irish government re-shuffle by Cromwell, also received former Franciscan land.[82] At the time of the dissolution of the Carmelite monastery of Whitefriars (18 August 1538), 'the church and all other buildings' were already 'thrown down', opportunists presumably having already moved to acquire building materials before the surrender of the buildings. Tellingly, the roofs of the church and other buildings, it was reported, were bought by Nicholas Stanyhurst from William Brabazon, the jurors adding 'but for how much we do not know'. Stanyhurst had earlier been a city bailiff in 1532, was a proctor in the church of St Werburgh in 1540 and became mayor of Dublin in 1542.[83] At the Hospital of St John outside Newgate, a somewhat similar situation was recorded in October 1540 at a sworn extent of its possessions – the church was thrown down after the dissolution and the 'roofing tiles, timber, glass and iron were sold by William Brabazon, sub-treasurer of the exchequer of Ireland, to diverse persons of the city of Dublin, their names and the sums of money paid, the jurors do not know'.[84] Finally, in an extent of the possessions of the convent of St Mary de Hogges, the jurors understood that the church and other buildings were broken down by William Brabazon and that the roofing tiles and timber were carried away by him to Dublin Castle 'where they are kept for the repair of the castle as is understood'. When, in 1550, the convent was in a ruined state with nothing remaining but the walls, Richard Tyant, a Dublin merchant, was successful in applying to the English privy council for permission to set up six looms of linen and woolen yarn on the site to create employment.[85]

It was clear that once the commission for the destruction of the images in Ireland began their work that three great shrines of the Pale would be targeted – the shrine of the *Baculus Ihesu* in Christ Church, Dublin, the Virgin's shrine at Trim, and the shine of the Holy Cross at Ballyboggan near the border of the Pale in Co. Meath. William Brabazon's accounts show that there were visits to these shrines, with a monetary value recorded for whatever precious stones or metals were taken at Trim (£40), at Christ Church (£36) and at Ballyboggan (26s.). When precisely these images were removed and destroyed is not known – Browne is reputed to have burned the *Baculus Ihesu*, possibly in August 1538, the cross at Ballyboggan was reported to have been burned at the suppression of the monasteries, and the statue of the Virgin Mary demolished in May 1539.[86] In England, in July 1538, a headline was set by the destruction of the shrine of Our Lady of Walsingham in Norfolk, a shrine of pilgrimage since the eleventh century. In March, the royal candle was burning before the statue of Our Lady but by July the shrine was dismantled and the statue of Our Lady was brought to London. By the end of the month the Virgin of Walsingham and other images were publicly burned at Chelsea on the instruction of Cromwell who justified his action by stating that 'the people should use no more idolatry unto them'.[87] In the same year, on 20 June, Browne wrote to Cromwell stating that there were rumours that he intended 'to pluck down [the shrine of] Our Lady of Trim' and other shrines of pilgrimage, such as the Holy Cross at Ballyboggan, adding that he had not tried to do so but that 'in conscience he would willingly oppress such idols'.[88] A further 29 shrines were visited and pillaged by the commissioners, with the true figure probably being close to 50 shrines. Many were humble and local in nature.[89]

The commissioners sought out shrines looking for 'jewels and ornaments on profane images'. They went through Crown lands, though not all the English territories, from Carlingford and Dundalk to Kildare, Leighlin and Holy Cross, Co. Tipperary. Churches in Dublin city and county were visited, but there is no record of the commissioners visiting St Canice's in Kilkenny or the shrines of the city of Waterford. The priory of Ballyboggan on the border of the Pale in Co. Meath was visited as were properties in Dublin city, the two cathedrals and St Mary's abbey and St Thomas's abbey from which valuables were removed from shrines. In Co. Dublin, the priory of Kilmainham was visited as were the following parish churches in counties Dublin and Meath whose shrines were stripped of their decoration – Ardcath, Castleknock, Coolmine, Donnybrook, Duleek, Fieldstown, Finglas, Garristown, Greenogue, Newcastle Lyons and Swords. The final return recorded in Brabazon's accounts for the sale of 'jewels and ornaments found on profane images' was £326 2s. 11d., about £450,000 in today's money. The figure could have been higher but for a number of reasons – the custodians of the shrines may have kept ahead of the commissioners and hidden the greater part of their valuables or the commissioners may have exercised moderation in a year of political crisis in which they did not wish to antagonize the colony too much.[90]

The reformers' break with the papacy in England and Ireland, the desecration of the shrine of St Thomas Becket, and the reforms rejecting the use of relics were reflected in the censorship of liturgical books used in Dublin. Deletions of references to the popes followed on from the declaration of the royal supremacy. The results of the work of the sixteenth-century censor can be seen in a number of manuscript volumes; occasionally he was not as diligent as he should have been and some erasures were not made. In a fifteenth-century antiphoner, TCD MS 79, containing a number of books, the property of the church of St John the Evangelist, Dublin, the censor deleted the word 'Pope' wherever it appeared in the calendar and in the same section the festival of the translation of St Thomas of Canterbury (Becket) on 7 July and the rubric directing that the Sunday following should be kept as the Feast of Relics were erased. The festival of the translation of St Thomas commemorated the reburial of the saint's relics at Canterbury on 7 July 1220. Oddly, the main feast day in honour of St Thomas Becket (29 December) and its octave (5 January) were missed by the censor, as were the readings for those saints described as 'Pope and martyr' in the *sanctorale* or book for the variable parts of the Mass peculiar to the saint or festival of the day.[91]

In MS 78 at Trinity College Dublin, an antiphoner discussed above at the beginning of a chapter on the Church, there were a number of erasures by the censor. In the calendar, the word 'Pope' was erased on the feasts of Leo (28 June), Stephen (2 August), Callixtus (14 October), Clement (23 November), Linus (26 November) and Sylvester (30 December). The feast of St Thomas of Canterbury and his translation were not erased.[92] Finally, in a portable breviary of Dublin provenance (*c.*1450–*c.*1500), probably owned by Thomas Pecoke who had served in the church of St Michan in 1477, the censors removed the feast of St Thomas of Canterbury and its octave day from the calendar. A reference to St Thomas's translation day in the calendar was left untouched by the censors (plates 13 & 14).[93]

Epilogue

Other Reformations would come to Dublin. The accession of Edward VI (1547–53) brought further church reform with the introduction of the Book of Common Prayer. Mary (1553–8) restored Catholic worship – there were 'general shouts and acclamations' in Dublin at her accession to the throne. Elizabeth (1558–1603) in turn restored Protestantism and the use of the Book of Common Prayer; traditional Mass vestments were retained for church services and Latin could be used in areas where English was not understood.[94] The privileged merchant class and city rulers in Dublin enjoyed 'a very large measure of independence of the royal administration in Ireland' into the 1570s but faced a downturn in their power in the Stuart period. But for the moment these were good times for the merchant and ruling class in Dublin, many enjoying urban residences, county properties and domestic affluence.[95]

A native of Dublin could be forgiven for enthusing about his home city, which Richard Stanihurst proudly did in Holinshed's Chronicles in 1577. Dublin's geographical setting was, he said, so pleasant, in the fresh water of the Liffey, the view of the sea and the nearness of the hills. Corn and meat were available in abundance in the markets and in the shambles and the mayor was hospitably generous to the nobility and to the powerful. Stanihurst regretted the 'only fault' of the city – the difficulty of navigation in Dublin bay, making the city less attractive to foreign merchants. He was correct in his assessment of Dublin's estuary, the old problem of silting still unsolved, ships sailing for Chester and Liverpool having to negotiate narrow channels around a sand-bar in the bay. Poverty was a problem in the city, the responsibility of alleviating it now falling on the municipal authorities and philanthropists in the absence of the monasteries. Despite the continued sense of decay that remained, with public buildings, walls, gates and towers in a poor state, and the fact that the city was in the first line of the defence of the Pale, Dublin was a place for opportunities – it was Ireland's primary service and administrative centre and a regional and colonial capital.[96]

Notes

INTRODUCTION

1   A.J. Otway-Ruthven, *A history of medieval Ireland* (2nd ed., London, 1980), pp 377–8, 406–8; Henry A. Jefferies, *The Irish Church and the Tudor Reformations* (Dublin, 2010), pp 71–87.
2   C.R. Cheney (ed.) and Michael Jones (rev.), *A handbook of dates for students of British history* (Cambridge, 2000), pp 36–8.
3   Mike Corbishley et al., *The history of Britain and Ireland* (Oxford, 2005), pp 157–60.
4   Ibid., p. 157; Otway-Ruthven, *Medieval Ireland*, p. 386.
5   Kenneth O. Morgan, *The Oxford illustrated history of Britain* (new ed., Oxford, 2009), p. 204.
6   Ibid., p. 204; Seán Duffy, *Ireland in the Middle Ages* (Basingstoke, 1997), p. 173.
7   Otway-Ruthven, *Medieval Ireland*, p. 388.
8   Morgan, *Illustrated history of Britain*, pp 204–7.
9   Art Cosgrove, 'The emergence of the Pale, 1399–1447' in *NHI*, ii, pp 533–56; Duffy, *Middle Ages*, pp 167–8, 170–1, 174–5; *NHI*, ix, pp 477–80.
10 Emmett O'Byrne, *War, politics and the Irish in Leinster* (Dublin, 2003), passim; Howard B. Clarke, 'Cities and their spaces: the hinterlands of medieval Dublin' in Michael Pauly and Martin Scheutz (eds), *Cities and their spaces: concepts and their use in Europe* (Cologne, Weimar and Vienna, 2014), pp 197–215, at pp 213–14.
11 *CARD*, i, pp 327, 328, 355, 357, 381.
12 *DIB*, iii, pp 844–7; Mary Clark and Raymond Refaussé (eds), *Directory of historic Dublin guilds* (Dublin, 1993), pp 41–2; Howard Clarke, 'From Dyflinnarskíri to the Pale: defining and defending a medieval city-state, 1000–1500' in J. Ní Ghrádaigh and E. O'Byrne (eds), *The march in the islands of the medieval West* (Leiden and Boston, 2012), pp 35–52, at p. 51.
13 Steven G. Ellis, *Reform and revival: English government in Ireland, 1470–1534* (Woodbridge, 1986), pp 49–66; Steven G. Ellis, *Ireland in the age of the Tudors, 1447–1603, English expansion and the end of Gaelic rule* (London, 1998), pp 98–118; Steven G. Ellis, 'The great earl of Kildare (1456–1513) and the creation of the English Pale' in Peter Crooks and Seán Duffy (eds), *The Geraldines and medieval Ireland: the making of a myth* (Dublin, 2017), pp 325–40, at p. 332.
14 Claire Walsh, 'Dublin's southern town defences, tenth to fourteenth centuries: the evidence for Ross Road' in Seán Duffy (ed.), *Medieval Dublin II* (Dublin, 2001), pp 88–127; Margaret Gowan, Linzi Simpson, et al., *Conservation plan: Dublin city walls and defences* (Dublin, 2004); Linzi Simpson, 'The medieval city wall and the southern line of defences: excavations at 14–16 Werburgh Street' in Seán Duffy (ed.), *Medieval Dublin VIII* (Dublin, 2008), pp 150–77.
15 Henry F. Berry (ed.), *Register of wills and inventories of the diocese of Dublin in the time of archbishops Tregury and Walton, 1457–1483* (Dublin, 1898), pp 83–5.
16 Walter Harris (ed.), *Hibernica; or, Some antient pieces relating to Ireland* (1st ed., Dublin, 1747–50), pp 59, 70–1; K.P. Wilson (ed.), *Chester customs accounts, 1301–1566* (Liverpool, 1969), pp 120–1.
17 Chester city records office, Chester: sheriffs' books, ZSB 3, ff 71–74 (1476–7); sheriffs' books, ZSB 3, ff 75–83 (1476–7), passim.
18 Colm Lennon and James Murray (eds), *The Dublin city franchise roll, 1468–1512* (Dublin, 1998), p. 77.

19   Berry, *Wills and inventories*, pp 8–11, 76–8, 128–33.

20   Lennon and Murray, *Dublin franchise roll*, p. 77.

21   J. Gilbart Smyly, 'Old deeds in the library of Trinity College – IV', *Hermathena*, 70 (1947), pp 1–21, at p. 17.

22   Lennon and Murray, *Dublin franchise roll*, pp xvii–xviii.

23   *CARD*, i, pp 139–40.

24   Lennon and Murray, *Dublin franchise roll*, p. xv.

25   *CARD*, i, pp 271–409, passim.

26   Giles Dawkes, 'Interim results of excavations at 152–5 Church Street, Dublin: St Michan's early enclosure and late medieval timber-framed buildings' in Seán Duffy (ed.), *Medieval Dublin X* (Dublin, 2010), pp 198–219, at pp 217–19.

27   Berry, *Wills and inventories*, pp 156–8; Howard Clarke, Sarah Dent and Ruth Johnson, *Dublinia: the story of medieval Dublin* (Dublin, 2002), p. 116.

28   Jefferies, *The Irish Church and the Tudor Reformations*, pp 77–8; *NHI*, viii, pp 198–9.

29   Myles V. Ronan, *The Reformation in Dublin, 1536–1558 (from original sources)* (London, 1926), pp 468–9.

30   Ibid., pp 493–4.

31   Ibid., pp 209–10, 179.

32   Charles McNeill, 'Accounts of sums realized by sales of chattels of some suppressed Irish monasteries', *JRSAI*, 6th series, 12:1 (June 1922), pp 11–37.

33   Fred E. Dukes, *Campanology in Ireland* (Dublin, 1994), pp 136–8; Clarke, Dent and Johnson, *Dublinia*, p. 116; Caitriona McLeod, 'Fifteenth-century vestments in Waterford', *JRSAI*, 82 (1952), pp 85–98; Eamonn McEneaney and Rosemary Ryan (eds), *Waterford treasures* (Waterford, 2004), pp 90–107; for frankincense, see Adrian Empey (ed.), *The proctors' accounts of the parish church of St Werburgh, Dublin, 1481–1627* (Dublin, 2009), pp 57, 63, 81; William Hawkes, 'The liturgy in Dublin, 1200–1500: manuscript sources', *Reportorium Novum*, 2:1 (1958), pp 33–67, passim.

34   M.J. McEnery and Raymond Refaussé (eds), *Christ Church deeds* (Dublin, 2001), no. 312; Empey, *Proctors' accounts*, pp 59–60, 62, 68, 75.

35   Henry A. Jefferies, *Priests and prelates of Armagh in the age of Reformations* (Dublin, 1997), pp 26–38; *Stat. Ire., Rich. III–Hen. VIII*, pp 129–31.

36   F.D. Logan, *Excommunication and the secular arm in medieval England* (Toronto, 1968), passim; *Stat. Ire., Hen. VI*, pp 655, 657.

37   Sparky Booker, 'An English city? Gaelicization and cultural exchange in late medieval Dublin' in Seán Duffy (ed.), *Medieval Dublin X* (Dublin, 2010), pp 287–98; Sparky Booker, 'Irish clergy and the diocesan church in the "four obedient shires" of Ireland, *c.*1400–*c.*1540', *IHS*, 39:154 (Nov. 2014), pp 179–209; Sparky Booker, *Cultural exchange and identity in late medieval Ireland: the English and Irish of the four obedient shires* (Cambridge, 2018); *CARD*, i, passim.

38   Howard B. Clarke, '*Angliores ipsis Anglis*: the place of medieval Dubliners in English history' in Howard B. Clarke, Jacinta Prunty and Mark Hennessy (eds), *Surveying Ireland's past: multidisciplinary essays in honour of Anngret Simms* (Dublin, 2004), pp 41–72, at pp 56, 58–60, 62–3.

39   Booker, *Cultural exchange and identity*, pp 219, 228–30, 235.

40   Lennon and Murray, *Dublin franchise roll*, pp 12, 16, 30, for members of the Harold family; Steven G. Ellis, *The Pale and the far north: government and society in two early Tudor borderlands* (Galway, 1988), pp 28–9.

41   Lennon and Murray, *Dublin franchise roll*, pp 22, 24–5, 28, for Leghlyn, Kenan, Berne, Neell; Booker, 'An English city?', pp 294–5.

42 Ronan, *Reformation in Dublin*, pp 156, 185–6, 191–2; for Alen, *DIB*, i, pp 69–70; for Cowley, *DIB*, ii, pp 927–8.

43 Charles Smith, 'Patricians in medieval Dublin: the career of the Sargent family' in Seán Duffy (ed.), *Medieval Dublin XI* (Dublin, 2011), pp 219–28; Brian Coleman, 'Urban elite: the county and civic elite of later medieval Dublin' in Seán Duffy (ed.), *Medieval Dublin XV* (Dublin, 2016), pp 293–304; Colm Lennon, *The lords of Dublin in the age of Reformation* (Dublin, 1989).

44 Lynda Conlon, 'Women in medieval Dublin: their legal rights and economic power' in Seán Duffy (ed.), *Medieval Dublin IV* (Dublin, 2003), pp 172–92, at pp 172–3, 176.

45 Conlon, 'Women in medieval Dublin', p. 179; Berry, *Wills and inventories*, p. 157.

46 Conlon, 'Women in medieval Dublin', pp 179–80, 182.

47 Conlon, 'Women in medieval Dublin', p. 185; Berry, *Wills and inventories*, passim.

48 Berry, *Wills and inventories*, pp 15–18, 38–41, 85–9.

49 Ibid., pp 13–15, 58–60, 102–3, 112–13, 142–4, 151–3.

50 Ibid., pp 128–33.

51 *Stat. Ire., John–Hen. V*, p. 489.

52 Mark Bailey, *Medieval Suffolk: economic and social history, 1200–1500* (Woodbridge, Suffolk, 2007), p. 159.

53 Berry, *Wills and inventories*, pp 65–6, 142–4.

54 Ibid., pp 113–15, 133–6.

55 Ibid., pp 41–5.

56 Barbara A. Hanawalt, *The ties that bound: peasant families in medieval England* (Oxford, 1986), p. 95.

57 Richard Britnell, *Britain and Ireland, 1050–1530: economy and society* (Oxford, 2004), p. 175.

58 Berry, *Wills and inventories*, passim.

59 Ibid., pp 128–33.

60 Ibid., passim.

61 John D. Seymour, 'James Yonge, a fifteenth century Dublin writer', *JRSAI*, 6th series, 16:1 (June 1926), pp 48–50, at p. 48; Caoimhe Whelan, 'James Yonge and the writing of history in late medieval Dublin' in Seán Duffy (ed.), *Medieval Dublin XIII* (Dublin, 2013), pp 183–95; Theresa O'Byrne, 'Manuscript creation in Dublin: the scribe of Bodleian e. Museo MS 232 and Longleat MS 29' in Kathryn Kerby-Fulton, John J. Thompson and Sarah Baechle (eds), *New directions in medieval manuscript studies and reading practices: essays in honour of Derek Pearsall* (Notre Dame, 2014), pp 271–91, at p. 284; Theresa O'Byrne, '*I. Yonge scripsit*: self promotion, professional networking, and the Anglo-Irish literary scribe' in Seán Duffy (ed.), *Medieval Dublin XVII* (Dublin, 2019).

62 O'Byrne, 'Manuscript creation in Dublin', pp 273, 279–81.

63 O'Byrne, 'Manuscript creation in Dublin', pp 273–4.

64 *CARD*, i, pp 237–8.

65 Ibid., pp 247–8.

66 Ibid., p. 249; H.B. Clarke, *IHTA, no. 11, Dublin part I, to 1610* (Dublin, 2002), map 4.

67 Paul Dryburgh and Brendan Smith (eds), *Handbook and select calendar of sources for medieval Ireland in the National Archives of the United Kingdom* (Dublin, 2005), pp 230–8.

68 Howard Clarke, 'Street life in medieval Dublin' in H.B. Clarke and J.R.S. Phillips (eds), *Ireland, England and the Continent in the Middle Ages and beyond: essays in memory of a turbulent friar, F.X. Martin OSA* (Dublin, 2006), pp 145–63, at pp 155–7.

69 Dianne Hall, 'Everyday violence in medieval Dublin' in Seán Duffy (ed.), *Medieval Dublin XV* (Dublin, 2016), pp 305–19, at pp 307–13.

70 Áine Foley, 'Violent crime in medieval Co. Dublin: a symptom of degeneracy?' in Seán Duffy (ed.), *Medieval Dublin X* (Dublin, 2010), pp 220–40, passim.

71 Alan J. Fletcher, 'What a performance!: street entertainment in medieval and Renaissance Dublin' in Máire Kennedy and Alastair Smeaton (eds), *The Sir John T. Gilbert commemorative lectures, 1998–2007* (Dublin, 2009), pp 27–43, at pp 29–31.

72 Howard B. Clarke, '*Urbs et suburbium*: beyond the walls of medieval Dublin' in Conleth Manning (ed.), *Dublin and beyond the Pale: studies in honour of Patrick Healy* (Bray, 1998), pp 45–58, at p. 56; Clarke, *IHTA, Dublin part I, to 1610*, p. 29; Henry Berry, 'History of the religious guild of St Anne in St Audoen's church, Dublin, 1430–1740, taken from its records in the Halliday collection, RIA', *PRIA*, 25C (1904–5), pp 21–106, at p. 66.

73 *CARD*, i, p. 383.

74 *CARD*, i, pp 326, 329, 333; Clarke, *IHTA, Dublin part I, to 1610*, map 4; James Mills (ed.), and James Lydon and Alan J. Fletcher (intro.), *Account roll of the priory of Holy Trinity, Dublin, 1337–1346* (Dublin, 1996), p. xli.

75 *Account roll of Holy Trinity priory*, pp xxxiii, xxxiv.

76 Newport B. White (ed.), *Extents of Irish monastic possessions, 1540–1541, from manuscripts in the Public Record Office, London* (Dublin, 1943), p. 57.

77 Howard B. Clarke, 'The mapping of medieval Dublin: a case-study in thematic cartography' in H.B. Clarke and Anngret Simms (eds), *The comparative history of urban origins in non-Roman Europe: Ireland, Wales, Denmark, Germany, Poland and Russia from the ninth to the thirteenth century* (2 parts, Oxford, 1985), part ii, pp 617–43, at pp 618–20.

78 J.H. Andrews, 'The oldest map of Dublin', *PRIA*, 53C (1983), pp 205–37, at p. 210.

79 Clarke, 'Mapping of medieval Dublin', p. 620.

80 John Montague, '"But what about the earlier city?": John Rocque's *Exact Survey* (1756) as a source for medieval Dublin' in Seán Duffy (ed.), *Medieval Dublin XIII* (Dublin, 2013), pp 196–245, at p. 245; Clarke, 'Mapping of medieval Dublin', pp 618, 629, 633.

81 Clarke, 'Mapping of medieval Dublin', pp 637–8; Clarke, *IHTA, Dublin part I, to 1610*, map 4, which carries a note on editions.

82 H.B. Clarke, *Dublin c.840 to c.1540: the medieval town in the modern city* (2nd. ed., Dublin, 2002).

83 Linzi Simpson, 'Forty years a-digging: a preliminary synthesis of archaeological investigations in medieval Dublin' in Seán Duffy (ed.), *Medieval Dublin I* (Dublin, 2000), pp 11–68; Linzi Simpson, 'Fifty years a-digging: a synthesis of medieval archaeological investigations in Dublin city and suburbs' in Seán Duffy (ed.), *Medieval Dublin XI* (Dublin, 2011), pp 9–112.

84 Clarke, *IHTA, Dublin part I, to 1610*, map 4.

85 Clarke, *Dublin, the medieval town in the modern city*, p. 10.

86 Giles Dawkes, 'Interim results of excavations at 152–5 Church Street, Dublin', pp 217–19.

87 Archaeological collection, DCAA 02.01, Dublin City Archaeological Archive, Dublin City Library and Archive.

88 Clarke, *IHTA, Dublin part I, to 1610*, p. 3.

89 Anngret Simms, 'Origins and early growth' in Joseph Brady and Anngret Simms (eds), *Dublin through space and time (c.900–1900)* (Dublin, 2001), pp 15–65, at p. 25.

90 Clarke, *IHTA, Dublin part I, to 1610*, pp 6–7, and map 4; Clarke, *Dublin, the medieval town in the modern city*, map 4, passim; Clarke, Dent and Johnson, *Dublinia*, pp 32–3.

91 Clarke, *IHTA, Dublin part I, to 1610*, p. 6 and map 4.

92 Ibid., map 4.

93 Berry, *Wills and inventories*, p. 202.

94 Clarke, *IHTA, Dublin part I, to 1610*, pp 6, 8, 9, 28, and map 4.

95 Ann Lynch and Conleth Manning, 'Excavations at Dublin Castle, 1985–7' in Seán Duffy (ed.), *Medieval Dublin II* (Dublin, 2001), pp 169–204, at pp 170, 172, 174; Clarke, *IHTA, Dublin part I, to 1610*, p. 6.

96 Ann Lynch and Conleth Manning, 'Dublin Castle: the archaeological project', *Archaeology Ireland*, 4:2 (summer 1990), pp 65–8, at p. 65; *NHI*, ii, p. 175; Clarke, *IHTA, Dublin part I, to 1610*, p. 6.

97 Conleth Manning and Emer Condit, 'Heritage guide no. 14: the Powder Tower, Dublin Castle', *Archaeology Ireland* (Sept. 2001), pp 1–5, at p. 3.

98 Lynch and Manning, 'Dublin Castle project', pp 65–6, 68.

99 Ibid., p. 66.

100 Philomena Connolly (ed.), *Irish exchequer payments, 1270–1446* (2 vols, Dublin, 1998), ii, pp 552, 564–5, 568–9.

101 *NHI*, ii, p. 664.

102 Simms, 'Origins and early growth', pp 49–50.

103 Richard Harris, *Discovering timber-framed buildings* (3rd ed., Oxford, 1993), pp 3, 20–1.

104 Simms, 'Origins and early growth', p. 49.

105 Ibid., pp 49–50.

106 Clarke, *IHTA, Dublin part I, to 1610*, pp 29–30.

107 *Christ Church deeds*, nos. 1011, 1047, 1072.

108 Peadar Slattery, 'The timber and wood trade, woodlands, house building and repairs in the English colony in Ireland, *c.*1350–*c.*1570, part II', *JRSAI*, 144–5 (2014–15), pp 90–9, at p. 91.

109 *CARD*, i, pp 12–18, 24–5, 28–9, 32.

110 Jane Laughton, *Life in a medieval city: Chester, 1275–1520* (Oxford, 2008), p. 61.

111 Alan J. Fletcher, *Drama, performance, and polity in pre-Cromwellian Ireland* (Cork, 2000), pp 109, 112–13.

112 *CARD*, i, p. 24.

113 Howard B. Clarke, 'The four parts of the city: high life and low life in the suburbs of medieval Dublin' in Kennedy and Smeaton (eds), *Gilbert commemorative lectures*, pp 57–78, at pp 63–4; Howard B. Clarke, 'Myths, magic and the Middle Ages: Dublin from its beginnings to 1577' in Howard B. Clarke, *Irish cities* (Cork and Dublin, 1995), pp 82–95, at p. 91; Simms, 'Origins and early growth', p. 50; Clarke, *IHTA, Dublin part I, to 1610*, map 4.

114 Clarke, 'The four parts of the city', pp 64–6; Clarke, 'Myths, magic and the Middle Ages', p. 92; Simms, 'Origins and early growth', p. 51; Clarke, *Dublin part I, to 1610*, map 4.

115 Clarke, 'The four parts of the city', p. 66; Clarke, 'Myths, magic and the Middle Ages', p. 92; Simms, 'Origins and early growth', p. 51; Clarke, *Dublin part I, to 1610*, map 4.

116 Clarke, 'The four parts of the city', pp 66–7; Simms, 'Origins and early growth', pp 50–1; Clarke, 'Myths, magic and the Middle Ages', p. 92; Clarke, *IHTA, Dublin part I, to 1610*, map 4; Áine Foley, *The abbey of St Thomas the Martyr, Dublin* (Dublin, 2017).

117 H.B. Clarke (ed.), *Medieval Dublin: the living city* (Dublin, 1990); H.B. Clarke, (ed.), *Medieval Dublin: the making of a metropolis* (Dublin, 1990); Seán Duffy (ed.), 'Medieval Dublin series I–X' (index to the first ten volumes) in Seán Duffy (ed.), *Medieval Dublin X* (Dublin, 2010), pp 313–26.

CHAPTER 1

Dublin, a Royal English City

1 Michael Bennett, *Lambert Simnel and the battle of Stoke* (Gloucester, 1987), pp 5–7.

2 Bennett, *Simnel*, p. 6; *NHI*, viii, p. 176.

3   F.X. Martin, 'The crowning of a king at Dublin, 24 May 1487', *Hermathena*, 144 (summer 1988), pp 7–34, at p. 12.

4   *NHI*, viii, p. 77; *NHI*, ii, p. 141.

5   James Lydon, 'Christ Church in the later medieval Irish world, 1300–1500' in Kenneth Milne (ed.), *Christ Church cathedral, Dublin* (Dublin, 2000), pp 75–94 at p. 85.

6   Milne, 'Priors and deans' in Milne, *Christ Church cathedral*, pp 391–2, at p. 391; Empey, *Proctors' accounts*, pp 47, 63, 72; rushes were used as a floor covering in St Werburgh's in the 1480s and 1490s, and regularly replaced.

7   Bennett, *Simnel*, pp 5–6; Martin, 'Crowning of a king' p. 23; *NHI*, ix, p. 506.

8   Martin, 'Crowning of a king', p. 26; Mary Hayden, 'Lambert Simnel in Ireland', *Studies: an Irish Quarterly Review*, 4:16 (Dec. 1915), pp 622–38, at p. 630.

9   Bennet, *Simnel*, p. 6; Hayden, 'Simnel in Ireland', pp 626–7; *NHI*, ii, p. 612, in which the priest is named as 'Richard Symonds'.

10 Hayden, 'Simnel in Ireland', pp 626–7; Mario Sughi, 'The appointment of Octavian de Palatio as archbishop of Armagh, 1477–8', *IHS*, 31:122 (1998), pp 145–64.

11 Bennett, *Simnel*, p. 6; Martin, 'Crowning of a king', pp 21–2, 28.

12 Martin, 'Crowning of a king', pp 19–21; Hayden, 'Simnel in Ireland', pp 624–5.

13 *NHI*, ii, p. 612.

14 Hayden, 'Simnel in Ireland', p. 626.

15 Bennett, *Simnel*, p. 6; Martin, 'Crowning of a king', pp 22–3.

16 Martin, 'Crowning of a king', pp 25–9.

17 Ibid., p. 28.

18 Hayden, 'Simnel in Ireland', pp 624, 632.

19 Bennett, *Simnel*, p. 123.

20 Hayden, 'Simnel in Ireland', p. 633.

21 Ibid.

22 *NHI*, ii, p. 613.

23 Ibid., p. 614.

24 Hayden, 'Simnel in Ireland', p. 634.

25 Harris (ed.), *Hibernica*, pp 62–3; Lennon and Murray, *Dublin franchise roll*, p. 13.

26 Harris (ed.), *Hibernica*, p. 63.

27 Ibid., pp 63–9; *NHI*, viii, p. 177.

28 *CARD*, i, p. 171.

29 Harris (ed.), *Hibernica*, p. 67.

30 *CARD*, i, pp 33, 171, 369–70.

31 Lennon and Murray, *Dublin franchise roll*, p. xv.

32 Ibid., p. 82; *NHI*, ii, pp 144–6; *CARD*, i, p. 287.

33 *NHI*, ii, pp 533, 536–7.

34 *CARD*, i, pp 30–1.

35 *NHI*, ii, pp 636–7.

36 Seán Duffy, 'Town and crown: the kings of England and their city of Dublin' in Michael Prestwich, Richard Britnell & Robin Frame (eds), *Thirteenth century England, X: Proceedings of the Durham conference, 2003* (Woodbridge, 2005), pp 95–117, at p. 95; Clarke, 'Myths, magic and the Middle Ages', pp 90–1; *NHI*, ii, pp 94–5.

37 Clarke, *Cities*, pp 90–1.

38 H.B. Clarke, 'The 1192 charter of liberties and the beginnings of Dublin's municipal life', *DHR*, 46:1 (spring 1993), pp 5–14, at pp 7–8.

39 *CARD*, i, pp 1–2.

40 Ibid., p. 2.

41   Clarke, 'The 1192 charter of liberties', pp 8, 9, 13.

42   Duffy, 'Town and crown', pp 106–7.

43   J.T. Gilbert (ed.), *Historical and municipal documents of Ireland, 1172–1320* (Dublin, 1870), p. 55; *NHI*, ix, p. 470.

44   *CARD*, i, pp 2–6.

45   Clarke, 'The 1192 charter of liberties', p. 5.

46   *CARD*, i, p. 4.

47   Ibid., i, p. 5; Clarke, 'The 1192 charter of liberties', p. 5.

48   John J. Webb, *Municipal government in Ireland: medieval and modern* (Dublin, 1918), p. 21; Duffy, 'Town and crown', p. 108.

49   Webb, *Municipal government*, p. 26.

50   Ibid., pp 23–4.

51   Ibid., pp 26–7.

52   *CARD*, i, pp 6–7.

53   Duffy, 'Town and crown', pp 110–11.

54   Gilbert, *Historical and municipal documents*, p. 64; I am grateful to Dr Peter Crooks for identifying the witnesses.

55   R. Dudley Edwards, 'The beginnings of municipal government in Ireland' in Clarke (ed.), *Medieval Dublin: the living city*, pp 145–52, at p. 149.

56   *CARD*, i, p. 8.

57   W.G. Strickland, 'The ancient official seals of the city of Dublin' in Clarke (ed.), *Medieval Dublin: the living city*, pp 163–71, at pp 163–4.

58   *CDI*, i, no. 935; Webb, *Municipal government*, p. 19; the terms 'jurat' or 'juré' are synonyms, both terms being used in this work depending on the contemporary source in use.

59   R. Dudley Edwards, 'An early town council in Dublin', letter to the editor of the *Times Literary Supplement*, 31 July 1937.

60   *CARD*, i, p. 231.

61   Webb, *Municipal government*, pp 19–20.

62   *CARD*, i, pp 219, 225.

63   Ibid., i, pp 271–408.

64   Ibid., i, pp 81–267.

65   *NHI*, ii, pp 714–15.

66   Lennon and Murray, *Dublin franchise roll*, p. 85; *CARD*, i, p. 334, for example.

67   *CARD*, i, p. 273.

68   Ibid., i, pp 305, 327, 334, 346, 368, 375.

69   Ibid., i, pp 222–3, 363–4, 367–8.

70   Lennon and Murray, *Dublin franchise roll*, p. 82.

71   *CARD*, i, p. 272.

72   Lennon and Murray, *Dublin franchise roll*, p. 82.

73   Ibid., p. xvi.

74   Ibid., p. 85.

75   *CARD*, i, p. 283.

76   *CARD*, i, pp 29–30.

77   *CARD*, i, p. 31.

78   Ibid., i, pp 31–2.

79   *CARD*, i, passim.

80   Ibid., i, pp 290, 336.

81   *CARD*, i, p. 314.

82   Ibid., p. 322; Clarke, *IHTA, Dublin part I, to 1610*, map 4.

83   *CARD*, i, pp 372, 374, 377.

84   Ibid., p. 287.

85   Ibid., i, pp 223, 296; generally, in the quoted material, place name spelling has been modernized or modern street names have been inserted in brackets to assist identification and location; 'Boue' Street had many spelling variations including, for example, 'Booth' Street.

86   *Stat. Ire., John–Hen. V*, pp 255–6.

87   *CARD*, i, p. 296.

88   Ibid., i, pp 320–1.

89   Ibid., pp 295–6, 320.

90   Barra Boydell, 'Dublin city musicians in the late Middle Ages and Renaissance, to 1660', *DHR*, 34:2 (Mar. 1981), pp 42–53, at pp 42–3.

91   *CARD*, i, p, 320; Fletcher, *Drama, performance, and polity in pre-Cromwellian Ireland*, pp 148–50.

92   *CARD*, i, p. 332; Lennon and Murray, *Dublin franchise roll*, p. 2, for Bennet, Clare and Talbot.

93   *CARD*, i, pp 242, 393.

94   Boydell, 'Dublin city musicians', pp 43–4.

95   Clarke, *IHTA, Dublin part I, to 1610*, map 4; H.F. Berry, 'The water supply of ancient Dublin', *JRSAI*, 1:7 (1891), pp 557–73, at p. 563; M.V. Ronan, 'The Poddle river and its branches', *JRSAI*, 17:1 (1927), pp 39–46, at p. 39.

96   Don McEntee and Michael Corcoran, *The rivers Dodder and Poddle* (Dublin, 2016), pp 56–7; Valentine Jackson, 'The inception of the Dodder water supply' in Clarke (ed.), *Dublin: the making of a metropolis*, pp 128–41, at pp 129–30, 135.

97   *CARD*, i, p. 92; Jackson, 'Dodder water', pp 130–3.

98   Ronan, 'Poddle river', p. 39.

99   *CARD*, i, pp 88–9, 96, 101–2.

100   Ibid., pp 292–3, 361.

101   Berry, 'Water supply of Dublin', pp 566–7.

102   *CARD*, i, pp 289, 372–3.

103   Ibid., pp 345–6.

104   Ibid., pp 325, 373–4.

105   *CARD*, i, pp 238–9; for the thirteenth-century development of the port of Dublin see: Andrew Halpin (ed.), *The port of medieval Dublin: archaeological excavations at the civic offices, Winetavern Street, Dublin, 1993* (Dublin, 2000), passim.

106   *CARD*, i, pp 274, 279.

107   Ibid., pp 295, 351.

108   Ibid., i, pp 286, 291, 295; I am grateful to Dr Theresa O'Byrne who has described Bellewe's profession as a scribe and his connection with Philip Bellewe, mayor, in her paper 'T. Yonge scripsit: self promotion, professional networking, and the Anglo-Irish scribe', delivered at Trinity College Dublin, on 21 May 2016 at the annual Medieval Dublin conference.

109   *CARD*, i, pp 310, 351.

110   Colin FitzPatrick, 'Food and drink: Ireland's overseas trade in the later Middle Ages' (PhD, TCD, 2015), pp 221–2.

111   *CARD*, i, p. 336.

112   FitzPatrick, 'Food and drink', p. 222.

113   *CARD*, i, p. 300.

114   Ibid., i, pp 299–300.

115   James Davis, *Medieval market morality* (Cambridge, 2012), p. 159.

116 *CARD*, i, p. 284.

117 Ibid., p. 312.

118 Ibid., pp 312, 318.

119 Ibid., pp 323, 324, 357 (1480), 364, 378 (1493).

120 Ibid., pp 278, 283, 286, 290, 329, 341, 380.

121 Ibid., p. 298.

122 Ibid., pp 139–40, 333, 375.

123 Ibid., p. 306.

124 Ibid., pp 221, 326–7.

125 Ibid., pp 328–9.

126 Ibid., p. 370.

127 *CARD*, i, p. 382; the word 'anent' means 'opposite'; see Terence Patrick Dolan, *A dictionary of Hiberno-English: the Irish use of English* (3rd ed., Dublin, 2012).

128 *CARD*, i, pp 139–40.

129 *Stat. Ire., Hen. VI*, pp 403, 405.

130 *CARD*, i, pp 280–1.

131 O'Byrne, 'Manuscript creation in Dublin', p. 272.

132 Booker, *Cultural exchange and identity*, pp 8–9.

133 Robin Frame, *Colonial Ireland, 1169–1369* (2nd ed., Dublin, 2012), pp 136–9.

134 Booker, *Cultural exchange and identity*, p. 9.

135 Ibid., pp 15, 45–7.

136 Ibid., pp 49–50; Dryburgh and Smith, *Handbook and select calendar*, pp 263–5; Edmund Curtis, ed., *Calendar of Ormond deeds*, iii (Dublin, 1935), no. 245, at pp 223–5.

137 Booker, *Cultural exchange and identity*, pp 52, 61–2, 64, 71.

138 Henry F. Berry, 'The records of the Dublin guild of merchants, known as the guild of the Holy Trinity, 1438–1671', *JRSAI*, 5th series, 10:1 (Mar. 1900), pp 44–68, at p. 49, for Shynnagh; Eoin C. Bairéad, 'The bailiffs, provosts and sheriffs of the city of Dublin' in Seán Duffy (ed.), *Medieval Dublin XIV* (Dublin, 2015), pp 210–309, at pp 290–1.

139 Lennon and Murray, *Dublin franchise roll*, p. 10 (Mulghan and Danyell), p. 11 (Ingerame).

140 *CARD*, i, p. 314; Booker, 'An English city?', p. 297.

141 *CARD*, i, p. 326; Booker, 'An English city?', pp 296–7.

142 Lennon and Murray, *Dublin franchise roll*, p. 21.

143 Ibid., p. 22.

144 Ibid., p. 2.

145 Booker, *Cultural exchange and identity*, pp 216, 220–1; Caoimhe Whelan, 'James Yonge and the writing of history in late medieval Dublin' in Seán Duffy (ed.), *Medieval Dublin XIII* (Dublin, 2013), pp 183–95, at p. 183.

146 Booker, *Cultural exchange and identity*, pp 219, 228–30, 235.

147 Lennon and Murray, *Dublin franchise roll*, pp 12, 16, 30, for the Harold family; Ellis, *The Pale and the far north*, pp 28–9.

148 Booker, 'An English city?', p. 294.

149 Ibid., p. 295.

150 *CARD*, i, p. 330.

151 Ibid., pp 352–3.

152 Lennon and Murray, *Dublin franchise roll*, pp 22, 25, 28; Booker, 'An English city?', p. 290.

153 *CARD*, i, p. 281.

154 Ibid., pp 281, 286–7.

155 Ibid., p. 298.

156 *Stat. Ire., 1–12 Edw. IV*, p. 291.

157 Steven G. Ellis and James Murray (eds), *Calendar of state papers, Ireland, Tudor period, 1509–1547* (rev. ed., Dublin, 2017), p. 141.
158 *CARD*, i, p. 328.
159 *Stat. Ire., 1–12 Edw. IV*, pp 809, 811.
160 Clark and Refaussé, *Historic Dublin guilds*, p. 41; *CARD*, i, p. 325; *Stat. Ire., 1–12 Edw. IV*, p. 293.
161 Clark and Refaussé, *Historic Dublin guilds*.
162 James Lydon, 'The defence of Dublin in the Middle Ages' in Seán Duffy (ed.), *Medieval Dublin IV* (Dublin, 2003), pp 63–78, at p. 77.
163 Clark and Refaussé, *Historic Dublin guilds*, pp 41–2.
164 *CARD*, i, pp 141–2.
165 Clark and Refaussé, *Historic Dublin guilds*, p. 42.
166 *Stat. Ire., 1–12 Edw. IV*, pp 797, 799; *CARD*, i, pp 360–1.
167 *CARD*, i, p. 355.
168 Ibid., p. 381.

CHAPTER 2

Merchants and Commerce in Dublin

1   The National Archives (London), indictments rolls, CHES 25/15, m. 30d, m. 31; Laughton, *Life in a medieval city*, p. 173.
2   Lennon and Murray, *Dublin franchise roll*, p. 10 (Cantwell), pp 7, 16 (Sweteman), p. 15 (Berefote), pp 4, 24 (West), pp 14, 19 (Bradok), pp 8, 16 (FitzLeones), p. 9 (Forster), p. 9 (Feypow), pp 6, 8, 12 (Parker), pp 1, 19, 59 (Walsh), pp 1, 16 (Hegley), p. 10 (Fouler), p. 14 (Denys).
3   See above list and its references.
4   Bairéad, 'Bailiffs, provosts and sheriffs', p. 291.
5   Chester city records, sheriffs' books, ZSB 3, ff 75–83 (1476–7).
6   Bairéad, 'Bailiffs, provosts and sheriffs', p. 291; Lennon and Murray, *Dublin franchise roll*, pp 8, 16, 18, 26, 31, for Patrick FitzLeones.
7   Lennon and Murray, *Dublin franchise roll*, p. xv.
8   *IHTA, Dublin part I, to 1610*, map 4.
9   L.F. Salzman, *English trade in the Middle Ages* (Oxford, 1931), pp 177–8.
10 Salzman, *English trade*, pp 171–2.
11 Ibid., pp 31–2.
12 Charles Gross, 'The court of pie powder', *Quarterly Journal of Economics*, 20:2 (Feb. 1906), pp 231–49, at p. 243.
13 Gross, 'Court of pie powder', p. 234.
14 Salzman, *English trade*, p. 161.
15 Gross, 'Court of pie powder', p. 231.
16 For a contemporary account of merchant law (in Latin) see *The little red book of Bristol*, ed. Francis B. Bickley (2 vols, Bristol and London, 1900), i, pp 57–84. In this present work, discussion and modern references to the quick justice courts are termed and spelled 'pie powder' while the spelling of all quoted historical references to the courts will be used as found.
17 *The statutes of the realm … to 1713* (9 vols in 10 + 2 index vols, Record Commission, London, 1810–28), ii, p. 461.
18 Salzman, *English trade*, p. 164.
19 Gross, 'Court of pie powder', pp 231, 234, 238.
20 Salzman, *English trade*, p. 172.
21 Ibid., p. 174.
22 Gross, 'Court of pie powder', p. 243.

23 Ibid., p. 237.

24 Salzman, *English trade*, pp 164–5.

25 *CIRCLE*, Close roll 17 Edward II, 13 Aug. 1323, no. 3.

26 Gross, 'Court of pie powder', p. 239.

27 *The great parchment book of Waterford, liber antiquissimus civitatis Waterfordiae*, ed. Niall J. Byrne (Dublin, 2007), p. 54.

28 *CARD*, i, p. 228.

29 *Stat. Ire., Hen. VI*, p. 215.

30 Liam Price, 'Powerscourt, and the territory of Fercullen', *JRSAI*, 83 (1953), pp 117–32, at pp 118, 132; Áine Foley, *The royal manors of medieval Co. Dublin: crown and community* (Dublin, 2013), p. 25; K.W. Nicholls, 'Three topographical notes', *Peritia: Journal of the Medieval Academy of Ireland*, 5 (1986), pp 409–15, in particular '1. Okelly: Uí Chellaig Chualann' at pp 409–13. Paul MacCotter, *Medieval Ireland: territorial, political and economic divisions* (Dublin, 2008), pp 164–5.

31 *Stat. Ire., Hen. VI*, pp 215, 217.

32 *Alen's reg.*, pp 229–30.

33 Britnell, *Britain and Ireland*, p. 255.

34 Salzman, *English trade*, p. 169; James Davis, *Medieval market morality* (Cambridge, 2012), p. 209.

35 *Stat. Ire., John–Hen. V*, pp 101–3.

36 Salzman, *English trade*, p. 169.

37 Salzman, *English trade*, pp 168–71; Davis, *Medieval market morality*, p. 200.

38 Salzman, *English trade*, pp 25–7.

39 These documents are to be found on the *CIRCLE* site.

40 *CIRCLE*, Close roll 20 Henry VI, 9 Nov. 1441, no. 33, Close Roll 20 Henry VI, 9 July 1442, no. 36, Close roll 20 Henry VI, 11 May 1442, no. 38, Close roll 20 Henry VI, 26 Jan. 1442, no. 39, Close roll 20 Henry VI, 18 Jan. 1442, no. 40, Close roll 20 Henry VI, 2 Aug. 1442, no. 41, Close roll 20 Henry VI, 2 Aug. 1441, no. 51.

41 Edwin S. Hunt and James M. Murray, *A history of business in medieval Europe, 1200–1550* (Cambridge, 1999), pp 66–7.

42 Dryburgh and Smith, *Handbook and select calendar*, pp 143–51, at p. 143.

43 *The statutes of the realm … [of England and Great Britain], to 1713*, vol. i, pp 332–43, at p. 332.

44 Ibid., vol. i, pp 332–43, with the pursuit of debtors at pp 336–7.

45 Dryburgh and Smith, *Handbook and select calendar*, p. 151.

46 Berry, *Wills and inventories*, pp 78–81, 128–33; Lennon and Murray, *Dublin franchise roll*, p. 79.

47 Lennon and Murray, *Dublin franchise roll*, pp 1 (Sawag), 3 (Ussher), 5 (Ludelow), 6 (Robert White), 8 (Sexe, Margaret White), 10 (Tu/Tyve), 11 (Rendill, Roche), 14 (Whiteacres); Berry, *Wills and inventories*, pp 71 (Barry), 80 (Tapister); Bairéad, 'Bailiffs, provosts and sheriffs', p. 291, for mayors and bailiffs of Dublin.

48 Salzman, *English trade*, pp 170–1.

49 Britnell, *Britain and Ireland*, p. 481.

50 Berry, *Wills and inventories*, pp 146–8.

51 Ibid., pp 8–11, 128–33.

52 Ibid., pp 15–18, 27, 31–4, 66–8, 83–5, 85–9, 149–51.

53 Ibid., pp 16, 31, 83, 85, 149.

54 Christopher Dyer, *Making a living in the Middle Ages: the people of Britain, 850–1520* (London, 2002), pp 266–7.

55 *Stat. Ire., 12–22 Edw. IV*, p. 255.

56 *Stat. Ire., Hen. VI*, p. 91.
57 *Stat. Ire., Hen. VI*, pp 445, 447.
58 *Stat. Ire., 1–12 Edw. IV*, pp 3, 5, 111, 113, 115, 117, 295, 297, 299, 439, 441, 443, 651, 653, 655, 657; *Stat. Ire., 12–22 Edw. IV*, pp 129, 131, 255, 257, 637.
59 Timothy O'Neill, 'A fifteenth century entrepreneur, Germyn Lynch, fl. 1441–1483' in John Bradley (ed.), *Settlement and society in medieval Ireland: studies presented to F.X. Martin OSA* (Kilkenny, 1988), pp 421–8, at p. 421.
60 S.G. Ellis, 'The struggle for control of the Irish mint, 1460–c.1506', *PRIA*, 78C (1978), pp 17–36, at p. 20.
61 O'Neill, 'Germyn Lynch', pp 423–4; Ellis, 'The Irish mint', pp 25–8; *Stat. Ire., Rich. III–Hen. VIII*, pp 21, 23.
62 *Stat. Ire., 1–12 Edw. IV*, pp 439, 441, 443.
63 *Stat. Ire., 1–12 Edw. IV*, pp 651, 653.
64 *Stat. Ire., 12–22 Edw. IV*, pp x, 129, 131.
65 *Stat. Ire., 12–22 Edw. IV*, p. 747.
66 *Stat. Ire., Rich. III–Hen. VIII*, pp 21, 23.
67 Berry, *Wills and inventories*, pp 15–18.
68 Ibid., pp 76–8; *CARD*, i, pp 349–50.
69 Lennon and Murray, *Dublin franchise roll*, pp 7, 50–1.
70 Berry, *Wills and inventories*, pp 128–33.
71 Ibid., p. 130.
72 Ibid., p. 131.
73 Coleman, 'Urban elite', pp 293, 298–9, and passim.
74 Berry, *Wills and inventories*, pp 8–11, 16.
75 Ibid., pp 154–5.
76 Lennon and Murray, *Dublin franchise roll*, pp 6, 18 (Kelly), 58–9 (Russell).
77 Ibid., pp 58–9.
78 Berry, *Wills and inventories*, pp 154–5.
79 Ibid., pp 128–33.
80 Ibid., pp 83–5.
81 John Bradley, 'The medieval boroughs of County Dublin' in Conleth Manning (ed.), *Dublin beyond the Pale: studies in honour of Patrick Healy* (Bray, 1998), pp 129–44, at p. 142 and passim; Niall Brady, 'Dublin's maritime setting and the archaeology of its medieval harbours' in John Bradley, Alan J. Fletcher and Anngret Simms (eds), *Dublin in the medieval world: studies in honour of Howard B. Clarke* (Dublin, 2009), pp 295–315, at p. 307; Foley, *The royal manors of medieval Dublin*, pp 38–9.
82 Berry, *Wills and inventories*, pp 94–7.
83 Ibid., pp 49–50.
84 Ibid., pp 31–2.
85 Ibid.
86 Berry, *Wills and inventories*, index, passim.
87 Ibid., pp 51–2, 92–3, 120–1, 123–4, 125–6, 151–3; for Dublin merchants see Lennon and Murray, *Dublin franchise roll*, pp 3 (Ussher), 8 (FitzLeones), 9 (Bartholomew Russell), 15 (Arland), 22 (Blanchevile).
88 Berry, *Wills and inventories*, for William Neill, Nicholas Keating, John Borrard and Margaret Browneusyn, pp 94–7, 112, 140–1, 144–5; for Dublin merchants see Lennon and Murray, *Dublin franchise roll*, pp 1 (Soggyn), 4 (Lye), 6 (Shynnagh, White), 7 (Fyan, Gerrot), 10 (John Russell), 12 (Nicholas Harold, Queytrot), 16 (Richard Harold); 'John Rosere' above is very likely a Dublin merchant, named John Rosseele or Russell.

89   *CARD*, i, pp 14–18.

90   Joy Bristow, *The local historian's glossary of words and terms* (Newbury, 2005); and see the glossaries in E.M. Carus-Wilson, *Overseas trade of Bristol in the later Middle Ages* (New York, 1967) and in Wilson, *Chester customs accounts*.

91   *CARD*, i, p. 15.

92   Berry, *Wills and inventories*, pp 11–13, 116–18, 125–7, 142–4, 159–62.

93   *CARD*, i, p. 15; for oxen in Co. Dublin, see Berry, *Wills and inventories*, pp 34, 129, 164.

94   *CARD*, i, p. 15.

95   Carus-Wilson, *Overseas trade of Bristol*, p. 337.

96   *CARD*, i, p. 15; *Webster's revised unabridged dictionary* (Springfield, MA, 1913).

97   *CARD*, i, p. 15.

98   Ibid., pp 15, 18.

99   Ibid., pp 15, 16, 18.

100   Britnell, *Britain and Ireland*, p. 333.

101   *CARD*, i, p. 18.

CHAPTER 3
Shipping, Navigation and the Irish Sea Trade

1   Bob Trett (ed.), *Newport medieval ship* (Newport, n.d.), p. 8.

2   Holger Schweitzer, 'Drogheda boat: a story to tell' in Nergis Günsenin (ed.), *Between continents: proceedings of the twelfth symposium on boat and ship archaeology, Istanbul 2009* (Istanbul, 2009), pp 225–31, passim.

3   Schweitzer, 'Drogheda boat', pp 225, 227, 228, 230, 231.

4   Wendy Childs, 'Ireland's trade with England in the later Middle Ages', *IESH*, 9 (1982), pp 5–33, at pp 5–6.

5   John J. O'Meara (trans. and intro.), *Gerald of Wales, The history and topography of Ireland* (London, 1982), p. 58.

6   Susan Rose, *The medieval sea* (London, 2007), pp 4–5.

7   J.T. Driver, *Chester in the later Middle Ages, 1399–1540* (Chester, 1971), pp 103–4; FitzPatrick, 'Food and drink', pp 15–17; Jan Bill, 'The cargo vessels' in Lars Berggren, Nils Hybel and Annette Landen (eds), *Cogs, cargoes and commerce: maritime bulk trade in northern Europe, 1150–1400* (Toronto, 2002), pp 92–112, at pp 96–7; Ian Friel, *The good ship: ships, shipbuilding and technology in England, 1200–1520* (London, 1995), p. 53.

8   Fitzpatrick, 'Food and drink', p. 22.

9   Ibid., pp 16–17.

10   Wilson, *Chester customs accounts*, pp 120–1; calculations are based on a horseload being equivalent to 2.5 hundredweight (cwt) and a cartload weighing 1 ton (2240 lbs) in Carus-Wilson, *Overseas trade of Bristol*, pp 335, 338.

11   Wilson, *Chester customs accounts*, pp 117–31, passim; Chester city records, sheriffs' books, ZSB 3, ff 75–83 (1476–7).

12   Driver, *Chester in the later Middle Ages*, ibid.; FitzPatrick, 'Food and drink', p. 18.

13   Wilson, *Chester customs accounts*, pp 122–5.

14   Ian Friel, *Maritime history of Britain and Ireland, c.400–2001* (London, 2003), pp 81–2; for the Howth ships, cargo sizes and passenger numbers, see Chester city records, sheriffs' books, ZSB 3, ff 75–83 (1476–7).

15   Smyly, 'Old deeds in the library of Trinity College', IV, p. 17.

16   Berry, *Wills and inventories*, p. 109.

17   *DIB*, ii, pp 927–8.

18 Fitzpatrick, 'Food and drink', pp 22–3.

19 Wilson, *Chester customs accounts*, pp 119–20, 120, 121, 125–6, 130.

20 *CARD*, i, p. 364.

21 *Alen's reg.*, p. 233.

22 Charles V. Smith, *Dalkey: society and economy in a small medieval Irish town* (Dublin, 1996), p. 47.

23 *Alen's reg.*, p. 233.

24 For the small ports of Co. Dublin see Brady, 'Dublin's maritime setting and the archaeology of its medieval harbours', pp 298–301.

25 Smith, *Dalkey*, p. 55.

26 Wilson, *Chester customs accounts*, pp 117–31; Chester city records, sheriffs' books, ZSB 3, ff 75–83 (1476–7).

27 Smith, *Dalkey*, p. 55.

28 *CARD*, i, pp 492–3.

29 Harris (ed.), *Hibernica*, pp, 59, 70.

30 Ibid.

31 Ibid., p. 70.

32 Ibid., pp 70–1.

33 Friel, *Maritime history of Britain and Ireland*, p. 85.

34 John H. Harvey (ed.), *William Worcestre: itineraries* (Oxford, 1969), p. 169; *ODNB*, H.C.G. Matthews and Brian Harrison, lx (Oxford, 2004), pp 294–5.

35 Thomas J. Westropp, 'Early Italian maps of Ireland from 1300 to 1600, with notes on foreign settlers and trade', *PRIA*, 30C (1912–13), pp 361–428, at p. 389 and at plates XLII to XLV.

36 Timothy O'Neill, *Merchants and mariners in medieval Ireland* (Dublin, 1987), pp 114–15; D.W. Waters (ed.), *The rutters of the sea: the sailing directions of Pierre Garcie* (New Haven and London, 1967), pp 181–95, at pp 191–3.

37 Modern versions of some place names above are listed here: Arglas/Ardglass; Clere/Cape Clear; Dalcay/Dalkey; Holbe/Howth; Skarris/Skerries; toure of Waterford/Hook lighthouse.

38 Wendy R. Childs, 'Irish merchants and seamen in late medieval England', *IHS*, 32:125 (May 2005), pp 22–43, at p. 24; Childs, 'Ireland's trade with England', p. 29; these references apply to the text and to the 'home ports' table in this work.

39 *CARD*, i, pp 30–1; Brady, 'Dublin's maritime setting and the archaeology of its medieval harbours', p. 299.

40 *CARD*, i, pp 25, 138.

41 Ibid., pp 30–1.

42 Ibid., pp 143–4.

43 See p. 43 above.

44 Ibid.

45 Ibid.

46 A.F. O'Brien, 'Commercial relations between Aquitaine and Ireland, *c.*1000–*c.*1550' in Jean-Michel Picard (ed.), *Aquitaine and Ireland in the Middle Ages* (Dublin, 1995), pp 31–80, at pp 46, 72–3.

47 Ibid., p. 73.

48 Ibid., passim.

49 Britnell, *Britain and Ireland*, pp 454–5.

50 *NHI*, ii, p. 496.

51 Britnell, *Britain and Ireland*, pp 454.

52 Childs, 'Ireland's trade with England', pp 7–12.

53 O'Brien, 'Commercial relations with Aquitaine', pp 37, 39.

54 Ibid., pp 44, 46–7.

55 Robert Bartlett, *England under the Norman and Angevin kings, 1075–1225* (Oxford, 2000), p. 22.

56 O'Brien, 'Commercial relations with Aquitaine', pp 59, 61; Jacques Bernard, 'The maritime intercourse between Bordeaux and Ireland, *c*.1450–*c*.1520', *IESH*, 7 (1980), pp 7–21, at p. 12.

57 O'Brien, 'Commercial relations with Aquitaine', pp 53–4, 59, 67, 71–2.

58 Ibid., pp 59, 61, 64–5; Bernard, 'Maritime intercourse', p. 14.

59 Bernard, 'Maritime intercourse', p. 16.

60 G.R. Elton, *England under the Tudors* (London, 1965), pp 72–4, 89–90.

61 Ibid., pp 93, 150–9, 196–7.

62 O'Brien, 'Commercial relations with Aquitaine', p. 41.

63 Ibid., p. 42; *NHI*, viii, p. 189.

64 Ellis and Murray, *Calendar of state papers, Ireland, Tudor period, 1509–1547*, no. 649.

65 Laughton, *Life in a late medieval city*, p. 174.

66 H.J. Hewitt, *Cheshire under the three Edwards* (Chester, 1967), pp 65–9.

67 Carus-Wilson, *Overseas trade of Bristol*, passim; E.M. Carus-Wilson, 'The overseas trade of Bristol' in Eileen Power and M.M. Postan, *Studies in English trade in the fifteenth century* (London, 1933), p. 195; Berry, *Wills and inventories*, pp 28, 83.

68 Susan Flavin and Evan T. Jones (eds), *British trade with Ireland and the Continent, 1503–1610: the evidence of the exchequer customs accounts* (Dublin, 2009), p. xv.

69 *CARD*, i, p. 322.

70 Laughton, *Life in a late medieval city*, p. 176.

71 Lennon and Murray, *Dublin franchise roll*, pp 1, 3; Wilson, *Chester customs accounts*, pp 117–31.

72 *CARD*, i, p. 327; Wilson, *Chester customs accounts*, pp 120–1.

73 Lennon and Murray, *Dublin franchise roll*, pp 4 (Eustace), 9 (FitzSymond), 10 (Fowler, Stanyhurst), 11 (West), 15 (Whiteacres).

74 Wilson, *Chester customs accounts*, pp 12, 120–1.

75 *Stat. Ire., 12–22 Edw. IV*, pp 785, 787.

76 Lennon and Murray, *Dublin franchise roll*, p. 1; Berry, *Wills and inventories*, pp 128–33.

77 Wilson, *Chester customs accounts*, pp 124–5.

78 Ibid., pp 119, 130–1.

79 Ibid., pp 120, 122, 128–9; Lennon and Murray, *Dublin franchise roll*, pp 2 (Rychman), 8 (FitzLeones).

80 Wilson, *Chester customs accounts*, p. 121.

81 Lennon and Murray, *Dublin franchise roll*, p. 1.

82 *CARD*, i, p. 323; John T. Gilbert, *A history of the city of Dublin* (3 vols, Dublin, 1854–9, facs. ed., Shannon, 1972), p. 162.

83 Wilson, *Chester customs accounts*, pp 120, 121 (*bis*), 123, 124, 125, 128 (*bis*), 129, 131.

84 Ibid., p. 128.

85 Ibid., pp 125, 128–9, 130–1.

86 Chester city records, sheriffs' books, ZSB 3, ff 75–83 (1476–7).

87 Ibid., passim.

88 Lennon and Murray, *Dublin franchise roll*, pp 1, 16, 31–2, for Christopher Higley; Chester city records, sheriffs' books, ZSB 3, ff 75–83 (1476–7).

89 Lennon and Murray, *Dublin franchise roll*, pp 1, 2, 11, 16, 17, 18, for John Savage; Chester city records, sheriffs' books, ZSB 3, ff 75–83 (1476–7).

90 Lennon and Murray, *Dublin franchise roll*, p. 16, for Thomas Higeley.

91 Chester city records, sheriffs' books, ZSB 3, ff 75–83 (1476–7); Lennon and Murray, *Dublin franchise roll*, pp 7, 16, 31, for John Sweteman.

92   Lennon and Murray, *Dublin franchise roll*, p. 16, for Richard Russell.
93   On examining the passenger lists of two Chester ships entering Chester in 1476–7, I have decided that there is a fair probability that the ships set out from Howth and I have treated them accordingly.
94   Chester city records, sheriffs' books, ZSB 3, ff 75–83 (1476–7).
95   Lennon and Murray, *Dublin franchise roll*, pp 6, 13, 18, 20, 22, for Stephen Harold; p. 6, for William Harold.
96   Chester city records, sheriffs' books, ZSB 3, ff 75–83 (1476–7).
97   Ibid.
98   Ibid.
99   Ibid.
100 Chester city records, sheriffs' books, ZSB 3, ff 71–4 (1476–7).
101 Ibid.
102 Ibid.; Chester city records, sheriffs' books, ZSB 3, ff 75–83 (1476–7).
103 *ODNB*, vol. 40, pp 294–5.
104 Harvey, *William Worcestre*, p. 169.
105 *ODNB*, vol. 40, pp 294–5; Harvey, *William Worcestre*, p. 169.
106 Lennon and Murray, *Dublin franchise roll*, p. 9.
107 Wilson, *Chester customs accounts*, pp 103–16, 132–42.
108 Ibid., pp 103, 106, 109; Carus-Wilson, *Overseas trade of Bristol*, pp 335, 337–8.
109 Wilson, *Chester customs accounts*, pp 103–16, passim.
110 Ibid., p. 103.
111 Ibid., p. 104.
112 Ibid., p. 109.
113 Ibid.
114 Ibid., pp 113–14.
115 Ibid., p. 109.
116 Ibid., pp 104–5, 107–9, 111–14, and pp 103–16, passim.
117 Driver, *Cheshire in the later Middle Ages*, pp 99–100, 103.

CHAPTER 4
Guilds and Apprentices

1   J.G. Smyly, 'Old deeds in the library of Trinity College – IV', *Hermathema*, 70 (1947), p. 17.
2   D. Hollis (ed.), *Calendar of the Bristol apprentice book, 1532–1565, part I, 1532–1542* (Bristol, 1949), p. 38.
3   Elizabeth Ralph and Nora M. Hardwick (eds), *Calendar of the Bristol apprentice book, 1532–1565, part II, 1542–1552* (Bristol, 1980), p. 76; Peadar Slattery, 'The timber and wood trade, woodlands, house building and repairs in the English colony in Ireland, *c.*1350–*c.*1570', part I, *JRSAI*, 142–3 (2012–13), pp 114–28, at p. 120.
4   Berry, 'Dublin guild of merchants', p. 51.
5   Ibid., pp 49, 51.
6   Ibid., p. 49.
7   Ibid.
8   Bartlett, *England under the Norman and Angevin kings*, pp 339–40.
9   *CARD*, i, p. 1.
10   John J. Webb, *The guilds of Dublin* (Dublin, 1929), pp 2–3.
11   *CARD*, i, p. 5.
12   Bartlett, *England under the Norman and Angevin kings*, p. 339.

13 Ibid., p. 340.

14 Salzman, *English trade*, pp 71–2.

15 *The Dublin guild merchant roll*, c. *1190–1265*, ed. Philomena Connolly and Geoffrey Martin (Dublin, 1992), p. 121.

16 Salzman, *English trade*, p. 74.

17 For the tailors' guild royal licence see *CIRCLE*, Patent roll 7 Henry V, 16 July 1419, no. 67.

18 Salzman, *English trade*, p. 71.

19 Connolly and Martin, *Dublin guild merchant roll*, passim.

20 Ibid., p. xiv.

21 Ibid., index, pp 133–56.

22 Ibid., pp xiv, xix, xxii.

23 Ibid., index, pp 133–56.

24 Salzman, *English trade*, p. 74.

25 Myles V. Ronan, 'Religious customs of Dublin medieval guilds', *IER*, 26 (1925), pp 225–47 and pp 364–85, at p. 230. For the tailors' guild licence see *CIRCLE*, Patent roll 7 Henry V, 16 July 1419, no. 67.

26 Henry S. Guinness, 'Dublin trade guilds', *JRSAI*, 6th series, 12:2 (Dec. 1922), pp 143–63, at p. 151; for the shoemakers royal licence see *CIRCLE*, Patent roll 5 Henry VI, 4 Dec. 1426, no. 44.

27 Ronan, 'Religious customs', p. 230.

28 Guinness, 'Dublin trade guilds', pp 148–9.

29 *Stat. Ire., 12–22 Edw. IV*, pp 769, 771, 773, 775, 777, 779, 781, 783, 785.

30 Henry F. Berry, 'The Dublin guild of carpenters, masons and heliers in the sixteenth century', *JRSAI*, 5th series, 35:4 (Dec. 1905), pp 321–37, at p. 325.

31 Berry, 'Dublin guild of merchants', p. 45.

32 Ibid., p. 52.

33 Ibid., p. 49.

34 *CARD*, i, p. 275.

35 Webb, *Dublin guilds*, pp 18–19.

36 Berry, 'Dublin guild of merchants', p. 52.

37 *Stat. Ire., 12–22 Edw. IV*, pp 769, 771; J.T. Gilbert, *A history of the city of Dublin* (3 vols, Dublin, 1861), i, p. 324.

38 *Stat. Ire., 12–22 Edw. IV*, p. 771.

39 Ibid., p. 773.

40 Ibid., p. 769.

41 Ronan, 'Religious customs', p. 229.

42 Ibid., p. 231.

43 Ibid., p. 232.

44 Aubrey Gwynn, 'Anglo-Irish church life: fourteenth and fifteenth centuries' in Patrick J. Corish, *A history of Irish Catholicism*, ii, fasciculus 4 (Dublin, 1968), pp 1–76, at p. 12.

45 Gwynn, 'Anglo-Irish church life', p. 18.

46 Aubrey Gwynn, 'Richard FitzRalph, archbishop of Armagh', part vi, *Studies: an Irish Quarterly Review*, 25 (1936), pp 81–96, at pp 90–1.

47 L.F. Salzman, *English industries of the Middle Ages* (London, 1970), pp 341–2.

48 Salzman, *English industries*, pp 340–41.

49 Ibid., p. 341; Ralph and Hardwick, *Calendar of the Bristol apprentice book, part II, 1542–1552*, p. 20.

50 For the shoemakers' guild royal licence, see *CIRCLE*, Patent roll 5 Henry VI, 4 Dec. 1426, no. 44.

51 Ibid.

52 Ibid.; William Cotter Stubbs, 'Weavers' guild', *JRSAI*, 6th series, 9:1 (June 1919), pp 60–86, at p. 61.

53 *CIRCLE*, shoemakers' guild royal licence, ibid.

54 Stubbs, 'Weavers' guild', p. 62.

55 *CIRCLE*, shoemakers' guild royal licence, ibid.

56 For the tailors' guild royal licence see *CIRCLE*, Patent roll 7 Henry V, 16 July 1419, no. 67.

57 Lennon and Murray, *Dublin franchise roll*, p. 85; *CARD*, i, p. 283.

58 Lennon and Murray, *Dublin franchise roll*; *CARD*, i, p. 331.

59 *CARD*, i, p. 338.

60 *CARD*, i, pp 382–3.

61 Smyly, 'Old deeds in the library of Trinity College – IV', p. 17.

62 Salzman, *English industries*, p. 341.

63 Smyly, 'Old deeds in the library of Trinity College – IV', p. 17.

64 *CARD*, i, pp 382–3.

65 Lennon and Murray, *Dublin franchise roll*, p. 77.

66 Ibid., pp 7, 8, 11, 13, 18, 22.

67 Ibid., p. 2.

68 Ibid., pp 1, 3, 19 (Sogyn), 12 (Harrold), 14 (Flemyng), 17 (Cruise).

69 *CIRCLE*, Patent roll 7 Henry V, 16 July 1419, no. 67 (tailors' guild); *CIRCLE*, Patent roll 5 Henry VI, 4 Dec. 1426, no. 44 (shoemakers' guild).

70 Patent roll 5 Henry VI, ibid.; Berry, 'Dublin guild of carpenters, millers, masons and heliers', p. 327.

71 Lennon and Murray, *Dublin franchise roll*, pp xxiii, 77–8.

72 Lennon and Murray, ibid., p. 78.

73 Ibid., p. xxiii; Patent roll 5 Henry VI, ibid.

74 Lennon and Murray, *Dublin franchise roll*, pp 1, 4, 5, 12, 15, 18, 25, 28, 32, 37.

75 *Stat. Ire., John–Hen. V*, pp 367, 369, 371, 389.

76 Ibid., pp 489, 491.

77 Ibid., pp 367, 369, 371, 389.

78 Ibid., pp 489, 491.

79 Ibid.

80 Hugh J. Lawlor, 'A calendar of the Liber Niger and Liber Albus of Christ Church, Dublin', *PRIA*, 27C (1908–9), pp 1–93, at pp 27–8.

CHAPTER 5

Provisioning Dublin

1   Berry, *Wills and inventories*, pp 58–60.

2   Clark and Refaussé, *Historic Dublin guilds*, p. 38.

3   Berry, *Wills and inventories*, pp 58–60.

4   Bruce M.S. Campbell, *English seignorial agriculture, 1250–1450* (Cambridge, 2000), pp 166–7.

5   Berry, *Wills and inventories*, pp 58–60.

6   Margaret Murphy and Michael Potterton, *The Dublin region in the Middle Ages: settlement, land-use and economy* (Dublin, 2010), p. 484.

7   Berry, *Wills and inventories*, passim; the writer has examined about sixty Co. Dublin farm inventories from the 1470s.

8   Murphy and Potterton, *The Dublin region*, p. 482.

9   *Stat. Ire., 1–12 Edw. IV*, pp 657, 659, 749.
10 *Stat. Ire., 1–12 Edw. IV*, pp 657, 659, 661 (1470); pp 747, 749, 751 (1471–2); all values in the text and comparative chart taken from parliamentary legislation are for the year 1470, with the exception of the price of a 'hog of the best' which is taken from the year 1471–2.
11 Berry, *Wills and inventories*, passim.
12 Berry, *Wills and inventories*, passim; *Stat. Ire.*, pp 657, 659, 749.
13 Mary C. Lyons, 'Weather, famine, pestilence and plague in Ireland, 900–1500' in E. Margaret Crawford (ed.), *Famine: the Irish experience, 900–1500: subsistence crises and famines in Ireland* (Edinburgh, 1989), pp 31–74, at pp 47, 69, 71.
14 Salzman, *English trade*, pp 75–80.
15 *CARD*, i, p. 287.
16 Ibid., pp 287–8.
17 Berry, *Wills and inventories*, passim; the wills and inventories of farmers from Co. Dublin drawn up in the 1470s identify the locations of farms of middle size and quantities and types of cereal produced.
18 Lennon and Murray, *Dublin franchise roll*, p. 77.
19 *CARD*, i, p. 308.
20 Ibid., pp 310–11.
21 Ibid., p. 311.
22 Ibid., pp 336–7.
23 Ibid., p. 337.
24 Ibid., p. 343.
25 Ibid.
26 Ibid., pp 346–7; Clarke, *IHTA, Dublin part I, to 1610*, map 4.
27 *Stat. Ire., 1–12 Edw. IV*, p. 753.
28 *CARD*, i, pp 220, 222, 224.
29 Judith M. Bennett, *Ale, beer and brewsters in England: women's work in a changing world, 1300–1600* (New York, 1996), p. 103.
30 Connolly and Martin, *Dublin guild merchant roll*, pp 157, 159, and passim.
31 Bennett, *Ale, beer and brewsters*, pp 35, 103, 164.
32 Henry F. Berry, 'Proceedings in the matter of the custom called tollboll, 1308 and 1385, St Thomas's abbey *v.* some early Dublin brewers, etc.', *PRIA*, 28C (1910), 169–73, passim.
33 *CARD*, i, pp 220, 222, 224; Bennett, *Ale, beer and brewsters*, see index, and passim.
34 *Stat. Ire., Hen. VI*, p. 193.
35 *CARD*, i, p. 288.
36 Dublin City Assembly Roll no. 02, membrane 10, paragraph 05, which clearly states 'a dozen of ther beest ale for ii d'. I am very grateful to Dr Mary Clark for finding this entry on the roll.
37 *CARD*, i, p. 342; a dozen of the best ale would have sold at about 2*d*., but the price stated in the reference is 2*s*., which is a typesetter's error. Berry, *Wills and inventories*, p. 80.
38 *CARD*, i, p. 360.
39 Berry, *Wills and inventories*, p. 80.
40 Bennett, *Ale, beer and brewsters*, pp 132–41.
41 Driver, *Cheshire in the later Middle Ages*, p. 142.
42 Berry, *Wills and inventories*, pp 156–8.
43 *Calendar of letter-books … of the city of London at the Guildhall, letter book K*, ed. Reginald R. Sharpe (London, 1911), p. 354.
44 Berry, pp 156–8.
45 *Stat. Ire., John–Hen. V*, p. 489.

46 Berry, *Wills and inventories*, pp 65–6, 112–13, 133–6.
47 Ibid., pp 41–5, 83–5, 109–11.
48 Ibid., pp 11–13 (Bennet), 13–15 (Kempe), 68–72 (Barret), 81–3 (Kenane), 102–3 (Kymore).
49 Ibid., pp 34–6 (Palmer), pp 58–60 (Delaber).
50 *CARD*, i, pp 274, 293, 304–5.
51 Ibid., p. 339.
52 Ibid., p. 342.
53 Ibid., p. 366.
54 Ibid., pp 233–4.
55 Salzman, *English industries*, pp 278–9.
56 *CARD*, i, p. 234.
57 Ibid., pp 233–4.
58 Salzman, *English industries*, pp 276–7.
59 *CARD*, i, pp 274, 293, 304–5.
60 Salzman, *English industries*, p. 274.
61 Lennon and Murray, *Dublin franchise roll*, pp 20, 77.
62 *CARD*, i, pp 239–41.
63 Ibid., pp 219, 234, 300–1, 303, 311–12.

CHAPTER 6

The Traditional Church

1 TCD MS 78, Trinity College Library, Dublin; William Hawkes, 'The liturgy in Dublin, 1200–1500', p. 46.
2 Ann Buckley, 'Music in Ireland to *c*.1500' in Dáibhí Ó Cróinín (ed.), *NHI*, i (Oxford, 2005), pp 744–813, at pp 790, 809, 812.
3 Marvin L. Colker (ed.), *Trinity College Library, Dublin: descriptive catalogue of the medieval and Renaissance Latin manuscripts* (Aldershot, 1991), pp 122–5.
4 Berry, *Wills and inventories*, pp 97–9.
5 Hawkes, 'Liturgy in Dublin, 1200–1500', p. 48.
6 Ibid., p. 47.
7 Ibid., pp 47–8.
8 Ibid., pp 48–9.
9 Ibid., p. 48; Pádraig Ó Riain, *A dictionary of Irish saints* (Dublin, 2012), pp 339–41.
10 Hawkes, ibid.; Ó Riain, *Irish saints*, pp 94–6.
11 Hawkes, ibid.; Ó Riain, *Irish saints*, p. 415.
12 Berry, *Wills and inventories*, pp 55–6.
13 Jefferies, *Priests and prelates*, p. 52.
14 Eamon Duffy, *The stripping of the altars: traditional religion in England, 1400–1580* (London, 2nd ed. 2005), p. 53; F.M. Powicke and C.R. Cheney (eds), *Councils and synods, with other documents relating to the English Church, II, 1205–1313* (2 vols, Oxford, 1964), part ii, pp 886–90, 900–5.
15 Jefferies, *Priests and prelates*, p. 52.
16 Duffy, *Stripping of the altars*, pp 53–4; *Lay folks' catechism*, intro. T.F. Simmons and H.E. Nolloth (London, 1901, facs. ed., New York, 1972), passim.
17 Clarke, *IHTA, Dublin part I, to 1610*, pp 17–20, map 4, and map 6, *Dublin 1610*; totals for church building types above are taken from map 4.
18 Fieldwork by the author in Baldoyle, Hollywood, Howth and Kinsaley; Tadhg O'Keeffe, *Medieval Irish buildings, 1100–1600* (Dublin, 2015), p. 128; Paul Duffy, 'The church of

Bearach, the grange of Baldoyle and the town of the dark stranger' in Seán Duffy (ed.), *Medieval Dublin XV* (Dublin, 2016), pp 89–118, at pp 111–13.

19 Mary McMahon, *St Audoen's church, Cornmarket, Dublin: archaeology and architecture* (Dublin, 2006), p. 101.

20 Ibid., p. 101; C. Platt, *The parish churches of England* (London, 1981), p. 15.

21 McMahon, *St Audoen's church*, pp 100–1.

22 Ibid., p. 99.

23 Clarke, Dent and Johnson, *Dublinia*, p. 116.

24 McMahon, *St Audoen's church*, p. 99; *The registers of Christ Church cathedral, Dublin*, ed. Raymond Refaussé and Colm Lennon (Dublin, 1998), p. 66.

25 The engraver mispelled '*nobis*'.

26 F. Elrington Ball, *Howth and its owners* (Dublin, 1917), pp 47–8; Fred E. Dukes, *Campanology in Ireland* (Dublin, 1994), pp 136–8.

27 Empey, *Proctors' accounts*, pp 44, 47, 49, 53, 55, 57, 63.

28 Peter M. Lefferts, 'England' in Mark Everist (ed.), *The Cambridge companion to medieval music* (Cambridge, 2011), pp 107–20, at p. 115: *ODCC*, pp 1446–7.

29 Aubrey Gwynn, *The Irish Church*, ed. Gerard O'Brien (Dublin, 1992), p. 307.

30 *NHI*, ix, p. 311; Tadhg O'Keeffe and Rhiannon Carey Bates, 'The abbey and cathedral of Ferns' in Ian W. Doyle and Bernard Browne (eds), *Medieval Wexford: essays in memory of Billy Colfer* (Dublin, 2016), pp 73–96, at pp 84, 92; *ODCC*, p. 320.

31 O'Keeffe and Bates, 'Abbey and cathedral of Ferns', p. 94.

32 Harry White and Barra Boydell (eds), *The encyclopaedia of music in Ireland* (Dublin, 2013), p. 917.

33 *ODCC*, pp 1671–2.

34 Ibid., p. 1308.

35 White and Boydell, *Encyclopaedia of music in Ireland*, p. 917.

36 Stuart Kinsella, 'From Hiberno-Norse to Anglo-Norman, c.1030–1300' in Milne (ed.), *Christ Church cathedral*, pp 25–52, at pp 49–50; Peadar Slattery, 'Woodland management, timber and wood production, and trade in Anglo-Norman Ireland, c.1170–c.1350', *JRSAI*, 139 (2009), pp 63–79, at p. 74; Roy Spring, *The new Bell's cathedral guides: Salisbury cathedral* (London, 1987), p. 12; D.W.H. Miles, *The tree-ring dating of the roof carpentry of the eastern chapels, north nave triforium, and north porch, Salisbury cathedral, Wiltshire* (English Heritage reports, no. 94, Portsmouth, 2002), pp 3, 20–22.

37 Alan J. Fletcher, 'Liturgy and music in the medieval cathedral' in John Crawford and Raymond Gillespie (eds), *St Patrick's cathedral, Dublin: a history* (Dublin, 2009), pp 120–48, at p. 123.

38 *ODCC*, pp 1177–8, 1191, 1335–6.

39 Margaret Fassler, *Music in the medieval west* (New York and London, 2014), pp 42–3; appendix, p. 26.

40 Andrew Brown, *Church and society in England, 1000–1500* (Basingstoke, 2003), pp 103–4; Duffy, *Stripping of the altars*, pp 95–6.

41 Empey, *Proctors' accounts*, pp 49, 53, 55, 57, 63.

42 *ODCC*, p. 1438.

43 Tadhg O'Keeffe, *Medieval Irish buildings, 1100–1600* (Dublin, 2015), pp 124–5.

44 Duffy, *Stripping of the altars*, pp 157–8.

45 Empey, *Proctors' accounts*, pp 44, 49, 53, 60, 68. 72.

46 Duffy, *Stripping of the altars*, p. 97.

47 Fieldwork by the writer at Whitechurch chapel, Rathfarnham, Co. Dublin.

48 I am grateful to Jean Farrelly of the National Monuments Service for information and discussion about this topic.

49 McMahon, *St Audoen's church*, pp 97–8.

50 Ibid., p. 96.

51 Philip Baxter, *Sarum Use: the development of a medieval code of liturgy and customs* (Salisbury, 1994), p. 45; *The Church of our fathers as seen in St Osmund's rite for the cathedral of Salisbury, by Daniel Rock D.D.*, ed. G.W. Hart and W.H. Frere (4 vols, London, 1903, 1904), ii, pp 213–18; W.H. St John Hope, 'On the English liturgical colours', *Transactions of the St Paul's Ecclesiastical Society*, 2 (1886–90), pp 345–86.

52 Baxter, *Sarum Use*, pp 45–6.

53 Ibid., p. 46.

54 *ODCC*, p. 379.

55 Rachel Moss (ed.), *Art and architecture of Ireland:* i, *medieval, c.400–c.1600*, (Dublin, 2014), pp 401–2.

56 Ibid., p. 405.

57 Ibid.; Berry, *Wills and inventories*, p. 24.

58 Berry, *Wills and inventories*, pp 167, 169. Altar cloths and vestments were made of this textile fabric, a kind of striped silk; an eastern fabric; *bord* in Arabic meaning striped cloth.

59 Moss, *Art and architecture*, i, pp 404–5.

60 Mary Anne Lyons, 'Sidelights on the Kildare ascendancy; a survey of Geraldine involvement in the Church, *c.*1470–*c.*1520', *Archivium Hibernicum*, 48 (1994), pp 73–87, at p. 82.

61 Lyons, 'Sidelights on the Kildare ascendancy', p. 81; Donough Bryan, *The Great Earl of Kildare, Gerald FitzGerald (1456–1513)*, (Dublin, 1933), p. 260; John T. Gilbert, *A history of the city of Dublin*, (Dublin, 1854–9, facs. ed., Shannon, 1972), p. 108.

62 Caitriona McLeod, 'Fifteenth-century vestments in Waterford', *JRSAI*, 82 (1952), pp 85–98, at p. 85.

63 McLeod, 'Fifteenth-century vestments', p. 85.

64 Ibid., pp 86–7.

65 Eamonn McEneaney, 'Politics and the art of devotion in late fifteenth-century Waterford' in R. Moss, C. Ó Clabaigh and S. Ryan (eds), *Art and devotion in medieval Ireland* (Dublin, 2006), pp 33–50, at p. 42.

66 Empey, *Proctors' accounts*, pp 48, 68, 71–2, 76, 82.

67 Baxter, *Sarum Use*, pp 39, 41.

68 Jefferies, *Priests and prelates*, pp 15–56.

69 Ibid., p. 39.

70 Colmán Ó Clabaigh, *The friars in Ireland, 1224–1540* (Dublin, 2012), p. 263.

71 Fergal McGrath, *Education in ancient and medieval Ireland* (Dublin, 1979), pp 185–6.

72 Lennon and Murray, *Dublin franchise roll*, p. 77.

73 Ibid., pp 11, 21.

74 Jefferies, *Priests and prelates*, pp 39, 42.

75 Ibid., p. 50.

76 *Stat. Ire., Rich. III–Hen. VIII*, pp 129, 131.

77 Jefferies, *Priests and prelates*, pp 51–2.

78 *Stat. Ire., Rich. III–Hen. VIII*, pp 129, 131.

79 Jefferies, *Priests and prelates*, pp 51–2.

80 Ibid., p. 53.

81 Ibid., pp 28–32.

82 Sam Barrett, 'Music and liturgy' in Everist (ed.), *Medieval music*, pp 185–204, at p. 195.

83 John Harper, *The forms and orders of Western liturgy from the tenth to the eighteenth century* (Oxford, 1991), p. 83.

84 Ó Clabaigh, *Friars in Ireland*, pp 170–1.

85 Clarke, *IHTA, Dublin part I, to 1610*, pp 17–20.

86 Lefferts, 'England', pp 116–18.

87 Roger Stalley, 'The architecture of the cathedral and priory buildings, 1250–1530' in Milne (ed.), *Christ Church cathedral*, pp 95–128, at p. 106.

88 Stalley, 'Cathedral and priory buildings', pp 104, 107.

89 Fletcher, 'Liturgy and music in the medieval cathedral', p. 129; *Alen's reg.*, p. 78.

90 Fletcher, ibid., p. 130.

91 Fletcher, 'Liturgy and music in the medieval cathedral', pp 131–3, 146.

92 Empey, *Proctors' accounts*, pp 43–5, 52, 56, 58, 62–3, 68–70, 75, 82.

93 Ibid., pp 81, 84 (*bis*), 85.

94 Lefferts, 'England', pp 114–15.

95 Hawkes, 'Liturgy in Dublin, 1200–1500', pp 44–6; TCD MS 79.

96 Ó Riain, *Irish saints*, pp 94–6, 138–40, 339–41, 424–5, 455, 457–8, 498–9.

97 Hawkes, 'Liturgy in Dublin, 1200–1500', pp 44–6; TCD MS 79.

98 Berry, *Wills and inventories*, pp 172–8.

99 Ibid., pp 172–4, 177–8.

100 Ibid., pp 176–7.

101 Ibid., pp 174–6.

102 Ibid.

103 Ibid., pp 172–5.

104 Ibid., pp 175–7.

105 John Begley, *The diocese of Limerick, ancient and medieval* (Dublin, 1906), pp 289–94.

106 *NHI*, ix, p. 302.

107 Begley, *Diocese of Limerick*, p. 290.

108 Ibid., pp 290–91.

109 Berry, *Wills and inventories*, pp xli, xlii, 179–84; Logan, *Excommunication*, p. 15.

110 Logan, *Excommunication*, p. 13.

111 Ibid., p. 14.

112 Ibid.

113 *CIRCLE*, Patent roll 5 Henry IV, 6 July 1404, no. 135.

114 *Stat. Ire., 1–12 Edw. IV*, pp 437, 439.

115 Logan, *Excommunication*, pp 44–5.

116 Ibid., p. 46.

117 Ibid., p. 24.

118 *CIRCLE*, Patent roll 20 Edward IV, January 1481, no. 4.

119 *Stat. Ire., 12–22 Edw. IV*, pp 617, 619.

120 *Stat. Ire., Hen. VI*, pp 655, 657.

121 Berry, *Wills and inventories*, pp xli, 180–1.

122 Ibid., pp 179–84.

123 Jefferies, *The Irish Church and the Tudor Reformations*, p. 50.

124 Ibid., pp 49–50.

125 Berry, *Wills and inventories*, pp 179–84.

126 Ibid.

127 Ibid.

128 Logan, *Excommunication*, pp 50–2, 64–5.

129 Jefferies, *The Irish Church and the Tudor Reformations*, p. 49.

130 Berry, *Wills and inventories*, pp 179–80.

131 Ibid., pp 182–3.

132 Ibid., p. 184.

133 Ibid., p. 181.
134 Ibid., pp 179, 180, 181, 184.
135 Ibid., pp 180–1, 183.
136 Ibid., pp 180–1.
137 *ODCC*, p. 23.
138 Salvador Ryan, 'Christ the wounded lover and affective piety in late medieval Ireland and beyond' in Henning Laugurud, Salvador Ryan and Laura Katrine Skinnebach (eds), *The materiality of devotion in late medieval northern Europe: images, objects, practices* (Dublin, 2016), pp 70–89, at p. 71.
139 Duffy, *The stripping of the altars*, p. 234.
140 Ibid., pp 234–5.
141 Ibid., p. 250.
142 Ryan, 'Christ the wounded lover', p. 71.
143 Duffy, *The stripping of the altars*, p. 238.
144 Ibid., pp 248–9; *ODCC*, pp 237–8, also known as the Bridgettines; *ODCC*, pp 1405–6 (Rolle).
145 O'Byrne, 'Manuscript creation in Dublin', pp 285–6; Theresa O'Byrne identified Bellewe as the scribe of two manuscripts, Longleat MS 29 and e. Museo MS 232; S.J. Ogilvie-Thomson, *Richard Rolle: prose and verse, edited from MS Longleat 29 and related manuscripts* (Oxford, 1988), p. xviii.
146 O'Byrne, 'Manuscript creation in Dublin', p. 279.
147 Ibid., pp 281–3, 285; the manuscript volume referred to here is known archivally as Longleat MS 29.
148 Duffy, *The stripping of the altars*, p. 250.
149 *ODCC*, pp 1405–6; Ogilvie-Thomson, *Richard Rolle*, pp 3–25, 34–9, 40, 64–8.
150 O'Byrne, 'Manuscript creation in Dublin', p. 283.
151 From a meditation in the Bodleian e. Museo MS 232 manuscript; communication from Dr Theresa O'Byrne.
152 Berry, *Wills and inventories*, p. 212; Ronan, *Reformation in Dublin*, p. 184.

CHAPTER 7
A Changing Growing Church

1 Adrian Empey, 'The lay person in the parish: the medieval inheritance, 1169–1536' in Raymond Gillespie and W.G. Neely (eds), *The laity and the Church of Ireland, 1000–2000: all sorts and conditions* (Dublin, 2002), pp 7–48, at p. 27; Empey, *Proctors' accounts*.
2 Empey, *Proctors' accounts*, passim.
3 Empey, 'The lay person in the parish', pp 25–7.
4 Ibid., pp 25–6, 29.
5 Empey, *Proctors' accounts*, pp 65–73.
6 Empey, 'The lay person in the parish', pp 29–30.
7 Empey, *Proctors' accounts*, p. 68.
8 Empey, 'The lay person in the parish', p. 16.
9 Ibid., p. 17; *ODCC*, p. 420.
10 Empey, 'The lay person in the parish', p. 17.
11 Adrian Empey, 'Intramural churches and communities in medieval Dublin' in Bradley, Fletcher and Simms (eds), *Dublin in the medieval world*, pp 249–76, at pp 256–7, and plate 15.
12 *NHI*, i, p. 800, and plate 121; British Library, Add. MS 24198.
13 Fassler, *Music in the medieval west*, pp 37–42.

14 Ibid., pp 36–7.

15 Barra Boydell, *A history of music at Christ Church cathedral, Dublin* (Woodbridge, Suffolk, 2004), p. 11; *NHI*, ix, p. 309.

16 Fletcher, 'Liturgy and music in the medieval cathedral', pp 130–5, 145–8; Hawkes, 'Liturgy in Dublin, 1200–1500', pp 35–8.

17 Hawkes, 'Liturgy in Dublin, 1200–1500', pp 46–9; TCD MS 78.

18 Ibid., pp 38–46.

19 Hawkes, 'Liturgy in Dublin, 1200–1500', pp 38–40 and Bodleian, Rawl. Liturg. d. 4; Hawkes, 'Liturgy in Dublin, 1200–1500', pp 40–4 and Marsh MS Z. 4.2.20; Hawkes, 'Liturgy in Dublin, 1200–1500', pp 44–6 and TCD MS 79.

20 Boydell, *History of music at Christ Church*, p. 11.

21 Lefferts, 'England', p. 115.

22 Boydell, *History of music at Christ Church*, p. 11.

23 Ann Buckley, 'Music and musicians in medieval Irish society', *Early Music*, 28:2 (May 2000), pp 165–76, 178–82, 185–90, at pp 178–9.

24 Buckley, 'Music and musicians', pp 179–180.

25 Fletcher, 'Liturgy and music in the medieval cathedral', pp 130–2.

26 British Library, London, Add. MS 24198.

27 A.J. Bliss, 'Smarmore inscribed slates: interim report', *CLAHJ*, 15:1 (1961), pp 21–2, at p. 21; A.J. Bliss, 'The inscribed slates at Smarmore', *PRIA*, 64C (1965–6), pp 33–60, at pp 42–3.

28 Stephen of Lexington, *Letters from Ireland, 1228–1229*, trans. with an intro. Barry W. O'Dwyer (Kalamazoo, 1982), p. 167.

29 Fletcher, 'Liturgy and music in the medieval cathedral', pp 132, 145–8.

30 Ibid., p. 135.

31 Roger Bowers, 'The musicians of the Lady Chapel of Winchester cathedral priory', *Journal of Ecclesiastical History*, 45 (1994), pp 210–37, at p. 214.

32 Boydell, 'Music in the medieval cathedral priory' in Milne (ed.), *Christ Church cathedral*, p. 148.

33 Fletcher, 'Liturgy and music in the medieval cathedral', pp 134–5; Boydell, *History of music at Christ Church*, p. 25; W.H. Grindle, *Irish cathedral music: a history of music in the Church of Ireland* (Belfast, 1989), pp 7–8.

34 Boydell, *History of music at Christ Church*, p. 25.

35 Roger Bowers, 'To chorus from quartet: the performing resource for English church polyphony, c.1390–1559' in John Morehen (ed.), *English church practice, 1400–1650* (Cambridge, 1995), pp 1–47, at p. 11.

36 Bowers, 'To chorus from quartet', pp 1, 12.

37 Barra Boydell, 'The establishment of the choral tradition, 1480–1647' in Milne (ed.), *Christ Church cathedral*, pp 237–51, at p. 237.

38 Boydell, *History of music at Christ Church*, p. 26; Barra Boydell, *Music in Christ Church before 1800: documents and selected anthems* (Dublin, 1999), p. 33.

39 Boydell, *History of music at Christ Church*, p. 27; Boydell, *Christ Church music documents*, pp 27–8; *Christ Church deeds*, no. 357.

40 Boydell, *History of music at Christ Church*, p. 30.

41 Jacques le Goff, *The birth of Purgatory* (Chicago, 1984, trans. Arthur Goldhammer), pp 1–3, 6, 7–8, 135, 210.

42 Ibid., pp 214–16.

43 Duffy, *Stripping of the altars*, p. 288.

44 Le Goff, *Purgatory*, p. 249.

45 *ODCC*, p. 1219.

46 Gerald Bray (ed.), *Records of convocation, XVI, Ireland, 1101–1690* (Woodbridge, Suffolk, 2006), p. 24.

47 Bray, *Records of convocation*, p. 25.

48 Ibid., p. 37.

49 Ibid., p. 49.

50 Christopher Wordsworth, 'Wiltshire pardons or indulgences', *Wiltshire Archaeological and Natural History Magazine*, 38:119 (1913–14), pp 15–33, at p. 18; Empey, *Proctor's accounts*, pp 59–60, 62, 68, 75.

51 Empey, ibid.

52 For Octavian de Palatio see *DIB*, vol. 7, pp 1043–4; *Christ Church deeds*, no. 312.

53 Lydon, 'Christ Church in the later medieval world, 1300–1500' in Milne (ed.), *Christ Church cathedral*, p. 85.

54 *DIB*, ibid.; *Christ Church deeds*, ibid.

55 Andrew Brown, *Church and society in England, 1000–1500* (Basingstoke, 2003), p. 104.

56 *ODCC*, pp 318–19.

57 Brown, *Church and society*, p. 127.

58 In *CIRCLE* there are nine documents, many quite similar, to do with a Carmelite chantry, the first and last being cited here: *CIRCLE*, Patent roll 9 Edward III, 16 June 1335, no. 10; Close roll 6 Henry VI, 23 Feb. 1428, no. 24.

59 For the Augustinian chantry see *CIRCLE*, Close roll 17 Richard II, 1 June 1394, no. 17.

60 For the chantry at Fore see *CIRCLE*, Patent roll 9 Richard II, 22 Oct. 1385, no. 54; O'Keeffe, *Medieval Irish buildings*, p. 52; Peter Harbison, *Guide to the national monuments of Ireland* (Dublin, 1970), pp 241–2.

61 For John Chevir's chantry see *CIRCLE*, Patent roll 36 Henry VI, 3 Feb. 1458, no. 4.

62 For Edward Somerton's chantry see *CIRCLE*, Patent roll 36 Henry VI, 3 Feb. 1458, no. 6.

63 Henry F. Twiss, 'Some ancient deeds of the parish of St Werburgh, Dublin, 1243–1676', *PRIA*, 35C (1919), pp 282–315, at pp 291–2; Empey, *Proctor's accounts*, pp 17–18.

64 For the chantry of St Doulagh's see *CIRCLE*, Patent roll 21 Henry VII, 22 Jan. 1506, no. 8.

65 Boydell, *Christ Church music documents*, pp 32–3.

66 *Christ Church deeds*, no. 1091.

67 Brown, *Church and society*, p. 104.

68 Ibid.

69 Duffy, *Stripping of the altars*, pp 142–3.

70 Ibid., p. 144.

71 Berry, *Wills and inventories*, pp 119–20; Clark and Refaussé, *Historic Dublin guilds*, p. 38.

72 Duffy, *Stripping of the altars*, p. 144.

73 Ibid., p. 142.

74 Clark and Refaussé, *Historic Dublin guilds*, pp 37–8.

75 Mary Esther Clark and Gael Chenard, 'The religious guild of St George Martyr, Dublin' in Salvador Ryan and Clodagh Tait (eds), *Religion and politics in urban Ireland, c.1500–c.1750: essays in honour of Colm Lennon* (Dublin, 2016), pp 31–50, at pp 33–4; Clark and Refaussé, *Historic Dublin guilds*, pp 35–7.

76 Clark and Refaussé, *Historic Dublin guilds*, pp 33–4, 39–40.

77 Ibid., p. 38.

78 Duffy, *Stripping of the altars*, p. 142.

79 For the guild at Drogheda see *CIRCLE*, Patent roll 16 Henry VI, Sept. 1437–Aug. 1438, no. 11.

80 For the guild at Dunsany see *CIRCLE*, Patent roll 5 Edward IV 17 Oct. 1465, no. 6; for the guild at Skreen see *CIRCLE*, Patent roll 14 Edward IV, Mar. 1474–Mar. 1475, no. 10.

81 For the chantry at Stamullin see *CIRCLE*, Patent roll 36 Henry VI, 3 Feb. 1458, no. 5.
82 *CIRCLE*, Patent roll 9 Henry VI, 16 Dec. 1430, no. 45.
83 Henry Berry, 'History of the religious guild of St Anne in St Audoen's church, Dublin, 1430–1740, taken from its records in the Halliday collection, RIA', *PRIA*, 25C (1904–5), pp 21–105, at pp 22–3.
84 Berry, 'Guild of St Anne', p. 94; *CIRCLE*, Patent roll 9 Henry VI, ibid.
85 Berry, 'Guild of St Anne', pp 23–4, 31.
86 *CIRCLE*, Patent roll 16 Edward IV, 12 June 1476, no. 5; Clark and Refaussé, *Historic Dublin guilds*, pp 39–40; Bairéad, 'Bailiffs, provosts and sheriffs', p. 291.
87 Colm Lennon, 'The foundation charter of St Sythe's guild, Dublin, 1476', *Archivium Hibernicum*, 48 (1994), pp 3–12, at p. 4.
88 Raymond Gillespie, 'The coming of reform, 1500–58' in Milne (ed.), *Christ Church cathedral*, pp 151–73, at p. 157.
89 James Lydon, 'Christ Church in the later medieval world, 1300–1500', p. 93.
90 Raghnall Ó Floinn, 'The late medieval relics of Holy Trinity church, Dublin' in Bradley, Fletcher and Simms (eds), *Dublin in the medieval world*, pp 369–89, at p. 372.
91 Ó Floinn, 'Medieval relics', pp 373–6; Raymond Refaussé with Colm Lennon (eds), *The registers of Christ Church cathedral, Dublin* (Dublin, 1998), pp 39–40.
92 Ó Floinn, 'Medieval relics', pp 371, 385–6.
93 Ibid., pp 376–84.
94 *ODCC*, pp 303–4, 1148.
95 Ó Floinn, 'Medieval relics' pp 386–9; Stalley, 'Architecture of the cathedral' in Milne (ed.), *Christ Church cathedral*, pp 95–128, at p. 108.
96 *CARD*, i, pp 383–4.
97 Ibid.; *Records of convocation, XVI, Ireland, 1101–1690*, p. 46.
98 *CARD*, i, pp 383–4.
99 *CARD*, i, pp 383–4.
100 Duffy, *Stripping of the altars*, p. 167.
101 Berry, *Wills and inventories*, pp 53, 67, 149, 163.
102 Ibid., p. 98; Duffy, *Stripping of the altars*, pp 113–14.
103 Mary Ann Lyons, 'The onset of religious reform: 1460–1550' in Brendan Smith (ed.), *The Cambridge history of Ireland*; i, 600–1550 (4 vols, Cambridge, 2018), pp 498–522, at pp 505–13.
104 Margaret Murphy, 'The high cost of dying: an analysis of *pro anima* bequests in medieval Dublin' in W.J. Shiels and Diana Woods (eds), *The Church and wealth: papers read at the 1986 summer meeting and the 1987 winter meeting of the Ecclesiastical History Society* (Oxford, 1987), pp 111–21, at p. 111.
105 Murphy, 'The high cost of dying', p. 112; Henry A. Jefferies, 'Men, women, the late medieval church and religion: evidence from wills from County Dublin', *Archivium Hibernicum*, 69 (2016), pp 355–65, at p. 357; Mary Ann Lyons, 'Lay female piety and church patronage in late medieval Ireland' in Brendan Bradshaw and Dáire Keogh (eds), *Christianity in Ireland: revisiting the story* (Dublin, 2002), pp 57–75, in which the piety of Gaelic noblewomen and of colonial women is discussed.
106 Duffy, *Stripping of the altars*, pp 310–13; Berry, *Wills and inventories*, pp xi–xiv, passim.
107 Fletcher, 'Liturgy and music in the medieval cathedral', p. 145; Cambridge University Library, MS Add. 710, f. 31.
108 Berry, *Wills and inventories*, pp 27, 104–5, 138–9.
109 Ibid., pp 56–8, 68–72, 78–81, 102–3, 115–16, 127–8; *CARD*, i, pp 332.
110 Berry, *Wills and inventories*, pp 56–8, 68–72, 78–81, 127–8.

111 Ibid., pp 68–72, 102–3, 127–8; *Christ Church deeds*, no. 955.

112 Berry, *Wills and inventories*, pp 7–8, 27–9, 38–41, 128–33.

113 Ibid., pp 8–11, 15–18, 76–8, 90–2.

114 Ibid., pp 23–7, 85–9, 146–8, 156–8.

115 Ibid., pp 15–18, 56–8, 68–72, 78–81, 102–3.

116 Duffy, *Stripping of the altars*, pp 357–8.

117 Berry, *Wills and inventories*, pp 81–3, 94–9, 112–13, 133–6.

118 Ibid., pp 8–11.

119 Ibid., pp 15–18.

120 Ibid., pp 159–62.

121 Duffy, *Stripping of the altars*, p. 365.

122 Berry, *Wills and inventories*, pp 109–11, and a survey by the writer of wills in Berry, *Wills and inventories*.

123 Duffy, *Stripping of the altars*, p. 293.

124 Berry, *Wills and inventories*, pp 11–13, 15–18, 51–3, 68–72, 94–9, 146–8.

125 Duffy, *Stripping of the altars*, p. 328.

126 Ibid., pp 327–8.

127 Ibid., p. 330.

128 Berry, *Wills and inventories*, pp 39–41.

129 Duffy, *Stripping of the altars*, p. 330: Berry, *Wills and inventories*, pp 63–4.

130 Berry, *Wills and inventories*, pp 25–7, 55–6, 150–51.

CHAPTER 8
Dramatic Presentations

1 *ODCC*, p. 507.

2 Phyllis Hartnoll, *The theatre: a concise history* (3rd ed., London, 1988), p. 33.

3 *ODCC*, p. 507; Hartnoll, *Theatre*, p. 32.

4 Hartnoll, *Theatre*, p. 32; J.J. Jusserand, *English wayfaring life in the Middle Ages* (4th ed., London, 1950), p. 115.

5 Lefferts, 'England', p. 116.

6 Nigel Davison, 'So which way round did they go? The Palm Sunday procession at Salisbury', *Music and Letters*, 61:1 (Jan. 1980), pp 1–14, at pp 1–2.

7 Fletcher, 'Liturgy and music in the medieval cathedral', pp 140–2.

8 Davison, 'The Palm Sunday procession', p. 2.

9 Fletcher, 'Liturgy and music in the medieval cathedral', p. 142.

10 Ibid., p. 140.

11 Frank Harrison, *Music in medieval Britain* (4th ed., London, 1980), pp 91–2.

12 Ibid., p. 92; Fletcher, 'Liturgy and music in the medieval cathedral', p. 141.

13 Fletcher, 'Liturgy and music in the medieval cathedral', p. 142.

14 Harrison, *Music in medieval Britain*, p. 92.

15 Fletcher, 'Liturgy in the late medieval cathedral priory', pp 140–1.

16 M. Egan-Buffet and Alan J. Fletcher, 'The Dublin "Visitatio Sepulcri" play', *PRIA*, 90C (1990), 159–241, at 159, 163–4, 167, 170–5; Clarke, *IHTA, Dublin part I, to 1610*, map 4, passim; Fletcher, *Drama, performance, and polity*, pp 68–70, 72–3

17 J.A. Burrow, *Medieval writers and their work: Middle English literature, 1100–1500* (2nd ed., Oxford, 2008), pp 62–3.

18 *CARD*, i, pp 239–42.

19 Ibid., pp 239–40.

20 Burrow, *Medieval writers*, p. 63.

21 Alan J. Fletcher, 'Dublin and the Pale' in David Wallace (ed.), *Europe: a literary history, 1348–1418* (2 vols, Oxford, 2016), vol. i, pp 401–13, at pp 410–11.

22 *Account roll of Holy Trinity priory*, p. xxii; Aubrey Gwynn, 'The origins of the Anglo-Irish theatre', *Studies*, 28:10 (1939), pp 260–74, at p. 262.

23 *Account roll of Holy Trinity priory*, p. xxxv.

24 *Account roll of Holy Trinity priory*, pp xxxvi–ix.

25 Ibid., pp xxxiii–xxxiv, xli; Alan J. Fletcher has pointed out that the number of stages used could have ranged from two to as many as five.

26 Clarke, *IHTA, Dublin part I, to 1610*, pp 31–2.

27 Seán Duffy, 'Town and crown', pp 96, 107; Clarke, 'The 1192 charter of liberties', p. 11; *CARD*, i, pp 2–6.

28 *CARD*, i, p. 285; Lennon and Murray, *Dublin franchise roll*, p. 22.

29 Clarke, *IHTA, Dublin part I, to 1610*, pp 31–2.

30 Ibid., p. 32.

31 Paul Ferguson, 'The custom of riding the franchises of the city of Dublin', *Sinsear*, 1 (1979), pp 69–79, at p. 71.

32 Clarke, *IHTA, Dublin part I, to 1610*; Ferguson, 'Riding the franchises', p. 71.

33 Driver, *Cheshire in the later Middle Ages*, pp 140–1.

34 Fletcher, *Drama, performance, and polity*, pp 93–4; *CARD*, i, p. 324.

35 Fletcher, *Drama, performance, and polity*, p. 98.

36 Hartnoll, *Theatre*, p. 44; Fletcher, *Drama, performance, and polity*.

37 *CARD*, i, pp 239–40; Fletcher, *Drama, performance, and polity*.

38 *CARD*, i, pp 239–40.

39 Ibid., i, p. 242.

40 Fletcher, *Drama, performance, and polity*, pp 107–9.

CHAPTER 9
Continuity and Religious Revolution

1 Otway-Ruthven, *Medieval Ireland*, p. 408.

2 R. Dudley Edwards and T.W. Moody, 'The history of Poynings' Law; part I, 1494–1615', *IHS*, 2:8 (Sept. 1941), pp 415–24, at pp 415–16.

3 Brendan Bradshaw, 'Cromwellian reform and the origins of the Kildare rebellion, 1533–34', *Transactions of the Royal Historical Society*, 27 (1977), pp 69–93, at p. 86.

4 E.H. Gombrich, *The story of art* (15th rev. ed., London, 1989), pp 224–8.

5 Ibid., pp 168, 202–4, 219.

6 *ODCC*, pp 1007–8.

7 Friel, *Maritime history of Britain and Ireland, c.400–2001*, pp 106–7; J.A. Williamson, *The voyages of John and Sebastian Cabot* (London, 1937), pp 8–10; Patrick O'Flaherty, *Old Newfoundland: a history to 1843* (St John's, 1999), p. 12; *NHI*, viii, p. 180.

8 Christopher Maginn and Steven G. Ellis, *The Tudor discovery of Ireland* (Dublin, 2015), pp 18, 64–5; *DIB*, viii, pp 735–8.

9 Maginn and Ellis, *Tudor discovery*, pp 18–19, 27, 40, 42, 65.

10 Maginn and Ellis, *Tudor discovery*, pp 27–34; *DIB*, iii, p. 788.

11 Maginn and Ellis, *Tudor discovery*, pp 35, 40, 42.

12 Ibid., pp 16–17, 50–51, 64; *DIB*, iii, pp 51–3.

13 Maginn and Ellis, *Tudor discovery*, p. 66.

14 *CARD*, i, pp 384–94.

15 *CARD*, i, pp 386, 388–90; Bairéad, 'Bailiffs, provosts and sheriffs', p. 292; Lennon and Murray, *Dublin franchise roll*, pp 38–9 (Moyr).

16 *CARD*, i, pp 390–3.

17 Empey, *Proctors' accounts*, pp 83–93.

18 Raymond Gillespie, 'The coming of reform, 1500–58' in Milne (ed.), *Christ Church cathedral*, pp 151–73, at pp 152–7.

19 Empey, *Proctors' accounts*, pp 91, 93–4.

20 Gillespie, 'Coming of reform', pp 159–61.

21 Lawlor, 'Liber Albus and Liber Niger', pp 26–7.

22 Raymond Gillespie, 'Reform and decay, 1500–1598' in Crawford and Gillespie (eds), *St Patrick's cathedral*, pp 151–73, at pp 152–6.

23 Fletcher, 'Liturgy and music in the medieval cathedral', pp 140–4.

24 *Alen's reg.*; Newport B. White (ed., introd. Aubrey Gwynn), The *'Dignitas decani' of St Patrick's cathedral, Dublin* (Dublin, 1957); Gillespie, 'Reform and decay, 1500–1598', p. 153.

25 Berry, 'Dublin guild of merchants', pp 54–5.

26 Berry, 'Carpenters, millers, masons', pp 322, 325–8.

27 Ibid., p. 328.

28 Fletcher, *Drama, performance, and polity*, p. 134.

29 Ibid., pp 134–6, 381 n. 42; *ODCC*, p. 958.

30 Fletcher, *Drama, performance, and polity*, p. 136; William Smith Clark, *The early Irish stage: the beginnings to 1720* (Oxford, 1955), p. 15.

31 Fletcher, *Drama, performance, and polity*, pp 136–7, 382 n. 45.

32 Wilson, *Chester customs accounts*, pp 132–42, 148 (map).

33 *CARD*, i, pp 395, 397; Bairéad, 'Bailiffs, provosts and sheriffs', pp 292–3.

34 Lennon and Murray, *Dublin franchise roll*, 36 (Wrentche), 41 (Gaydon), 43 (Fyan), 45 (Queytrot).

35 *NHI*, ii, pp 501–2.

36 Wilson, *Chester customs accounts*, pp 132–42, passim, and 135–8.

37 Ibid., pp 135–7, 141.

38 Ibid., p. 142.

39 Ibid., pp 137, 141.

40 Ibid., pp 133, 135–8, 141–2.

41 Bairéad, 'Bailiffs, provosts and sheriffs', p. 293.

42 Lennon and Murray, *Dublin franchise roll*, pp 31 (Beswick), 39 (Beswyke and Michael FitzSymon), 69 (Beswik), 75 (Beswyk); Wilson, *Chester customs accounts*, p. 141; Driver, *Cheshire in the late Middle Ages*, p. 105.

43 Lennon and Murray, *Dublin franchise roll*, p. 77; Connolly and Martin, *Dublin guild merchant*, passim; Wilson, *Chester customs accounts*, pp 132–42, passim.

44 The figures in the table, taken from the *Chester customs accounts*, are interesting and useful; however, they do not give the full picture of imports, because quantities of other cargoes arriving in Chester are hidden in collective words such as 'fardel' and 'pack' used by Chester customs officers.

45 Jenny Kermode, 'The trade of late medieval Chester, 1500–1550' in Richard Britnell and John Hatcher (eds), *Progress and problems in medieval England: essays in honour Edward Miller* (Cambridge, 1996), pp 286–307, at p. 287; Driver, *Cheshire in the later Middle Ages*, p. 106.

46 Driver, *Cheshire in the late Middle Ages*; Kermode, 'The trade of late medieval Chester', pp 289, 305.

47 Kermode, 'The trade of late medieval Chester', p. 290; Driver, *Cheshire in the late Middle Ages*.

48 Kermode, 'The trade of late medieval Chester', pp 289, 294.

49 Driver, *Cheshire in the late Middle Ages*; Kermode, 'The trade of late medieval Chester', pp 290, 294; K.P. Wilson, 'The port of Chester in the later Middle Ages' (PhD, University of Liverpool, 1965), p. 91.

50 Driver, *Cheshire in the late Middle Ages*; Kermode, 'The trade of late medieval Chester', pp 289, 294, 306.

51 Elton, *Tudors*, p. 134; *ODCC*, pp 428, 433, 752–4.

52 Elton, *Tudors*, pp 130–6, 141; *ODCC*, p. 1552.

53 Elton, *Tudors*, p. 153; *ODCC*, pp 832–3, 1587–8.

54 Elton, *Tudors*, pp 154–5; Duffy, *Stripping of the altars*, p. 412.

55 Áine Foley, *The abbey of St Thomas the Martyr, Dublin* (Dublin, 2017), pp 12–13.

56 Elton, *Tudors*, p. 156.

57 Elton, *Tudors*, pp 141, 144, 149; *ODCC*, pp 433, 490.

58 Elton, *Tudors*, pp 145, 146–8; *ODCC*, pp 1287–8.

59 *DIB*, i, pp 909–11.

60 Brendan Bradshaw, 'George Browne, first Reformation archbishop of Dublin, 1536–1554', *Journal of Ecclesiastical History*, 21:4 (Oct. 1970), pp 301–26, at p. 306.

61 *DIB*, i, pp 909–11; Bradshaw, 'George Browne', pp 310–12.

62 Henry A. Jefferies, 'The early Tudor Reformations in the Irish Pale', *Journal of Ecclesiastical History*, 52:1 (Jan. 2001), pp 34–62, at pp 51, 53–4.

63 Jefferies, *The Irish Church and the Tudor Reformations*, pp 80–81; Ronan, *Reformation in Dublin*, pp 121–3; 'The second Royal Injunctions of Henry VIII, 1538', *English historical documents, V, 1485–1558*, ed. C.H. Williams (London, 1971), pp 811–14.

64 Ronan, *Reformation in Dublin*, pp 81–4.

65 Robert E. Scully, 'The unmaking of a saint: Thomas Becket and the English Reformation', *Catholic Historical Review*, 86:4 (Oct. 2000), pp 579–602, at p. 592.

66 Ibid., p. 593.

67 Ibid., p. 595.

68 Williams, *English historical documents, V*, p. 813.

69 Brendan Bradshaw, 'The opposition to the ecclesiastical legislation in the Irish Reformation parliament', *IHS*, 16:3 (Mar. 1969), pp 285–303, at pp 290–4.

70 Bradshaw, 'Opposition to ecclesiastical legislation', pp 294–9; Jefferies, 'Tudor Reformations in the Irish Pale', pp 47–8.

71 Ronan, *Reformation in Dublin*, pp 143–4; Brendan Bradshaw, *The dissolution of the religious orders in Ireland under Henry VIII* (Cambridge, 1974), p. 118.

72 *DIB*, i, pp 909–11.

73 Robert Dudley Edwards, *Church and state in Tudor Ireland: a history of penal laws against Irish Catholics, 1534–1603* (Dublin, 1935), p. 59.

74 Ronan, *Reformation in Dublin*, pp 154–5.

75 Ibid., pp 166, 168.

76 Ibid., pp 156, 196–7; *DIB*, i, pp 69–70.

77 Ronan, *Reformation in Dublin*, pp 183–7, 465; Jefferies, 'Tudor Reformations in the Irish Pale', p. 49; Brendan Scott, 'The religious houses of Tudor Dublin: their communities and resistance to the dissolution, 1537–41' in Seán Duffy (ed.), *Medieval Dublin VII* (Dublin, 2006), pp 214–32, at pp 225–6.

78 Ronan, *Reformation in Dublin*, pp 191–2; *DIB*, ii, pp 927–8.

79 Ronan, *Reformation in Dublin*, p. 199; *DIB*, i, pp 752–4.

80 Ronan, *Reformation in Dublin*, pp 209–10, 496.
81 Ibid., pp 171, 179.
82 Ibid., pp 202–3, 491–2; Brendan Bradshaw, 'Cromwellian reform and the origins of the Kildare rebellion, 1533–4', *Transactions of the Royal Historical Society*, 27 (1977), pp 69–93, at p. 84.
83 Ronan, *Reformation in Dublin*, pp 162–4, 449; Bairéad, 'Bailiffs, provosts and sheriffs', p. 293; Empey, *Proctors' accounts*, p. 153.
84 Ronan, *Reformation in Dublin*, pp 468–9.
85 Ibid., pp 205–7, 493.
86 Bradshaw, *Dissolution of the religious orders*, pp 102–4; Ronan, *Reformation in Dublin*, pp 114–19; Charles McNeill, 'Accounts of sums realized by sales of chattels of suppressed Irish monasteries', *JRSAI*, 6th series, 12:1 (June 1922), pp 11–37, at p. 15.
87 Scully, 'The unmaking of a saint', pp 591–2; *ODCC*, p. 1718.
88 Ellis and Murray, *Calendar of state papers, Ireland, Tudor period, 1509–1547*, no. 402.
89 Bradshaw, *Dissolution of the religious orders*, p. 104.
90 McNeill, 'Accounts of monastery chattel sales', pp 13–15; Bradshaw, *Dissolution of the religious orders*, pp 103–7; Ronan, *Reformation in Dublin*, p. 144.
91 Hawkes, 'Liturgy in Dublin, 1200–1500', p. 45, and TCD MS 79; *ODCC*, p. 1637.
92 Hawkes, 'Liturgy in Dublin, 1200–1500', p. 48, and TCD MS 78.
93 Hawkes, 'Liturgy in Dublin, 1200–1500', pp 51–2, and Emmanuel College, Cambridge, MS I 3.11.
94 Jefferies, *The Irish Church and the Tudor Reformations*, pp 104, 125, and passim.
95 Colm Lennon, 'The beauty and eye of Ireland: the sixteenth-century' in Art Cosgrove (ed.), *Dublin through the ages* (Dublin, 1988), pp 46–62, at pp 46–8, 50–1, 55–6, 60.
96 Liam Miller and Eileen Power (eds), *Holinshed's Irish Chronicle ... by Richard Stanyhurst* (New York, 1979), pp 39–40, 42.

Bibliography

MANUSCRIPT SOURCES

Bodleian Library, Oxford
Rawl. Liturg. d. 4.

British Library
Add. MS 24198.

Cambridge University Library
MS Add. 710, f. 31.

Chester City Records Office, Chester
Sheriffs' books, ZSB 3, ff 71–74 (1476–7).
Sheriffs' books, ZSB 3, ff 75–83 (1476–7).

Dublin City Library and Archive
Dublin City Assembly Roll, 1454, 1456, 1470

Dublin City Archaeological Archive, Dublin City Library and Archive
Archaeological collection, DCAA 02.01.

Emmanuel College, Cambridge
MS I 3.11

National Archives, London
NA, indictment rolls, CHES 25/15, m. 30d, m. 31.

Trinity College, Dublin
TCD MS 78.
TCD MS 79.

PUBLISHED PRIMARY SOURCES

Berry, Henry F. (ed.), *Register of wills and inventories of the diocese of Dublin in the time of archbishops Tregury and Walton, 1457–1483* (Dublin, 1898).
— (ed.), *Statutes and ordinances and acts of the parliament of Ireland, King John to Henry V* (Dublin, 1907).
— (ed.), *Statute rolls of the parliament of Ireland, reign of King Henry VI* (Dublin, 1910).
— (ed.), *Statute rolls of the parliament of Ireland, 1st to the 12th years of the reign of King Edward IV* (Dublin, 1914).
Bickley, Francis B. (ed.), *The little red book of Bristol* (2 vols, Bristol and London, 1900).
Byrne, Niall J. (ed.), *The great parchment book of Waterford, liber antiquissimus civitatis Waterfordiae* (Dublin, 2007).

Carus-Wilson, E.M. (ed.), *The overseas trade of Bristol in the later Middle Ages* (2nd ed., New York, 1967).

Connolly, Philomena, and Geoffrey Martin (eds), *The Dublin guild merchant roll, c.1190–1265* (Dublin, 1992).

Connolly, Philomena (ed.), *Irish exchequer payments, 1270–1446* (2 vols, Dublin, 1998).

— (ed.), *Statute rolls of the parliament of Ireland, Richard III–Henry VIII* (Dublin, 2002).

Crooks, Peter (ed.), *Calendar of Irish chancery letters c.1244–1509*, an online source known as *CIRCLE*.

Dryburgh, Paul, and Brendan Smith (eds), *Handbook and select calendar of sources for medieval Ireland in the National Archives of the United Kingdom* (London and Dublin, 2005).

— (eds), *Inquisitions and extents of medieval Ireland* (London, 2007).

Ellis, Steven G., and James Murray (eds), *Calendar of state papers, Ireland, Tudor period, 1509–1547* (Dublin, 2017).

Empey, Adrian (ed.), *The proctors' accounts of the parish church of St Werburgh, Dublin, 1481–1627* (Dublin, 2009).

Flavin, Susan, and Evan T. Jones (eds), *Bristol's trade with Ireland and the Continent, 1503–1601: the evidence of the exchequer customs accounts* (Dublin, 2009).

Gilbert, John T. (ed.), *Calendar of ancient records of Dublin*, i (Dublin, 1889).

Harris, Walter (ed.), *Hibernica; or, Some antient pieces relating to Ireland* (1st ed., Dublin, 1747–50)

Hart, G.W., and W.H. Frere (eds), *The Church of our fathers as seen in St Osmund's rite for the cathedral of Salisbury, by Daniel Rock D.D.* (4 vols, London, 1903, 1904).

Hollis, D. (ed.), *Calendar of the Bristol apprentice book, 1532–1565, part I, 1532–1542* (Bristol, 1949).

Lennon, Colm, and James Murray (eds), *The Dublin city franchise roll, 1468–1512* (Dublin, 1998).

McEnery, M.J., and Raymond Refaussé (eds), *Christ Church deeds* (Dublin, 2001).

McNeill, Charles (ed.), *Calendar of Archbishop Alen's register* (Dublin, 1950).

Miller, Liam, and Eileen Power (eds), *Holinshed's Irish Chronicle … by Richard Stanyhurst* (New York, 1979).

Mills, James (ed.), and James Lydon and Alan J. Fletcher (intro.), *Account roll of the priory of Holy Trinity, Dublin, 1337–1346* (Dublin, 1996).

Morrissey, James (ed.), *Statute rolls of the parliament of Ireland, 12th and 13th to the 21st and 22nd years of the reign of King Edward IV* (Dublin, 1939).

O'Meara, John J. (trans. and intro.), *Gerald of Wales, The history and topography of Ireland* (London, 1982)

Ogilvie-Thomson, S.J., *Richard Rolle: prose and verse, edited from MS Longleat 29 and related manuscripts* (Oxford, 1988).

Powicke, F.M., and C.R. Cheney (eds), *Council and synods, with other documents relating to the English Church, II*, 1205–1313 (2 vols, Oxford, 1964).

Ralph, Elizabeth, and Nora M. Hardwick (eds), *Calendar of the Bristol apprentice book, 1532–1565, part II, 1542–1552* (Bristol, 1980).

Refaussé, Raymond, and Colm Lennon (eds), *The register of Christ Church cathedral* (Dublin, 1998).

Sharpe, Reginald R. (ed.), *Calendar of letter-books … of the city of London at the Guildhall, letter book K* (London, 1911).

Simmons, T.F., and H.E. Nolloth (introd.), *The lay folks' catechism* (London, 1901, facs. ed., New York, 1972).

Smyly, J. Gilbart, 'Old deeds in the library of Trinity College' – V, *Hermathena*, 70 (1937), pp 1–21.

—, 'Old deeds in the library of Trinity College' – IV, *Hermathena*, 70 (1947), pp 1–21.

Statutes of the realm … [of England and Great Britain], to 1713 (9 vols in 10 + 2 index vols, Record Commission, London, 1810–28).

Sweetman, H.S. (ed.), *Calendar of documents relating to Ireland* (5 vols, London, 1875–86).

Waters, D.W. (ed.), *The rutters of the sea: the sailing directions of Pierre Garcie* (New Haven, 1967).

White, Newport B. (ed.), intro., Aubrey Gwynn, *The 'Dignitas decani' of St Patrick's cathedral, Dublin* (Dublin, 1957).

Williams, C.H. (ed.), *English historical documents, V, 1485–1558* (London, 1971).

Wilson, K.P. (ed.), *Chester customs accounts, 1301–1566* (Liverpool, 1969).

SECONDARY SOURCES

Andrews, J.H., 'The oldest map of Dublin', *PRIA*, 83C (1983), pp 205–37.

Bailey, Mark, *Medieval Suffolk: economic and social history, 1200–1500* (Woodbridge, Suffolk, 2007).

Ball, F. Elrington, *Howth and its owners* (Dublin, 1917).

Bairéad, Eoin C., 'The bailiffs, provosts and sheriffs of the city of Dublin' in Seán Duffy (ed.), *Medieval Dublin XIV* (Dublin, 2015), pp 210–309.

Barrett, Sam, 'Music and liturgy' in Mark Everist (ed.), *The Cambridge companion to medieval music* (Cambridge, 2011), pp 185–204.

Bartlett, Robert, *The making of Europe: conquest, colonization and cultural change, 950–1350* (London, 1993).

—, *England under the Norman and Angevin kings, 1075–1225* (Oxford, 2000).

Begley, John, *The diocese of Limerick, ancient and medieval* (Dublin, 1906).

Bennett, Judith M., *Ale, beer and brewsters in England: women's work in a changing world, 1300–1600* (New York, 1996).

Bennett, Michael, *Lambert Simnel and the battle of Stoke* (Gloucester, 1987).

Berggren, Lars, Nils Hybel and Annette Landen (eds), *Cogs, cargoes and commerce: maritime bulk trade in northern Europe* (Toronto, 2002).

Bernard, Jacques, 'The maritime intercourse between Bordeaux and Ireland, *c*.1450–*c*.1520', *IESH*, 7 (1980), pp 7–21,

Berry, Henry F., 'The water supply of ancient Dublin', *JRSAI*, 1:7 (1891), pp 557–73.

—, 'The records of the Dublin guild of merchants, known as the guild of the Holy Trinity, 1438–1671', *JRSAI*, fifth series, 10:1 (Mar. 1900), pp 44–68.

—, 'History of the religious guild of St Anne in St Audoen's church, Dublin, 1430–1740, taken from its records in the Halliday collection, RIA', *PRIA*, 25C (1904–5), pp 21–105.

—, 'The Dublin guild of carpenters, masons and heliers in the sixteenth century', *JRSAI*, fifth series, 35:4 (Dec. 1905), pp 321–37.

—, 'Proceedings in the matter of the custom called tollboll, 1308 and 1385, St Thomas's abbey *v.* some early Dublin brewers, etc.', *PRIA*, 28C (1910), pp 169–73.

Bill, Jan, 'The cargo vessels' in Lars Berggren, Nils Hybel and Annette Landen (eds), *Cogs, cargoes and commerce: maritime bulk trade in northern Europe, 1150–1400* (Toronto, 2002), pp 92–112.

Bliss, A.J., 'Smarmore inscribed slates: interim report', *CLAHJ*, 15:1 (1961), pp 21–2.

—, 'The inscribed slates at Smarmore', *PRIA*, 64C (1965–6), pp 33–60.

Booker, Sparky, 'An English city? Gaelicization and cultural exchange in late medieval Dublin' in Seán Duffy (ed.), *Medieval Dublin X* (Dublin, 2010), pp 287–98.

—, 'Irish clergy and the diocesan church in the 'four obedient shires' of Ireland, *c.*1400–*c.*1540', *IHS*, 39:154 (Nov. 2014), pp 179–209.

—, *Cultural exchange and identity in late medieval Ireland: the English and Irish of the four obedient shires* (Cambridge, 2018).

Bowers, Roger, 'The musicians of the Lady Chapel of Winchester cathedral priory', *Journal of Ecclesiastical History*, 45 (1994), pp 210–37.

—, 'To chorus from quartet: the performing resource for English church polyphony, *c.*1390–1559' in John Morehen (ed.), *English church practice, 1400–1650* (Cambridge, 1995), pp 1–47.

Boydell, Barra, 'Dublin city musicians in the late Middle Ages and Renaissance, to 1660', *Dublin Historical Record*, 34:2 (Mar. 1981), pp 42–53.

—, *Music in Christ Church before 1800: documents and selected anthems* (Dublin, 1999).

—, *A history of music at Christ Church cathedral, Dublin* (Woodbridge, Suffolk, 2004).

—, 'Music in the medieval cathedral priory' in Milne (ed.), *Christ Church cathedral*, pp 142–8.

Bradshaw, Brendan, 'The opposition to the ecclesiastical legislation in the Irish Reformation parliament', *IHS*, 16:63 (Mar. 1969), pp 285–303.

—, 'George Browne, first Reformation archbishop of Dublin, 1536–1554', *Journal of Ecclesiastical History*, 21:4 (Oct. 1970), pp 301–26.

—, *The dissolution of the religious orders in Ireland under Henry VIII* (Cambridge, 1974).

—, 'The Edwardian Reformation in Ireland, 1547–53', *Archivium Hibernicum*, 34 (1976–7), pp 83–99.

—, 'Cromwellian reform and the origins of the Kildare rebellion, 1533–4', *Transactions of the Royal Historical Society*, 27 (1977), pp 69–93.

Bradley, John, 'The medieval boroughs of County Dublin' in Conleth Manning (ed.), *Dublin beyond the Pale: studies in honour of Patrick Healy* (Bray, 1998), pp 129–44.

—, Alan J. Fletcher and Anngret Simms (eds), *Dublin in the medieval world: studies in honour of Howard B. Clarke* (Dublin, 2009).

Brady, Joseph, and Anngret Simms (eds), *Dublin through space and time (c.900–1900)* (Dublin, 2001).

Brady, Niall, 'Dublin's maritime setting and the archaeology of its medieval harbours' in John Bradley, Alan J. Fletcher and Anngret Simms (eds), *Dublin in the medieval world: studies in honour of Howard B. Clarke* (Dublin, 2009), pp 295–315.

Bray, Gerald (ed.), *Records of convocation, XVI, Ireland, 1101–1690* (Woodbridge, Suffolk, 2006).

Britnell, Richard, *Britain and Ireland 1050–1530: economy and society* (Oxford, 2004).

Brown, Andrew, *Church and society in England, 1000–1500* (Basingstoke, 2003).

Bryan, Donough, *The Great earl of Kildare, Gerald FitzGerald (1456–1513)*, (Dublin, 1933).

Buckley, Ann, 'Music and musicians in medieval Irish society', *Early Music*, 28:2 (May 2000), pp 165 76, 178 82, 185 90.

—, 'Music in Ireland to *c.*1500' in Dáibhí Ó Cróinín (ed.), *A new history of Ireland*, i (Oxford, 2005), pp 744–813.

— (ed.), *Music, liturgy, and the veneration of the saints of the medieval Irish Church in a European context* (Turnhout, 2017).

—, 'From hymn to *historia*: liturgical veneration of local saints in the medieval Irish Church' in Buckley (ed.), *Music, liturgy, and the veneration of the saints*, pp 161–83.

Burrow, J.A., *Medieval writers and their work: Middle English literature, 1100–1500* (2nd ed., Oxford, 2008).

Byrne, Francis J., *Irish kings and high-kings* (2nd ed., Dublin, 2001).

Campbell, Bruce M.S., *English seignorial agriculture, 1250–1450* (Cambridge, 2000).

Carus-Wilson, E.M., 'The overseas trade of Bristol' in Eileen Power and M.M. Postan (eds), *Studies in English trade in the fifteenth century* (London, 1933), pp 183–246.

Chart, David A., *The story of Dublin* (London, 1932).

Childs, Wendy R., 'Irish merchants and seamen in late medieval England', *IHS*, 32:125 (May 2005), pp 22–43.

Childs, Wendy, 'Ireland's trade with England in the later Middle Ages', *IESH*, 9 (1982), pp 5–33.

Clark, Mary, and Raymond Refaussé (eds), *Directory of historic Dublin guilds* (Dublin, 1993).

Clark, Mary Esther, and Gael Chenard, 'The religious guild of St George Martyr, Dublin' in Salvador Ryan and Clodagh Tait (eds), *Religion and politics in urban Ireland, c.1500–c.1750: essays in honour of Colm Lennon* (Dublin, 2016), pp 31–50.

Clark, William Smith, *The early Irish stage: the beginnings to 1720* (Oxford, 1955).

Clarke, H.B., and Anngret Simms (eds), *The comparative history of urban origins in non-Roman Europe: Ireland, Wales, Denmark, Germany, Poland and Russia from the ninth to the thirteenth century* (2 parts, Oxford, 1985).

Clarke, Howard B., 'The mapping of medieval Dublin: a case-study in thematic cartography' in Clarke and Simms (eds), *The comparative history of urban origins in Europe*, part ii, pp 617–43.

—, 'Gaelic, Viking and Hiberno-Norse Dublin' in Art Cosgrove (ed.), *Dublin through the ages* (Dublin, 1988), pp 5–24.

—, (ed.), *Medieval Dublin: the living city* (Dublin, 1990).

—, (ed.), *Medieval Dublin: the making of a metropolis* (Dublin, 1990).

—, 'The 1192 charter of liberties and the beginnings of Dublin municipal life', *Dublin Historical Record*, 46:1 (spring 1993), pp 5–14.

—, (ed.), *Irish cities* (Cork and Dublin, 1995).

—, 'Myths, magic and the Middle Ages: Dublin from its beginnings to 1577' in Howard B. Clarke (ed.), *Irish cities* (Cork and Dublin, 1995), pp 82–95.

—, '*Urbs et suburbium*: beyond the walls of suburban Dublin' in Conleth Manning (ed.), *Dublin and beyond the Pale: studies in honour of Patrick Healy* (Bray, 1998), pp 45–58.

—, *Irish historic town atlas no. 11, Dublin part I, to 1610* (Dublin, 2002).

—, *Dublin c.840 to c.1540: the medieval town in the modern city* (2nd. ed., Dublin, 2002).

—, '*Angliores ipsis Anglis*: the place of medieval Dubliners in English history' in Howard B. Clarke, Jacinta Prunty and Mark Hennessy (eds), *Surveying Ireland's past: multi-disciplinary essays in honour of Anngret Simms* (Dublin, 2004), pp 41–72.

—, 'Street life in medieval Dublin' in H.B. Clarke and J.R.S. Phillips (eds), *Ireland, England and the Continent in the Middle Ages and beyond: essays in memory of a turbulent friar, F.X. Martin OSA* (Dublin, 2006), pp 145–63.

—, 'The four parts of the city: high life and low life in the suburbs of medieval Dublin' in Kennedy and Smeaton (eds), *The Sir John T. Gilbert commemorative lectures, 1998–2007*, pp 57–78.

—, 'From Dyflinnarskíri to the Pale: defining and defending a medieval city-state, 1000–1500' in J. Ní Ghrádaigh and E. O'Byrne (eds), *The march in the islands of the medieval west* (Leiden and Boston, 2012), pp 35–52.

Clarke, Howard, Sarah Dent and Ruth Johnson, *Dublinia: the story of medieval Dublin* (Dublin, 2002).

Conlon, Lynda, 'Women in medieval Dublin: their legal rights and economic power' in
    Seán Duffy (ed.), *Medieval Dublin IV* (Dublin, 2003), pp 172–92.
Corbishley, Mike, et al., *The history of Britain and Ireland* (Oxford, 2005).
Coleman, Brian, 'Urban elite: the county and civic elite of later medieval Dublin' in Seán
    Duffy (ed.), *Medieval Dublin XV* (Dublin, 2016), pp 293–304.
Cosgrove, Art (ed.), *A new history of Ireland*, ii, *medieval Ireland* (Oxford, 1987).
—, 'The emergence of the Pale, 1399–1447', *NHI*, ii, pp 533–56.
— (ed.), *Dublin through the ages* (Dublin, 1988).
Crawford, John, and Raymond Gillespie (eds), *St Patrick's cathedral, Dublin: a history*
    (Dublin, 2009).
Crooks, Peter, and Sean Duffy (eds), *The Geraldines and medieval Ireland: the making of a
    myth* (Dublin, 2017).
Davis, James, *Medieval market morality* (Cambridge, 2012).
Davison, Nigel, 'So which way round did they go? The Palm Sunday procession at
    Salisbury', *Music and Letters*, 61:1 (Jan. 1980), pp 1–14.
Dawkes, Giles, 'Interim results of excavations at 152–5 Church Street, Dublin: St Michan's
    early enclosure and late medieval timber-framed buildings' in Seán Duffy (ed.),
    Medieval Dublin X (Dublin, 2010), pp 198–219.
Dolley, Michael, *Medieval Anglo-Irish coins* (London, 1972).
Doyle, Ian W., and Bernard Browne (eds), *Medieval Wexford: essays in memory of Billy Colfer*
    (Dublin, 2016).
Driver, J.T., *Cheshire in the later Middle Ages* (Chester, 1971).
Dublin vocational schools committee (curriculum development unit), *Viking settlement to
    medieval Dublin* (Dublin, 1978).
Duffy, Eamon, *The stripping of the altars: traditional religion in England, 1400–1580* (New
    Haven and London, 2nd ed., 2005).
—, *Royal books and holy bones: essays in medieval Christianity* (London, 2018).
Duffy, Paul, 'The church of Bearach, the grange of Baldoyle and the town of the dark
    stranger' in Seán Duffy (ed.), *Medieval Dublin XV* (Dublin, 2016), pp 89–118.
Duffy, Seán, *Ireland in the Middle Ages* (Basingstoke, 1997).
—, 'Town and crown: the kings of England and their city of Dublin' in *Thirteenth century
    England, X: proceedings of the Durham conference, 2003* (Woodbridge, 2005), pp 95–117.
— (ed.), '*Medieval Dublin* series I–X' (index to the first ten volumes) in Seán Duffy (ed.),
    Medieval Dublin X (Dublin, 2010), pp 313–26.
Dukes, Fred E., *Campanology in Ireland* (Dublin, 1994).
Dyer, Christopher, *Making a living in the Middle Ages: the people of Britain, 850–1520* (New
    Haven & London, 2002).
Edwards, Robert Dudley, *Church and state in Tudor Ireland: a history of penal laws against
    Irish Catholics, 1534–1603* (Dublin, 1935).
—, and T.W. Moody, 'The history of Poynings' Law; part I, 1494–1615', *IHS*, 2:8 (Sept.
    1941), pp 415–24.
—, 'The beginnings of municipal government in Ireland' in Howard Clarke (ed.), *Medieval
    Dublin: the living city* (Dublin, 1990), pp 145–52.
—, 'An early town council in Dublin', letter to the editor of the *Times Literary Supplement*,
    31 July 1937.
Egan-Buffet, M., and Alan J. Fletcher, 'The Dublin "Visitatio Sepulcri" play', *PRIA*, 90C
    (1990), pp 159–241.
Ellis, Steven G., 'The struggle for control of the Irish mint, 1460–c.1506', *PRIA*, 78C
    (1978), pp 17–36.

—, *Reform and revival: English government in Ireland, 1470–1534* (Woodbridge, 1986).

—, *Ireland in the age of the Tudors 1447–1603, English expansion and the end of Gaelic rule* (London, 1998).

Elton, G.R., *England under the Tudors* (London, 1965).

Empey, Adrian, 'The lay person in the parish: the medieval inheritance, 1169–1536' in Gillespie and Neely (eds), *The laity and the Church of Ireland*, pp 7–48.

—, 'Intramural churches and communities in medieval Dublin' in Bradley, Fletcher and Simms (eds), *Dublin in the medieval world*, pp 249–76.

Everist, Mark, (ed.), *The Cambridge companion to medieval music* (Cambridge, 2011).

Fassler, Margaret, *Music in the medieval west* (New York and London, 2014).

Ferguson, Paul, 'The custom of riding the franchises of the city of Dublin', *Sinsear*, 1 (1979), pp 69–79.

Fletcher, Alan J., *Drama, performance, and polity in pre-Cromwellian Ireland* (Cork, 2000).

—, *Drama and the performing arts in pre-Cromwellian Ireland: sources and documents from the earliest times until c.1642* (Cambridge, 2001).

—, 'Liturgy in the late medieval cathedral priory' in Milne (ed.), *Christ Church cathedral*, pp 129–41.

—, 'Liturgy and music in the medieval cathedral' in Crawford and Gillespie (eds), *St Patrick's cathedral*, pp 120–48.

—, 'What a performance! street entertainment in medieval and Renaissance Dublin' in *The Sir John T. Gilbert commemorative lectures, 1998–2007* (Dublin, 2009), pp 27–43.

—, 'Dublin and the Pale' in David Wallace (ed.), *Europe: a literary history, 1348–1418* (2 vols, Oxford, 2016), i, pp 401–13.

Foley, Áine, 'Violent crime in medieval Co. Dublin: a symptom of degeneracy?' in Seán Duffy (ed.), *Medieval Dublin X* (Dublin, 2010), pp 220–40.

—, *The royal manors of medieval Co. Dublin: crown and community* (Dublin, 2013).

—, *The abbey of St Thomas the Martyr, Dublin* (Dublin, 2017).

Frame, Robin, *Colonial Ireland, 1169–1369* (2nd ed., Dublin, 2012).

Friel, Ian, *The good ship: ships, shipbuilding and technology in England, 1200–1520* (London, 1995).

—, *Maritime history of Britain and Ireland, c.400–2001* (London, 2003).

Gilbert, John T. (ed.), *Historical and municipal documents of Ireland, 1172–1320* (Dublin, 1870).

—, *A history of the city of Dublin* (3 vols, Dublin, 1854–9, facs. ed., Shannon, 1972).

—, *A history of the city of Dublin* (3 vols, Dublin, 1861).

Gillespie, Raymond, 'The coming of reform, 1500–58' in Milne (ed.), *Christ Church cathedral*, pp 151–73.

— and W.G. Neely (eds), *The laity and the Church of Ireland, 1000–2000: all sorts and conditions* (Dublin, 2002).

—, 'Reform and decay, 1500–1598' in Crawford and Gillespie (eds), *St Patrick's cathedral*, pp 151–73.

Gombrich, E.H., *The story of art* (15th rev. ed., London, 1989).

Gowan, Margaret, Linzi Simpson, et al., *Conservation plan: Dublin city walls and defences* (Dublin, 2004).

Grindle, W.H., *Irish cathedral music: a history of music in the Church of Ireland* (Belfast, 1989).

Gross, Charles, 'The court of pie powder', *Quarterly Journal of Economics*, 20:2 (Feb. 1906), pp 231–49.

Guinness, Henry S., 'Dublin trade guilds', *JRSAI*, sixth series, 12:2 (Dec. 1922), pp 143–63

Günsenin, Nergis (ed.), *Between continents, proceedings of the twelfth symposium on boat and ship archaeology, Istanbul 2009* (Istanbul, 2009).

Gwynn, Aubrey, 'Richard FitzRalph, archbishop of Armagh, part vi', *Studies: an Irish Quarterly Review*, 25 (1936), pp 81–96.

—, 'The origins of the Anglo-Irish theatre', *Studies*, 28:10 (1939), pp 260–74.

—, 'Anglo-Irish church life: fourteenth and fifteenth centuries' in Patrick J. Corish (ed.), *A history of Irish Catholicism*, ii, fasciculus 4 (Dublin, 1968), pp 1–76.

—, *The Irish Church*, ed. Gerard O'Brien (Dublin, 1992).

Hall, Dianne, 'Everyday violence in medieval Dublin' in Seán Duffy (ed.), *Medieval Dublin XV* (Dublin, 2016), pp 305–19.

Halpin, Andrew (ed.), *The port of medieval Dublin: archaeological excavations at the civic offices, Winetavern Street, Dublin, 1993* (Dublin, 2000).

Hanawalt, Barbara A., *The ties that bound: peasant families in medieval England* (Oxford, 1986).

Harbison, Peter, *Guide to the national monuments of Ireland* (Dublin, 1970).

Harper, John, *The forms and orders of western liturgy from the tenth to the eighteenth century* (Oxford, 1991).

Harris, Richard, *Discovering timber-framed buildings* (3rd ed., Oxford, 1993).

Harris, Walter, *The history and antiquities of the city of Dublin* (Dublin, 1766).

Harrison, Frank, *Music in medieval Britain* (4th ed., London, 1980).

Hartnoll, Phyllis, *The theatre: a concise history* (3rd ed., London, 1988).

Harvey, John H. (ed.), *William Worcestre: itineraries* (Oxford, 1969).

Hawkes, William, 'The liturgy in Dublin, 1200–1500: manuscript sources', *Reportorium Novum*, 2:1 (1958), pp 33–67.

Hayden, Mary, 'Lambert Simnel in Ireland', *Studies: an Irish Quarterly Review*, 4:16 (Dec. 1915), pp 622–38.

Hewitt, H.J., *Cheshire under the three Edwards* (Chester, 1967).

Hunt, Edwin S., and James M. Murray, *A history of business in medieval Europe, 1200–1550* (Cambridge, 1999).

Jackson, Valentine, 'Dodder water supply' in Howard B. Clarke (ed.), *Medieval Dublin: the making of a metropolis* (Dublin, 2012), pp 128–41.

Jefferies, Henry A., *Priests and prelates of Armagh in the age of Reformations* (Dublin, 1997).

—, *The Irish Church and the Tudor Reformations* (Dublin, 2010).

—, 'The early Tudor Reformations in the Irish Pale', *Jour. Eccles. Hist.*, 52:1 (Jan. 2001), pp 34–62.

—, 'Men, women, the late medieval church and religion: evidence from wills from County Dublin', *Archivium Hibernicum*, 69 (2016), pp 355–65.

Jones, Randolph, 'Hys worthy seruice done in that vpror: Sir John Whyte and the defence of Dublin during Silken Thomas' rebellion, 1534' in Seán Duffy (ed.), *Medieval Dublin XI* (Dublin, 2011), pp 275–97.

—, 'Janico Markys, Dublin, and the coronation of "Edward VI" in 1487' in Seán Duffy (ed.), *Medieval Dublin XIV* (Dublin, 2015), pp 185–209.

Jusserand, J.J., *English wayfaring life in the Middle Ages* (4th ed., London, 1950).

Kennedy, Máire, and Alastair Smeaton (eds), *The Sir John T. Gilbert commemorative lectures, 1998–2007* (Dublin, 2009).

Kermode, Jenny, 'The trade of late medieval Chester, 1500–1550' in Richard Britnell and John Hatcher (eds), *Progress and problems in medieval England: essays in honour Edward Miller* (Cambridge, 1996), pp 286–307.

Kinsella, Stuart, 'From Hiberno-Norse to Anglo-Norman, c.1030–1300' in Milne (ed.), *Christ Church cathedral*, pp 25–52.

Laughton, Jane, *Life in a late medieval city: Chester, 1275–1520* (Oxford, 2008).

Lawlor, H.J., 'A calendar of the Liber Niger and Liber Albus of Christ Church, Dublin', *PRIA*, 27C (1908–9), pp 1–93.

Lefferts, Peter M., 'England' in Everist (ed.), *Medieval music*.

Le Goff, Jacques, *The birth of Purgatory* (Chicago, 1984, trans. Arthur Goldhammer).

Lennon, Colm, 'The beauty and eye of Ireland: the sixteenth-century' in Cosgrove (ed.), *Dublin through the ages*, pp 46–62.

—, *The lords of Dublin in the age of Reformation* (Dublin, 1989).

—, 'The foundation charter of St Sythe's guild, Dublin, 1476', *Archivium Hibernicum*, 48 (1994), pp 3–12.

Lewis, Samuel, *A history and topography of Dublin city and county* (London, 1837).

Lexington, Stephen of, *Letters from Ireland, 1228–1229*, trans. with an intro. Barry W. O'Dwyer (Kalamazoo, 1982).

Logan, F.D., *Excommunication and the secular arm in medieval England* (Toronto, 1968).

Lydon, James, 'Christ Church in the later medieval world, 1300–1500' in Milne (ed.), *Christ Church cathedral*, pp 75–94.

—, 'The defence of Dublin in the Middle Ages' in Seán Duffy (ed.), *Medieval Dublin IV* (Dublin, 2003), pp 63–78.

Lynch, Ann, and Conleth Manning, 'Dublin Castle: the archaeological project', *Archaeology Ireland*, 4:2 (summer 1990), pp 65–8.

— and Conleth Manning, 'Excavations at Dublin Castle, 1985–7' in Seán Duffy (ed.), *Medieval Dublin II* (Dublin, 2001), pp 169–204.

Lyons, Mary Ann, 'Sidelights on the Kildare ascendancy; a survey of Geraldine involvement in the Church, *c*.1470–*c*.1520', *Archivium Hibernicum*, 48 (1994), pp 73–87.

—, 'Maritime relations between Ireland and France, *c*.1480–*c*.1630', *IESH*, 27 (2000), pp 1–24.

—, 'Lay female piety and church patronage in late medieval Ireland' in Brendan Bradshaw and Dáire Keogh (eds), *Christianity in Ireland: revisiting the story* (Dublin, 2002), pp 57–75.

—, 'The onset of religious reform: 1460–1550' in Smith (ed.), *Cambridge history of Ireland*, i, pp 498–522.

Lyons, Mary C., 'Weather, famine, pestilence and plague in Ireland, 900–1500' in E. Margaret Crawford (ed.), *Famine: the Irish experience 900–1900: subsistence crises and famines in Ireland* (Edinburgh, 1989), pp 31–74.

MacCotter, Paul, *Medieval Ireland: territorial, political and economic divisions* (Dublin, 2008).

McEneaney, Eamonn, and Rosemary Ryan (eds), *Waterford treasures* (Waterford, 2004).

—, 'Politics and the art of devotion in late fifteenth-century Waterford' in R. Moss, C. Ó Clabaigh and S. Ryan (eds), *Art and devotion in medieval Ireland* (Dublin, 2006), pp 33–50.

McEntee, Don, and Michael Corcoran, *The rivers Dodder and Poddle: mills, storms, droughts and the public water supply* (Dublin, 2016).

McGrath, Fergal, *Education in ancient and medieval Ireland* (Dublin, 1979).

McLeod, Caitriona, 'Fifteenth-century vestments in Waterford', *JRSAI*, 82 (1952) pp 85–98.

McMahon, Mary, *Church sites of north County Dublin: a heritage trail* (Dublin, 1991).

—, *St Audoen's church, Cornmarket, Dublin: archaeology and architecture* (Dublin, 2006).

McNeill, Charles, 'Accounts of sums realized by sales of chattels of suppressed Irish monasteries' in *JRSAI*, 6th series, 12:1 (June 1922), pp 11–37.

Maginn, Christopher, and Steven G. Ellis, *The Tudor discovery of Ireland* (Dublin, 2015).

Manning, Conleth, and Emer Condit, *Archaeology Ireland*, 'Heritage guide no. 14: the Powder Tower, Dublin Castle' (Sept. 2001).

Martin, F.X., 'The crowning of a king at Dublin, 24 May 1487', *Hermathena*, 144 (summer 1988), pp 7–34.

Miles, D.W.H., *The tree-ring dating of the roof carpentry of the eastern chapels, north nave triforium and north porch, Salisbury cathedral, Wiltshire* (Portsmouth, 2002).

Mills, James (ed.), and James Lydon and Alan J. Fletcher (intro.), *Account roll of the priory of Holy Trinity, Dublin, 1337–1346* (Dublin, 1996).

Milne, Kenneth (ed.), *Christ Church cathedral, Dublin: a history* (Dublin, 2000).

Montague, John, '"But what about the earlier city?": John Rocque's *Exact Survey* (1756) as a source for medieval Dublin' in Duffy (ed.), *Medieval Dublin XIII* (Dublin, 2013), pp 196–245

Moody, T.W., F.X. Martin and F.J. Byrne (eds), *A new history of Ireland*, viii, *a chronology of Irish history to 1976* (Oxford, 1989).

—, F.X. Martin and F.J. Byrne (eds), *A new history of Ireland*, ix, *maps, genealogies, lists* (Oxford, 1989).

Morgan, Kenneth O., *The Oxford illustrated history of Britain* (new ed., Oxford, 2009).

Moss, Rachel, C. Ó Clabaigh and S. Ryan (eds), *Art and devotion in medieval Ireland* (Dublin, 2006).

Moss, Rachel (ed.), *Art and architecture of Ireland: i, medieval c.400–c.1600* (Dublin, 2014).

Moylan, T.K., 'Vagabonds and sturdy beggars: poverty, pigs and pestilence in medieval Dublin' in Howard Clarke (ed.), *Medieval Dublin: the living city* (Dublin, 1990), pp 192–9.

Murphy, Margaret, 'The high cost of dying: an analysis of *pro anima* bequests in medieval Dublin' in W.J. Shiels and Diana Woods (eds), *The Church and wealth: papers read at the 1986 summer meeting and the 1987 winter meeting of the Ecclesiastical History Society* (Oxford, 1987), pp 111–21.

—, and Michael Potterton, *The Dublin region in the Middle Ages: settlement, land-use and economy* (Dublin, 2010).

Nicholls, K.W., 'Three topographical notes', *Peritia: journal of the Medieval Academy of Ireland*, 5 (1986), pp 409–15.

Ní Mharchaigh, Máirín, 'Medieval parish churches of south-west Co. Dublin', *PRIA*, 97C (1997), pp 245–96.

O'Brien, A.F., 'Commercial relations between Aquitaine and Ireland, *c.*1000–*c.*1550' in Picard (ed.), *Aquitaine and Ireland*, pp 31–80.

O'Byrne, Theresa, 'Manuscript creation in Dublin: the scribe of Bodleian e. Museo MS 232 and Longleat MS 29' in Kathryn Kerby-Fulton, John J. Thompson and Sarah Baechle (eds), *New directions in medieval manuscript studies and reading practices* (Notre Dame, Indiana, 2014), pp 271–91.

—, '*I. Yonge scripsit*: self promotion, professional networking, and the Anglo-Irish literary scribe' in Seán Duffy (ed.), *Medieval Dublin XVII* (Dublin, 2019).

Ó Clabaigh, Colmán, *The friars in Ireland, 1224–1540* (Dublin, 2012).

Ó Cróinín, Dáibhí, *A new history of Ireland*, i (Oxford, 2005).

O'Flaherty, Patrick, *Old Newfoundland: a history to 1843* (St John's, 1999).

Ó Floinn, Raghnall, 'The late medieval relics of Holy Trinity church, Dublin' in John Bradley, Alan J. Fletcher and Anngret Simms (eds), *Dublin in the medieval world: studies in honour of Howard B. Clarke* (Dublin, 2009), pp 369–89.

O'Keeffe, Tadhg, *Medieval Irish buildings, 1100–1600* (Dublin, 2015).

—, and Rhiannon Carey Bates, 'The abbey and cathedral of Ferns' in Ian Doyle and Bernard Browne (eds), *Medieval Wexford*, pp 73–96.

Ó Lochlainn, Colm, 'Roadways in ancient Ireland' in John Ryan (ed.), *Essays and studies presented to Professor Eoin McNeill … 15 May 1938* (Dublin, 1940), pp 465–74.

O'Neill, Timothy, *Merchants and mariners in medieval Ireland* (Dublin, 1987).

—, 'A fifteenth century entrepreneur, Germyn Lynch, fl. 1441–1483' in John Bradley (ed.), *Settlement and society in medieval Ireland: studies presented to F.X. Martin OSA* (Kilkenny, 1988), pp 421–8.

Otway-Ruthven, A.J., *A history of medieval Ireland* (2nd ed., London, 1980).

Picard, Jean-Michel (ed.), *Aquitaine and Ireland in the Middle Ages* (Dublin, 1995).

Platt, C., *The parish churches of England* (London, 1981).

Power, Eileen, and M.M. Postan (eds), *English trade in the fifteenth century* (London, 1933).

Price, Liam, 'Powerscourt, and the territory of Fercullen' *JRSAI*, 83 (1953), pp 117–32.

Reeves, William, 'Octavianus Del Palacio, archbishop of Armagh', *JRSAI*, 4th series, 3:21 (Jan. 1875), pp 341–52.

Ronan, Myles V., 'Religious customs of Dublin medieval guilds', *Irish Ecclesiastical Record*, 24 (1925), pp 225–47 and pp 364–85.

—, *The Reformation in Dublin, 1536–1558 (from original sources)* (London, 1926).

—, 'The Poddle river and its branches', *JRSAI*, 17:1 (1927), pp 39–46.

Rose, Susan, *The medieval sea* (London, 2007).

Ryan, Salvador, 'Christ the wounded lover and affective piety in late medieval Ireland and beyond' in Henning Laugerud, Salvador Ryan and Laura Katrine Skinnebach (eds), *The materiality of devotion in late medieval northern Europe: images, objects, practices* (Dublin, 2016), pp 70–89.

St John Hope, W.H., 'On the English liturgical colours', *Transactions of the St Paul's Ecclesiological Society*, 2 (1886–90), pp 345–86.

Salzman, L.F., *English trade in the Middle Ages* (Oxford, 1931).

—, *English industries of the Middle Ages* (new ed., London, 1970).

Schweitzer, Holger, 'Drogheda boat: a story to tell' in Nergis Günsenin (ed.), *Between continents, proceedings of the twelfth symposium on boat and ship archaeology, Istanbul 2009* (Istanbul, 2009), pp 225–31.

Scott, Brendan, 'The religious houses of Tudor Dublin: their communities and resistance to the dissolution, 1537–41' in Seán Duffy (ed.), *Medieval Dublin VII* (Dublin, 2006), pp 214–32.

Scully, Robert E., 'The unmaking of a saint: Thomas Becket and the English Reformation', *Catholic Historical Review*, 86:4 (Oct. 2000), pp 579–602.

Seymour, John D., 'James Yonge, a fifteenth-century Dublin writer', *JRSAI*, 6th series, 16:1 (June 1926), pp 48–50.

Simms, Anngret, 'Origins and early growth' in Joseph Brady and Anngret Simms (eds), *Dublin through space and time*, pp 15–65.

Simpson, Linzi, 'Forty years a-digging: a preliminary synthesis of archaeological investigations in medieval Dublin' in Seán Duffy (ed.), *Medieval Dublin I* (Dublin, 2000), pp 11–68.

—, 'The medieval city wall and the southern line of defences: excavations at 14–16 Werburgh Street' in Seán Duffy (ed.), *Medieval Dublin VIII* (Dublin, 2008), pp 150–77.

—, 'Fifty years a-digging: a synthesis of medieval archaeological investigations in Dublin city and suburbs' in Seán Duffy (ed.), *Medieval Dublin XI* (Dublin, 2011), pp 9–112.

Slattery, Peadar, 'Woodland management, timber and wood production, and trade in Anglo-Norman Ireland, c.1170–c.1350', *JRSAI*, 139C (2009), pp 63–79.

—, 'The timber and wood trade, woodlands, house building and repairs in the English colony in Ireland, c.1350–c.1570, part I', *JRSAI*, 142–3 (2012–13), pp 114–28.

—, 'The timber and wood trade, woodlands, house building and repairs in the English colony in Ireland, *c.*1350–*c.*1570, part II', *JRSAI*, 144–5 (2014–15), pp 90–9.

Smith, Brendan (ed.), *The Cambridge history of Ireland*, i, *600–1550* (4 vols, Cambridge, 2018).

Smith, Charles V., *Dalkey: society and economy in a small medieval Irish town* (Dublin, 1996).

—, 'Patricians in medieval Dublin: the career of the Sargent family' in Seán Duffy (ed.), *Medieval Dublin XI* (Dublin, 2011), pp 219–28.

Somerville-Large, Peter, *Dublin* (London, 1979).

—, *Dublin: the fair city* (London, 1996).

Spring, Roy, *The new Bell's cathedral guides: Salisbury cathedral* (London, 1987).

Stalley, Roger, 'The architecture of the cathedral and priory buildings, 1250–1530' in Milne (ed.), *Christ Church cathedral*, pp 95–128.

Strickland, W.G., 'The ancient official seals of the city of Dublin' in Clarke (ed.), *Medieval Dublin: the living city*, pp 163–71.

Stubbs, William Cotter, 'Weavers' guild', *JRSAI*, 6th series, 9:1 (June 1919), pp 60–86.

Sughi, Mario, 'The appointment of Octavian de Palatio as archbishop of Armagh, 1477–8', *IHS*, 31:122 (1998), pp 145–64.

—, 'The Italian connection: the great earl and archbishop Octavian', *History Ireland*, 7:2, (summer 1999), pp 17–21.

Twiss, Henry F., 'Some ancient deeds of the parish of St Werburgh, Dublin, 1243–1676', *PRIA*, 35, sect. C (1919), pp 282–315.

Wallace, David (ed.), *Europe: a literary history, 1348–1418* (2 vols, Oxford, 2016).

Walsh, Claire, 'Dublin's southern town defences, tenth to fourteenth centuries: the evidence for Ross Road' in Seán Duffy (ed.), *Medieval Dublin II* (Dublin, 2001), pp 88–127.

Warburton, John, and James Whitelaw, *History of the city of Dublin from the earliest accounts to the present time* (London, 1818).

Watts, John, *The Church in medieval Ireland* (2nd ed., Dublin, 1998).

Webb, John J., *Municipal government in Ireland: medieval and modern* (Dublin, 1918).

Westropp, Thomas J., 'Early Italian maps of Ireland from 1300 to 1600, with notes on foreign settlers and trade', *PRIA*, 31C (1912–13), pp 361–428.

Whelan, Caoimhe, 'James Yonge and the writing of history in late medieval Dublin' in Seán Duffy (ed.), *Medieval Dublin XIII* (Dublin, 2013), pp 183–95.

White, Newport B. (ed.), *Extents of Irish monastic possessions, 1540–1541, from manuscripts in the Public Record Office, London* (Dublin, 1943).

Williamson, J.A., *The voyages of John and Sebastian Cabot* (London, 1937).

Wilson, K., 'The port of Chester in the fifteenth century', *Transactions of the Historic Society of Lancashire and Cheshire*, 67 (1965), pp 1–15.

Wordsworth, Christopher, 'Wiltshire pardons or indulgences', *Wiltshire Archaeological and Natural History Magazine*, 38:119 (1913–14), pp 15–33.

THESES

FitzPatrick, Colin, 'Food and drink: Ireland's overseas trade in the later Middle Ages' (PhD, Dublin University, 2015).

Wilson, K.P., 'The port of Chester in the later Middle Ages' (PhD, University of Liverpool, 1965).

DICTIONARIES, ENCYCLOPAEDIAS & GUIDES

Bristow, Joy, *The local historian's glossary of words and terms* (Newbury, 2005).

Chambers concise dictionary (London, 1988).

Cheney, C.R. (ed.) and Michael Jones (rev.), *A handbook of dates for students of British history* (Cambridge, 2000).

Colker, Marvin L. (ed.), *Trinity College Library, Dublin: descriptive catalogue of the medieval and Renaissance Latin manuscripts* (Aldershot, 1991).

Cross, F.L., and E.A. Livingstone, *The Oxford dictionary of the Christian Church* (3rd ed., New York, 1997).

Dictionary of Irish biography from the earliest times to the year 2002 (Cambridge, 2009).

Dolan, Terence Patrick, *A dictionary of Hiberno-English: the Irish use of English* (3rd ed., Dublin, 2012).

Latham, R.E., *Revised medieval word-list from British and Irish sources with supplement* (Oxford, 2004).

Ó Riain, Pádraig, *A dictionary of Irish saints* (Dublin, 2012).

Oxford dictionary of national biography, in association with the British Academy (Oxford, 2004).

Webster's revised unabridged dictionary (Springfield, MA, 1913).

White, Harry, and Barra Boydell (eds), *The encyclopaedia of music in Ireland* (Dublin, 2013).

Index

by Eileen O'Neill

Tables are indexed in *italics*; Figures are indexed in **bold**